Globalization and Economic Nationalism in Asia

Globalization and Economic Nationalism in Asia

Edited by
Anthony P. D'Costa

OXFORD
UNIVERSITY PRESS

OXFORD
UNIVERSITY PRESS

Great Clarendon Street, Oxford, OX2 6DP,
United Kingdom

Oxford University Press is a department of the University of Oxford.
It furthers the University's objective of excellence in research, scholarship,
and education by publishing worldwide. Oxford is a registered trade mark of
Oxford University Press in the UK and in certain other countries

First Edition published in 2012

Published in the United States of America by Oxford University Press
198 Madison Avenue, New York, NY 10016, United States of America

British Library Cataloguing in Publication Data
Data available

Library of Congress Cataloguing in Publication Data
Data Available

ISBN 978-0-19-964621-0

Foreword

This book investigates the interactions between globalization and economic nationalism in Asian countries, an important subject, especially in the context of contemporary capitalism and the financial crisis that has dogged most of the advanced capitalist countries today. Here I consider the question of economic nationalism through the lens of economic openness.[1] Full globalization, which connotes total integration of national economies with that of the world economy, is the antonym of economic nationalism. I argue that economic openness is a multidimensional concept. A country can be open or not so open, in trade, exports, imports, finance, science, culture, education, migration, foreign investment, and investment by its citizens and companies abroad, among other things. There is no economic theory that suggests that a country has to be open in all dimensions simultaneously. Given its economic and geographical situation, a country may choose to be open in some areas and not at all, or only partially in others. I briefly present a discussion of the economic terrain in which the optimum degree of openness is an important issue.[2]

At the simplest level a policy of total autarky is not necessarily one that coincides with economic nationalism. National economic benefits may increase with some trading compared to no trade at all. Orthodox economists would argue that a nation's gains from trade with the rest of the world are best enhanced by the policy of free trade. I challenge this proposition by arguing that there are only narrow circumstances in which the orthodox stance is either analytically or historically valid, with the clear implication that states, other institutions, politics, and policies are all critical spheres of integration with the world economy. These are the themes that are discussed in this volume by Anthony D'Costa and his colleagues by richly illustrating the ways in which Asian states remain active even as they whole-heartedly play the globalization game.

One way of defining the optimum degree of openness is by using the theory of national planning. Despite our increasing ability to handle complex optimization models on more powerful computers, there are many reasons to believe that the approach is not entirely satisfactory. While a planning approach avoids easy and facile identification of the optimal degree of openness with a regime of "free trade," it suffers from a number of limitations. First, planning analysis cannot take into account issues connected with irreversibility over time except by resorting to very ad hoc procedures. Second, the only connection of this approach with history is through initial specification of vectors of primary factors, which are easily quantifiable. There are no simple and convenient ways of quantifying the states of knowledge in the community or its degree of absorptive capacity if inflows of factors from the outside world are considered to be relevant. Third, national planning models are rich in details for a single country. However, to be operationally meaningful they have to assume that the rest of the world is either going to stay constant or change only in a predetermined way. Strategic choices are excluded.

If one were to take these criticisms seriously then the alternative to planning exercises would be a somewhat looser but a more historically grounded approach, which emphasizes the advantages of trade and identifies certain factors that may make the country more vulnerable to outside influences. These may produce long-term, irreversible effects on the country's pattern of production and its ability to generate productive employment, among other things. It is important to note that such an alternative approach is quite consistent with the paradigm of classical economics, including in this respect not only Ricardo, but also Marshall. Ricardo was interested not in the artificial example of trade in wine and cloth between Portugal and England so mechanically reproduced in standard economics textbooks, but in the need to capitalize on the emerging revolution in textile production in the British economy. Marshall understood this very well, appreciating the historical specificity of the maxims of a policy of free trade, which have been treated by many as historical truths.

While Marshall clearly recognized how the changes in configuration of production forces can alter the degree and character of openness of the economy, Keynes, it would appear, was worried about schemes for post-World War II national reconstruction in maintaining equilibrium in the balance of payments of different countries. As he once put it, "To suppose that there exists some smoothly functioning automatic mechanism of adjustment which preserves equilibrium if only we trust to methods of 'laissez-faire' is a doctrinaire delusion which denigrates the lessons of historical experience without having behind it the support of sound theory" (Keynes 1980: 21–2). Now it is clear that in history there have been periods, in which, as Keynes himself acknowledged, payment arrangements have worked out satisfactorily. This permitted large expansions of trade and trade-induced growth. However, these have been episodes characterized by the presence of suitable conjunctures, as the study of the economy for the period after World War II, the "golden age," demonstrates (Glyn, Hughes, Lipietz, and Singh 1992).

A country wishing to open up when the conjuncture is adverse in Keynes's sense (that different economies are characterized by "persistent surpluses" or "deficits" without any mechanism to restore global equilibrium) may benefit much less and, in certain cases, may end up being much worse off than if its opening-up process were differently timed. If timing makes a difference—and timing is important—and if returns to scale are increasing, openness by virtue of assuring higher levels and growth rates of external demand may facilitate major structural changes in the economy, and induce higher labor productivity and growing per capita consumption. If on the other hand the timing is wrong, a country may have to go through painful processes of adjustment precisely because it is more "open" than not. This would once again suggest that we ought to deal with the problem of openness in terms of rate and pattern of growth of output with due recognition to carry out structural changes as and when circumstances warrant.

The traditional economic answer to the question of the optimal degree of openness for the economy is given in terms of the theory of free trade. This theory is, however, extremely restrictive. Its validity depends on various neoclassical assumptions such as full employment, no externalities or information asymmetries, and perfect knowledge about goods and services being traded. However, the benefits of free trade can be realized only under specific world economic conjunctures coupled with domestic policies that go considerably beyond the limits of commercial policy as traditionally defined. For example, two well-documented historical episodes where trade and growth-promoting forces interacted in a positive manner were linked to the hegemonic roles played by Britain and the USA respectively. Economic historians have pointed out that Britain's decision to adopt "free trade" as the major thrust of its commercial policy helped to trigger the secular boom of the second half of the nineteenth century. But changes in the geopolitical situation, coupled with altered industrial leadership consequent on the maturing of major new innovations during the second Kondratieff, as described by Schumpeter, led to severe strains towards the end of the nineteenth century and to the violent demise of the free trade system.

Openness can benefit an economy if relatively specialized resources are concentrated in production whose world demand: is highly income- and price-elastic; leads to diffusion of knowledge and thus upgrading of the quality of local factors of production; enhances efficiency due to increased competition, and alters the distribution of income, which can lead to greater share of production over time. The question of increasing returns to scale and imperfect competition has received considerable attention in the recent developments in the theory of free trade. This literature has been reviewed by Paul R. Krugman (1987).

However, as Krugman (1987) noted, in the type of "second-best" world relevant in the contemporary context, there is no automatic tendency for gains from trade to be realized. The scope of gains from trade does not necessarily decrease but the composition of trade changes significantly from inter-industry to intra-industry trade. Furthermore the need for government intervention can no longer be ignored. While Krugman himself ends up with a justification for free trade, he noted that "this is not the argument that free trade is optimal because markets are efficient. Instead, it is a sadder but wiser argument for free trade as a rule of thumb in a world whose politics are as imperfect as its market" (Krugman 1987: 143). The main reason behind Krugman's cautionary ending is that sophisticated interventionism is likely to be a difficult exercise in political economy. However, because of "nationalist" sentiments, the world trading system cannot be expected to gravitate to free trading. Instead, the argument better meets the need for "managed trade."

There are several reasons why trade needs to be managed. These have to deal with the fact that "openness" can be a mixed blessing. The point was well understood by Keynes when he changed his position from being a champion of free trade to that of an advocate for "national self-sufficiency" in the midst of depression during the 1930s. However, Keynes's argument was more subtle than that of simple-minded economic nationalism. He was all in favor of free movement of people between countries, freedom from passport controls, free educational and cultural exchange. But he was opposed to the free movement of capital and goods, as that led to mass unemployment. Furthermore, there are situations in which increasing the openness of the economy may harm the quality of locally available factors. The classic example of this is the adverse impact of British cotton textiles on Indian cotton weavers in the nineteenth century.

Generally, it has been seen that "openness" works positively if "learning" from contacts with the rest of the world is suitably institutionalized, and there is appropriate adaptation of policies involving strategic government interventions that make the domestic economy more responsive to change. The experience of Japan and the newly industrialized countries of Asia, and now China and India, seem to suggest that home market expansion can often trigger growth-promoting investment, which then leads sequentially to import and export substitution along highly efficient lines. In its turn, home market expansion may have much to do with increases in food productivity levels. Arthur Lewis (1966) strongly underlined the importance of food productivity growth as a mechanism of overcoming the terms of trade loss suffered by many tropical countries that specialized in primary commodity exports.

In the absence of a growing home market accompanied by suitable diversification of the industrial structure, the effect of "openness" can at best be a "once-for-all gain" from increased openness. On occasion it may lead to pronounced economic difficulties for the country, which liberalized its trade and investment policies in the expectation of sustained growth but without adequate preparation on the knowledge absorption side. To sum up, the phenomenon of learning over time is a more relevant paradigm for development gains through trade as distinct from the neoclassical emphasis on exploitation of arbitrage opportunities based on comparative advantage.

Since the demise of the golden age in the 1970s, the world economy has evolved. Most developed countries have adopted more or less free trade and more or less free capital movements since the 1980s. A number of developing countries have done the same since the 1990s. It is this regime of globalization integrating national product and capital markets that provides the backdrop to the discussion of issues of economic nationalism addressed in this book. The editor is quite right to point out that economic nationalism is still widely practiced, notwithstanding globalization, by most successful as well as unsuccessful countries. And there are political and institutional reasons why states continue their activism.

This book provides an analysis of economic nationalism in five leading Asian countries: India, China, South Korea, Japan, and Singapore. Each of these countries has adapted its interventions to the requirements of the new international trading and financial regime and changing domestic class forces. The detailed analysis offered indicates that globalization has not been negated by economic nationalistic measures adopted in one form or another by all five nations; nor has economic nationalism been able to overcome the institutional framework of globalization. To use a different language, what has happened is that Asian countries have sought not close integration with the world economy but strategic integration. They have been open in some spheres and not in others according to their national advantage. Before globalization, strategic integration or managed trade was relatively easy. However, under a revamped World Trade Organization (formerly the GATT) and international legislation, the policy space for most developing countries has been considerably reduced.

It is widely believed that financial globalization and the world financial system have been responsible for the most acute economic crisis to hit the international economy since the Great Depression 60 years ago (Singh 1997). The particularly poor performance of the advanced capitalist countries is regarded as proof of the failure of globalization. This is, however, a one-sided view that ignores the fact that the crisis occurred only in rich countries and not in poor countries. In fact, Asian countries have performed well prior to and during the crisis. Since the beginning of the new millennium and until 2007, the world economy grew at a historically unprecedented pace. Between 2003 and 2005, the world economy grew at a rate of 5% per annum in PPP terms, a rate never before achieved. The economic performance of India and China, the two most populous and hitherto among the poorest countries in the world, was stellar. Overall, the growth rate for developing countries was twice that of rich countries, thereby reducing the distance between the two groups of countries. In general, the level of poverty (defined as earnings below a dollar a day) fell by a large margin in many countries and in the world as a whole.

The essential reason for the good performance of Asian countries lies in the measures adopted by these countries following the lessons they learned from the Asian crisis of 1997–9 (Singh 2002). Since the crisis, these countries started to strive for current account surpluses and to accumulate reserves, which stood them in very good stead during the current crisis. Additionally, most of these Asian countries inherited the institutional basis for industrial learning and strategic intervention, which was established during the heady days of import substitution industrialization and mercantilist trade policies in East Asia. This was a triumph of economic nationalism over globalization. Developing countries did not repudiate globalization but took advantage of it while protecting themselves against its dangers by adopting nationalistic economic policies towards reserves, balance of payments, and strategic industrial policy.

What is crucial today is that both the North and South grow. The North needs full employment (Singh 1995) and the South high rates of growth to minimize poverty and improve the desperately low living standards of the people. Recent research indicates that if developing countries such as India and China were to grow at the desired rate, this would be incompatible with full employment growth in developed countries (Izurieta and Singh 2010; Cripps, Izurieta, and Singh 2011). However, the research also indicates that cooperation between rich and poor countries, particularly India, China, and the USA over technical progress (such as energy saving) can resolve these difficulties. Such cooperation is to be preferred to the narrow economic nationalism of the 1930s, which led to stagnation and crisis. A globalized world economy is in the interest of developing countries provided they have the policy space to enable them to achieve fast growth, reduce poverty, generate quality jobs, and ensure relatively equitable distribution of the benefits of growth. Globalization, together with international economic cooperation among nation states, is a far better goal for developing and emerging countries as long as they are able to manage strategically the economic vulnerabilities associated with international integration. More importantly, by regaining the policy space lost through globalization and committing to spread the benefits of growth widely to their citizenry, states will have justified their nationalist interventions.

Ajit Singh
Emeritus Professor of Economics, University of Cambridge
Life Fellow Queens' College Cambridge
Tun Ismail Ali Chair, University of Malaya

Notes

1. This is a condensed version of a keynote address delivered at the conference "Globalization and Economic Nationalism in Asia," organized by the Asia Research Centre, Copenhagen Business School, December 3, 2009. Financial support from Cambridge Endowment for Research in Finance, the Malaysian Commonwealth Trust, and the Centre for Business Research at Cambridge is gratefully acknowledged.
2. Views on the optimal degree of openness and the subsequent discussion on free trade are adaptations of those first presented in Chakravarty and Singh (1988).

References

Chakravarty, S. and Singh, A. (1988). "The Desirable Forms of Economic Openness in the South." *World Institute for Development Economics Research.* Helsinki: WIDER.

Cripps, F., Izurieta, A., and Singh, A. (2011). "Global Imbalances, Under-consumption and Over-borrowing: The State of the World Economy and Future Policies." *Development and Change*, 42 (1): 228–61.

Glyn, A., Hughes, A., Lipietz, A., and Singh, A. (1992). "The Rise and Fall of the Golden Age," in S.A. Marglin and J. Schor (eds.), *The Golden Age of Capitalism*, 39–125, New York: Oxford University Press.

Izurieta, A. and Singh, A. (2010). "Does Fast Growth in India and China Help or Harm US Workers?" *Journal of Human Development and Capabilities: A Multi-Disciplinary Journal for People-Centered Development*, 11 (1): 115–41.

Keynes, J.M. (1980). *Collected Writings*, ed. Donald Moggridge, Vol. XXV.

Krugman, P.R. (1987). "Is Free Trade Passé?" *Journal of Economic Perspectives*, 1 (2): 131–43.

Lewis, W.A. (1966). *Development Planning* (library edition). London: Routledge.

Singh, A. (2002). "Asian Capitalism and the Financial Crisis," in J. Eatwell and L. Taylor (eds.), *International Capital Markets: Systems in Transition*, 339–67. Oxford: Oxford University Press.

Singh, A. (1997). "Financial Liberalisation, Stockmarkets and Economic Development." *The Economic Journal*, 107: 771–82.

Singh, A. (1995). "Institutional Requirements for Full Employment in Advanced Economies." *International Labour Review*, 134 (4–5): 471–95.

Preface

The global financial crisis of 2008 is a harsh reminder that capitalism as an economic system is still vulnerable to the whims of market dynamics. It is the convergence of the economic motives and aspirations of individuals, households, corporations, and governments that generates the systemic forces of capitalism and also drives economic growth and structural change at the global and national levels. There are occasions when structural imbalances between supply and demand and the inability of the regulatory institutions to stabilize the runaway economic forces produce periodic slumps, which sometimes are severe enough to warrant a depression-like economic stagnation. The recent "Great Recession" led by the housing bubble and Wall Street's financial excess in an era of deregulation and international economic integration is of crisis proportion even though unemployment has not been as severe as that of the Great Depression of the 1930s. However, the prognosis for the USA and the world economy in 2011 is for continuing slow growth and economic misery at least through 2013. The European financial crisis and sluggish Japanese growth—made worse by the recent tsunami and nuclear plant disaster—have added to global economic woes. In this sense, this may turn out to be the worst economic crisis to date.

In the midst of such a crisis, can we expect states to remain aloof and let the economic crisis run its course with the belief that the economy will right itself? But governments cannot watch from the sidelines, since states have a national responsibility to manage their economies and ensure social stability. Ambitious states have political legitimacy concerns and hence cannot remain passive in the face of the economic turbulence or the sluggish pace of change. Even those states that profess excessive allegiance to the virtues of free markets intervene when compelled. It is instructive that governments of varying political persuasions have responded with swift institutional moves to the recent financial crisis, including the USA, whose political distaste for regulation is widely known. Bank and industry bailouts, fiscal stimulus and monetary expansion, and re-regulation of financial institutions have been the principal forms of state intervention. Curiously, there was no talk of protectionism even though the *Economist* (February 9, 2009) sounded alarm bells, predicting economic nationalism would go wild and drag the world economy even further down. What is now evident is that states, despite neoliberal leanings more or less across the board, have become far more active in economic and financial management than they were before the crisis.

The 1980s neoliberal reforms rested on the presumed confidence in the workings of an unbridled market system, which added an unusual sense of invincibility among politicians, business, financial, and policy economists. Markets were seen as the answer to economic and social problems and orthodox protectionism in the post-WTO era was passé. The argument was that it was difficult to micromanage specific sectors in light of globalization, difficult to select national champions, and nearly impossible to wean vested interests that have become accustomed to state largesse in the form of subsidies. All of this was true. The economic development narratives were replete with stories of failed states, the exhaustion of import substitution industrialization, rent-seeking activities, and low economic growth. Furthermore, countries that allegedly pursued free markets and free trade policies were positioned better to grow rapidly and experience widespread social development. The high performing East Asian economies were exemplars of such virtuous change. Of course, this was a misreading of the development process. These countries did well because they avoided unproductive state intervention and not because they abandoned state activism; they exported not because of free trade policies but because of national concerns about balance of payments, benchmarking their competitiveness through aggressive exports. The story is thus nuanced: states remained active in these countries but they were reinventing their role by working with the market and seeking out global economic opportunities in a pragmatic fashion.

The common and mostly correct argument that economic performance in the first three decades of the founding of two of the world's largest countries, China and India, has been less than impressive was mainly due to unbridled state intervention. Notwithstanding their very different political systems, once the shackles of state ownership, rigid price controls, production regulations, and import tariffs were removed, both of these countries have taken off economically. This too is mostly correct. The 1978 reforms in China and the 1991 reforms in India have paved the way for high rates of economic growth and market deepening. However, aside from the thorny questions of determining when exactly higher growth rates began to occur and why, the story is largely—but still only partially—correct. Gradually freeing markets has been beneficial to both countries. But this popular view overlooks the fact that deregulation and liberalization have been engineered and orchestrated by the states themselves and at a pace that has been appropriate to particular political and institutional contexts. Governments in these countries continue to influence economic outcomes even though they have slowly, but not completely, moved out of direct production and removed many of the earlier policy instruments that regulated economic output and protected domestic business. Hence, though globalization has transformed the role of states, it has not eliminated the state in its pursuit of national economic interests. Instead, states have internalized global economic forces to the extent that they themselves are contributors to international economic integration.

In this volume, we address the basic question as to how Asian states today pursue economic nationalism: what do they do and how do they bolster their economies in the larger global system? Attention to this issue is prompted by two reasons: (1) Asian economies are dynamic and actively engaged with the world economy and thus presumed to be bereft of active states; and (2) most predictions indicate that they will constitute a new growth pole of the world economy. In this volume we undertake an inquiry into the nature of state activism under globalization in major Asian economies. As a region, Asia in the post-World War II period has quite solidly demonstrated the significance of the state's role in economic transformation. Today the region continues to be dynamic with new players such as China and India, whose penchant for state intervention is legendary, and who continue to use the state for national economic purposes.

Anthony P. D'Costa
Copenhagen
September 2011

Acknowledgements

The inspiration for this project came from an earlier paper, "Economic Nationalism in Motion: Steel, Auto and Software Industries in India" (D'Costa 2009),[1] where I argued that globalization has not made economic nationalism theoretically redundant or practically impossible. Rather, states have been active in carving out a role for national development as new opportunities and challenges emanated from the world economy, even as the coherence of their actions weakened due to their reinvented roles in working with the market. This paper was previously presented at the Asia Research Institute, National University of Singapore, and subsequently published as a working paper there. However, the paper itself was a product of a conference panel "Foreign Companies and Economic Nationalisms in the Third World," at the 2006 International Economic History Association Congress in Helsinki. I am grateful to Rory Miller of the University of Liverpool and co-editor of the *Journal of Latin American Studies* for inviting me and putting together a fine conference panel. But evidence from a single country such as India, analyzing only a handful of sectors, was clearly not adequate for an understanding of the continued role of the state in a highly integrated international economy. To broaden the scope and to capture the patterns and nuances of state intervention in promoting national interests in the twenty-first century, I organized a conference on "Globalization and Economic Nationalism in Asia" in Copenhagen in December 2009. This volume is a result of that conference. Most of the papers from the conference are included and two additional researchers were invited to contribute to the project.

The conference was financially supported by the Asia Research Centre at the Copenhagen Business School. Kjeld Erik Brødsgaard, Director of the center, wholeheartedly supported this project. Also, FUHU (the Danish Society for the Advancement of Business Education) and ØKs Almennyttige Fond (the East Asiatic Company Foundation) in Copenhagen co-sponsored the conference with financial contributions. I acknowledge the administrative support received from Niels Mygind, Head of the International Economics and Management Department, to pursue my scholarly engagement with India and Asia and for appreciating the intellectual and practical importance of the study of Asia in the department. Without their support it would not have been possible to organize the conference and invite scholars—both seasoned and upcoming—from the USA, Europe, India, Japan, and Australia. I am also grateful to the A.P. Møller-Mærsk Foundation for establishing an endowed professorship in Indian Studies, allowing me to pursue not just interesting intellectual questions about contemporary political economy of India, but also more generalized concerns about globalization and Asia's and China's place in the world economy today. I believe this is a good beginning to what I hope is a wide range of projects covering what is now a very dynamic part of the global economy.

At the Asia Research Centre, Bente Faurby, then Program Coordinator, organized and handled most of the logistical details of the conference. She was assisted by Koen Ruttan, now pursuing his Ph.D. at the London School of Economics. Janette Rawlings, also of the Asia Research Centre, generously provided invaluable editorial support. At Oxford University Press, it has been a pleasure to work with Adam Swallow, Commissioning Editor. We worked together on an earlier edited volume, *The New Economy in Development: Challenges and Opportunities,* when he was at the UN University's World Institute of Development Economics Research in Helsinki. Jenny Townshend and Aimee Wright at Oxford oversaw the finer details of bringing the project to completion. Three anonymous reviews helped greatly in the final shaping of this project.

I would like to thank Alan Irwin, Dean of Research at CBS, for giving me some time off from teaching to pursue several time-consuming editing projects. This is the second volume completed under his tenure. I also thank my colleagues at the Asia Research Centre who presented or served as officiating members at the conference, the invited participants, and a lively audience, representing faculty, students, and corporate executives. Alice Amsden of MIT, who passed away in early 2012, was aware of this project and left an intellectual imprint through her personal communications as well an incisive analysis of the role of the state in Asia and the "rise of the rest." Lastly, I deeply appreciate Ajit Singh's active participation in the conference as a keynote speaker and his willingness to write the Foreword to the book. A committed scholar and a true gentleman who shows no signs of slowing down, I believe he is also a great institutional bridge-builder between Copenhagen Business School and Cambridge University. None of the individuals or institutions bears any responsibility for any inadvertent errors or omissions.

Note

1. D'Costa, A.P. (2009). "Economic Nationalism in Motion: Steel, Auto, and Software Industries in India." *Review of International Political Economy*, 16 (4): 618–46.

Contents

List of Figures

List of Tables

List of Contributors

Alan Chong is Associate Professor at the S. Rajaratnam School of International Studies in Singapore. He has published widely on the notion of soft power and the role of ideas in constructing the international relations of Singapore and Asia. His publications have appeared in *The Pacific Review*, *International Relations of the Asia-Pacific*, *Asian Survey*, *East Asia: an International Quarterly*, *Journal of International Relations and Development*, *Review of International Studies*, and *Cambridge Review of International Affairs*. He is the author of *Foreign Policy in Global Information Space: Actualizing Soft Power* (Palgrave, 2007). He is currently working on several projects exploring the notion of "Asian international theory." His interest in soft power has also led to inquiry into the sociological and philosophical foundations of international communication. He is working on his next book entitled *The International Politics of Communication: Representing Community in a Globalizing World*. Professor Chong has been interviewed frequently in the Asian media and think tanks in the region.

Anthony P. D'Costa holds the Professorship in Indian Studies endowed by the A.P. Møller-Mærsk Foundation and serves as the Research Director of the Asia Research Centre, Department of International Economics and Management, Copenhagen Business School. Prior to this appointment in 2008 he was with the University of Washington for 18 years. As a political economist working with steel, auto, and IT sectors, he has written extensively on globalization, development, innovation, and industrial restructuring in India and other Asian countries. Of his eight books, his most recent are: *Transformation and Development: The Political Economy of Transition in India and China* (co-edited with Amiya Bagchi, forthcoming), A *New India? Critical Reflections in the Long Twentieth Century* (edited 2010), and *The New Asian Innovation Dynamics: China and India in Perspective* (co-edited with G. Parayil, 2009). He is currently working on his next book, *Global Capitalism and the Mobility of Technical Talent*. He has been a fellow of the Abe Program, Japan Foundation; American Institute of Indian Studies; Fulbright-Hays; Korea Foundation; Social Science Research Council, NY; and UN University's World Institute of Development Economics Research (WIDER) in Helsinki. He has also conducted commissioned projects for the ILO, World Bank, and WIDER. He served on the Board of Trustees of the American Institute of Indian Studies and currently serves on the International Advisory Board of India-US World Affairs Institute, Washington, DC, and the Nordic Centre in India.

Karl Gerth 's latest book is *As China Goes, So Goes the World: How Chinese Consumers are Transforming Everything*. After receiving his Ph.D. from Harvard in 2000, he taught at the University of South Carolina until his 2007 move to Oxford University, where he is a fellow and tutor at Merton College and Lecturer in Modern Chinese History. His previous book, published by Harvard University Press, focused on the role of nationalism in forming a consumer culture in pre-World War II China, *China Made: Consumer Culture and the Creation of the Nation*. Dr. Gerth grew up in Chicago and has conducted research in China and Japan on consumerism for over 25 years.

You-il Lee is Associate Professor and Associate Director of the Center for Asian Business, leading research on globalization and Asian capitalism in the International Graduate School of Business at the University of South Australia. Professor Lee is a political economist, who works on socio-economic and political changes, foreign direct investment, and political and economic dynamics of globalization in Northeast Asia. His research findings have appeared in a number of academic journals including *Journal of Contemporary Asia, Asian Studies Review, Asia-Pacific Business Review, Asian Perspectives,* and *Pacific Affairs*, and he has authored/co-authored three scholarly books with Edward Elgar Publishing, Ashgate, and *The Financial Times*. Professor Lee is currently working on a book for Edward Elgar Publishing entitled, *The Impact of Foreign Multinational Corporations in South Korea: Evolution, Dynamics and Contradictions*.

Surajit Mazumdar is with the Ambedkar University in New Delhi, India. Before joining the University in 2011, he was with the Institute for Studies in Industrial Development (ISID), New Delhi, from 2007. Prior to that, for 14 years he taught economics at Hindu College, University of Delhi. Professor Mazumdar studied at the University of Delhi and then at the Centre for Economic Studies and Planning, Jawaharlal Nehru University, Delhi, receiving his Ph.D. from the latter. His research, from a historical perspective, focuses on the corporate sector and the political economy of Indian industrialization, patterns of growth and structural change in India, and the impact of globalization on India's economy.

Toshiya Ozaki is Professor of International Business at College of Business, Rikkyo University, Tokyo, Japan. His recent publications include "Path Dependence as a Political Construct" (co-authored with Steve McGuire and Felicia Fei), *International Journal of Technology Management* (2010), and "The Effect of Multinationality on Firm Performance: An Examination of Japanese Service Firms" (co-authored with Nobuaki Endo), *Asian Business and Management* (2011). His research interests include the globalization of business and its impacts on corporate strategy. Before joining the faculty of Rikkyo University, he worked for IBM for 20 years in varied and increasing responsibilities in business management in Japan, Southeast Asia, and the USA. He received his Ph.D. in International Political Economy from George Washington University, Washington, DC. He regularly advises a number of major Japanese multinational corporations.

Rongfang Pan is currently a Ph.D. student at the Department of International Relations of the Australian National University. She has worked as a research assistant at the East Asian Institute of the National University of Singapore, and received her M.Sc. degree from the S. Rajaratnam School of International Studies at the Nanyang Technological University. She was awarded the Lion Group Gold Medal for being the most outstanding student in the IPE program during the academic year 2008–9. Her publications have appeared as book chapters and in journals such as *World Economics* and *China & World Economy*. Her research interests cover international political economy, economic nationalism, and the political economy of Asian countries and particularly China's integration into the world economy.

Keikoh Ryu is an executive in charge of Chinese business promotion at a major Japanese multinational corporation in Tokyo, and a visiting research scholar at the Institute of Public Policy of Waseda University. Prior to graduating from Waseda University with a Ph.D. in public management, Dr. Ryu received his Master's degree in International Finance and Business from Columbia University. His research has primarily dealt with cross-cultural research methodology in international business and the management of multinational firms. In 2010, Waseda University Press published Dr. Ryu's monograph, *Creating Public Value: The Challenges of Localization for Japanese Corporations in China,* which was also selected as a winner of the 2010 Emerald/EFMD Outstanding Doctoral Research Awards. He has published in *Rikkyo Business Review, Corporate Communication Studies, Journal of International Business,* and other scholarly journals. Recently, he served as a member of the editorial board for the *Annals of the University of Bucharest.*

Mark Selden is a senior research associate in the East Asia Program at Cornell University, Professor Emeritus of Sociology at Binghamton University, and Coordinator of the *Asia-Pacific Journal: Japan Focus* (at http://www.japanfocus.org), which provides in-depth critical analysis of the forces shaping the Asia-Pacific and the world. He is editor of book series at Rowman & Littlefield, Routledge, and M.E. Sharpe publishers. A specialist on the modern and contemporary geopolitics and political economy of the Asia Pacific, his books include: *Chinese Society: Change, Conflict and Resistance; Censoring History: Citizenship and Memory in Japan, China and the United States; China, East Asia and the Global Economy; The Resurgence of East Asia: 500, 150 and 50 Year Perspectives; China in Revolution: The Yenan Way Revisited; and Chinese Village: Socialist State.*

Ajit Singh has taught economics at Cambridge University for the last 45 years. In October 2007 he was made Professor Emeritus by Cambridge University and is now a Life Fellow of Queens' College Cambridge and the Central Bank's Tun Ismail Ali Chair at the University of Malaya as well. He has been a senior economic adviser to the governments of Mexico and Tanzania and has advised almost all the UN developmental agencies, including the ILO, UNCTAD, UNIDO, the World Bank, and the International Finance Corporation. He was elected as an Academician of the UK Academy of Social Sciences in 2004. In 2008, he was inducted into the Hall of Fame of the Department of Economics of Howard University, Washington, DC, where he had completed his Master's degree before going on to do a Ph.D. in Economics at Berkeley. Professor Singh has published 17 books and monographs, and more than 200 research papers, of which nearly 100 are in leading refereed economic journals. He continues to research the modern business enterprise, including corporate organization and finance, takeovers, the stock market, theory of the firm, de-industrialization, and long-term structural changes in advanced and emerging economies, North–South competition, and issues of employment and unemployment, and liberalization and globalization of financial and product markets.

Takaaki Suzuki is the Director of East Asian Studies and an associate professor of political science at Ohio University. His book, *Japan's Budget Politics: Balancing International and Domestic Interests*, is published by Lynne Rienner Publishers as part of Columbia University's East Asian Institute Series. The book examines the interplay of the international and domestic forces that have shaped Japanese macroeconomic policy. Some of his other recent publications include: "Nationalism, Identity and Security in Post Cold War Japan" (2008); "The East Asian Developmental Model in the Era of Global Finance: The Case of Japan" (2007); "Global Finance, Democracy, and the State in Japan" (2006); "Modernity and the Transformation of the Japanese State" (2006); "Keynesianism, Monetarism, and the Contradiction of Japan's Modern Welfare State" (2003).

Yongnian Zheng is Professor and Director of the East Asian Institute, National University of Singapore. He is the series editor for Contemporary China (World Scientific Publishing) and editor of the China Policy Series (Routledge). He is also the editor of *China: An International Journal* and the coeditor of *East Asian Policy*. He has studied both China's transformation and its external relations. He is the author of numerous books, including *The Chinese Communist Party as Organizational Emperor; Technological Empowerment, Discovering Chinese Nationalism in China*; and *Globalization and State Transformation in China*. He is also a coeditor of 12 books on China's domestic development and international relations including the latest volumes: *China and the New International Order* (2008) and *China and International Relations: The Chinese View and the Contribution of Wang Gungwu* (2010).

1

Capitalism and economic nationalism: Asian state activism in the world economy

Anthony P. D'Costa

1.1 Introduction

Not a day goes by in the business press without mentioning China and India, and on most days commentators continue to lament Japan's "lost decade." While China's global presence in terms of exports, with the world's second-highest gross domestic product and the highest economic growth rates, is now routine news, the story of India's rise is also making the rounds. Both countries are trying to shed whatever form of "socialism" they might have claimed to have fostered in the past and they "appear" to have enthusiastically embraced capitalism's best known institution—the market system. Atul Kohli's (2009) collection of essays on India's democracy and development, subtitled "from socialism to pro-business," reflects such a sentiment. Leaving aside the question of whether India was indeed socialist, there is the larger question: by abandoning "socialism" has the Indian state also given up economic nationalism? We intend to show that states in both India and China, as well as others in Asia, continue to influence critical economic, technological, industrial, and financial decisions. These countries have no doubt moved away from the orthodox versions of economic nationalism as practiced through blatant protectionism, but they continue to influence industrial development, export growth, and research and development (R&D) promotion.

These states are enmeshed in the workings of an integrated world economy and thus directly contributing to it, but are also engaged in leveraging the global market system with their internal deregulation and external liberalization. To take advantage of the economic, technological, and other opportunities offered by globalization, they are engaged in re-engineering their economic and political institutions to adjust flexibly to the changing dynamics of the world economy. The national purpose behind economic nationalism has not vanished, rather the approach to realizing such a purpose has changed to account for the wider processes of international economic integration. Japan and other countries in Asia, especially those that have pursued export-oriented, often mercantilist economic policies, have also altered their institutions through deregulation, liberalization, and selective privatization to make their capitalist economic systems work more efficiently and flexibly.

However, the persistence of the belief that, with international integration, economic nationalism has been on the retreat is still strong. Using the case of Japan, an exemplar in the practice of economic nationalism, it has been argued that the institutions behind economic nationalism are no longer fit to cope with the contemporary challenges of globalization or for that matter able to lift Japan out of the now two-decades-old recession (see Hall 2004). Whatever the merits of this argument, Hall (2004) shows that it is economic nationalism itself that is driving Japan's integration with the world economy. Reading closely, this position suggests that economic nationalism is not incompatible with globalization. As Bresser-Pereira succinctly puts it, "Despite conventional wisdom, globalization and nation-states are phenomena that do not contradict each other but are rather part of a same universe, which is the universe of capitalism" (2010: 19). Globalization (or world capitalism to be more precise) can be credited with Asia's economic, political, technological, and cultural resurgence, albeit some still in their nascent forms. The four "Asian dragons," of South Korea, Taiwan, Hong Kong, and Singapore followed by Southeast Asian economies such as Malaysia, Thailand, and Indonesia, China since 1970 with its export push, and India with its economic reforms of the 1980s, are all beneficiaries of the world economy. With major policy turning points—1978 for China and 1991 for India—global economic forces have been embraced and accommodated with great intensity. But this does not mean they have discarded state intervention. On the contrary, as competition increases with globalization, states take on new roles in supporting their national firms to compete in and benefit from the global economy (Bresser-Pereira 2010: 23–7) and both the sophisticated and mundane practices of economic nationalism that have been a factor behind Asian development are still relevant today. And in the context of the 2008 global financial crisis, state intervention has become commonplace even in the USA, the bastion of free markets, which has had to economically and politically accept the importance of state bailouts in an effort to get out of its current financial malaise.[1]

Economic nationalism does not mean economic autarky. On the contrary, it is about national unity and thus quite consistent with international economic interaction (Nakano 2004: 224, 226). We define economic nationalism as a set of state practices, policies, and strategies, often in concert with private capital and politically supported generally by organized labor, to protect and promote national economic interests such as national well being (wages and income). It also aims to foster national competitiveness (efficiency, technological advances), induce growth and structural change (economic development and high value production), and promote particular "national champions" (firms), sectors (such as information technology or aerospace), and products (national brands) vis-à-vis foreign products and foreigners.[2] Globalization is the context in which we argue economic nationalism is practiced, not one in which it dissolves. Globalization is defined as the ongoing, contested process of international economic integration through which flows of trade, investment, technology, and people expansively and intensely interconnect national economies. Thus state action, in promoting the productive powers, can be seen to be integral to the process of globalization (Levi-Faur 1997). The difference with earlier forms of intervention is that states today do not practice economic nationalism in conventional ways, such as tariff protection or discriminate outright against multinational firms. Rather the interventions are more subtle and generally more in consonance with international norms and behavior such as those imposed by the World Trade Organization (WTO) or they are focused on investing in the national workforce to support national firms or wealth creation at home by foreign firms.

Do globalization and deregulation signal that we can expect all vestiges of economic nationalism to disappear? How strong are the historical legacies of economic nationalism in Asia that explain its rise today? More specifically, do the Asian economies that have done extremely well on the economic front because of an interventionist state no longer practice the art of economic nationalism? The rising stars of Asia—China and India—once vilified for their past state actions, are now poster boys of the global economy, though we know that both, but especially China, still intervene in currency markets, the internet, and green technology. Have they embraced market capitalism to the point that state intervention in economic matters (other than macroeconomic policy) has faded away? And where does Japan stand? After relentless badgering from the West to mend its illiberal, inefficient, bureaucratic ways in managing its recession-prone economy, has Japan swerved more toward the market to get its economy humming again?[3] More generally, how have Asian states adjusted to the reality of global and regional economic integration? Has economic nationalism become passé or do states intervene more selectively, surreptitiously, and pragmatically for twenty-first century capitalist development?

This volume examines the persistence of economic nationalism in Asia, its forms, how it differs from past practice, and its implications for the functioning of the world economy. These speak directly to the fact that the world has changed from an era of economic nationalism of the orthodox kind, when infant-industry protection was intellectually justified and routinely practiced (Grieco and Ikenberry 2003: 46–7, 100, 125), to an era of deep international integration with states seemingly retreating from the economy. Today, national capitalist markets have been consolidated in Asia and have become global in scope. For example, today the former Soviet Union and China are very much part of the capitalist world economy. They have shed a good part of their statist ideology to participate actively in the global market. Of course the results of both market participation and economic nationalism across nations have been mixed and their outcomes contested. Some argue that without past intervention many countries would not be where they are today, while others counter that those countries would be much better off had their governments not intervened. Our concern here is less with judging the merits of economic nationalism and more about accounting for its persistence in an era of globalization. Consequently, we hope to further our understanding of why states continue to intervene in the economy and how the modes of intervention have changed due to shifting conditions.

We argue that many Asian states have been active with industrial, trade, investment, and technology policy with the intent to promote domestic capitalists and thus national economic development. One could argue that economic nationalism is so loosely defined that looking for the continuity and new forms of economic nationalism might indicate that any form of state intervention might be interpreted as purposeful (see Nakano 2004: 212).[4] However, we only examine those forms of intervention in different Asian countries that have an explicit economic bearing aimed at either protecting or promoting national business, industry, and economy. The relative success of several Asian countries in supporting capitalist maturity and dynamic market development with wage repression has now enmeshed them globally (Coates 2001: 77–106). Yet, the "triumph" of neoliberalism as an ideology (Biersteker 1992) and associated policy practices have yet to dissuade these erstwhile statist regimes to abandon the pursuit of economic nationalism. These countries in Asia, as will be shown, play it both ways: they selectively pursue economic nationalism while remaining some of the most aggressive players in the world economy. This is in contrast to the Latin American countries whose enthusiastic embrace of globalization after an era of import substitution industrialization was not supplemented by an activist state (see Pedersen 2008; Amsden 2009; Bresser-Pereira 2010).

To understand this seeming paradox between globalization and state activism it is necessary to appreciate what states actually do for national well-being.[5] Without a doubt, the regulatory mechanisms generally available to states are becoming less effective due to the porosity of national borders, facilitated by multilateral organizations such as the WTO and Bretton Woods institutions. Also, inward-looking models of development have been challenged by newer forms of outward-looking competitive strategies in the global economy (Reich 1992). There are many well known reasons for this shift in economic policy in favor of greater reliance on the market for economic coordination. These include ideological shifts with greater public receptivity for a reduced role of the state and the structural inflexibility of states that constrain capital accumulation. The key reasons for this rightward shift include high wages in the OECD, increased financial burden due to government deficits everywhere, and pervasive technological change facilitating the mobility of capital on the world stage and thus relative redundancy of state coordination.

The purpose of this compilation is to document the different ways by which Asian governments have been pursuing economic nationalism even as they have been economically integrating with the world economy. On this point, this project is different from the detailed discussion of state-directed development and the patterns of intervention by select late industrializers in the pre-neoliberal phase (see Kohli 2007: 20–3). The thorny question is how weakening states in a neoliberal era can practice economic nationalism, given that states must adapt to global market forces by maintaining open trade and investment regimes. It means that states cannot have discriminatory policies in favor of national capital and keep the same latitude or inclination in their social spending priorities. Yet, as we will illustrate, at least for business, states do favor domestic capital in their expansion, increasingly by tailored deregulation and liberalization and less by orthodox protectionism. So it is not a question of whether economic nationalism has disappeared altogether, rather how it operates today and under what guises.

By adopting a non-rigid understanding of economic nationalism we expect to uncover newer forms of its practice. This is consistent with the writings of Alexander Hamilton and Friedrich List, the eighteenth-century American and nineteenth-century German economic nationalists respectively (see Harlen 1999: 741–2; Ho 2005). Although they are erroneously perceived as orthodox protectionists, they were interested in the international economic linkages that would spring from the domestic market. By this Listian logic, economic nationalism via tariffs and subsidies at an earlier phase of capitalist development was expected to lead to international competitiveness (Ho 2005). While List could not foresee the contemporary form of global capitalism, he was a "tactical" protectionist, which meant that he believed that when capitalists had matured, protection ought to be removed (Crane 1999: 223; see also Robison and Goodman 1996: 12–13). Under this type of government-business institutional alliance, the state could be expected to pursue new complementary policies that had not been part of the policy repertoire of an earlier form of economic nationalism. For example, unlike in the past, today the Indian state is leveraging its expatriate population for investment, remittance income, knowledge transfer, and even to lobby foreign governments on behalf of national businesses (D'Costa 2009). Similarly, the Chinese diaspora has become an important medium for China's economic resurgence and expressions of nationalism—economic or otherwise—in an integrating East Asian regional economy (see Dent 2008).

These developments are counterintuitive since international economic integration implies the increasing inability of the state to orchestrate economic activities, due to both macroeconomic instability and a changing business environment, which is no longer confined to national boundaries or national firms. But this reading of the tension between state intervention and globalization implies that there is a zero-sum game between globalization and economic nationalism. Our argument is that globalization does not erase economic nationalism wholesale. Rather, it forces states to find wedges of intervention pragmatically since national goals such as economic development, technological advance, job protection, and promotion of national business in a competitive world economy remain (see Amsden 2001). China's one-party state provides the litmus test as it continues its gradual but definitive turn away from orthodox economic nationalism to a more pragmatic form by playing the globalization process. Thus, promoting inward foreign direct investment (FDI), joining the WTO, and abandoning economic autarky (Crane 1999: 230) are consistent with the pressures of globalization but also reflect clever positioning by the Chinese state to enhance its national economic interests.

We argue that globalization selectively compels economic nationalism and in tandem selectively undercuts it because of the structural imperatives accompanying international economic integration. States facilitate the process of adjustment to globalization through selective reforms and continued protection of domestic firms (Nayar 2001), allowing for flexible evolution of the relationship between the state and economic nationalism (Bhaduri 2002: 39–40). But what is shed and what is retained is very much an empirical matter. States pursue economic objectives both defensively and offensively, protecting as well as promoting national assets and resources, at home and abroad. States, like other institutions, are also subject to failure, hence economic nationalism, despite being purposeful in design and intent, does not guarantee preferred outcomes. For example, the Chinese state is seen as quite capable of pursuing its goals whether in its export strategy, organization of the Olympics, or high-speed rail systems. Yet it has not been very successful in consolidating and streamlining its state-owned steel industry (Sun 2007), or supporting an effective science and technology policy (Cao, Suttmeier, and Simon 2009: 249–50).[6] However, both policy successes and failures enable institutional learning, where the shifting terrain of economic nationalism suggests holding on to some areas, discarding others, and picking new areas of promotion. We view this as "economic nationalism in motion" (D'Costa 2009), a dynamic concept that presumes that economic nationalism under globalization is a response to the changing opportunities and challenges offered by the world economy (Marshall 1996; Jones 2000; Helleiner and Pickel 2005).

Capturing the details of this dynamic phenomenon among Asian economies is the central task of this book. The rest of this chapter is divided into three main sections. In the next section, I briefly relate Asian states to global capitalism to bring out some of the common as well as diverse features of Asian economies in their quest for economic development. In Section 1.3, I provide a brief discussion of both familiar and new types of economic nationalism in Asia. Section 1.4 presents an outline of the chapters, which investigate a range of Asian countries and the varied ways of practicing economic nationalism in an era of globalization. The final section concludes.

1.2 Global Capitalism and Asian Economic Nationalism

Globalization is both the process and consequence of systemic expansion of national capitalism, which is an economic system that rests on accumulation based on private property and wage labor. The relationship between capitalism and economic nationalism is open-ended. Capitalism is a worldwide system of markets in which production relations are organized to yield the largest economic surplus for the owners of capital. Economic nationalism, on the other hand, is a practice adopted by states to generate and retain as much of the surplus as possible within the confines of the national territory. A priori, there is no reason for economic nationalism to mesh with the goals of capital accumulation since the former is a collective project while the latter is a private one. However, under globalization the process of generating economic surplus is not limited to the nation-state since economic nationalism as practiced by the state is an attempt to capture the surplus generated by national business operating at home or abroad. Hence, behind economic nationalism lies not just the state but also national business and elites since state support of accumulation directly favors business classes. Of course there are factions within the business and entrepreneurial groups, but in the contestation over capital accumulation large firms with their powerful associations are better able to mobilize the state on their behalf. In fact, not only does successful accumulation by business require nurturing by the state (leading to capitalist maturity) as evident in the earlier incarnations of intervention, capable states themselves can engineer their retreat from markets and partner with business to serve national accumulation. Hence, under globalization, economic nationalism increasingly entails strategic collaboration with capital (Rodrik 2007: 7).

The formation of capitalist markets in Asia has varied roots and thus substantial heterogeneity. However, colonialism and the Cold War, along with lateness of entry to modern industrialization, have left a deep imprint on the economic and political trajectory of the continent. In this context, East Asia has a special place in global capitalism because, as late industrializers, they more or less shared highly competent states (Amsden 1989; Evans 1995; Fitzgerald 2006). The region operated under the successive tutelage of China, Japan, and the USA. Now, increasingly the region is under Chinese influence in competition with a declining USA and Japan. Hence, the integral nature of contemporary East Asian capitalism, shaped historically by industrial modernity during the Cold War phase, cannot be erased from current discussions of economic nationalism in the region and beyond. After all, contemporary East Asian development is a realignment of the flying geese model established by nationalist and imperialist Japan since the early twentieth century and the hegemonic USA since World War II (Cumings 1984; Hatch and Yamamura 1997), incorporating both East and Southeast Asia into the larger global economic system.

The emerging regional order continues to be tense through latent nationalist conflicts anchored around unresolved issues of colonialism and war, including territorial conflicts between the Koreas and among China, Japan, South Korea, Taiwan, and Vietnam. Such conflicts often take on economic overtones, as evident from China's recent strategic export embargo of rare earth metals to Japan over disputed islands. Notwithstanding the conflicts, or perhaps because of them, the imbrications of these economies suggest an ongoing division of labor leading to a regional order. For China and other countries in the region, economic nationalism in its myriad forms has been the backbone of their ascendance and, for some, a tool to manage their international relations. Other areas of Asia are also linked to global capitalism, such as India with an overdeveloped state (Alavi 1972), albeit selectively. In the post-independence period the Indian state had a penchant for orthodox forms of economic nationalism (D'Costa 1995). However, today its economic and political trajectory is more in tune with globalization and has added to the heterogeneity of Asian capitalism. But just as in East Asia, the practice of economic nationalism has not disappeared; instead it now serves to push for integration with the world economy (D'Costa 2009; see also Mazumdar, Chapter 3) on its own national terms.

The recent active engagement of China in Africa to secure raw materials is an example of how far the state will go to protect its place in the global economic system by ensuring critical supplies of natural resources for its own firms. The embargo by China on rare earth metals, of course, has less to do with "economic" nationalism per se and more to do with *realpolitik*. Thus, the line between economic nationalism and nationalism as a broader sentiment is admittedly quite thin.[7] However, all nationalism is fundamentally political and in these times economic nationalism is a political expression of regulating or rather fostering national capitalism and facilitating its expansion externally. Of course this point stirs a hornet's nest since we are still confounded by what China represents: is it market socialism with Chinese characteristics, capitalism with socialist characteristics, state capitalism, or just simply capitalism? For our purposes, we do not enter this debate but we assume China is capitalist, albeit its capitalism takes a novel form, given that it increasingly organizes its economy around markets even though the state with its one-party apparatus remains an important shaper of society. China provides an interesting case to understand economic nationalism under globalization since it is leveraging its entrenched statist legacies on its own terms while integrating with the world capitalist economy.

Does this mean that global capitalism is a singular system with multiple states converging with similar economic policies, all designed to make markets work seamlessly? The "varieties of capitalism" (VOC) school suggests otherwise (Hall and Soskice 2001). Based on a comparative analysis of principal OECD economies, this school of thought argues that institutional differences in coordinating markets give rise to different economic and social outcomes. The heterogeneity of national capitalism is a product of the diverse legacies of history, culture, and institutional learning. But under capitalism, coordination is necessary to preempt market failure and minimize the instability associated with capitalist swings of boom and bust.[8] Though not stated explicitly, coordination is undertaken with *national* stability in mind, albeit with international coordination in times of severe financial crisis. Under globalization, state intervention is best justified for outcomes that markets fail to produce. Markets fail because of "information externalities" and "coordination externalities" and thus call for direct state intervention in the form of industrial policy (Rodrik 2007: 102–4). Technical advance, which may entail subsidies, protection, and government support for research and development (R&D), is promoted by states themselves (Ostry and Nelson 1995: 31). For example, China recently overtook the USA in solar panel manufacturing, capturing half the global output of US$29 billion, due to "lavish government subsidies"[9] and "loans at very low rates from state-owned banks in Beijing, cheap or free land from local and provincial governments" (Bradsher 2011a). Understanding the nature of global capitalism in general and specifically in the Asian context is a good starting point to appreciate the heterogeneity of Asian capitalism and by extension the relationship between economic nationalism and globalization. This relationship is a consequence of the continuity of state activism typically found in late industrializing countries under changing opportunities and challenges in the global economy. By supporting national capital accumulation, through critical investments in industry, human capital, and infrastructure, late industrializing states in Asia are contributing to the development of national capitalism.

Japanese capitalism is an exemplar of state activism in both overt and subtle ways. However, many of the institutions that served post-World War II economic nationalism in Japan have come under massive stress with globalization. With the intensification of international competition, institutional arrangements such as the *keiretsu* (vertically and horizontally integrated business groups) and lifetime employment are under pressure. These challenges to Japanese capitalism suggest that the earlier forms of state activism may not serve domestic business effectively in an increasingly integrating global economy. However, as new industrial and economic sectors emerge as part of the national portfolio, state activism can be expected to continue. As shown by Suzuki (Chapter 5) and Ozaki (Chapter 6), the role of the Japanese state under a liberalizing economy should not be underestimated. Both finance and high-tech industrial sectors remain very much part of the state's portfolio for intervention.

What Asian countries share is their late entry to industrialization and economic development and their penchant for intervention in practicing economic nationalism (see Amsden 2009). Competitive nationalism has been a feature of an East Asian regional order where geopolitics and economic hegemony have been persistent features. However, beginning with Japan, whose interventions date back to the late nineteenth century, economic nationalism in other Asian countries has been mostly a post-World War II nation-building phenomenon.[10] Anti-colonialism, combined with the *swadeshi* (self-reliance) movement in India to rid the British, has been very much part of India's political and economic nationalism. Post-independence state-led rapid industrialization in varying forms complemented such anti-colonial, nationalist legacies and was aimed to nurture and deepen national capitalism. In the 1980s, when globalization was in full swing, the Bharatiya Janata Party (BJP) mobilized the *swadeshi* nationalist strategy politically and ideologically by advancing the idea of "India First" in the world economy (Nayar 2000: 799). The major economies of Asia have all practiced economic nationalism with an active state. Even tiny Singapore, which is highly internationalized, shares partly with Japan and Korea the initial export drive of labor-intensive manufactures and gradually, with state sponsorship, a shift toward high-technology production and services. Singapore rode the wave of foreign direct investment under a state-mediated liberal economic environment (Huff 1995), while both Japan and South Korea shunned FDI and adopted explicit industrial policies and sectoral targeting in the complex capital goods sector. All three countries, being natural-resource-poor, utilized their human resources effectively through state-supported basic education and infrastructure development. It was also a way for these countries to pre empt any kind of leftist, pro-labor, pro-peasant dissent.

China and India, with different political systems, initially had similar impulses toward economic nationalism undergirded by strong statist systems but they differed markedly in their operationalization of policies. Their paths diverged with the onset of the Cultural Revolution in China. However, more or less at the same time—in the late 1970s—they began to undo their statist systems in favor of greater reliance on the market, first gradually and then quite rapidly (Bardhan 2010). They diverged considerably with the pace, content, and sequencing of deregulation and liberalization, with China more or less following the East Asian export-oriented model since the export growth spurt of the 1990s, albeit on a much larger scale, while India, except in a handful of sectors, remained very much a domestically driven economy. India, despite state intervention, inherited and fostered a mature capitalist class whose forays now extend to the world economy, while China has gradually transformed its state managers and others connected to the party apparatus into ambitious entrepreneurs. Both countries continue to adopt policies that aim to expand the national capitalist system.

All five countries under study provide various shades of the practice of economic nationalism in the form of pragmatic measures to cope with changes in the global capitalist system. Each one of these countries, whether through import substitution industrialization or an export-oriented model, contributed to the maturity of their capitalist classes. In India, business groups (often associated with particular ethnic communities) and industries got their start with government investment projects and handouts for their global expansion (Damodaran 2008). China's private capitalist class as an independent social class may be the least developed, given its heavy statist past and state-controlled enterprises today. But Chinese entrepreneurs, through family networks and state enterprises, are intricately interlinked. They are increasingly cashing in on opportunities with strategies and policies that are consistent with capitalist market imperatives.[11] The development of Asian capitalism suggests that the practice of economic nationalism, even as these states continue to actively engage with the world economy, has not been dampened. The rise of their capitalist classes is part of the reason for their ongoing participation in the world economy, just as new forms of emerging systemic vulnerabilities contribute to the persistence of economic nationalism in Asian countries.

1.3 Continuity and Change in Economic Nationalism

From an instrumentalist point of view, states pursue economic policies for national economic advantage and for achieving social goals. However, actual state action is politically derived mainly as a response to national societal forces. This is because the state is generally constrained by dominant classes and social groups. Furthermore, as international economic integration becomes a de facto structural requirement for accumulation, systemic or external economic and political pressures become additional sources for state action or incapacity. In this vortex of endogenous and exogenous drivers, the national capitalist class and its particular factions in a dynamic market system pull and push the state to support their accumulation agenda. Under such circumstances there could be some convergence of goals of the state and capital if supporting domestic capital is perceived as good for the country, akin to the "what is good for General Motors is good for America" dictum. This is also seen in contemporary China, India, and other Asian countries where state intervention in favor of private capital, often at the expense of rural and urban poor, migrants, and other disadvantaged social groups, is justified on the basis of national interest with the expectation that some benefits would also accrue to the poor.

The relationship between the state and capital is dynamic, especially under international economic integration since businesses are no longer "national" in outlook or origin. Domestic businesses expand and seek foreign markets just as multinationals from abroad aim to capture a share of the growing emerging market economies. In fact, the changing relationship between the state and the capitalist class is also accompanied by shifts within the capitalist class and between domestic and international capitalists (Evans 1979). For example, the export-oriented capitalist class could find increasing opportunities in the world economy as long as it continues to upgrade economic activities through technological learning and innovations and continues to attract state support because of its structural position in the economy. Domestically centered businesses, if unable to make a successful adjustment, may continue to seek state protection or succumb to international competition.

With the entry of multinational corporations (MNCs), the state is compelled to mediate between domestic and foreign capital and between different fractions of capital, weighing politically and economically the relative welfare effects of the two. The state is interested in reproducing the structure of accumulation as a whole, not supporting each and every fraction of capital. Propping up some capital (i.e., leading sectors) could be seen as strategic. The very firms that might have been protected, when mature, could become the internal agents of liberalization and globalization. This is further reinforced with internalization of neoliberal reforms by the state itself, albeit unevenly. Thus, when neoliberal reforms in India were well underway and multinational investments became integral to the globalization process, the BJP selectively sought foreign capital, captured best by its slogan "computer chips, yes, potato chips, no" (Nayar 2000: 800). As neoliberal ideology was absorbed by Bretton Woods institutions and by economics departments in the USA, policy makers, and students now serving in their home countries (for South Korea see Amsden 1992), economic nationalism as conventionally understood has been significantly weakened. But rather than disappear, it has taken different forms. Increasingly, sheltering weak firms is no longer the preferred option. Instead, the state, collaboratively with capital, attempts to forge new areas of intervention in the economy such as emerging product markets, branding, technological advance, currency controls, and internationalization of domestic firms. Below I discuss several areas in which economic nationalism can be found, not all of which are new.

1.3.1 *Classical Industrial Policy*

Classical industrial policy has been used by much of the world. For example, the Japanese, South Korean, and Taiwanese states have intervened relentlessly to strategically exploit opportunities available in the global economy for national development (Johnson 1982; Gold 1986; Amsden 1989). The major Asian countries—India and China—since their founding as republics in the late 1940s, and Japan and Korea in the post-World War II era, were cold to inward FDI, fearing weakened national control. During the decade-long recession of the 1990s, the Japanese saw foreigners buying what they perceived as prized assets, leading to a sense of national loss and intense nationalist feelings (Suginohara 2008: 844). The system of intra-*keiretsu* shareholding helped protect Japanese businesses from foreign acquisitions and competition for several decades. However, globalization has pushed states to dismantle both tariff and non-tariff barriers. The protection of domestic agriculture is a good example of classical industrial policy. The rich countries continue to protect their agriculture for economic, political, and social reasons even though the contribution of agriculture to national income and employment has fallen drastically. In 2007, the share of agriculture to GDP in both the USA and Japan was about 1% (World Bank 2010), while estimates of US employment in agriculture and allied industries in the sector was 1.5% of the total workforce in 2008 (US Census Bureau 2010), and 3.6% in Japan (calculated from Government of Japan, Ministry of Agriculture, Forestry, and Fisheries 2010). Despite the low value and employment contribution, agriculture has been protected due to the political influence of this sector. The failure of the 1999 Seattle WTO negotiations was partly due to the participants' inability to negotiate the terms of dismantling the agricultural subsidies of the rich countries. In this context, Japan still stands out with a 777.7% tariff on imported rice (Tabuchi 2010). Despite the high economic cost to Japanese consumers, agricultural interests in Japan still wield considerable political power over trade policy.

With globalization, the footloose character of investments and the fine-tuning of the production chain through offshoring strategies render traditional industrial policy less effective (Naudé 2010a). Hence, states find new ways to practice economic nationalism. For example, special economic zones, perfected by China, are a carryover of the export processing zones but on a much larger scale and scope (Naudé 2010b).[12] They have become a novel vehicle to jump-start domestic industrialization that is globally oriented. The usual kinds of subsidies, government-provided infrastructure, wage and labor control, and appropriation of agricultural land, are all part of the interventionist package. India has attempted to revive a relatively stagnant industrial sector through special economic zones by providing a wide variety of incentives to businesses including infrastructural support, income tax holidays, and questionable forms of agricultural land acquisition (Palit and Bhattacharjee 2008).

Furthermore, orthodox industrial policies are not completely discarded even in an age of globalization. For example, the Chinese government has continued to favor local suppliers over foreign ones, especially in technology. Procurement policy continues to favor domestic companies in energy production, such as producers of solar panels and wind turbines, which are both technologically and commercially new emerging sectors (Browne and Dean 2010; Bradsher 2011b). Until 1990, Japan had restrictions on large foreign retail stores, which were negotiated away under the structural impediments initiative. Such restrictions persist in India today, where companies such as Walmart are not allowed to operate. The fear of job losses for the less educated and less skilled makes states wary of large-scale multinational retailers. In Japan and India, small, individual, family-owned businesses are protected from big retailers. The Indian government does not yet allow multinationals to retail multiple brands under the same roof. However, Indian retail business is expanding and hence the protective policy could be lifted if the small sector loses its political clout or big retail businesses with market growth override such protectionist sentiments.

1.3.2 *Techno-nationalism*

As globalization makes the practice of conventional industrial policy difficult and imposes fierce competitive pressure, arising not from cost pressures alone but from technical advance, states are compelled to intervene in the broader areas of science and technology. This is particularly salient as new developments in technology require massive R&D efforts, new institutional mechanisms, and government support for private initiatives to create a viable competitive economy in knowledge-intensive sectors. For example, industrial targeting, a longstanding practice, persists in emerging sectors such as biotechnology, medical equipment, information technology, and aerospace (for aerospace see McGuire 2007; Vertesy and Szirmai 2010). While Japan has moved away from traditional protectionism, it continues to work with its giant *keiretsu* firms such as Mitsubishi to develop a new kind of energy-efficient regional aircraft (see Ozaki, Chapter 6). China has ambitious plans to increase its R&D expenditure to 2.5% of GDP by 2020 (Cao, Suttmeier, and Simon 2009: 247), a ratio matched only by a handful of countries thus far.

This techno-nationalism is justified on the same grounds as industrial policy, namely market failure, though the complexity of technical advance and anticipated losses in rents demand new forms of state regulation (Ostry and Nelson 1995). Thus anti-trust policy, as in the Microsoft case in Europe, and intellectual property rights protection in the USA and its extension to all other countries, are ways to protect and promote what are private rents that are also presumed to contribute to national economic welfare. The formation of Sematech in 1987 in the USA, a consortium of semiconductor firms with public funding, is an example of state-industry cooperation in a high-technology sector (Ostry and Nelson 1995: 57). Over time, Sematech has extended its partnership to universities and state governments and in 2004 set up an Advanced Materials Research Center (AMRC) to jointly "accelerate commercialization of research on new materials and nanostructures for future transistors and their interconnection, as well as the advanced patterning and measurement of future materials and structures" (Sematech 2010). Another instance of techno-nationalism can be seen in the USA blocking the sale of Fairchild Semiconductor in 1987 to Japan's Fujitsu on national security grounds, though trade friction was alleged to be another motive behind this measure (Sanger 1987).

1.3.3 *Support for Internationalization of National Firms*

Since international economic integration in the current phase of global capitalism is a given, states have recognized the importance of playing the market system by supporting their national businesses in their expansion abroad. The East Asian economies, through their mercantilist strategies, initially pushed exports and restricted imports and inward FDI. Japan and South Korea are examples par excellence of this approach. As businesses matured and export revenues soared, governments of these countries liberalized their economies selectively. Rising wage costs and currency appreciation compelled governments to encourage national business to expand overseas. For example, Suzuki Motors, one of the smallest auto producers in Japan, was encouraged by the government to invest in India in the early 1980s (D'Costa 2005). Today, Suzuki produces more cars in India than it does in Japan. Outward FDI became a Japanese national strategy to promote domestic business overseas, while inward FDI policy in Japan was designed to protect domestic business and thus remained low key. This is also visible in the case of South Korea, whose push for Korean investments abroad is predicated on mercantilist policies (see Lee, Chapter 7), a view not shared by all (Pirie 2005). However, by creating the "foundations of a new neoliberal regime of accumulation" (Pirie 2005: 371) the Korean state has repositioned itself in the world economy, which is an action consistent with the argument advanced here.

China still has vast pools of poor communities but it has amassed sizable foreign exchange reserves through exports and inward FDI, and is engaged in promoting outward FDI to compensate for the economy's competitive disadvantages (Luo, Xue, and Han 2010). Furthermore, the macroeconomic imbalance in China due to massive foreign exchange reserves, which must be recycled to contain inflationary pressures and currency appreciation, is in itself an arena for creative intervention. Such a pragmatic turnaround in state action is not an Asian phenomenon alone. It is exemplified by the recent visit to India of US president Barack Obama, the leader of one of the most liberal capitalist states. Accompanied by representatives of American business, Obama's mission was to help American businesses sell to India and generate jobs at home (Stolberg and Bajaj 2010).

Another novel approach to promote national businesses has been branding, a growing commercial endeavor (Ogilvy and Mather 2008) where ambitious states have begun to intervene. While promoting national brands is an extension of supporting national products and thus the companies that produce them, branding today has taken on added significance due to the slicing of value chains across national boundaries, which pits high-value segments against low-value ones. Thus the production or, more accurately, the assembly of Apple's iPhone, yields a mere 7% of the final sale price to China, demonstrating low value added to a high-value product (Barboza 2010). In this case, China cannot cash in on the Apple brand itself and reap the higher revenues. Branded products in the Asian context are particularly relevant, as Western design companies, confronted with stagnant OECD markets, have targeted growing Asian markets.[13] Furthermore, successful brands from France, Italy, Japan, South Korea, and Taiwan have had a demonstration effect. Some of these brands have been products of industrial policies, which have nurtured many of the name-brand-producing companies in Japan and South Korea.

In this era of globalization, where competition for markets is fierce, a lack of brands creates a sense of economic inferiority and outflows of resources.[14] It is therefore not surprising to witness China clamping down on foreign brands and trying to foster national brands (see Gerth, Chapter 9). In fact nationalism can be strong enough to force foreign companies hawking branded products to take unusual positions, as in the Carrefour case in 2008 when the French company explicitly distanced itself from the French government's relationship with the Dalai Lama (Ogilvy 2008: 3). Recently the Chinese government complained about foreign luxury goods not meeting domestic standards, charging that branded products were over-hyped through labeling. Since foreign branded products sell at a premium compared to domestically produced ones, with the difference in price attributed to quality, the Chinese government ingeniously disputed the superiority of foreign brands (Canaves 2010).[15] In a similar vein, the Indian Ministry of Industry and Commerce, in partnership with the Confederation of Indian Industry, has established an India Brand Equity Foundation (IBEF), which works to "brand" India for its "distinctive" qualities, perhaps in contrast to China. These qualities include democracy and freedom, spirit of entrepreneurship, intellectual capital, and global integration (IBEF 2010). Such public–private partnerships to market India as well as China's quest for national brand development are indicative of new forms of state intervention.

1.3.4 *Leveraging the Diaspora*

Supporting national businesses overseas is an aggressive form of economic nationalism. Consider the successful Indian software industry, which is an export-driven business sector that makes use of the international mobility of Indian technical talent (D'Costa 2008). As the volume of offshoring has increased and the global demand for Indian professionals has expanded, the Indian state is able to take advantage of a large pool of technical talent for export. The presence of highly educated Indian professionals overseas, especially in the USA, and its large pool of English speakers at home, gives the Indian state an unexpected source of national strength (D'Costa 2009). Reaping the economic benefits from the global economy is possible, in part, due to India's diaspora of expatriates, professionals, and students. India is able to leverage its talent pool at home and abroad with roughly 14 million young graduates with less than seven years of experience in India and 14% of the 3.1 million foreign-born science and engineering graduates in the USA being Indians (Bound 2007: 9, 11). The Indian state today is pragmatically trying to extract the commercial, technological, and intellectual contributions of Indian talent and claim a nation abroad through its émigré population of highly skilled professionals (Dickinson and Bailey 2007).[16] The government of India has offered various financial incentives for non-resident Indians (NRIs), Persons of Indian Origin (PIO), and Overseas Citizens of India (OCI) (D'Costa 2009). The latter two categories are entitled to 15-year and life-long visas respectively, clearly suggesting that in an age of globalization economic nationalism can still be practiced by leveraging its diaspora. China is also leveraging its diaspora, beckoning overseas Chinese to contribute to their country's transformation (Crane 1999: 227) and creating an "imagined nation" (Crane 1998; also Selden, Chapter 2).

1.3.5 *Financial and Currency Controls*

With increasing volatility and unpredictability, many governments continue to keep a tight control on the balance of payments by regulating current and capital accounts and maintaining fixed exchange rates. However, with globalization and liberalization, Asian governments have become more confident in interacting with the world economy. The USA–China trade relationship is a case in point where China's massive trade surplus has given it new confidence. However, the USA's massive deficits in the context of the current global financial crisis have also introduced mistrust between the two countries. China's low wages, various government interventions, and its policy of tying the yuan to the US dollar, have all contributed to the perceived unfairness of China's trade when it comes to American jobs and competitiveness. If the US dollar declines, the Chinese yuan also declines, thereby sustaining its export competitiveness, when by market logic, with high rates of economic growth and massive foreign exchange reserves, the Chinese currency ought to be appreciating relative to the dollar and thus easing the USA's trade deficit. China's trade surplus and its nearly three trillion dollars worth of foreign exchange reserves have not had immediate impact on the appreciation of the yuan (at least in the eyes of the USA), though it has been gradually rising over the years. The Chinese government appears intent on controlling its currency as an instrument of export competition and protection of its US dollar assets.

The practice of economic nationalism, intended to benefit the national economy, can adversely impact other countries. Singapore, one of the most agile economies with a strong liberal economic approach, nevertheless uses the state to manage its sizable sovereign wealth funds abroad. But in doing so it has faced challenges abroad. For example, Singapore's Temasek Holdings had bought shares in Thailand's Shin Corporation, a telecommunications company in which Thaksin Shinawatra, the ousted prime minister, was a partner. The Thai government reacted strongly against the selling of strategic national assets to a foreign government, leading to a coup in 2006. The fact that Temasek was a state-owned entity made economic nationalism in Thailand even more severe as a neighboring state had control over an important national asset in Thailand (Sam 2008). Nationalist sentiments from foreign governments have been expressed elsewhere. For example, Japanese multinationals operating in China have faced pressure from the Chinese government to alter their ways of doing business to achieve Chinese goals, including siting plants locally, recruiting local talent, promoting energy efficiency, and protecting the environment (see Ryu, Chapter 10). At first cut, the entry of foreign companies signals a diluted form of economic nationalism in the host economy, but making them conform to national goals is indicative of strengthening such nationalism. Overall, these examples serve to illustrate the new kinds of challenges posed by both the process of globalization and the practice of economic nationalism in the internationalized environment.

1.4 Chapter Outlines

How economic nationalism has changed in the last 60 years in Asia and what contemporary forms economic nationalism has taken are central questions in this study. Since East Asia displays a distinct form of regionalized geopolitics, we begin the discussion with a historical analysis of the interplay of economic and geopolitical nationalism and regionalism involving Japan, Korea, China, and the USA (Chapter 2). This is followed by three chapters, one each on India, China, and Japan, that form the crux of our argument, namely, that globalization and economic nationalism are not contradictory: rather, their coexistence is a reflection of capitalist maturity on the one hand and incremental pragmatic adjustments to the imperatives of globalization and market liberalization on the other (Chapters 3, 4, 5). In this transition the state does not disappear though the forms of its engagement change in ways that internalize the mechanisms of globalization. This argument is elaborated in the next three chapters (Chapters 6, 7, 8) discussing in turn: Japan's use of industrial policy in new emerging sectors such as innovation-driven, energy-efficient commercial aircraft; South Korea's pursuit of globalization with neo-mercantilist strategies; and Singapore's pragmatic mercantilism in trying to cope with new challenges spurred by economic globalization. Chapters 9 and 10 discuss two contemporary developments in the area of economic nationalism in Asia. The first presents a historical account of how China is practicing economic nationalism by promoting national brands and discouraging foreign brands. The second discusses the growing nationalism in China and the response of Japanese multinationals in adjusting to the Chinese economic and political environment. This is a critical development where further research is warranted since we anticipate increasing inter-nationalist frictions accompanying the intensification of globalization. In all, these ten chapters comprehensively cover economic nationalism in the selected countries in Asia and offer a window on the future of globalization in the region. Given the nature of the theme, the thrust is an interdisciplinary, political-economic, sociological, and historically sensitive analysis at the macrogeopolitical, regional, and micronational levels.

In Chapter 2, Mark Selden explores the interplay of economic and geopolitical nationalism and regionalism in contemporary East Asia. A brief survey of East Asia from the sixteenth to the late twentieth century, covering the Sinocentric tributary trade system, colonial rule, world wars, and the rise of revolutions and nationalism sets the stage for the analysis of the resurgence of contemporary East Asia and the changing face of regional geopolitics and political economy. He notes that a new East Asian regional order rests on foundations of dynamic economic growth but is framed within the structure of US global power. The central question he asks is how the post-1970s resurgence and transformation of East Asia can be conceptualized in relation to three major forces: economic and geopolitical nationalism, regionalism, and globalism, with the last understood in relation to the US bid for hegemony. According to Selden, the new regional order, far from transcending competitive nationalisms, is the expression of latent nationalist and economic conflicts pivoting on unresolved tensions rooted in historical experiences of colonialism and war. Tensions also include territorial conflicts and the perpetuation of national divisions involving China and Taiwan and the Korean peninsula that reflect the outcomes of World War II and postwar revolutionary movements. The East Asian order continues to be driven by competitive nationalisms and the role of the USA as a participant or partner in an emerging East Asian order, which is simultaneously framed by China's rise as a dominant regional and international economic power.

Surajit Mazumdar in Chapter 3 argues that economic nationalism in India contributed to and coexists with the liberalization process initiated in 1991, which marked a decisive break in India's economic policy and pushed the country towards increased integration with the global economy. India's capitalists embraced this process, in contrast to their active support for a strategy of autonomous development at the time of independence. He focuses on this shift by examining the outlook of the capitalist class as represented by India's big business and argues that this transformation reflects the development and evolution of Indian capitalism resulting from industrialization under the older autonomous strategy. Furthermore, embracing liberalization became both possible and necessary for India's capitalists with the Indian state also adjusting to the imperatives of national capitalist development. The state has continued to assist the capitalist class in different ways and in turn Indian capital has gained increased leverage with the state. With state support it has expanded globally and become less industrial and more integrated into global production and financial systems. This growth and transformation of Indian big business due to past economic nationalism in turn has reinforced its support for liberalization and globalization.

In continuing this thread of the relationship between globalization and economic nationalism, Yongnian Zheng and Rongfang Pan in Chapter 4 show that while liberalism seems to have dominated China's integration with the world economy, economic nationalism continues to play a significant role in the process. In tandem with the three distinct periods of opening and reform, Zheng and Pan demonstrate that economic nationalism in China has undergone three phases, reflecting a gradual transition from a "defensive" phase, shielding the domestic market from foreign competition, to the present "aggressive" phase, venturing into the global market. The authors point out that while economic nationalism has remained in existence throughout China's economic modernization, its origins, forms of presentation, and themes have been constantly changing. In each of the three distinct phases, economic nationalism is examined conceptually and empirically: economic nationalism as an ideology of the state, as industrial policies on the part of the government, and as industrial practices of the individual firms. In the process, the Chinese state has continuously made proactive adjustments to the institutions to cushion the negative impact of global integration and offset the potential risks of liberalization. The chapter also stresses that these efforts by the government have been embedded in a constantly evolving process of political contention, intellectual discourse, and institutional change.

In Chapter 5, Takaaki Suzuki turns to Japan, a nation well known for its particular brand of economic nationalism. Its determined effort to expand militarily in the region and beyond and catch up economically and technologically with the West since the Meiji Restoration of 1868 and after the departure of the US occupation forces in 1951 was successful. Suzuki begins the chapter by addressing how economic nationalism in Asia and Japan has changed in the last 30 years and where it might be heading in the future. He looks at the "East Asian developmental state model" driven by state intervention rather than laissez-faire approaches. Japan has been credited with perfecting this approach, deftly combining state action with large private corporations. However, this model came under increasing criticism as Japan's economy slid into a prolonged period of stagnation in the late 1980s and neoliberal policies were embraced by the political establishment. The key issue Suzuki raises is counterintuitive: despite scaling back the role of the state in many economic regulatory and welfare-related areas, the state took on a much greater though often hidden role in areas that helped preserve the stability of a more liberalized and finance-driven market. Hence, the actual size and role of the state has expanded. Relying on financial and macroeconomic policies since the early 1980s, he demonstrates that globalization and greater financial liberalization were accompanied by the creation of several powerful state-backed institutions entrusted with substantial financial resources and a wide range of regulatory authority that go well beyond what is deemed "prudential regulatory" safeguards. These included protecting depositors of failed banks, recovering bad loans, liquidating and temporarily nationalizing failed banks, and strengthening the capital-adequacy ratio of solvent banks. Consequently, the role of the state as lender, depositor, guarantor, and investor rose dramatically during this period, and the overall size of the state as a percentage of GDP has grown considerably. Although Suzuki recognizes that the rhetorical justifications made to support this transition were often consistent with economic nationalist claims, he suggests that neoliberalism has failed to deliver on its promises of growth and social stability.

Toshiya Ozaki in Chapter 6 also takes up the Japanese case and asks whether Japan can and should pursue economic nationalism in the twenty-first century, or whether it should commit itself to the liberal multilateralism that has been the foundation of the post-war international economic system. These questions imply that economic nationalism is fundamentally at odds with the liberal multilateralism on which today's international economic relations have been founded. Using the latest round of Japanese policy debate as a case study, the chapter highlights the potential opportunity for a mature and advanced industrial economy such as Japan to pursue economic nationalism while at the same time embracing liberal multilateralism. The Japanese government understood that dismantling tariff and non-tariff barriers would not result in a level playing field across countries and individual sectors. Rather it believed that removal of these barriers would expose firms more directly to national differences that were once obscured by these barriers. In this chapter Ozaki examines the Japanese search for answers to cope with these challenges by conducting a case study entailing both industrial and trade policy. He explores the intense debate between the Japanese government and its counterparts in the civil aircraft manufacturing industry sector as they searched for a new source of industrial competitiveness. Government and business redefined economic nationalism so that they could develop nationalist industry policies while simultaneously embracing the liberal trade regime of the WTO. The Japanese government embarked on a new and different nationalist economic policy: helping Japanese firms establish their advantages by embedding their competitive strength in national institutions. Thus economic nationalism continues to matter substantially for Japanese firms to compete in the age of liberal and multilateral global markets.

After the Asian financial crisis of 1997, South Korea was compelled to adopt IMF-style liberalization policies and, by implication, to abandon economic nationalism. In Chapter 7, You-il Lee argues otherwise. He explores the process by which economic nationalism as an economic trajectory was challenged in South Korea in the post-World War II era of globalization, but makes the case that no economic shift has occurred in the course of South Korea's neoliberal economic trajectory. *Segyehwa* (globalization), initiated by the Kim Young-sam regime (1993–8) in 1994, entailed globalization by way of outward foreign direct investment. The regimes that followed (Kim Dae-jung

(1998–2003) and Roh Moo-hyun (2003–8)) encouraged inward FDI. These neoliberal policies of deep international economic integration, he argues, have not reversed the traditional nationalist development course, rather they have strengthened the state's capacity. Globalization policies of the previous regimes still remain subordinate to the goal of state building and the interests of the state. In other words, the Korean state remains developmental and neo-mercantilist. Economic nationalism in South Korea should be understood as a political phenomenon rather than simply being anti-neoliberal.

Chapter 8 by Alan Chong examines one of the world's most globalized nation-states, Singapore. The remarkable aspect of Singapore's development is a curious blend of economic nationalism with a globalization-friendly government. However, this blending has not been forged without contradictions and political slippage. Rather, the Singaporean "model" of "mercantilism with a global face," as Chong argues, should be seen as a test of how economic nationalism can exploit globalization's promise of liberal economic access. As a result, Singapore is practicing a globalization strategy that is chameleon in nature by disciplining national factors of production and investment to integrate with the liberal economic currents of a global economy. The roots of this blending experiment lie in the foundational visions of its dominant party government's leaders since 1965. Increasingly, this blending has been tested through the extemporaneous compromises made in dealing with antagonisms over living spaces between locals and foreigners, mediating housing market controversies, extending sovereign wealth funds overseas, and hosting globalization-friendly summitry. These dimensions in Singapore illustrate some negative externalities to even the most nationalistically directed globalization process. At some point in the future, despite the sterling growth rates of the Singaporean economy, the ruling party will have to account for the strains on the citizenry arising from the peculiar formula of globalization-friendly economic nationalism.

Paralleling Zheng and Pan's treatment of Chinese economic nationalism (Chapter 4) as one of gradual adjustment on increasingly aggressive footing, Karl Gerth in Chapter 9 documents how, since the early 1990s, economic nationalism in China has evolved away from orthodox economic nationalist concerns about protecting the home market from foreign products, services, and capital toward owning and managing domestically and internationally competitive brands. Gerth shows that this transition is not accidental but is an explicit goal of current Chinese state policy. Since Beijing decided to join the WTO in the early 1990s, the country has had to comply with new trade rules liberalizing its markets for goods and services. WTO membership was often heralded as the quintessential symbol of the demise of economic nationalism, something that would create a "flat world" wherein borders and nationalities finally surrendered to competitive advantage. Ironically, though, the chapter shows that the obligations of WTO membership have actually helped push China toward a newer, more sophisticated form of economic nationalism. This newer form stresses the control of the higher value-added portions of the value chain, branding, rather than simply production with the use of local labor and capital.

We continue with China in the final chapter, an economy whose limits seem boundless and whose state appears equally ambitious. This is evident from its renewed anti-Japanese sentiment, exacerbated by recent territorial disputes involving the Senkaku Islands and natural resources of the East China Sea. Following the violent anti-Japanese demonstrations of 2005, China's hostility towards Japan has also had an effect on the economic prospects of Japanese corporations, creating apprehension over the future of Japanese corporate and trade relations in China. This pervasive climate of anti-Japanese sentiment, often couched in economic nationalist terms, has forced Japanese companies seeking to expand their businesses abroad to grapple with the unique challenges of navigating the highly politicized environment. Kei-koh Ryu in Chapter 10 asks how Japanese corporations should respond to China's economic nationalism. Based on data obtained from field research, his chapter begins with an analysis of the impact of Chinese economic nationalism on the commercial prospects of Japanese businesses with operations in China. He then discusses the importance of "business–society relations" for the localization of Japanese corporations in the Chinese market, concluding with some recommended strategies for social engagement. Still, the success of any localization strategy for foreign companies in China fundamentally depends on whether China's market economy continues to develop in the face of harsh political conditions and growing social unrest. Ryu fills an important scholarly void by analyzing the effects of Chinese economic nationalism on the performance of Japanese corporations operating in China. We believe future research on economic nationalism ought to take up multicountry experiences of how states treat multinationals as the latter become more entrenched in national economies.

1.5 Conclusion

From the descriptions above it seems that the early twenty-first century may be the era of economic nationalism because of vulnerabilities associated with globalization, and in tandem, the availability of new opportunities in the world economy. In other words, economic nationalism is expected to coexist with globalization as disputes over trade, investment, balance of payments, exchange rate controls, immigration, and intellectual property rights persist.

This new nationalism is not expected to be practiced with the usual tariff- and non-tariff-based instruments or with disincentives to foreign investment. Rather, both instability and opportunities will demand state orchestration and global negotiations, both of which are subject to considerable structural impediments. Some states, such as China, seem better able to pursue their goals, though there are international and domestic challenges that make even the Chinese state defensive. Thus, in an era of economic integration anti-foreigner sentiment, backlash against offshoring, pressure to revalue currencies, focus on domestic development, branding, techno-nationalism, and leveraging ethnic-based social networks and diasporas for economic and political gains are some of the contemporary forms of both defensive and offensive economic nationalism.

As I have argued and as the chapters demonstrate in the rest of the volume, economic nationalism in practice is a dynamic process—from one of protecting domestic capital from foreign capital to making domestic capital compete with foreign capital in the global economy. As will be shown in the chapters ahead, China's practice of economic nationalism can be captured dynamically in three phases, moving initially from gradual, defensive engagement to aggressive expansion. This is also evident in the case of Japan and South Korea, although the sequencing of strategies has been different in these countries in part because of a unified regional political economy. In parallel fashion, Singapore seems to display a happy blend of global-friendly policies with economic nationalism. But the constraints faced by the mature economy in the context of the wider changes in the structure of global economy have introduced new contradictions for the small island. In India, the earlier nationalist policies that contributed to capitalist maturity also unleashed the political and economic forces of global integration, though pockets of resistance remain as new challenges of "exclusive" growth worsen. In each of these cases, the dynamic of economic nationalism has its own momentum interacting with the rhythm, pace, and pressures of globalization.

Two issues that have not been explicitly addressed in this volume but which remain implicit in the discussion of economic nationalism are: (1) whether economic nationalism as practiced actually improves the material conditions of citizens or simply creates an aura of expectations of trickle-down effects by the explicit support of national capital; and (2) to what extent contemporary economic nationalism alters the structure of the world economy from its status quo of triad dominance to unprecedented rivalries and collaboration between the West and Asia, and for that matter induce capitalist competition and national rivalry within Asian economies. In other words, as Asian economies gain stature, could the pursuit of economic nationalism consistent with globalization also be consistent with inclusive development policies for those sectors that are peripherally touched by the benefits of globalization or marginalized by the very process of globalization? In the concluding chapter, these issues are briefly introduced to propose future areas of research and advance further our understanding of the very dynamic phenomenon of economic nationalism in motion (D'Costa 2009).

The current global financial crisis has wrought substantial economic havoc in the OECD economies and is forcing states to correct for some of the past excesses of a deregulated capitalist economic system, which has focused more on growth and less on social policy. Hence, economic nationalism, in new ways through national policies of "inclusive" growth and development, could be resurrected in the future. At the same time, nationalist sentiments in a climate of low global economic growth, rising joblessness in the OECD, and bilateral macroeconomic imbalances between China and the USA could spark an unprecedented spate of orthodox protectionist policies not witnessed since the Great Depression of the 1930s. There is a decline in the support for free trade in the USA and other OECD economies just as prominent economists have reassessed the virtues of untrammeled international trade (Woo 2008: 89). The challenge for Asian countries now and in the near future will be how best to juggle national development with a highly competitive and interdependent capitalist world economy and capitalists who know no bounds to their accumulation agenda. Clever and sophisticated economic nationalism could be one limited solution for tackling national development concerns, but the fallacy of composition suggests otherwise. A rethinking of the relationship between the state and capitalism is imperative for a better appreciation of the workings of globally integrated markets and state responses to the exclusive nature of contemporary capitalism. The chapters ahead are expected to contribute to that agenda.

Notes

1. Witness the "buy American program" for solar panels for the defense industry, discouraging Chinese exports of such panels to the USA (Bradsher 2011a).
2. Amsden and Hikino (2006) emphasize the importance of local firms and national champions as part of economic nationalism. They also suggest that initial favorable distribution of income allows the state to create national champions (Amsden and Hikino 2006: 190).
3. The slowness of Japanese bureaucrats to restructure the banking sector was not due to incompetence but an attempt to minimize the impact of liberalization on the lifetime employment system (Weiss 2000; Walter 2006).
4. We are aware of the contingent dimension of economic nationalism in particular moments and hence do not always presume the purposeful nature of economic nationalism. For example, in Thailand the emergent economic nationalism since

2001 was a product of a confluence of particular political forces, designed to favor certain groups, and was politically expedient (Glassman 2004).

5. We are aware that states are complex institutions. We also acknowledge that national well being is a nebulous term. However, we here focus on the relatively "hard" dimensions of economic nationalism, principally the economy, technology, finance, and policy interventions. Softer categories, such as branding, are also included but they sit squarely within the economic dimension. We are also aware of the real possibility and actual practice of economic nationalism not benefiting citizens (as in India and China for example, where income inequalities have worsened). We take up this issue briefly in Chapter 11.
6. The recent accident of its high-speed train has been a temporary setback to such bold initiatives.
7. In a recent textbook on nationalism, the economic dimension was altogether missing and the discussion centered on the relationship between ethnic/social identity and nationalism (Özkirimli 2010).
8. For an alternative and pro-market view on market failure and state intervention, see Tanzi (2011: 13–31).
9. "Solar Energy." *New York Times*, 6 September 2011. http://topics.nytimes.com/top/news/business/energy-environment/solar-energy/index.html?scp=1&sq=solar%20energy%20china&st=cse [Accessed January 25, 2012].
10. India had a well-developed economic nationalist movement during the colonial period.
11. This partnership could degenerate into "crony" capitalism as being increasingly witnessed in China and India under economic liberalization. Elsewhere in South and East Asia such forms of capitalism, where the public treasury effectively becomes a private domain, has been astutely observed (see Khan and Sundaram 2000).
12. Globalization and outsourcing also put organized labor on the defensive (Candland and Sil 2001) as union density has sharply declined around the world and China does not have any independent unions.
13. Of course, strong brands can have their downside as anti-foreign sentiments can be targeted at particular foreign brands. The smashing of Toyota cars in the USA at the height of trade friction with Japan in the 1980s and citizen opposition to KFC in India due to perceived animal rights violations in the 1990s are two cases of economic nationalism targeted at countries via national brands.
14. From a corporate point of view, brands for individual consumers are seen as providing an identity that meets human emotional inadequacies and vulnerabilities, and the objective is to exploit such weakness with brands.
15. China has also attempted to limit US entertainment products on "nationalist" grounds. It has lost WTO panel rulings "...in the last 13 months, regarding high taxes on imported auto parts and lax enforcement of counterfeiting laws, (but) has not changed its policies in either case" (Bradsher 2009).
16. Successful lobbying by non-resident Indians in the USA to forge a USA–India Nuclear Treaty after India refused to sign the Comprehensive Test Ban Treaty (Narlikar 2006: 73) speaks volumes about leveraging expatriate populations.

References

Alavi, H. (1972). "The State in Postcolonial Societies: Pakistan and Bangladesh." *New Left Review*, 74: 59–81.

Amsden, A.H. (1989). *Asia's Next Giant: South Korea and Late Industrialization*. New York: Oxford University Press.

Amsden, A.H. (2009). "Nationality of Firm Ownership in Developing Countries: Who Should 'Crowd Out' Whom in Imperfect Markets?" in M. Cimoli, G. Dosi, and J.E. Stiglitz (eds.), *Industrial Policy and Development: Political Economy of Capabilities Accumulation*, 409–23. Oxford: Oxford University Press.

Amsden, A.H. (2001). *The Rise of the "Rest": Challenges to the West from Late-Industrializing Economies*. Oxford: Oxford University Press.

Amsden, A.H. (1992). "The South Korean Economy: Is Business-Led Growth Working?" in D.N. Clark (ed.), *Korea Briefing, 1992*. Boulder: Westview Press.

Amsden, A.H. and Hikino, T. (2006). "Economic Nationalism and Income Distribution in Late-Industrializing Countries," in S.Y.S. Chien and J. Fitzgerald (eds.), *The Dignity of Nations: Equality, Competition, and Honor in East Asian Nationalism*, 189–205. Hong Kong: Hong Kong University Press.

Barboza, D. (2010). "Supply Chain for iPhone Highlights Costs in China." *New York Times*, 5 July 2010. http://www.nytimes.com/2010/07/06/technology/06iphone.html?_r=1&scp=1&sq=supply%20chain%20for%20iphone&st=cse [Accessed January 25, 2011].

Bardhan, P. (2010). *Awakening Giants, Feet of Clay: Assessing the Economic Rise of China and India*, Princeton: Princeton University Press.

Bhaduri, A. (2002). "Nationalism and Economic Policy in the Era of Globalization," in D. Nayyar (ed.), *Governing Globalization: Issues and Institutions*, 19–48. Oxford: Oxford University Press.

Biersteker, T.J. (1992). "The 'Triumph' of Neoclassical Economics in the Developing World: Policy Convergence and Bases of Governance in the International Economic Order," in J.N. Rosenau and E.-O. Czempiel (eds.), *Governance without Government: Order and Change in World Politics*, 102–31. Cambridge: Cambridge University Press.

Bound, K. (2007). *India: The Uneven Innovator*. London: Demos.

Bradsher, K. (2011a). "China Benefits as U.S. Solar Industry Withers." *New York Times*, 1 September 2011. http://www.nytimes.com/2011/09/02/business/global/us-solar-company-bankruptcies-a-boon-for-china.html?_r=1&ref=solarenergy [Accessed January 25, 2012].

Bradsher, K. (2011b). "Pentagon Must 'Buy American,' Barring Chinese Solar Panels." *New York Times*, 9 January 2011. http://www.nytimes.com/2011/01/10/business/global/10solar.html?pagewanted=1&_r=1&emc=etal [Accessed January 25, 2012].

Bradsher, K. (2009). "W.T.O. Rules against China's Limits on Imports." *New York Times*, 12 August 2009. http://www.nytimes.com/2009/08/13/business/global/13trade.html?pagewanted =2&emc=eta1 [Accessed January 25, 2012].

Bresser-Pereira, L.C. (2010). *Globalization and Competition: Why Some Emergent Countries Succeed while Others Fail*. Cambridge: Cambridge University Press.

Browne, A. and Dean, J. (2010). "Business Sours on China: Foreign Executives Say Beijing Creates Fresh Barriers; Broadsides, Patent Rules." *Wall Street Journal*, 17 March: p. A. 1. http://online.wsj.com/article/SB20001424052748704688604575125650352968686.html#mod=todays_us_page_one [Accessed January 25, 2012].

Canaves, S. (2010). "China Slams Luxury Goods' Quality." *Wall Street Journal*, 17 March: p. B. 2. http://online.wsj.com/article/SB10001424052748704688604575125422114724504.html?mod=todays-us-page-one [Accessed January 25, 2012].

Candland, C. and Sil, R. (eds.) (2001). *The Politics of Labor in a Global Age: Continuity and Change in Late-industrializing and Post-socialist Economies*. New York: Oxford University Press.

Cao, C., Suttmeier, R.P., and Simon, D.F. (2009). "Success in State-Directed Innovation? Perspectives on China's Medium and Long-Term Plan for the Development of Science and Technology," in G. Parayil and A.P. D'Costa (eds.), *The New Asian Innovation Dynamics: China and India in Perspective*, 247–64. Basingstoke: Palgrave Macmillan.

Coates, D. (2001). *Models of Capitalism: Growth and Stagnation in the Modern Era*. Oxford: Polity Press.

Crane, G.T. (1998). "Economic Nationalism: Bringing the State Back In." *Millennium, Journal of International Studies*, 27: 55–75.

Crane, G.T. (1999). "Imagining the Economic Nation: Globalisation in China." *New Political Economy*, 4 (2): 215–32.

Cumings, B. (1984). "The Origins and Development of the Northeast Asian Political Economy: Industrial Sectors, Product Cycles, and Political Consequences." *International Organization*, 38 (1): 1–40.

Damodaran, H. (2008). *India's New Capitalists: Caste, Business, and Industry in a Modern Nation*. Basingstoke: Palgrave Macmillan.

D'Costa, A.P. (2008). "The Barbarians are Here: How Japanese Institutional Barriers and Immigration Policies Keep Asian Talent Away." *Asian Population Studies*, 4 (3): 311–29.

D'Costa, A.P. (2009). "Economic Nationalism in Motion: Steel, Auto, and Software Industries in India." *Review of International Political Economy*, 16 (4): 618–46.

D'Costa, A.P. (2005). *The Long March to Capitalism: Embourgeoisment, Internationalization, and Industrial Transformation in India*. Basingstoke: Palgrave Macmillan.

D'Costa, A.P. (1995). "The Long March to Capitalism: India's Resistance to and Reintegration with the World Economy." *Contemporary South Asia*, 4 (3): 257–87.

Dent, C.M. (2008). *East Asian Regionalism*. Milton Park: Routledge.

Dickinson, J. and Bailey, A.J. (2007). "(Re)membering Diaspora: Uneven Geographies of Indian Dual Citizenship." *Political Geography*, 26: 757–74.

Evans, P. (1979). *Dependent Development: The Alliance of Multinational, State, and Local Capital in Brazil*. Princeton: Princeton University Press.

Evans, P. (1995). *Embedded Autonomy: States and Industrial Transformation*. Princeton: Princeton University Press.

Fitzgerald, J. (2006). "Introduction: the Dignity of Nations," in S.Y.S. Chien and J. Fitzgerald (eds.), *The Dignity of Nations: Equality, Competition, and Honor in East Asian Nationalism*, 1–22. Hong Kong: Hong Kong University Press.

Glassman, J. (2004). "Economic 'Nationalism' in a Post-nationalist Era." *Critical Asian Studies*, 36 (1): 37–64.

Gold, T.B. (1986). *State and Society in the Taiwan Miracle*. Armonk, N.Y.: M.E. Sharpe.

Government of Japan, Ministry of Agriculture, Forestry, and Fisheries (2010). "Statistical Tables, Labor Force and Employment(EXCEL:49KB)." http://www.maff.go.jp/e/tokei/kikaku/monthly_e/index.html [Accessed January 25, 2012].

Grieco, J.M. and Ikenberry, G.J. (2003). *State Power and World Markets: The International Political Economy*. New York: W.W. Norton and Company.

Hall, D. (2004). "Japanese Spirit, Western Economics: The Continuing Salience of Economic Nationalism in Japan." *New Political Economy*, 9 (1): 79–99.

Hall, P.A. and Soskice, D. (2001). "An Introduction to Varieties of Capitalism," in P.A. Hall and D. Soskice (eds.), *Varieties of Capitalism: The Institutional Foundation of Comparative Advantage*, 1–68. Oxford: Oxford University Press.

Harlen, C.G. (1999). "A Reappraisal of Classical Economic Nationalism and Economic Liberalism." *International Studies Quarterly*, 43 (4): 733–44.

Hatch, W. and Yamamura, K. (1997). *Asia in Japan's Embrace: Building a Regional Production Alliance*. Cambridge: Cambridge University Press.

Helleiner, E. and Pickel, A. (eds.) (2005). *Economic Nationalism in a Globalizing World*. Ithaca: Cornell University Press.

Ho, P.S. (2005). "Distortions in the Trade Policy for Development Debate: A Re-examination of Friedrich List." *Cambridge Journal of Economics*, 29 (5): 729–45.

Huff, W.G. (1995). "What is the Singapore Model of Economic Development?" *Cambridge Journal of Economics*, 19 (6): 735–59.

India Brand Equity Foundation (IBEF) (2010). "Brand Development." http://www.ibef.org/aboutus.aspx [Accessed 25 January 2012].

Johnson, C.A. (1982). *MITI and the Japanese Miracle: The Growth of Industrial Policy, 1925–1975*. Stanford: Stanford University Press.

Jones, R.J.B. (2000). *The World Turned Upside Down? Globalization and the Future of the State*. Manchester: Manchester University Press.

Khan, M.H. and Sundaram, J.K. (2000). *Rents, Rent-seeking and Economic Development: Theory and Evidence in Asia*. Cambridge: Cambridge University Press.

Kohli, A. (2009). *Democracy and Development in India: From Socialism to Pro-Business*. New Delhi: Oxford University Press.

Kohli, A. (2007). *State-Directed Development: Political Power and Industrialization in the Global Periphery*. Cambridge: Cambridge University Press.

Levi-Faur, D. (1997). "Economic Nationalism: From Frederich List to Robert Reich." *Review of International Studies*, 23 (3): 359–70.

Luo, Y., Xue, Q., and Han, B. (2010)."How Emerging Market Governments Promote Outward FDI: Experience from China." *Journal of World Business*, 45 (1): 68–79.

Marshall, D.D. (1996). "National Development and the Globalisation Discourse: Confronting 'Imperative' and 'Convergence' Notions." *Third World Quarterly*, 17 (5): 875–901.

McGuire, S. (2007). "The United States, Japan and the Aerospace Industry: From Capture to Competitor." *The Pacific Review*, 20 (3): 329–50.

Nakano, T. (2004). "Theorising Economic Nationalism." *Nations and Nationalism*, 10 (3): 211–29.

Narlikar, A. (2006). "Peculiar Chauvinism or Strategic Calculation? Explaining the Negotiating Strategy of a Rising India." *International Affairs*, 82 (1): 59–76.

Naudé, W. (2010a). "New Challenges for Industrial Policy." WIDER Working Paper No. 2010/107 (September).

Naudé, W. (2010b). "Industrial Policy: Old and New Issues." WIDER Working Paper No. 2010/106 (September).

Nayar, B.R. (2001). *Globalization and Nationalism: The Changing Balance in India's Economic Policy, 1950–2000*. New Delhi: Sage Publications.

Nayar, B.R. (2000). "The Limits of Economic Nationalism in India: Economic Reforms under the BJP-Led Government, 1998–1999." *Asian Survey*, 40 (5): 792–815.

Ogilvy (2008). *Chinese Nationalism and Its Impact on Brands*. Shanghai: Ogilvy and Mather Greater China.

Ogilvy and Mather (2008). *China's Prosumers*. Shanghai: Ogilvy and Mather Greater China.

Ostry, S. and Nelson, R.R. (1995). *Techno-Nationalism and Techno-Globalism: Conflict and Cooperation*, Washington, DC: The Brookings Institution.

Özkirimli, U. (2010). *Theories of Nationalism: A Critical Introduction* (2nd edn). Basingstoke: Palgrave Macmillan.

Palit, A. and Bhattacharjee, S. (2008). *Special Economic Zones in India: Myths and Realities*. New Delhi: Anthem Press.

Pedersen, J.D. (2008). *Globalization, Development and the State: The Performance of India and Brazil since 1990*. Basingstoke: Palgrave Macmillan.

Pirie, I. (2005). "Better By Design: Korea's Neoliberal Economy." *The Pacific Review*, 18 (3): 355–74.

Reich, R.B. (1992). *The Work of Nations: Preparing Ourselves for 21st Century Capitalism*. New York: Vintage Books.

Robison, R. and Goodman, D.S.G. (1996). "The New Rich in Asia: Economic Development, Social Status and Political Consciousness," in R. Robison and D.S.G. Goodman (eds.), *The New Rich in Asia: Mobile Phones, McDonalds, and Middle-Class Revolution*, 1–18. London: Routledge.

Rodrik, D. (2007). *One Economics, Many Recipes: Globalization, Institutions, and Economic Growth*. Princeton: Princeton University Press.

Sam, C.Y. (2008). "Economic Nationalism in Singapore and Thailand: The Case of the Shin Corporation-Temasek Holdings Business Deal." *South East Asia Research*, 16 (3): 433–59.

Sanger, D.E. (1987). "Japanese Purchase of Chip Maker Canceled after Objections in U.S." *New York Times*, 17 March. http://www.nytimes.com/1987/03/17/business/japanese-purchase-of-chip-maker-canceled-after-objections-in-us.html [Accessed January 25, 2012].

Sematech (2010). http://www.sematech.org/corporate/history.htm [Accessed January 25, 2012].

Stolberg, S.G. and Bajaj, V. (2010). "In India Obama Courts Corporate America." *New York Times*, 6 November. http://www.nytimes.com/2010/11/07/world/asia/07prexy.html?emc=eta1 [Accessed January 25, 2012].

Suginohara, M. (2008). "The Politics of Economic Nationalism in Japan: Backlash against Inward Foreign Direct Investment." *Asian Survey*, 48 (5): 839–59.

Sun, P. (2007). "Is the State-led Industrial Restructuring Effective in Transition China? Evidence from the Steel Sector." *Cambridge Journal of Economics*, 31: 601–24.

Tabuchi, H. (2010). "Japan's Farmers Oppose Pacific Free-Trade Talks." *New York Times*, November 11. http://www.nytimes.com/2010/11/12/business/global/12yen.html?%2339;s%20agriculture=&_r=1&sq=japan&st=cse&adxnnl=1&scp=1&adxnnlx=1291900158-G3STHgtgGKaukUVM8vUVbg&pagewanted=print [Accessed January 25, 2012].

Tanzi, V. (2011). *Government versus Markets: The Changing Economic Role of the State*. Cambridge: Cambridge University Press.

US Census Bureau (2010). "The 2010 Statistical Abstract." http://www.census.gov/compendia/statab/2010/tables/10s0603.pdf [Accessed January 25, 2012].

Vertesy, D. and Szirmai, A. (2010). "Interrupted Innovation: Innovation System Dynamics in Latecomer Aerospace Industries." United Nations University MERIT (Working Paper Series #2010-059).

Walter, A. (2006). "From Developmental to Regulatory State? Japan's New Financial Regulatory System." *The Pacific Review*, 19 (4): 405–28.

Weiss, L. (2000). "Developmental States in Transition: Adapting, Dismantling, Innovating, Not 'Normalizing'." *The Pacific Review*, 13 (1): 21–55.

Woo, W.T. (2008). "Understanding the Sources of Friction in US–China Trade Relations: The Exchange Rate Debate Diverts Attention from Optimum Adjustment." *Asian Economic Papers*, 7 (3): 61–95.

World Bank (2010). http://data.worldbank.org/indicator/NV.AGR.TOTL.ZS/countries/1W-JP-US?display=default [Accessed January 25, 2012].

2

Economic nationalism and regionalism in contemporary East Asia

Mark Selden

2.1 Introduction

Regions are socially constructed areas defined by state, supra-state, and societal agents, with shifting territorial, economic, and socio-political parameters. In contrast to the dominant literature, which has focused on states and state-constructed regions, we assess multiple forces in defining, constructing, and deconstructing regional formations in an epoch in which competing definitions of, and approaches to, region and nation challenge the reigning order (Gamble and Payne 1996; Katzenstein and Shiraishi 1997; Hamanaka 2009). Political, geostrategic, economic, social, and cultural factors may all shape a regional order and its position in the world economy. In light of competing claims of national, regional, and global forces, we inquire into the possibility of contemporary region formation that does not rest on the hegemony of a single nation or power, that is, an imperium whether formal or informal, and which serves, in varying degrees, the interests of the nations and peoples that comprise it. In particular, we consider the interplay between economic nationalism and region formation, including China, Japan, Korea, and the USA.

Yet spatial conceptions of the East Asia region remain contested. While it is obvious to discuss the East Asian countries, especially in the context of the region's economic dynamism and China's economic might and growing political influence, why include the USA? The relationship between East Asian regionalism and the continued salience of American power or Pacific Ascendancy—as Bruce Cumings observes, the USA is the first world power to exploit the fact that it borders both the Atlantic and Pacific—is a defining question for the emerging regional and global conjuncture and a direct challenge to the economic nationalism that shapes important outcomes (Cumings 2009). Stated differently, there are competing definitions of East Asia and the East Asian region, and our approach, which weds geopolitics and political economy, brings out the tensions between them.

The territories that comprise East Asia as defined here are China, Japan, the Koreas (North and South), and Taiwan. Our focus is on the burgeoning economies, and the deepening economic interpenetration of all of the above with the exception of North Korea, which alone has been excluded from the regional growth and economic interpenetration of recent decades. In geopolitical terms it is important to include North Korea since Korea's division, together with the China–Taiwan division and the geopolitical dominance of the USA in East Asia and the Asia Pacific, are at the heart of regional and global tensions that both define the region and drive economic nationalism. Above all in geopolitical terms, but also in economics, regional dynamics cannot be grasped without due attention to the role of the USA.

East Asia as a region is notable because of its recent resurgence to a position at the center of the global economy following a protracted decline from the heights achieved during a previous period of regional peace and prosperity under the China-centered tributary trade system of the eighteenth century (Arrighi, Hamashita, and Selden 2003; Hamashita 2008). Following a brief survey of East Asia in the era framed by the Sinocentric tributary trade system (sixteenth–eighteenth century), I show how the stage was set for the decline and subsequent resurgence of East Asia and how the character of regional geopolitics and political economy changed in the current epoch of economic nationalism, region formation, and globalization (Sugihara 2005; Beeson 2007; Wang 2007; Yoshimatsu 2008; Duara 2010). This historical survey permits consideration of whether economic nationalism should be understood as a specifically modern concept or whether its roots can be traced to earlier dynamics.

The interaction and tension between economic nationalism and regional and global forces that are integral to the resurgence of the region have strengthened linkages between the nations that comprise the region and fostered growing bonds with neighboring regions including Southeast Asia, Northeast Asia, South Asia, and the global economy. However, such links do not imply the demise, or even a reduction, of economic nationalism. Rather they point to the changing character of economic nationalism, which may be pursued through policies that are statist, collective, and autarchic, but can also be directed in ways compatible with an expansive market and wide scope for domestic and international capital. China, as we will see, well illustrates the range of possibilities.

However, in contemporary East Asia an array of historical legacies, including territorial and cultural conflict, war, and international geopolitics, drive economic nationalism and threaten to undermine regional harmony. In recent years, sharply juxtaposed images of the regional future have surfaced: including deepening intraregional economic and financial ties on the one hand, and on the other renewed geopolitical challenges that pose mounting risks of war in the wake of clashes involving Japan and South Korea over the Dokdo/Takeshima islands, North and South Korea at sea near the Northern Limit Line, the China–Japan imbroglio over the Senkaku/Diaoyu Islands, and clashes involving China and various nations in the South China Sea. In each of these, geopolitical conflict is wedded to economic conflict. A central fact pertaining to these clashes is that they are not merely bilateral. The USA and to a lesser extent Russia play a major role so that the arena of conflict extends to the Asia-Pacific and the world.

The chapter is divided into three main sections. In Section 2.2, I show that East Asia was already an economic and geopolitical center and a major actor in the global political economy from at least the sixteenth to the eighteenth century. In Section 2.3, I examine the interplay and tensions between economic nationalism and regional and global forces in driving the economic resurgence of East Asia since the 1970s, with an eye to defining distinctive features of the region and the interplay of economic nationalism, regional, and global forces. Section 2.4 shows that the historical legacies including territorial and cultural conflict, war, and international rivalry in the context of economic and financial integration of the region continue to fuel economic nationalism and geopolitics that threaten to undermine regional harmony. Today several emergent clashes over competing claims over neighboring islands pose new geopolitical challenges for the Asia-Pacific, including the USA.

2.2 Historical Perspectives on East Asian Regionalism

Throughout the nineteenth and well into the twentieth century, the dominant view in both East and West privileged a dynamic Western world order over a weak, inward-looking and conservative East Asia that collapsed in the face of an expansive Western capitalism cum imperialism. This Eurocentric world vision reified the perspective of the colonial powers and their successors and ignored the substantial long-term developmental trajectory of East Asia and its parity with Europe as recently as the eighteenth century (Rostow 1962; Landes 1969, 2003). The essentialist presumption that continues to pervade a substantial literature—that Western superiority is a historical constant, once and forever immutable—is now being tested.

An alternative paradigm recognizes East Asia as an economic and geopolitical center and a major actor in the global political economy from at least the sixteenth to the eighteenth century or even the mid-nineteenth century.

Interestingly, the avatars of this approach, frequently framed as a China-centered perspective on East Asia and the world economy, emerged primarily not from Chinese scholarship but from the writings of Japanese and American researchers (Grove and Daniel 1984; Bray 1985; Reid 1988, 1993; Wong 1997; Brook 1998; Frank 1998; Pomeranz 2000; Sugihara 2005; Hamilton 2006; Beeson 2007; Wang 2007; Yoshimatsu 2008; Duara 2010). China's economic strides of recent decades and, above all, the resurgence of East Asia with China, Japan, and Korea as an expansive regional center of the capitalist world economy in the final decades of the long twentieth century, lend plausibility to this perspective.

Between the sixteenth and eighteenth century, at the dawn of European capitalism, East Asia was the center of a vibrant economic and geopolitical zone with its own distinctive characteristics. Among the most important linkages that shaped the political economy and geopolitics of the East Asian world was the China-centered tributary trade order,[1] pivoting on transactions negotiated through formal state ties as well as providing a venue for informal trade conducted at the periphery of tributary missions. The system was also sustained by a wide range of legal and illegal trade, much of it linking port cities that were beyond the reach of the Chinese imperial state. Korea, Vietnam, the Ryūkyūs, and a number of kingdoms of Central and Southeast Asia actively engaged in tributary trade with China.

East Asian linkages with the world economy from the sixteenth century forward, via both the land silk road and the sea, transformed East–West trade as well as the domestic Chinese and regional economies. Silver flows, to pay for tea, silk, ceramics, and opium among other products, bound Europe and the Americas with East Asia, particularly China, with Manila as the key port of transit. Indeed, the large-scale flow of silver from the Americas to China beginning in the sixteenth century and peaking in the mid-seventeenth century linked major world regions and transformed both intra-Asian trade and China's domestic economy. If the dominant scholarship on world capitalist development from the sixteenth century—both its celebratory and its critical strains—has emphasized overwhelmingly the outward thrust of European military and economic power, it is more fruitful to recognize a two-way flow of resources and people (Gresh 2009). Reid, for example, writes of Chinese–Southeast Asian–South Asian trade in global perspective in the years 1450–1680:

> The pattern of exchange in this age of commerce was for Southeast Asia to import cloth from India, silver from the Americas and Japan and copper cash, silk, ceramics and other manufactures from China, in exchange for its exports of pepper, spices, aromatic woods, resins, lacquer, tortoiseshell, pearls, deerskin, and the sugar exported by Vietnam and Cambodia. (Reid 1993: 33)

The result was massive silver flows into China from other parts of Asia, Europe, and the Americas in exchange for silk, tea, porcelain, and other manufactures. Takeshi Hamashita shows how the articulation of Asian silver markets with Euro-American silver dynamics shaped world financial flows and facilitated the expansion of trade that took place in the sixteenth and seventeenth centuries (Frank 1998: 131–64; Pomeranz 2000: 159–62, 267–74; Hamashita 2008: 39–56). China's domestic economy was simultaneously transformed as silver became the medium for taxation in the Ming's single whip tax reform, which mandated that all land taxes be paid in silver. This stimulated commodification of the agrarian economy and rural–urban exchange. Silver also provides a thread to link Europe, the Americas, and Asia as well as a means to deconstruct Eurocentric history and to chart profound changes internal to the Chinese and Asian regional economy and society.

We cannot limit discussion of intra-Asian trade to the formal parameters of the tributary order or discipline that the imperial Chinese state sought to impose. Consider, for example, the fact that, while the Ryūkyūs actively participated in tributary relations with China, in order to obtain pepper and other products that were mandated by the Chinese tributary relationship, Ryūkyūan merchants traded far and wide throughout Southeast and Northeast Asia and the Pacific Islands from at least the fifteenth century. Likewise, Nola Cooke and Tana Li highlight the autonomous trade patterns that gave rise to the "water frontier" linking southern coastal China and Indochina in the eighteenth century, thereby contributing to the transformation of the domestic economies of the Mekong region and their links to regional and global markets, much of the trade independent of tributary missions (Cooke and Li 2004).

Asia, like all world regions, was subject to periodic wars and conquests. At its height in the eighteenth century, however, in the wake of the Manchu conquest of China, and the expansion of the Chinese empire into Inner Asia, large regions of East Asia experienced a long epoch of peace and prosperity on the foundation of a tributary trade order. The contrast to a Europe that was perpetually engulfed by war and turmoil is striking.[2] If tributary and private trade lubricated the regional order, so too did common elements of statecraft in the neo-Confucian orders that linked China, Japan, Korea, the Ryūkyūs, and Vietnam. In contrast to European colonialism in the eighteenth and nineteenth century, it might also be argued that this Manchu–Mongol–Sinic order placed fewer demands for assimilation on China's neighbors when contrasted with European conquerors, was less exploitative in economic terms, and displayed a capacity to secure general peace throughout large areas of East and Southeast Asia for protracted periods.

Indeed, at the height of its power, China subsidized regional stability through the tributary trade order. This meant investing in the regimes of favored local rulers as well as assuring a sustained transfer of resources to them via direct subsidies and guaranteed access to lucrative trade with Korea, Vietnam, and the Ryūkyūs among others. Even Japan, which sent no direct tributary missions to China during the Tokugawa period (1600–1868), bought into the system through trade with China at Nagasaki as well as through covert domination of Ryūkyū tribute missions that enabled Japan to secure lucrative trade with China while covertly subordinating the Ryūkyūs to its own sub-tributary order during the seventeenth and eighteenth centuries. Similarly, Vietnam implemented a sub-tributary order with Laos. In other words, the tributary model extended beyond China's own framing of that order.

In these and other ways, a distinctive regional geopolitics and political economy emerged in a prosperous East Asia whose population far exceeded that of Europe and North America, whose wealth in core areas was comparable to that of leading Western nations, and was linked to other parts of Asia, Europe, and North America in the world economy of the sixteenth to eighteenth centuries. That order anticipated certain elements of modern economic nationalism: Chinese rulers in particular sought to order geopolitical and exchange relations across a broad region and invested favored rulers with power and authority. Yet, following the literature on nationalism that privileges state and societal responses to imperialism and dynamic state efforts to promote and shape economic development, I emphasize the fact that the earlier tributary trade order, while serving Chinese state interests, differed in fundamentals from modern and contemporary incarnations.

2.3 Economic Resurgence, Complementarity, and the Sprouts of Regionalism in East Asia

Contemporary East Asian development is best understood not as a series of discrete national phenomena but as a regional and global process whose distinctive feature is economic integration and the growing economic role of the region in the world economy. Within the processes of global and intra-regional integration, the practice of economic nationalism has varied in part due to persistence of divided nations and intranational conflict notable in the case of the two Koreas, China and Taiwan, as well as in mutual suspicion between Japan and China and between Japan and the two Koreas. The economic rise of China and conflictual geopolitics has added additional layers of complexity to the region, including US engagement. If East Asian regionalism has achieved impressive gains since the 1970s, it differs in fundamentals both from historical patterns of East Asia and the European Union variant that has dominated global understanding of regionalism. It should come as no surprise that there is a lack of institutionalization underpinning East Asian regionalism when compared to Europe. First, Europe has been free of major wars for two generations while the East has been at peace only since 1975. Second, China and Korea remain divided two decades after German reunification and a transformed united Europe. Third, territorial and historical memory conflicts continue to divide China, Japan, and Korea.[3] There is, of course, no East Asian Union, no common currency, parliament, or high court. Nor do we find a military equivalent of NATO or other effective security structure. In East Asia and the Pacific, the character of regionalism is conditioned simultaneously not only by the economic dynamism of the nations and their deepening ties with neighboring states, but also by the position and policies of the USA, which continues to exercise geopolitical domination.

The stage was set in 1970 for new East Asian regional possibilities and a global reconfiguration of power with geopolitics in command: in the wake of the China–Soviet rift of the 1960s and the looming US defeat in Indochina, the US–China entente and a burgeoning economic relationship opened the way for ending the bifurcation that had characterized not only postwar Asia but East–West global relations. The end of China's isolation and pariah status from 1970, its assumption of a UN Security Council seat, above all its accelerated economic growth fueled by expansive markets, foreign trade and investment, and wide access to US markets, capital, and technology, opened the way not only to China's economic rise but also to the re-knitting of economic and political bonds across Asia and the strengthening of intra-Asian linkages with the global economy. Specifically, Japan and China quickly established diplomatic relations following the US opening, South Korea–China economic relations grew rapidly in the 1980s, with diplomatic ties established in 1992, and Taiwan–China relations similarly warmed in the 1990s. This emphatically did not bring about the demise of economic nationalism, specifically of national economic, financial, and technology policies designed to boost the competitiveness of national economies. Rather, competing nationalisms and the development paradigms to which they gave rise, remain strong in an epoch characterized by growing interpenetration of East Asian and Asia-Pacific economies, polities, and cultures and the expansive role of the region in global perspective.

2.3.1 *China's Reintegration in the World Economy*

China's reintegration into Asian and the world economy is central to defining the character of East Asian regionalism, both in light of China's primacy in historical patterns of Asian regionalism and the geopolitics of the post-World War II international order in Asia, particularly of the long-term clash between the USA and China spanning the Chinese Civil War, the US–Korean War, and the US–Indochina War. Among critical developments since the 1970s were

China's full engagement in, indeed, its eventual emergence as the motor driving, the Asian and world economies. At a time of growing regional development, economic nationalism has remained powerful across East Asia in three important respects. Not only has each nation sought to maximize its economic position vis-à-vis others, but the role of the state in directing economic development trajectories remains striking while mass nationalism remains a force that states can manipulate, but which can also threaten the state. This is most evident in the case of China, but it applies to Japan, the two Koreas, and Taiwan as well. For China, the role of both national and local (provincial, city) governments has been and remains critical, or, stated differently, it has been the symbiosis of private and international capital with government, that is pivotal in defining China's trajectory (Lee and Selden 2007; Huang 2011). This continues to hold in a period in which the direct control of the state over industry and agriculture has been reduced while private (including international) capital is regulated and markets replace collectives and state enterprises as the local engine of economic growth.

Regional development has taken off due to expansive trade and investment involving Asian economies, overseas Chinese who have linked China with Asian and other economies, China's entry into the World Trade Organization in 2001, and by its emergence as the leading trade surplus nation. In effect, China has become the banker to the USA, the world's leading deficit nation. This reminds us that throughout the long twentieth century, no country approaching China's size has succeeded in moving from the periphery to the semi-periphery (in world-system categories), or from the ranks of the poor to middle-income countries, in standard parlance. What has made this possible in geopolitical terms is the extraordinary symbiosis of the Chinese and US economies, what I call "codependence" to emphasize both the distinction from classical dependency theory and to highlight the fact that the economies of the two nations are so deeply imbricated.

One distinctive feature of economic and geopolitical nationalism in East Asia is a product of the national divisions of the post-World War II and postcolonial eras. With the reunification of Vietnam (1975), of Germany (1989), and subsequently of China with Hong Kong (1997) and Macau (1999), only the two Koreas and China–Taiwan remain divided among the major national ruptures that were the legacy of World War II and subsequent conflicts in Asia and Europe. With the active role both of China and the Chinese overseas, with economics and finance as the driving force, the China–Taiwan division would narrow sharply from the 1990s. These changes illustrate the interface of geopolitics and political economy both in global (particularly USA–China) and regional (China–Japan–South Korea as well as mainland China–Taiwan) terms, making the emergence of regional bonds spanning East Asia possible.

Among the remarkable geopolitical and economic changes in the wake of the post-1970 USA–China opening has been the emergence and deepening of China–Republic of Korea (ROK) relations. From an anti-communist mecca, a South Korea that fought China in the US–Korean War and then joined the USA to fight in Vietnam, would emerge, to the chagrin of the rival Democratic People's Republic of Korea (DPRK), one of China's most important trade and investment partners, beginning in the 1980s. Within a few decades, Japan, China, and South Korea would become closely linked by trade and investment, surpassing in significant ways even their bonds with the USA. For example, in 2010, China was South Korea's largest trade partner, accounting for 30% of its exports. Korea's total trade with China of 152 billion euros exceeded that of the combined totals with Japan and the USA. In addition, by 2009, more than 41,000 Korean enterprises operated in China (South Korea Main Economic Indicators 2010; Snyder and Byun 2010).

In 2010, China, Japan, and Korea were the world's second, third, and fifteenth largest economies by IMF reckoning measured by nominal gross domestic product (GDP).[4] All were closely linked with not only one another but also with the economies of Taiwan, Hong Kong, and Singapore in particular, and Southeast Asia in general. China, moreover, also displaced the USA as India's leading trade partner from 2008 (Financial Express 2009).

One development strengthening regional bonds has been the trade, investment, technological partnership, and associated movement of people that links Taiwan and mainland China. In less than two decades, the core of Taiwan's high-tech production migrated across the Straits. Approximately one million Taiwanese workers, engineers, managers, and family members presently work and live on the mainland, most of them in Guangdong, Fujian, and especially the Shanghai–Suzhou corridor, the center of Taiwan's high-tech export-oriented enterprise in China. Taiwanese capital and technology are central to China's industrialization and export drive, and increasingly to domestic consumption in China. Taiwan's Foxconn, with approximately one million mainland employees, dominates production of the leading electronic products for Apple, Nokia, HP, and other top global brands whose production in China has fueled Chinese growth and superprofits for multinational corporations. In addition, other leading multinationals in China are also based in Taiwan and South Korea (Zhou 2008; Chan and Pun 2010). In turn, Taiwan's economic future rests firmly on the performance of mainland industry, both its exports and, increasingly, the expansion of China's domestic market. The political gulf between the two claimants to the Chinese mantle has not substantially slowed their economic integration.

Taiwan–China relations, and the role of the global Chinese diaspora, offer insight into questions of economic as well as geopolitical nationalism. The 2008 electoral victory of the Kuomintang's Ma Ying-jeou as President strengthened cross-straits ties, as indicated by the initiation of regularly scheduled flights as well as direct shipping and postal links between Taiwan and mainland China, the signing of oil development agreements, and China's offer of a US$19 billion loan package to Taiwanese enterprises in China—all factors suggestive of further possibilities for economic, social, and political integration (Sun and Tang 2008). With both China and Taiwan entering the World Trade Organization (WTO) in 2001 (the latter, with PRC support, as Chinese-Taipei), China swiftly became Taiwan's leading trade partner, a position that has steadily strengthened. Taiwanese firms invested more than US$150 billion in the mainland between 2001 and 2008 while a US$13.3 billion investment in 2010 marked an increase of 120% over the preceding year (Roberge 2009). The memorandums of understanding between China and Taiwan that came into effect in January 2010 extended the scope of economic and financial interpenetration to the insurance, banking, and securities sectors (Yadav 2010).

The issue of economic nationalism is characteristically posed in terms of state policies geared to competing *national* interests. In East Asia, however, in both China and Korea, the issues are exacerbated and given distinctive form by the existence of divided nations with competing claims of sovereignty rooted in wars and revolutions that span a century, or have roots in economic and geopolitical conflicts involving external powers, notably Japan and the USA. The Taiwan case illustrates important facets not only of deepening economic ties across the Straits but also regional development. There, what is perhaps most notable is the economic interpenetration of China and Taiwan facilitated by a worldwide Chinese diaspora linking the two and creating economic and financial ties to Southeast Asia, the USA, Europe, and beyond. At play is simultaneously competing Chinese nationalisms, as well as Taiwanese nationalism, and attempts to overcome political divisions through appeals to common goals based in culture and shared economic interests with China's Confucius Institutes, framing the mainland's bid for global cultural hegemony in the Sinic world using the twin tools of cash and culture.

China's reentry into the world economy and the formation of a dynamic interconnected East Asian economic zone from the 1970s coincided with, and was made possible by, two developments of global significance. First, the primary global war zone, which had centered on East and Southeast Asia since the 1940s—the Pacific War followed by Chinese, Korean, and Indochinese revolutionary wars as well as independence struggles in the Philippines, Malaysia, and the Dutch East Indies among others—shifted to the Middle East and Central Asia. If intra-Asian politics has remained contentious, the growth and deepening of the Asian regional economy since the 1970s has taken place in the midst of a general peace, widening cultural and economic exchange, and easing of tensions throughout East Asia.[5] Second, China's full entry into the world economy occurred at precisely the moment when the postwar global economic expansion came to an end, the B-phase in the Kondratieff cycle began, the dollar plummeted in value, and the USA sought to prevent economic collapse through the expansion of a world economy that included China. Indeed, in subsequent decades the USA would shift substantial sectors of its industry to China, while its domestic economy became ever more dependent on finance and services (Brenner 2009; Murphy 2009; Wallerstein 2009; Arrighi 2010).

In the years 1988–2004, as world trade expanded at an annual rate of 9.5%, intra-East Asian trade grew by 14% per year, compared with 9% for that of the European Union. East Asia's share of world exports increased by 6% in the course of those years, while that of the European Union decreased by 3% (Brooks and Hua 2008: 10). In contrast to the autarky of East Asia at the height of the Japanese empire between 1931 and 1945, since the 1970s the region, this time with the inclusion of China and Greater China (Hong Kong, Taiwan, Singapore) as well as Vietnam (but not North Korea), has been fully enmeshed in global trade and financial and investment networks.

The interplay of national economies and economic nationalism is both intensified and made more complex by the role of international diasporas, notably in the cases of China, Japan, Korea, Taiwan, Vietnam, and India. It is a story that is deeply influenced by the era of European and Japanese colonialism and its aftermath. We focus discussion on the Chinese diaspora, the most important of these, because of its centrality to the performance and character of East Asian economies as well as its complex role in mediating between China and Taiwan and between China and the USA. The role of Chinese diasporic capital, technology, and labor, including a major role for returnees from North American and European graduate schools and corporations, has been large, multidirectional, and embracing the full range of activities spanning investment, technological transfer, networking, and labor migration back and forth across the Pacific and throughout Asia. The USA, Taiwan, Hong Kong, and Singapore are among the most important interlinked sites for movement of entrepreneurial capital, researchers, and intellectuals from and to Chinese cities, suggesting that while each of these Chinese communities bids for capital, technology, contacts, and contracts, the contrast to decades of deep divisions across Cold War lines, and earlier across colonial divides, is striking.

One important dimension of the multidirectional and multidimensional flow of Chinese diasporic people, capital, and technology, is the large and growing numbers of Chinese, Hong Kong, Taiwan, and Singapore undergraduate and graduate students studying abroad, particularly in the USA, Canada, Europe, Japan, and Australia. Together with numerous technologically advanced students graduating from Chinese universities, these are among the most geographically and upwardly mobile groups in the world system. Many now pursue careers that take them in and out of China and across the Asia-Pacific, moving back and forth between universities, government, and the private sector, organizing and leading their own enterprises and creating cross-national networks. Simultaneously internationalists by education, lifestyle, and movement, Chinese diaspora nationalism has been striking, as in the rallying in support of Chinese positions on Diaoyutai/Senkaku islands, and in criticism of Japanese wartime atrocities.

Economic nationalism and developmental strategies in the early postwar years frequently took distinctive shape in East Asia. They were predicated on state-led accumulation and investment, social change strategies that pivoted on land reform, and measures that blocked takeover by international capital while seeking to create firm foundations for the domestic economy. The developmental state model that Chalmers Johnson etched for Japan applies, but with significant variations, for China, North and South Korea, Taiwan, and Singapore. In no other region did the state so effectively capture the surplus and direct it toward capital construction (roads, railways, dams, irrigation systems) and heavy-industry-led industrialization (Johnson 1982; Selden with Ka 1993). In the case of China, economic nationalism has continued but with important new features from the period of revolution to the era of markets, mobility, and capital's ascendance since the 1970s.

In recent decades, China has both strengthened and deepened economic and financial ties with neighboring countries throughout Asia and the Pacific and spearheaded important regional initiatives: these include efforts to bring about an ASEAN + 3 arrangement involving China, Japan, and Korea to unify East and Southeast Asia and an agreement on an ASEAN–China Free Trade Area which, at its inception in January 2010, created the world's third largest Free Trade Area. Here, too, we note a new phase in the playing out of economic nationalism with regional characteristics.

It is interesting to note that in contrast to China's centrality in the tributary trade order of the eighteenth century, Southeast Asian nations, through ASEAN, have come to play a proactive role in the emerging regionalism in the new millennium. Nevertheless, China has again emerged as the largest regional power, arguably the driving force behind such regional initiatives as ASEAN +3 and, above all, in expansive bilateral trade relations. Geoffrey Wade has documented the powerful economic and geopolitical thrust of a resurgent China in its relations with its major Southeast Asian neighbors, a pattern that is likewise evident with respect to East, South, and Inner Asia (Wade 2010).

Surveying China's expansive relations with the major ASEAN nations, Wade shows that for most nations in the region, and indeed all those with shared borders with China, economic ties with China now overshadow those with ASEAN, and in almost every instance, with other East Asian nations as well as the USA and Europe. In some instances, new economic subregions promote vibrant but sometimes one-sided bonds. For example, the Greater Mekong Subregion (GMS), comprised of Cambodia, Laos, Myanmar, Vietnam, Thailand, and the two Chinese provinces of Yunnan and Guangxi, was initiated and led by the Asian Development Bank in 1992. The Bank continues to provide an important source of funding, including for infrastructure development in China. However, regional outcomes are now significantly shaped by Chinese planners and technocrats, Chinese-supported infrastructure development, and the infusion of Chinese capital, labor, and expertise, with projects ranging from roads and railroads, hydropower dams and ports, to resource and industrial development. Some of these, however, as in China's dam building on the Mekong, are contentious: threatening, for example, the flow of water downstream in Indochina (Osborne 2007; Hirsch 2011). Wade, for example (2010: 3), talks about China's "bridgehead strategy" of building transportation infrastructure linking to Southeast Asia, a course that is producing myriad roads, railroads, and harbors. Precisely such a bridgehead strategy can be seen on numerous Chinese borderlands, notably in the Northeast (Russia, North Korea, South Korea, and, across the sea, Japan), in South Asia (India, Pakistan, Bangladesh), and Central Asia (Kazakhstan, Russia, and other former Soviet territories).[6]

Consider China's impoverished neighbor, Cambodia. A Cambodia–China economic agreement signed in December 2009 involved agreements valued at US$1.9 billion. By November 2010, more than US$9.4 billion worth of deals had been signed in infrastructure construction, communication technology, and energy exploration, and China waived US$4 billion in Cambodian debt. Chinese firms now dominate Cambodian oil exploration, highway construction, and hydropower projects, and Chinese banks have made large inroads. The Chinese government, moreover, has reportedly pledged to provide US$600 million to finance a railroad from Phnom Penh to the Vietnam border. Within a brief period of time, China has become the major trade and investment partner for many ASEAN countries, including those such as Laos, Cambodia, and Burma that are relatively poor and isolated. Its infrastructure projects, pivoting on rail transport and port construction, will connect China and ASEAN countries including Laos, Vietnam, Burma, and Thailand and further boost their burgeoning trade. In short, even as it cooperates with ASEAN, China threatens to overshadow the smaller and weaker ASEAN economies, with the GMS countries constituting a direct challenge to the regional group. Wade concludes (2010: 13) that "Myanmar, Cambodia and Laos are already virtual client states of China, and Vietnam and Thailand are increasingly tied (and in some ways beholden) to the economic giant to the north."

For all its dynamism and growing power, arguably, in contrast with the eighteenth century, China has not, or not yet, achieved regional dominance, still less hegemony. This is both because of the continued (if declining) geopolitical primacy of the United States in the region, and because of the fact that both Japan and South Korea, the other two leading East Asian nations, are allied with the US even as their economic and financial ties with China grow.

As China's power has grown in regional and global affairs, Japan, the world's second economic power, and the motor that drove region-wide economic growth in the 1960s and 1970s, has virtually disappeared from much analysis of Asian regionalism and global geopolitics. In the 1970s, Japan played a critical role in stoking global overproduction posing a fundamental challenge to the global economy, as China does in the new millennium. Indeed, analysts find it all too easy to ignore the wealth and technological edge that Japan maintains over other regional states. In short, Japan remains a powerful regional force.

In the course of the postwar era, Japan promoted no less than 30 regional projects in the realms of finance, trade, and summitry, notably in the founding and leadership of the Asian Development Bank in the 1960s (Hamanaka 2009: 6). Yet Japan is no longer the leader in East Asian trade or in promoting major regionalism projects. Above all, this is because of the surge in China's economic and financial strength over the last two decades, with China's economy outstripping the size of Japan's in 2010, as Japan has never recovered momentum since the bubble burst in 1990 resulting in the collapse of stock market and real estate values and more than a decade of stagnation followed by slow and sporadic growth. Viewed from another angle, as Andrew Kennedy points out, "Between 2000 and 2008, China's demand for energy grew so quickly that it single-handedly accounted for 51% of world demand growth," and in 2010 it overtook the USA as the world's largest energy consumer and the number two economic power measured by GDP (Kennedy 2010). The result of this Chinese dynamism is that the USA–China relationship has become the single most important in the world, and China's role is equally evident in regional initiatives.

In recent years, East Asia has taken steps toward interregional cooperation in such areas as economic and financial security, nuclear nonproliferation, resource management, fishing, counterterrorism, drugs, smuggling, piracy, human trafficking and organized crime control, disaster relief, environmental degradation, and container security. The 1997 Asian financial and currency crisis provided impetus for regional responses, the most important of which was the currency swaps starting with the Chiang Mai initiative of May 2005 to help shore up nations facing currency and financial crises (efforts to do so at the time of the 1997 Asian financial crisis were blocked by the USA), an initiative reinforced in 2008 (Beeson 2009). Clearly, major obstacles challenge the further development of East Asian regionalism, obstacles that are in part a result of the region's rapid growth and interpenetration, which has transformed not only East Asia, but the nature of the world system. They are also, however, a product of historical legacies and conflicts that challenge a system-in-formation that extends from economics and finance to nascent yet frequently contested geopolitical arrangements.

2.4 Geopolitical and Historical Conflicts: Challenges to East Asian Regional Development

If economic change has come swiftly to shape an emerging region since the 1970s, and if the protracted wars that took so heavy a toll over the preceding century have ended, the challenges of bridging such divides as China–ROK, China–Japan, ROK–Japan, and China–Taiwan remain formidable. This is among the reasons why region-wide institutional frameworks to mediate political and economic conflict have been slow to form. We consider the geopolitics of the region in light of three intertwined sets of issues: (1) history and memory conflicts; (2) territorial conflicts; and (3) the role of the USA in shaping regional outcomes.

China since the 1970s has set out to resolve or defuse important territorial disputes including border disputes with India, Russia, Japan, Vietnam, and the Philippines, some involving disputes over potentially oil rich islands and fishing grounds, such as the Spratlys and Paracels, by multiple nations. Illustrative of the possibilities for adjudicating conflict is the vision advanced by Deng Xiaoping in 1978 that for a time provided a basis for China and Japan to put aside permanent resolution of territorial issues involving the Diaoyutai/ Senkaku Islands and Okinotorishima, while cooperating in the region in fishing and joint oil exploration (Zhao 2008: 207–27). Despite resolution or partial resolution of a number of these issues, including China–Russia and some China–India border issues, many remain contentious, even volatile. Below we consider some of these and their implications for economic nationalism.

First, however, consider a number of regional initiatives. The first summit of the three East Asian nations, China, Japan, and South Korea, held in Fukuoka, Japan on 13 December 2008 constituted an effort to frame a common policy in response to the world recession. The brief meeting was indicative, however, of the obstacles to framing common policies at a time when world recession presented severe challenges to their high-flying economies with heavy reliance on export markets and foreign investment. It also illustrated competitive Chinese and Japanese positions concerning the summit including the participants and the nature of the meeting, which would determine the ability of China or Japan to lead. China insisted that it be no more than a forum for dialogue, and it succeeded in bringing in countries such as Russia (as an observer) that it anticipated would be supportive of its agenda. For its part, Japan proposed inviting the USA in an observer status. In this as in much else, the divide of the postwar, enacted in the US–Korean War and since, reveals its imprint. Both the East Asian Summit and the ASEAN +3 summit became arenas for contesting Chinese and Japanese leadership, displaying features of economic and geopolitical nationalism during an era in which regional economic penetration was rapidly deepening (Hamanaka 2009: 70–6).

At the ASEAN meeting in Hanoi in July 2009, Japan met separately with five Mekong delta nations, deliberately excluding Beijing, at a time when tensions were high over competing claims to the Spratly Islands and Chinese arrest of Vietnamese fishermen. That month the USA angered China when Secretary of State Hillary Clinton attempted to shape regional outcomes by expressing US concerns over Chinese claims to special interest in the South China Sea. In September 2010, when Japan arrested the captain of a Chinese fishing trawler near the Senkaku/Diaoyu islands, Clinton stated that the US would support Japanese claims under the Ampo treaty while calling for peaceful resolution of the dispute. The incident revealed not only tensions involving conflicting territorial claims to the islands, but undermined attempts to resolve both oil and gas drilling and fishing rights conflicts in the region (Bland 2010; Wada 2010; Acheson 2011). In 2011, however, China and ASEAN reached agreement to develop an approach to resolve the territorial impasse (Quijano 2011; cf. ASEAN and China 2002).

By 2010, the East Asian Summit had increased to two days and the primary agenda was a preliminary discussion of the thorny issue of a free trade agreement (FTA) among the three nations of China, Japan, and South Korea, a forum that excludes North Korea (Agence France Presse 2010; Xetrade 2010). To date, however, there has been little indication of progress toward such an agreement and the accomplishments of the summit pale not only compared with those of the European Union and NATO, but even with those of ASEAN. This despite the fact that the economic interrelationships among China, Japan, and South Korea far surpass those among the ASEAN states and rival those of the most closely intertwined members of the EU. By contrast, the ROK entered into an FTA with ASEAN in July 2009. Their trade, which had doubled between 2004 and 2008 to US$90 billion, is projected to reach US$150 billion by 2015 (*The Nation* 2009).

One important reason for lagging regional political achievements or institutionalization of the relationships binding the East Asian powers, is interstate tensions whose origins can be traced in some instances to territorial and cultural conflicts of the dynastic period, exacerbated by unresolved issues from the period of colonialism and war, particularly those associated with the rise of the Japanese empire in the years 1895–1945, as well as the legacies of the US–Korean War, US–Indochina War, and the international Cold War.

Despite such signs of progress toward framing a common future as a joint China–Japan textbook commission charged with writing a common modern history of the two nations, intra-Asian issues, historical memories associated with the Asia-Pacific War and colonial rule, continue to surface, poisoning interstate relations and fueling nationalist conflicts. This was the case for China–Japan relations in the tenure of Prime Minister Koizumi (2001–6) as a result of his annual visits to Yasukuni Shrine, preeminent symbol of Japanese war making and emperor-centered nationalism. These conflicts were intensified by numerous territorial conflicts discussed below. However, perhaps the most important challenges pertain to the role of the USA in East Asian and Asia-Pacific geopolitical outcomes. To the extent that the USA, whose empire of bases and alliance politics incorporates both Japan and the Republic of Korea, dominates the geopolitics of the region, high-level cooperation among China, Japan, and ROK is likely to remain limited to the economic sphere while geopolitical divisions rooted in the alliance structure of the USA–Korea and USA–Indochina wars dominate (deLisle 2011). Some nationalist acts, like Koizumi's Yasukuni performance, may be good theatre and good politics at home but have the effect of impeding economic advance.

The rudimentary institutional arrangements among East Asian states contrast with a preponderance of "US-led security architecture across Asia. This system includes five bilateral alliances in East Asia; non-allied security partnerships in Southeast Asia, South Asia and Oceania; a buildup of US forces in the Pacific; US–India and US–Pakistan military relations; and the US military presence and defense arrangements in Southwest and Central Asia" (Shambaugh 2004). That formulation needs supplementing with reference to the network of US military bases throughout the region and beyond, encircling China and with plans for the expansion of the US military presence on Guam, a new base in Okinawa, the militarization of space where the USA has a virtual monopoly, and the predominance of US sea-launched ballistic missiles and aircraft carriers deployed in the Pacific maritime region, another US monopoly. Equally important is the expansive conception of the US–Japan Security Treaty (Ampo), which has led Japan to extend its naval reach to the Indian Ocean and its military involvement in the service of the USA to the Iraq and Afghanistan Wars. Japan has also explored security arrangements with India, Australia, and South Korea designed to shift the center of its defense from Hokkaido in the North (directed toward the Soviet Union) to the South, among many moves in the years 2008–11 to target China (Gurtov 2008; Katzenstein 2008; McCormack 2008; Tanter 2008). For its part, China has no comparable alliance structure or effective network of military bases. And despite its rapidly growing military budget, its military spending remains a small fraction of that of the USA and its air and naval power is still rudimentary compared with that of the USA.

In spring 2009, China, Japan, and South Korea all responded to Somalian piracy with the dispatch of ships to patrol off the coast of Africa, involving a major expansion of the military trajectory of each of these nations. In April 2010, Japan announced establishment of a US$40 million military base in Djibouti, its first military base abroad (Yu 2010). The base opened in July 2011 (Farah 2011). Most important, perhaps, has been the South Korean and Japanese response to the conflicts of 2010 involving the China–Japan dispute over the Senkakus/Diaoyu, and North and South Korean clashes involving the sinking of the South Korean warship Cheonan and the Yeonpyeong Island shelling in the contested area around the Northern Limit Line dividing North and South. In both cases, the USA responded with massive military exercises involving Japan and South Korea, with the US battleship George Washington sending powerful warning messages to China and North Korea and indicating the fragility, in geopolitical terms, of East Asian regionalism. Viewed from another angle, the conflicts mirrored the alliance structure of the US–Korean War of 1950, with US allies rallying to the ROK–US position to pin responsibility on North Korea, with China and Russia opposing UN sanctions on North Korea. All of these incidents reinforce nationalist response and challenge the emerging East Asia region-in-formation, or confine it to the economic realm.

We have located the re-emergence of the East Asian region from the 1970s in the context of the USA–China entente. Was the shift emblematic of US weakness at a time of looming defeat in the Indochina Wars, the collapse of the dollar, the end of the postwar boom, and growing recognition of multipolarity? Or was it a brilliant USA–China strategic move to isolate the Soviet Union, one that would simultaneously secure Chinese access to US markets and bring the Chinese economy within the purview of the capitalist world economy? It was in fact each of these. A critical point is that then, as now, US initiatives would substantially shape regional outcomes even as they opened the way for the resurgence of China and East Asia that could eventually challenge US supremacy.

Forty years later, signs abound of the further weakening of American power in East Asia and globally. The economic surpluses generated by China, Japan, and South Korea account for the largest part of the massive US trade deficit, yet in turn, these nations have made it possible for the USA to continue to live beyond its means as dollar surpluses are recycled back to the USA, primarily in the form of Treasury bonds but also as direct and indirect investment. As of April 2011, according to the US Treasury Department, China with US$1,153 billion and Japan with US$906 billion in US treasuries ranked first and second in the world, accounting for nearly half of the US$4.5 trillion total (US

Treasury Department 2011). Chinese, Japanese, and Korean purchases of Treasury bonds over the last decade have helped to hold down US interest rates and the yuan–dollar and yen–dollar ratio, boosting the trade and growth of all three economies. This has helped the USA to finance the Iraq and Afghanistan Wars at the same time that US manufacturing jobs continued their inexorable migration to China and elsewhere, leaving some 15 million Americans unemployed by official figures in 2010, figures last seen in the Great Depression of the 1930s (Fallows 2008; Landler 2008; Murphy 2008; Takahashi and Murphy 2008; Bureau of Labor Statistics 2011). In this way, too, East Asia plays a systemic regional role in the world economy, though not one that is premised on cooperation of the East Asian nations. In the case of China and the USA in particular, we note the extraordinary level of codependence—all the more intriguing as the USA narrowly averted default in August 2011, a prospect that threatened the value of China's US$2 trillion investment in Treasuries—at a time of widespread recognition that the world's two largest and now intertwined economies are geopolitical rivals (Barboza 2011; Ewing and Dempsey 2011). In both nations, geopolitical and economic nationalisms drive the relationship. In the economic sphere, this has resulted in ever-deepening trade and investment and, at times, even security relations, while each government remains wary.

The collapse of the Soviet Union in 1989 left the USA without serious geopolitical constraints. At the same time, 15 years after East and Southeast Asia ceased to be a major war zone, the rationale for permanent stationing of US forces—in Japan/Okinawa, in South Korea, in Taiwan, and in Guam, for example—was simultaneously weakened. Yet Pentagon planners and weapons and aircraft manufacturers have continued to thirst for an expansive US military presence, smoothly shifting gears from the threat of a Soviet evil empire to the "war on terror" after 9/11, and continuing to press for new base construction in, for example, Okinawa and Guam. While no nation or group of nations has attained the military power to directly challenge US military might or diplomatic clout, US military budgets from the mid-1990s have continued their relentless surge, even excluding the gargantuan costs of fighting simultaneous wars in Iraq and Afghanistan and Pakistan. Indeed, with the USA accounting for close to half of global military spending, if no nation can rival its military prowess, its ability to effectively dominate geopolitics has been undermined by successive protracted stalemated wars over six decades. The USA now faces the world's largest trade and budget deficits that are in part the product of the attempt to overcome the present economic and financial crisis, while paying for two decade-long wars with an annual cost approximating one million dollars per soldier—and the US military stretched thin, and a political system that is in gridlock over deficits, taxes, and job creation to address a double-dip recession.

To be sure, the weaknesses of other nations and emerging regional formations including ASEAN + 3 and the Shanghai Group (China, Russia, and four Central Asian states of Kazakhstan, Kyrgyzstan, Tajikistan, and Uzbekistan, with India, Iran, Pakistan, and Mongolia as observers), and the South Asian Association for Regional Cooperation (with China and the USA among the observers) are palpable. New regional bonds, moreover, face demanding tests with the world economy entering its most difficult period since the depression/World War of the 1930s–40s, posing formidable challenges to Asia's high-flying export-oriented economies after several decades of sustained expansion.

2.5 Conclusion

We have reviewed important steps that East Asian nations have taken to overcome the fragmentation and division associated with several centuries of colonial rule and the postwar US–Soviet division to re-emerge as a major world region. We have shown the articulation since the 1970s of economic nationalism and geopolitical nationalism nevertheless resulting in a vibrant East Asian economic regionalism. The combination of deepening intraregional economic bonds in the world's most dynamic economic zone, together with region-wide efforts that have begun to confront acute environmental, territorial, and security issues, suggest possible futures compatible with substantially reduced USA- and USA–Japan-dominated dynamics and momentum toward expanded regional coordination. However, the divisive legacies of colonialism and war, a host of new conflicts rooted in part in economic and geopolitical nationalisms, and the destabilizing and divisive role of a US superpower in decline, all challenge the emergence of an effective regional polity.

Once again, China is central to regional outcomes as it has been over the *longue durée*, and its reach is powerful not only in the 14 nations with which it has common borders and the surrounding seas. This is palpable in China's search for resources and markets in Africa, Latin America, Central Asia, and the Middle East. If its dynamism captures world attention, it is important to recognize also that after decades of high-speed growth, capitalist transition and integration in the global economy, China continues to lag far behind such competitors as Japan and Korea as well as the USA in its level of development as measured by per capita income, even in purchasing power parity terms, in its share of global income and its technological level. Equally important, China's continued dramatic rise is far from assured given its own formidable developmental problems, including the enormous toll on land, water, and air, and profound structural inequalities, of which the plight of rural migrant workers is emblematic, with an export-dependent economy and with domestic consumption lagging, and with internal divisions of region, ethnicity, and class (Harris 2005; Selden and Wu 2011). Indeed, by many measures, Japan and the USA remain the major powers in the region, indicative of the fact that, for all its gains in regional and global perspective, notably the expansion of its economic and military reach, China cannot dominate the region. Indeed, China's advance has had the effect of strengthening the geopolitical ties of East and Southeast Asian nations to the USA.

In contrast to realist international relations analysts such as John Mearsheimer, who, based on simplistic projections and assumptions about China's economic growth, project the emergence of a hegemonic China in East Asia, a more likely prospect for the coming decades is a regional order in which the pace of China's development slows, no single nation reigns supreme, and the USA maintains an important, if declining geopolitical role (Mearsheimer 2001: 402; Beeson 2009: 95–112). Meanwhile, immediate challenges both to national development trajectories and to regional accord will come from economic recession and geopolitical conflicts, of which a divided Korea remains the most dangerous. In these circumstances, American challenges to Asian regionalism, and historical divisions among the nations of East Asia, inflamed by economic and geopolitical nationalism, will continue to divide China, Japan, and Korea.

Notes

1. China was arguably the geopolitical center of East Asia in the eighteenth century, but it is important to note that at that time, as during the Mongol dynasty earlier, it was ruled by a steppe people, the Manchus, thereby lending a distinctive character to the Qing empire and its dealings with peoples on its borders, notably the Mongols, Tibetans, and Uyghurs of Central Asia, but also the peoples of Southeast and South Asia as well.
2. This is certainly not to suggest that Asia was free of wars or conquest. China under Manchu, or more accurately Manchu-Mongol rule, achieved the peak of territorial expansion during the eighteenth century, extending the reach of empire north and west into Inner Asia including incorporation of Tibet, Mongolia, and Xinjiang, and China's informal reach extended into Southeast Asia as well. Most of China south of the Great Wall, and particularly coastal China, by contrast enjoyed protracted peace together with East Asia writ large.
3. Katzenstein (2005) emphasizes fundamental systemic differences between the nature of regional development in Europe and East Asia. Yet the question remains: is this systemic, or are the differences in part a product of earlier moves toward regional development in the EU on the one hand and the character of historic

patterns of regionalism in the China-centered tributary trade system of the sixteenth to eighteenth century and earlier on the other?

4. In GDP measured in purchasing power parity (PPP) terms, in 2010 as calculated by the IMF, China ranked first, Japan second, Republic of Korea fourth, and Taiwan eighth among Asian countries with China's US$8.7 trillion more than twice Japan's US$4.3 trillion (Wikipedia http://en.wikipedia.org/wiki/List_of_Asian_countries_by_GDP_PPP).

   World figures for nominal GDP in 2010 (as calculated by the IMF) show China ranked second and Japan third with South Korea 15th, if we exclude the European Union (http://en.wikipedia.org/wiki/List_of_countries_by_GDP_(nominal)). For per capita GDP (PPP) figures, see http://en.wikipedia.org/wiki/List_of_countries_by_GDP_(PPP)_per_capita For per capita GDP (nominal) world figures for 2010 (IMF), Japan ranked 24th, Republic of Korea 25th, and China 93rd with US$7,518 compared with Japan's US$33,828 (see http://www.nationmaster.com/encyclopedia/List-of-countries-by-GDP-(nominal)-per-capita).
5. This is not to suggest that rapid economic growth can only occur in a peaceful milieu. Japan's post-World War II recovery and economic growth was in part a product of an industrialization fostered by the USA as a means to support the Korean and Vietnam Wars. Japan's gain was bought at the price of devastation of Korea and Indochina. Japan itself was not only protected from the devastation of war, but enjoyed economic resurgence as a consequence of massive war procurements and was able to recover from the devastation of the Asia-Pacific War without having to divert substantial resources to its own defense. The price has been a permanent subordinate status within a USA–Japan client relationship.
6. On Northeast Asia (China, North Korea, South Korea, Russia, and Japan), that is, the Tumen river delta region, see Freeman (2010: 137–57). While slow to gain momentum, here too China has led, and continues to lead, the effort, the implications of which span the economic and geopolitical.

References

Acheson, C. (2011). "Disputed Claims in the East China Sea. An Interview with James Manicom." *Japan–US Discussion.* Forum.file:///Users/markselden/Desktop/1.M.docs/1.Focustexts/5801-5825/5816.manicom.c.j.e.chi.seaclaims/manicom.c.j.eastchiseaclaims.html [Accessed January 25, 2012].

Agence France Presse. (2010). "S. Korea, China, Japan Move Towards Free Trade Bloc." May 29. http://www.france24.com/en/20100529-skorea-china-japan-move-towards-free-trade-bloc [Accessed January 25, 2012].

Arrighi, G. (2010). *The Long Twentieth Century: Money, Power and the Origins of Our Times* (2nd edn). London: Verso.

Arrighi, G., Hamashita, T., and Selden, M. (eds.) (2003). *The Resurgence of East Asia: 500, 150 and 50 Year Perspectives.* London: Routledge.

ASEAN and China. (2002). "Declaration on the Conduct of Parties in the South China Sea." http://www.aseansec.org/13163.htm [Accessed January 25, 2012].

Barboza, D. (2011). "China's Treasury Holdings Make U.S. Woes Its Own." *New York Times*, July 19.

Beeson, M. (2009). "East Asian Regionalism and the Asia-Pacific: After American Hegemony." *The Asia-Pacific Journal*, January 10. http://japanfocus.org/-Mark-Beeson/3008 [Accessed January 25, 2012].

Beeson, M. (2007). *Regionalism and Globalization in East Asia: Politics, Security and Economic Development*. Basingstoke: Palgrave Macmillan.

Bland, B. (2010). "US Warning to China on Maritime Rows." *Financial Times*, October 11. *http://www.ft.com/cms/s/0/ac600588-d4fa-11df-ad3a00144feabdc0.html#axzz1Ax6g7zDi* [Accessed January 25, 2012].

Bray, F. (1985). *The Rice Economies: Technology and Development in Asian Societies*. New York: Oxford University Press.

Brenner, R. interviewed by Jeong, Seong-jin. (2009). "Overproduction not Financial Collapse is the Heart of the Crisis: the US, East Asia, and the World." http://japanfocus.org/-Robert-Brenner/3043

Brook, T. (1998). *The Confusions of Pleasure; Commerce and Culture in Ming China*. Berkeley: University of California Press.

Brooks, D.H. and Hua, C. (2008). "Asian Trade and Global Linkages." ADB Institute Working Paper No. 122, December, "Intra-regional Trade of Major Regions (1988–2007)."

Bureau of Labor Statistics, US Department of Labor. (2011). "Economic News Release, Employment Situation Summary." January 7. http://www.bls.gov/news.release/empsit.nr0.htm [Accessed January 25, 2012].

Chan, J. and Pun, N. (2010). "Suicide as Protest for the New Generation of Chinese Migrant Workers: Foxconn, Global Capital, and the State." *The Asia-Pacific Journal*, September 13. http://japanfocus.org/-Jenny-Chan/3408 [Accessed January 25, 2012].

Cooke, N. and Li, T. (eds.) (2004). *Water Frontier: Commerce and the Chinese in the Lower Mekong Region, 1750–1880*. Lanham, Md.: Rowman and Littlefield.

Cumings, B. (2009). *Dominion from Sea to Sea. Pacific Ascendancy and American Power*. New Haven: Yale University Press.

deLisle, J. (2011). "Regional Security in East Asia: An FPRI Conference Report." January 7. http://www.fpri.org/research/asia/regionalsecurityineastasia1011/_ [Accessed January 25, 2012].

Duara, P. (2010). "Asia Redux: Conceptualizing a Region for Our Times." *Journal of Asian Studies* 69 (4): 959–1029.

Ewing, J. and Dempsey, J. (2011). "Europe's Economic Powerhouse Drifts East." *New York Times*, July 18. http://www.nytimes.com/2011/07/19/business/global/Germany-Europers-Powerhouse-Drifts-East.html?scp=1&sq=Jack%20Ewing%20and%20Judy%20Dempsey&st=cse

Fallows, J. (2008). "Be Nice to the Countries That Lend You Money." *Atlantic Monthly*, December. http://www.theatlantic.com/doc/200812/fallows-chinese-banker [Accessed January 25, 2012].

Farah, M.O. (2011). "Japan Opens Military Base in Djibouti to Help Combat Piracy." *Bloomberg*, July 8. www.bloomberg.com/news/2011/-07-08/japan-opens-military-base-in-Djibouti-to-help-combat-piracy.html [Accessed January 25, 2012].

Financial Express. (2009). "China Replaces US as India's Largest Trade Partner." *Financial Express*, July 28.

Frank, A.G. (1998). *ReORIENT: Global Economy in the Asian Age*. Berkeley: University of California Press.

Freeman, C.P. (2010). "Neighborly Relations: the Tumen Development Project and China's Security Strategy." *Journal of Contemporary China*, 19 (63): 137–57.

Gamble, A. and Payne, A. (eds.) (1996). *Regionalism and World Order*. Basingstoke: Macmillan.

Gresh, A. (2009). "From Thermopylae to the Twin Towers: The West's Selective Reading of History." *Le Monde Diplomatique*, January.

Grove, L. and Daniel, C. (eds.) (1984). *State and Society in China: Japanese Perspectives on Ming-Qing Social and Economic History*. Tokyo: University of Tokyo Press.

Gurtov, M. (2008). "Reconciling Japan and China." *Japan Focus*, January 5. http://japanfocus.org/-Mel-Gurtov/2627 [Accessed January 25, 2012].

Hamanaka, S. (2009). *Asian Regionalism and Japan. The Politics of Membership in Regional Diplomatic, Financial and Trade Groups*. London: Routledge.

Hamashita, T. (2008). *China, East Asia and the Global Economy: Regional and Historical Perspectives*, ed. M. Selden and L. Grove. London: Routledge.

Hamilton, G. (2006). *Commerce and Capitalism in Chinese Societies*. London: Routledge.

Harris, P. (2005). *Confronting Environmental Change in East and Southeast Asia: Eco-politics, Foreign Policy, and Sustainable Development*. Tokyo: UN University Press.

Hirsch, P. (2011). "China and the Cascading Geopolitics of Lower Mekong Dams." *The Asia-Pacific Journal*, 9 (20/2), May 16. http://japanfocus.org/-Philip-Hirsch/3529 [Accessed January 25, 2012].

Huang, P.C. (2011). "The Theoretical and Practical Implications of China's Development Experience: The Role of Informal Economic Practices." *Modern China* 37 (1): 3–43.

Johnson, C. (1982). *MITI and the Japanese Miracle: The Growth of Industrial Policy, 1925–1975*. Stanford: Stanford University Press.

Katzenstein, P. (2008). "Japan in the American Imperium: Rethinking Security." *Japan Focus*, October 14. http://japanfocus.org/-Peter_J_-Katzenstein/2921 [Accessed January 25, 2012].

Katzenstein, P. (2005). *A World of Regions*. Ithaca: Cornell University Press.

Katzenstein, P. and Shiraishi, T. (eds.) (1997). *Network Power: Japan and Asia*. Ithaca: Cornell University Press.

Kennedy, A. (2010). "Rethinking Energy Security in China." East Asia Forum, June 6. http://www.eastasiaforum.org/2010/06/06/rethinking-energy-security-in-china/ [Accessed January 25, 2012].

Landes, D. (1969). *The Unbound Prometheus. Technological Change and Industrial Development in Western Europe from 1750 to the Present*. Cambridge: Cambridge University Press.

Landes, D. (2003). *The Unbound Prometheus. Technological Change and Industrial Development in Western Europe from 1750 to the Present* (2nd edn). Cambridge: Cambridge University Press.

Landler, M. (2008). "Dollar Shift: Chinese Pockets Filled as Americans' Emptied." *The New York Times*, December 25. http://www.nytimes.com/2008/12/26/world/asia/26addiction.html?pagewanted=1&th&emc=th [Accessed January 25, 2012].

Lee, C.K. and Selden, M. (2007). "China's Durable Inequality: Legacies of Revolution and Pitfalls of Reform." *The Asia-Pacific Journal*, January 21. http://japanfocus.org/-Mark-Selden/2329 [Accessed January 25, 2012].

McCormack, G. (2008). "Conservatism" and "Nationalism." The Japan Puzzle, *Japan Focus*, June 22. http://japanfocus.org/-Gavan-McCormack/2786 [Accessed January 25, 2012].

Mearsheimer, J. (2001). *The Tragedy of Great Power Politics*. New York: Norton.

Murphy, R.T. (2008). "Asia and the Meltdown of American Finance." *Japan Focus*, October 24. http://japanfocus.org/-R_Taggart-Murphy/2931 [Accessed January 25, 2012].

Murphy, R.T. (2009). "In the Eye of the Storm: Updating the Economics of Global Turbulence, an Introduction to Robert Brenner's Update." http://japanfocus.org/-R_Taggart-Murphy/3265 [Accessed January 25, 2012].

Osborne, M. (2007). "The Water Politics of China and Southeast Asia: Rivers, Dams, Cargo Boats and the Environment." *The Asia-Pacific Journal*, June 11. http://japanfocus.org/-Milton-Osborne/2448 [Accessed January 25, 2012].

Pomeranz, K. (2000). *The Great Divergence: China, Europe, and the Making of the Modern World Economy*. Princeton: Princeton University Press.

Quijano, K. (2011). "China, ASEAN Agree on Plans to Solve South China Sea Dispute." July 21. http://edition.cnn.com/2011/WORLD/asiapcf/07/21/china.sea.conflict/ [Accessed January 25, 2012].

Reid, A. (1988 and 1993). *Southeast Asia in the Age of Commerce, 1450–1680* (2 vols). New Haven: Yale University Press.

Richardson, M. (2008). "A Southward Thrust for China's Energy Diplomacy in the South China Sea." *Japan Focus*, November 7. http://japanfocus.org/-Michael-Richardson/2949 [Accessed January 25, 2012].

Roberge, M. (2009). "China–Taiwan Relations." Council on Foreign Relations (backgrounder) August 11. http://www.cfr.org/publication/9223/chinataiwan_relations.html#p4 [Accessed January 25, 2012].

Rostow, W.W. (1962). *The Stages of Economic Growth. A Non-Communist Manifesto.* Cambridge: Cambridge University Press.

Selden, M. with Ka, C. (1993). "Original Accumulation, Equality and Late Industrialization: The Cases of Socialist China and Capitalist Taiwan," in M. Selden (ed.), *The Political Economy of Chinese Development*, 109–36. Armonk, N.Y.: M.E. Sharpe.

Selden, M. and Wu, J. (2011). "The Chinese State, Incomplete Proletarianization and Structures of Inequality in Two Epochs." *The Asia-Pacific Journal*, 9 (5/1), January 3. http://japanfocus.org/-Jieh_min-Wu/3480 [Accessed January 25, 2012].

Shambaugh, D. (2004). "China Engages Asia: Reshaping the Regional Order." *International Security*, 29 (3): 64–99.

Snyder, S. and Byun, S. (2010). "China–ROK Trade Disputes and Implications for Managing Security Relations." *Korean Economic Institute Academic Paper Series*, 5 (8), September. http://www.keia.org/Publications/AcademicPaperSeries/2010/APS-Snyder-2010.pdf [Accessed January 25, 2012].

South Korea Main Economic Indicators. (2010). http://trade.ec.europa.eu/doclib/docs/2006/september/tradoc_113448.pdf [Accessed January 25, 2012].

Sugihara, K. (ed.) (2005). *Japan, China and the Growth of the Asian International Economy, 1850–1949*. Oxford: Oxford University Press.

Sun, Y. and Tang, E. (2008). "Taiwan, China Start Direct Links as Relations Improve." Bloomberg, December 15. http://www.bloomberg.com/apps/news?pid=20601080&sid=aeoan51P.sBg&refer=asia/ [Accessed January 25, 2012].

Takahashi, K. and Murphy, R.T. (2008). "The US and the Temptation of Dollar Seignorage." *Japan Focus*. http://japanfocus.org/-Kosuke-TAKAHASHI/3028 [Accessed January 25, 2012].

Tanter, R. (2008). "The Maritime Self-Defence Force Mission in the Indian Ocean: Afghanistan, NATO and Japan's Political Impasse." *Japan Focus*, September 2. http://japanfocus.org/-Richard-Tanter/2868 [Accessed January 25, 2012].

The Nation (Thailand). (2009). June 5.

UPI. (2010), "Japan to Build Navy Base in Gulf of Aden." May 11. http://www.upi.com/Business_News/Security-Industry/2010/05/11/Japan-to-build-navy-base-in-Gulf-of-Aden/UPI-60511273596816/. [Accessed January 25, 2012].

US Treasury Department. (2011). "Major Foreign Holders of Treasury Securities." http://www.treas.gov/tic/mfh.txt [Accessed January 25, 2012].

Wada, H. (2010). "Resolving the China–Japan Conflict Over the Senkaku/Diaoyu Islands." *The Asia-Pacific Journal*, 43-3-10, 25 October. http://japanfocus.org/-Haruki-Wada/3433 [Accessed January 25, 2012].

Wade, G. (2010). "ASEAN Divides," *New Mandala*, December. http://asiapacific.anu.edu.au/newmandala/ [Accessed January 25, 2012].

Wallerstein, Immanuel, interviewed by Suh, Jae-Jung. (2009). "Capitalism's Demise?" *Japan Focus*. http://japanfocus.org/-I-Wallerstein/3005 [Accessed January 25, 2012].

Wang, H. (2007). "The Politics of Imagining Asia: Empires, Nations, Regional and Global Orders." *Inter-Asia Cultural Studies*, 8 (1): 1–34.

Wong, R.B. (1997). *China Transformed: Historical Change and the Limits of European Experience*. Ithaca: Cornell University Press.

Xetrade. (2010). "Japan, South Korea, China: Trilateral Ties, Tensions." http://www.xe.com/news/Fri%20Dec%2012%2020:48:00%20EST%202008/129221.htm?categoryId=5¤tPage= [Accessed January 25, 2012].

Yadav, M. (2010). "International Trade in Taiwan and Taiwan China Trade Relations." Suite 101.com, May 11. http://www.suite101.com/content/international-trade-in-taiwan-and-taiwan-china-relationship-a236159 [Accessed January 25, 2012].

Yoshimatsu, H. (2008). *The Political Economy of Regionalism in East Asia. Integrative Explanations for Dynamics and Challenges*. Basingstoke: Palgrave Macmillan.

Yu, Z. (2010). "Japan's First Overseas Base Aimed at Expanding Military Boundaries," 28 April. http://news.xinhuanet.com/english2010/indepth/2010-04/28/c_13270876.htm [Accessed January 25, 2012].

Zhao, S. (2008). "China's Global Search for Energy Security: Cooperation and Competition in the Asia-Pacific." *Journal of Contemporary China*, 55: 207–27.

Zhou, Y. (2008). *The Inside Story of China's High Tech Industry*. Lanham, Md.: Rowman and Littlefield.

3

Big business and economic nationalism in India

Surajit Mazumdar

3.1 Introduction

The conventional wisdom about globalization—namely, that it is synonymous with the "retreat of the state" and the demise of economic nationalism—has been questioned by many (Patnaik 1992; Wood 1999; Shulman 2000; Helleiner 2002; Pickel 2003; D'Costa 2009). This chapter shares this skepticism of a one-dimensional interpretation of increased international economic integration. Specifically, I emphasize the class dimension of the phenomenon to reinforce the view that while economic nationalism is intrinsic to capitalism, the ways in which it manifests itself are historically contingent. Economic nationalism is neither the exclusive pursuit of statist and protectionist economic policies nor incompatible with economic liberalism. This chapter demonstrates this through the example of India's transition from autonomous development to liberalization by highlighting the continuity between these phases.

The nature of the Indian economy's relationship with the global economy, as well as Indian capitalist opinion about it, has changed over the different stages of Indian capitalism. Born in the context of a colonial economy, the Indian capitalist class came to oppose the economic liberalism imposed by a foreign power and contributed to crafting the strategy of autonomous development that was adopted after India's independence in 1947. The abandonment of this strategy in 1991 marked the return of liberalism as the underlying philosophy of economic policy. This time around, however, it was a national state that pushed India's economy towards increased international integration. India's capitalists, too, in contrast to their earlier attitude, embraced rather than resisted this new liberalism. This chapter focuses on this shift in the outlook of the capitalist class represented by India's big business. I try to identify the reasons why it initially emerged and why it has gathered strength over time. The objective is to bring out important national factors working with external pressures to bring about the swing towards economic liberalism by a quintessentially developing country capitalist state. The emphasis on the capitalist class is due to the premise that it has always constituted a powerful social force in shaping independent India's economic policy. To understand the historical dynamics of economic nationalism in India, therefore, the development of this class and its changing attitude towards the Indian economy's external economic relationship merits examination.

The central argument of this chapter is that economic nationalism in India both contributed to and coexists with the liberalization process. Indian capitalist opinion moved away from old-style economic nationalism because industrialization after independence altered the business environment. Embracing liberalism became both possible and necessary for India's capitalists, who then gained tremendously from increased integration. Like the earlier strategy of autonomous development, liberalization, too, can be seen as a response of the Indian state to the imperatives of national capitalist development. Precisely for that reason, state support for such development did not cease but adapted to the new context paralleling the apparent retreat of the state. This dual role has been as important to the post-liberalization success of India's capitalists as it was for their preceding development.

Economic nationalism has thus remained a key influence on economic policy making in India, but the forms in which it is expressed have changed as a result of capitalist development. India remains a poor capitalist country still with very high levels of economic backwardness. The modern capitalist sector of its economy, however, has experienced growth, which brought about an advance of its capitalist class. This changed rather than eliminated the nature of support the capitalist class needed from the state, which in turn has tended to intensify uneven or dualistic development.

The chapter is divided into three main sections. The first section underscores the significance of Indian liberalization as a case study for examining the relationship between economic nationalism and globalization in less advanced capitalist countries. The second brings out the role of import-substituting industrialization in generating the internal impetus towards liberalization in Indian capitalism. Two main outcomes are emphasized: the increasing technological requirements of a technologically dependent economy; and the strengthening of Indian big business within the limits of such dependence. The former inclined Indian capitalists towards the opening-up of India's economy; the latter made the resultant exposure to global competition less threatening. The third section shows how and in what manner Indian big business has benefited from liberalization. I argue here that the processes of liberalization and the ceding of space by the state to the private sector have been designed and carried out in a manner that has made increased international integration complementary to Indian capital's growth. This has imparted durability to the liberal course of Indian economic policy.

3.2 Globalization, Third World Economic Nationalism, and Indian Liberalization

Economic nationalism can be said to result from the contradictory combination of a political division of the world into nations and a capitalist economic system whose spontaneous tendencies are toward global expansion rather than being confined within individual nations. Capitalist states are class states—protecting and advancing the interests of dominant capitalist classes is their prime function—but they also come into being as national states. This is true of states in the advanced regions where capitalism first emerged, in latecomer countries after they achieved political independence, or more recently in transition economies. National states have often erected barriers to interaction across national economies and have been key instruments of capitalism's internationalization. The point is that in acting in either manner, all states are always motivated by *national* imperatives—the promotion of national economic performance and of the interests of national capital at home or abroad. Hence, internationalization of capitalism has reinforced economic nationalism, which is also naturally a dynamic phenomenon. The specific measures that states take in order to promote national economic interests, and the ideologies rationalizing these measures, change in response to shifting contexts.

These general propositions laid out above should characterize contemporary capitalism as they did earlier phases of capitalism's history. Globalization does, however, pose a specific challenge. How does one explain the trajectories of the economic nationalisms of so many diverse countries coalescing into the global triumph of economic liberalism that made globalization possible? A rough-and-ready generalization derivable from historical experience is that the proclivity of states towards liberalism or protectionism is dependent on the levels of *relative* development of their national capitalism. While advanced forms of capitalism would tend to favor economic liberalism, those seeking to develop in the shadow of more developed rivals would be inclined towards protectionism. This generalization, however, does not explain why the shifts in so many developing countries from the strategies of autonomous development were their initial response to their subordinate position in capitalism's global order. Part of the explanation for this of course lies in precisely the unequal position of less advanced forms of capitalism in developing countries, which makes them subject to significant external pressure. However, their crossover to liberalism cannot be explained simply by the lack of development and external pressure. The relationship between the interests of their national capitalist development and the transition to liberalization has to be examined.

India represents an important case study to examine this phenomenon. India's history until 1991 made it one of the least obvious cases for adopting liberal economic policies in that year. An extremely large country, India had experienced one of the longest histories of colonial subjugation by a capitalist power. After independence, it was one of the most statist, autonomous, and inward-looking of Third World capitalisms. It was also politically distanced from the leading capitalist powers to a greater extent, and for a longer period of time, than any other major non-socialist developing world. Its domestic market, based on industrial growth, created a fairly large and diverse industrial sector. Industrialization in India, however, did not produce a transformation of the kind seen in some other East and Southeast Asian developing countries. It remained one of the most agrarian and poorest countries at the time it made its rather dramatic shift towards liberalization. Nor did Indian industry manage to create a sufficiently strong base for the self-development of technology (Alam 1985; Tyabji 2000).

In short, India was not among the likes of South Korea, which had built internationally competitive firms and industrial structures, but it was also not a "banana republic" that could be simply bullied into responding to the dictates of international capital. Yet its economic policy regime made a shift that has survived way beyond the passing of the foreign exchange crisis in 1991 that was its immediate trigger.

Judged in terms of purely aggregate economic performance, Indian capitalism's integration into the global economy also appears to have been extremely successful. India has been, along with China, one of the fastest growing economies of the world in the last two decades.[1] It has also escaped so far the currency crises that have struck so many of its developing country counterparts, and apparently weathered the storm of the global economic crisis better than most countries.

The Indian case therefore is of a less developed capitalist country opening up when it was still a fair distance behind advanced capitalisms and yet managing to hold its own under globalization.[2] A deeper investigation of this case can therefore contribute to a better understanding of the relationship between the evolution of economic nationalism across capitalist economies in an unequal world and the unfolding of the globalization process itself.

3.3 Capitalist Development after Independence and the Shift to Liberalism

In the colonial era, the rising class of Indian capitalists reflected, as well as reinforced, Indian nationalism that grew in opposition to India's political and economic subjugation (Ray 1985). As the end of British rule approached, Indian businesses participated actively in the process of shaping the form and substance of the post-independence strategy of planned development. Their attitude towards other elements of that strategy, specifically the disciplining of private capital by the state that was implied in it, is a subject of some debate (Chibber 2004). However, beyond doubt, they were firmly in favor of protection and autonomous development. Indeed, greater protection from foreign competition had been virtually the sole objective that India's capitalists had pursued in the battles on economic policy in the colonial period (Bagchi 1980).

Until 1991, Indian economic policy retained its original broad framework of economic nationalism. The relative autonomy of the Indian economy was maintained and the public sector share in the economy steadily increased. Limited external sector liberalization in the 1980s only enlarged a little the window for sourcing foreign technology that had existed throughout the life of the import-substituting industrialization strategy. It was the liberalization of the 1990s that more comprehensively opened India to international trade and capital flows. Fiscal conservatism, privatization, and ultimate abandonment of the attempt to direct private investment also came as part of the package. The 1991 reforms must therefore be considered the decisive turning point in the history of Indian economic policy. With these, the trajectory of the Indian economy became subject much more than before to the operation of international economic forces.

The 1991 liberalization also revealed a remarkable metamorphosis in the attitude of Indian capitalists. The change in the policy paradigm was somewhat abrupt, and implemented without much warning. Indian big business took some time to adjust and some sections did initially raise concerns about the pace of change, particularly of external sector liberalization (Tyabji 2000; Chandrasekhar and Ghosh 2002). An informal group of industrialists, the "Bombay Club," lobbied for a "level playing field."[3] The head of one of the major Indian industry associations later also criticized what he called the "cowboy" tactics of foreign partners in joint ventures.[4] However, the resistance to liberalization came from other segments of Indian society rather than its business class. Any initial ambiguity in the capitalist attitude towards liberalization soon disappeared, and Indian big business came to eventually actively push the "reform" agenda (Pedersen 2007; Kohli 2009).

3.3.1 *Import-substituting Industrialization and Private Capital*

Until 1991, the chief propeller of the growth and development of Indian big business was industrialization. Manufacturing was earmarked within the industrialization strategy mainly for private sector development, and Indian private business in fact became highly concentrated in the manufacturing sector.

Manufacturing growth was marked by instability but the tempo of industrial growth picked up greatly after independence (Sivasubramonian 2000). A considerable expansion and diversification of the industrial sector by the end of the 1980s was the result. A structure initially dominated by light industries was transformed to one where chemical and engineering industries became predominant. This diversification represented the typical pattern associated with the diffusion of industrialization to the Third World in the second half of the twentieth century, which brought their industrial structures closer to that of advanced countries (Table 3.1).

The extent of Indian industrialization measured in terms of diversification of its industrial structure was greater than in terms of the growth of industrial output or its share in aggregate output. Industrialization had been based on a growing but nevertheless narrow domestic market (D'Costa 2005). Diversification consequently had major weight in the long-run expansion of industrial output even without achieving very high per capita levels. In the formal or organized manufacturing sector, the sphere of big business activity, the transformation in the pattern of manufacturing output in India (Table 3.2) was even greater. At independence, the organized mills accounted for four-fifths of fabric production in India's large textile industry. A combination of government policy and prolonged crisis in the industry, however, led to a massive

Table 3.1. Structure of manufacturing value added in 1991 (percentage shares)

Branch (ISIC)	Developed market economies	Developing countries	World	India
31—Food, beverages, and tobacco	11.9	17.3	13.3	11.9
32—Textiles, wearing apparel, leather, and footwear	5.5	12.6	7.1	15.9
33—Wood products including furniture	3.1	2.3	2.9	0.4
34—Paper, printing, and publishing	9.1	4.6	7.9	3.8
35—Chemicals, petroleum, rubber, and plastic products	17.1	23.1	17.7	21.9
36—Non-metallic mineral products	3.9	5.1	4.1	5.1
37—Basic metals	5.3	7.1	5.8	13.8
38—Metal products, including machinery and equipment	43.0	26.6	39.8	26.8
39—Other manufacturing industries	1.2	1.4	1.4	0.4

Note: ISIC International Standard Industrial Classification.
Source: UNIDO, Industrial Country Statistics.

Table 3.2. Composition of gross value added of registered manufacturing in India, 1950–1 and 1990–1, at current prices (percentages to total)

Industry group	1950–1	1990–1
food products	15.62	8.10
beverages and tobacco products	2.84	2.37
textile products	42.60	13.47
leather and fur products	0.81	0.89
wood and wood products, furniture, fixtures, etc.	0.81	0.39
paper and printing, etc.	5.07	4.27
Total of above six industry groups	**67.75**	**29.50**
rubber, petroleum products, etc.	2.64	8.22
chemical and chemical products	7.30	14.63
non-metallic products	3.45	5.47
basic metals	4.67	12.85
metal products and machinery	3.04	11.20
electrical machinery	0.81	7.01
other manufacturing	2.23	3.47
transport equipment	7.91	7.65
Total of above eight industry groups	**32.05**	**70.50**

Source: CSO, National Accounts Statistics.

shift in fabric production to the informal or unorganized power loom sector (Misra 1993).

In line with the features of Indian industrialization, the industrial spread of corporate capital changed more visibly than its relative size within the economy. The organized private sector share in net domestic product (NDP) stayed at around or below 15%,[5] but the industries that were prominent for private corporate capital changed. At independence, large business firms were concentrated in a few traditional industries such as the cotton and jute textile industries, mining, and tea manufacture. By the 1980s, their presence in many of these had become limited or absent and these industries were rarely important for large firms. Instead, big businesses were often built around their presence in one or more of a range of other industries that had grown over different time periods, such as steel and steel products, chemicals, cement, automobiles and automobile products, industrial and other machinery, and consumer electronics.

With changes in the pattern of control over corporate capital and industrial assets, Indian big business consolidated its position and reflected most the shift in the industrial spread (Mazumdar 2006). The final demise by the mid-1970s of surviving old European-controlled firms reduced the significance of direct foreign control. The presence of multinational companies (MNCs) fluctuated somewhat in response to policy shifts.[6] Pervasive, however, was their indirect presence in the technical collaborations and joint ventures of Indian business groups. Indian family-controlled business groups clearly took a lion's share of the expansion opportunities that arose in non-traditional industries of the kind mentioned earlier. Elements in the policy regime reining in MNCs also helped Indian capital make major inroads into industries where MNC dominance had been marked for long stretches of time (Encarnation, 1989).

These changes in the industrial spread of Indian big business as a result of import substitution brought about its development along many additional dimensions. Expansion in newer and more "modern" industries increased the level of technological sophistication that Indian big business dealt with. They learned to find, absorb, adapt, and use technologies and technological advances across the industrial spectrum even if they themselves did not develop them. The kind of demand that their production was geared towards also changed. For the cotton textile industry, a populous but poor country had provided a mass market. The ultimate markets for the products most big Indian firms produced on the eve of liberalization were generally narrower but with considerably higher average incomes. Big business and oligopolistic dominance also came in closer contact with each other as the industries into which Indian corporate capital spread by the end of the 1980s had a more concentrated character than the older textile industries.

3.3.2 *The Transformation of Indian Capitalism and the Transition to Liberalization*

Import-substituting industrialization enhanced Indian capitalism's strengths even as some old weaknesses persisted. There was a coming-of-age of Indian corporate capital as it acquired new capabilities. Collectively, Indian big business had to an extent "caught up" with its international counterparts in terms of the industries in which it operated, the kind of technologies it handled, the demand pattern it responded to, and in its oligopolistic character. The supporting institutions of Indian capitalism, in particular the financial sector, were also considerably more developed by the end of the 1980s. But this maturing of Indian capitalism had remained limited. The new and old constituents of Indian big business on the eve of liberalization had all grown in the sheltered environment provided by protectionism. They had built businesses that were mainly "national," producing in, selling in, and raising finances from the domestic economy.[7] Their scales of operation were considerably smaller than international scales and technological gaps still existed. The most important weakness, however, was the continued dependence on foreign technologies.

By 1991, import-substituting industrialization had also increased the scale and frequency at which technological advances needed to be introduced. Catching up with the structure of industries at the international level had reduced the scope for industrial expansion through a successive diffusion of industries. Continued expansion had to be based primarily on existing industries rather than on new ones, and that too under conditions of a narrow domestic market. Such an expansion had to follow the international pattern or constitute a niche within it. Either way, the technological requirements were different from those of the past. Under import-substituting industrialization, the critical requirements of technology or know-how were usually at the point of entry into a new industry and limited to the firms making such an entry. Expansion on the basis of existing industries, however, meant that all firms in all industries required recurrent technological advances.

The strengths and weaknesses of Indian capital worked in tandem to move Indian business opinion towards favoring a greater degree of integration with the world economy. As subsequent experience proved, industrial development had enhanced the general ability of Indian big business to confront international competition. However, that could not have been sufficient reason for it to welcome such competition, particularly because of its technological weakness. This very weakness, however, made freer interaction with the international economy imperative for meeting the new technological requirements of Indian capitalist development. This collective need of the Indian industrial capitalist class, under conditions of oligopolistic rivalry in markets reflecting international demonstration effects, would have also been felt as an individual need by its different constituents. The threat from international competition strengthened rather than weakened this orientation towards liberalization. The challenge of withstanding it created an additional need for greater "freedom" being accorded to Indian business firms to pursue their strategic imperatives. Thus, old economic nationalism and the entire edifice of state regulations through which it had been given effect became an anachronism for Indian big business. The self-realization of this by the class may not have been instantaneous in 1991 and developed unevenly across its different segments. Nevertheless, this was the reason that a stiff resistance to liberalization by Indian big business never materialized.

3.4 Liberalization, Indian Big Business, and the New Economic Nationalism

Thus, both the old form of economic nationalism and newly instituted liberalization had the objective of maximizing the scope for capitalist development within the historical limits of Indian capitalism's prevailing context. One gave way to the other only because it had served its purpose. In the process, some overt forms of past economic nationalism had to be abandoned or toned down. The new economic nationalism also has a less explicit appearance of a strategy of guiding the economy in a definite direction. Yet Indian liberalization has always been justified by the state in terms of "national interest."[8] It has been increasingly portrayed as a means of national economic success setting India on the path to becoming an economic superpower. The nationalist element is, however, not limited to the ideological discourse on liberalization. Its substantive appearance is in the tailoring of the process of liberalization to enable Indian capital to succeed in competition at home and abroad.

That economic liberalism marks the demise of economic nationalism is based on a misconception that the state's role in the economy becomes very limited under liberalization. Liberalization is a process that can take place in many ways with results that are not identical. Its speed, its degree and sequencing, the pattern of variations in its extent across different spheres, the extent to which the state retreats from some roles and the new tasks it assumes: these are all sources of such variability. In choosing their specific path towards liberalization, individual states may not be entirely free of external constraints. Indeed liberalization itself results in some constraints once undertaken. However, this does not mean that states are reduced to being simply passive instruments of liberalization.

The Indian state has played an important role in the post-liberalization story and not as a representative of capital shorn of any national identity. Precisely because it has played such a part, heightened integration of India into the global economy has been complementary rather than antithetical to the growth of Indian big business in at least quantitative terms. It has helped Indian capital face the new challenges posed by liberalization and take advantage of new opportunities. In that process the state has also tilted more in favor of capital relative to the rest of Indian society. The results have been more rapid growth of corporate capital and profits, which has reinforced big business endorsement of liberalization.

3.4.1 *The Transition to Corporate-led Growth*

After 1991, the long-standing stability in the share of the Indian private organized sector in India's aggregate NDP gave way to a rapid rising trend (Figure 3.1). From a little over 14% in 1990–1, it went up to over 23% by 2007–8.[9] The private corporate sector's role in determining the tempo of investment in the economy also increased. It has been responsible for a third of the increase in the net fixed capital stock (at 1999–2000 prices) since 1991, raising its share from less than 11% in the early 1990s to over 26% by 2008.

A striking aspect of corporate growth in India is that surplus incomes have been the main beneficiaries. The share of employee compensation in the private organized sector to the economy's aggregate NDP has on average been *lower* after 1991 than in the 1980s. In other words, there has been a

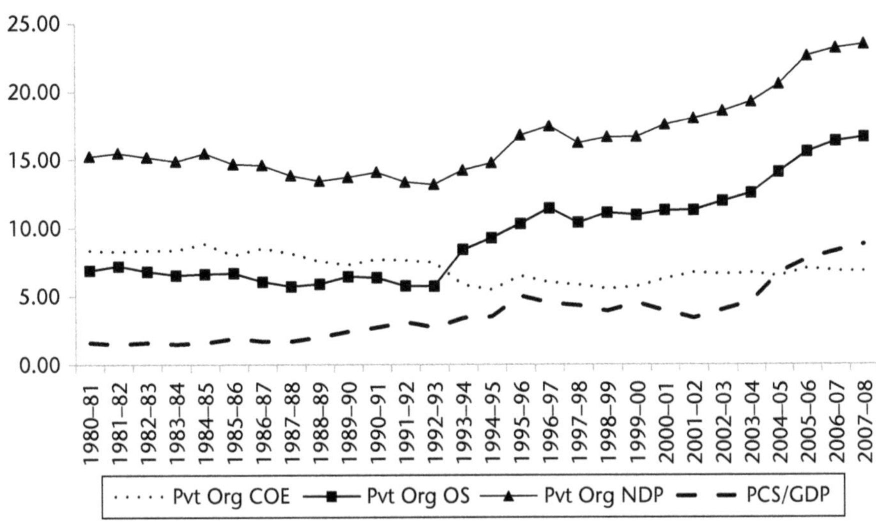

Figure 3.1. Shares of the private organized sector and its components in aggregate net domestic product and of private corporate savings in gross domestic product, 1980–1 to 2007–8 (percentages).

Notes: COE = Compensation of Employees; OS = Operating Surplus; PCS = Private Corporate Savings.

Source: CSO, National Accounts Statistics.

massive redistribution of incomes within the organized private sector, with the operating surplus share increasing from just above 45% to nearly 71%. This is also reflected in the quite dramatic increase in private corporate savings. In the four decades before liberalization, such savings were generally below 2% of gross domestic product (GDP). In 2007–8, this figure stood at 8.8%.[10]

Corporate growth under liberalization has also been highly concentrated. Nearly 55% of the total profits of over 400,000 companies filing income tax returns in 2007–8 was accounted for by just 190 companies with profits over Rs. 5 billion.[11] Some of these were of course public sector companies. However, since all 1,808 public sector companies together accounted for less than 22% of the total profits, private corporate profits clearly were highly concentrated in a few companies and even fewer business groups.

3.4.2 *The Shift to Services-Dominated Growth*

While corporate growth outpaced the rest of the economy after 1991, industrial growth did not. Leaving aside construction, the slow post-independence rise in the share of the industrial sector in aggregate GDP completely ceased after the mid-1990s (Mazumdar 2010). Industrial expansion continued to be plagued by demand-related instability, and two episodes of faster growth were separated by a six-year period of slowdown from the second half of the 1990s (Table 3.3). The largest component of industry, the manufacturing sector, exhibited an identical pattern.

It is expansion in services rather than in industry that has made possible the enlarging of the share of the private organized sector in the Indian economy's production. Private business firms have found lucrative opportunities in externally as well as domestically demanded services, and of late also in construction. Services have consequently decisively displaced manufacturing as the principal sphere of private corporate activity (Table 3.4). This change in the distribution of its output would suggest that private corporate capital in India has been *de-industrializing* during the liberalization process.

This should not be construed to mean that private capital is abandoning manufacturing activity or that manufacturing in India is dying. Indian manufacturing has survived import liberalization and continued to expand. Manufactured exports have grown after liberalization and diversified somewhat away from India's traditional labor-intensive products. Many major Indian business enterprises are still mainly manufacturing firms, and in

Table 3.3. Annual average rates of growth of real gross domestic product in Indian industry (percent per annum)

Sector	1991–2 to 1996–7	1997–8 to 2002–3	2003–4 to 2007–8
Mining & quarrying	3.87	3.97	6.02
Manufacturing	8.10	4.07	9.11
Electricity, gas & water supply	7.68	4.50	5.74
Construction	3.37	6.92	13.68
Industry	6.58	4.71	9.69

Source: CSO, National Accounts Statistics.

Table 3.4. Distribution of private organized net domestic product (NDP) (percentage shares)

	Distribution of private organized NDP				Private organized NDP to aggregate NDP			
Sector	1990–1	1996–7	2002–3	2007–8	1990–1	1996–7	2002–3	2007–8
Agriculture	15.49	12.44	7.49	5.14	2.21	2.18	1.39	1.21
Industry	57.32	55.06	46.05	45.76	8.18	9.66	8.55	10.72
Industry excl. Construction	*45.13*	*45.77*	*36.77*	*31.53*	*6.44*	*8.03*	*6.83*	*7.39*
Services	27.19	32.50	46.45	49.10	3.88	5.70	8.62	11.51
Services and Construction	*39.38*	*41.79*	*55.73*	*63.33*	*5.62*	*7.33*	*10.35*	*14.84*
Total	100.00	100.00	100.00	100.00	14.26	17.55	18.56	23.44

Source: CSO, National Accounts Statistics.

some industries, such as pharmaceuticals, Indian firms are competing globally. Much of the invested private corporate capital is also in the manufacturing sector; whereas the growing services sector is generally not capital intensive. In fact, private corporate ascendancy in India's investment process has actually found its fullest expression in the manufacturing sector. The share of organized manufacturing in the increase in fixed capital stock between 1990–1 and 2007–8 went up to nearly 30% from less than 19% in the 1980s. A lack of private interest and investment has thus not been the problem for industrial expansion.

Despite these qualifications, the rising importance of services in the Indian corporate scene is undeniable. The major firms that have risen from a relatively modest size to the top rungs of the Indian corporate hierarchy in the liberalization era have achieved this through growth in services. Examples of this are Infosys (software) and Bharti (communication). Others such as Wipro (software), and HDFC and ICICI (financial services) have also moved up into the top league through services. Big industrial groups such as Tata, AV Birla, and Reliance have also built up a substantial presence in a range of services including software, communication, retail, and financial services.

The manufacturing sector's rising share in investment has not been matched by its contribution to India's aggregate output growth. Instead, organized manufacturing's share in GDP growth fell from 13% in the 1980s to under 9% in the period after 1991. This imbalance has undermined the sustainability of corporate and manufacturing investment growth (Mazumdar 2008). These investments have also exhibited instability with a similar time pattern as manufacturing growth but of a higher order—a period of complete collapse between two phases of extremely rapid growth (Table 3.5).

Compared with many other developing countries, India is still a minor location of production of manufactured products for the world market. Growth of exports has also been accompanied by a sharp rise in manufactured

Table 3.5. Annual rates of growth of gross fixed capital formation at constant prices in India (percent per annum)

At 1993–4 prices			At 1999–2000 prices		
Period	Registered manufacturing	Private corporate sector	Period	Registered manufacturing	Private corporate sector
1990–1 to 1996–7	19.50	21.94	1999–2000 to 2002–3	−4.91	−2.02
1996–7 to 2002–3	−6.06	−3.75	2002–3 to 2007–8	28.51	31.39

Note: The series with base year 1993–4 does not extend up to 2007–8 while that with the base year 1999–2000 also begins from 1999–2000.

Source: CSO, National Accounts Statistics.

imports. Relative to India's GDP, its aggregate merchandise deficit as well as its non-oil component have, after liberalization, attained levels far beyond those witnessed in the run-up to the balance of payments crisis of 1991. If no such crisis has hit India after liberalization it is because of a large surplus in its invisibles trade based on services exports and income remittances.

Deindustrialization of corporate capital and the rise of services in India are products of the same set of conditions that have generated rapid corporate growth. They reflect the combined operation of domestic income-distribution trends and the position in globalization's international division of labor that India is being slotted into. A highly concentrated process of growth in incomes (Sengupta, Kannan, and Raveendran 2008; D'Costa 2010) on one side has held back the expansion of a mass market for industrial consumer goods. Increasing incomes of a minority on the other has led to a greater diversification in their demand in favor of services. In external markets too, India's spectacular success has been in services rather than in manufactured exports. Public investment, capable of both generating demand for industry as well as contributing to the international competitiveness of domestic industry, has become a victim of fiscal conservatism. Given these fundamental demand constraints, manufacturing growth has relied heavily on corporate investment to generate demand. That is why the two have moved up and down together.

The trajectory of a services-dominated growth, and its impact on corporate capital, has great significance for the post-liberalization course of economic nationalism in India. The rapid growth of services has enabled a national capitalist expansion to a degree that would have been impossible relying mainly on industry. This has contributed to the sustained endorsement of liberalization by big business. The deindustrialization of corporate capital is also, however, changing the context for economic nationalism in a fundamental long-term sense, weakening the link between the advance of capitalism and a national *industrialization* process. In time this may weaken the commitment of the capitalist class to industrialization, which was the central concern of old economic nationalism. Key elements of that nationalism, such as trade protection, have few positives but many negatives for the growth of important services. Software, for instance, is mainly reliant on external markets, while communication and trade are not subject to import competition. At the same time, the software and communication sectors rely heavily on import of equipment, thus undermining national production.

3.4.3 *Foreign Capital and Indian Big Business after Liberalization*

With liberalization, the growth of Indian capital became dependent on the degree and nature of success it could achieve against international competition at home and abroad. The domestic economic space was no longer reserved for it in the way it was under old economic nationalism. Yet Indian capital has been the principal beneficiary of rapid corporate growth in India and much of the Indian corporate sector has remained in "national" hands. At the same time, Indian firms have taken important steps in the direction of greater internationalization, mainly through acquisitions abroad (Nayyar 2008; Athukorala 2009).

One implication of capital account liberalization has been the tying together of Indian corporate capital and global financial interests in a mutually beneficial relationship. A major part of capital inflows into India after 1991 has consisted of portfolio capital or private equity. Volatility associated with such flows has created problems of exchange-rate instability and narrowing of the policy space of the state. However, Indian big business firms have also derived benefits from financial globalization. Foreign institutional investors (FIIs) have become important movers of the Indian stock market and have helped create conditions whereby Indian firms can raise cheap capital. The financing options of Indian private firms have also increased through better access to foreign finance, and their recourse to such sources has been quite significant in some years (Reserve Bank of India 2009). These have also facilitated foreign acquisitions by Indian firms. Large capital inflows have indirectly also financed internationalization of Indian firms by covering India's current account deficit and allowing accumulation of reserves, enabling thereby the easing of norms for acquisitions abroad.

Foreign direct investment (FDI) by multinational firms in India and their presence there has also certainly become more pronounced after liberalization. An increasing number of leading MNCs from diverse sectors now have Indian affiliates (Table 3.6). Liberalization has also enabled and induced multinationals to increase the level of control in their Indian affiliates (Basant 2000; Nagaraj 2003), buying out their partners in joint ventures or becoming the dominant partner, and acquiring other firms. From Parle and Tomco in the early part of the liberalization era to the more recent cases of ACC and Ranbaxy, a number of prominent Indian firms have passed into foreign hands. In some individual industries, the extent of MNC presence has increased after liberalization and they completely dominate some such as passenger cars, scooters, consumer electronics, and soft drinks.

However, rather than any foreign takeover of the Indian corporate sector, it is the lack of FDI into India that has been the chief concern of Indian big business and the state. Underlying this is the reality that India has not emerged as a very important FDI destination, and MNCs have played a very limited role in drawing Indian manufacturing into global production networks. The scale of foreign affiliate presence in India's economy has remained restricted and the degree of their export orientation even more so.

Table 3.6. Illustrative list of MNCs in different sectors in India

Sector	Prominent MNCs
Financial services	Citigroup, HSBC, Merrill Lynch, Goldman Sachs
IT services	IBM, Microsoft, Adobe, Oracle, Cisco, Hewlett-Packard
Media	News Corp, Sony
Electronics including consumer electronics	Nokia, Whirlpool, Samsung, LG, Motorola, Sony, Hitachi, Canon
Automobiles	Suzuki, Honda, Toyota, Ford, GM, Hyundai Kia Automotive, Daimler Chrysler, BMW
Consumer goods	Unilever, Proctor and Gamble, Colgate-Palmolive, Nestle, Cadbury, Johnson and Johnson, Henkel
Machinery and equipment	Robert Bosch, Siemens, Caterpillar, JCB, SKF, Alfa-Laval, ABB, Cummins
Chemicals	Bayer, Mitsubishi Chemical, Monsanto, Akzo Nobel, BASF
Drugs and pharmaceuticals	Pfizer, Novartis, GlaxoSmithKline, Sanofi-Aventis
Non-metallic mineral products	Holcim, Lafarge, Saint-Gobain
Petroleum and products	ExxonMobil, BP, Royal Dutch Shell, Total
Outsourced services	Convergys, Sykes, Accenture
Contract manufacturers	Flextronics, Jabil Circuits

Source: Author's compilation.

Multinational interest in India has not only been mainly of the market-seeking variety, it has also remained limited in spread. In many sectors, a large part of selling activity in India is still done mainly by Indian firms.

Indian firms have been more prominent than MNCs in pushing Indian manufactured exports. The same is actually also true in the case of services. However, in the IT-BPO (information technology-business process outsourcing) sector, while Indian firms are the main suppliers of services, multinational firms are their major clients, many of whom have also set up their own captive units (Rajeevan et al. 2007). Such outsourcing has also happened to an extent in manufactured products. A prominent example is the automobile components sector where leading Indian groups such as Kalyani (Bharat Forge), TVS, Mahindra, Rane, and Amtek have succeeded in establishing themselves as suppliers to global auto companies. However, manufacturing outsourcing to India is not comparable in scale to that in services.[12]

Indian firms have also played a dominant role in other expanding services sectors and those where public sector prominence has tended to recede. These include sectors such as telecommunications, banking, construction, retail, and oil and gas. In banking for instance, it is Indian private banks that have displaced the public sector to some extent, with foreign banks remaining a somewhat peripheral segment (Table 3.7).

The success of Indian firms in the liberalization era has not been achieved by eliminating the old weakness in the technological sphere, but despite it. Indeed, the evidence suggests that, barring the pharmaceutical industry, there has been no significant increase in the innovative capacity of the Indian

Table 3.7. Distribution pattern of bank deposits and credit in India (percentage shares)

	Deposits			Credit		
Bank group	March 1991	March 2002	March 2009	March 1991	March 2002	March 2009
SBI and associates	26.5	24.1	24.1	27.9	25.0	23.1
Nationalized banks	60.9	51.0	49.5	57.4	47.3	50.5
Foreign banks	5.6	5.0	5.2	7.5	7.3	5.9
Regional rural banks	2.4	3.9	3.0	3.0	2.9	2.3
Other scheduled commercial banks	4.3	16.0	18.2	4.0	17.5	18.2

Source: Reserve Bank of India: Banking Statistics March 1991 and March 2002; and Quarterly Statistics on Deposits and Credit of Scheduled Commercial Banks March 2009.

Table 3.8. R&D intensity of Indian business groups and independent companies, 2008–9

R&D expenditure to net-income ratio range	No. of groups	No. of companies	Average R&D expenditure to net-income ratio (%)	Share in total income (%)	Share in total R&D expenditure (%)
> 10%	4	6	11.87	0.42	8.79
5–10%	7	21	6.87	1.33	16.17
3–5%	5	12	4.56	0.53	4.25
2–3%	3	8	2.33	1.06	4.39
1–2%	25	154	1.67	10.48	30.97
0.5–1%	31	155	0.73	4.76	6.16
0–0.5%	146	639	0.15	44.1	11.59
0%	211	441	0.00	9.64	0.00
All groups	432	1436	0.64	72.31	82.32
Other companies		2854	0.36	27.69	17.68
TOTAL		4290	0.56	100.00	100.00

Source: CMIE, Prowess Database (full citation in reference list).

private sector (Mani 2009). Table 3.8 shows that most Indian firms have very low levels of research and development (R&D) expenditure. Moreover, all of the 16 groups with an R&D expenditure to net income ratio above 3% are pharmaceutical firms. Even in pharmaceuticals, however, Indian firms lack drug development capabilities. They have therefore basically utilized their established strength in generics due to India's earlier protective patent regime, and licensing of molecules developed by their own R&D efforts (Jha 2007; Chaudhuri 2008). In the other highly internationalized sector, software, innovative activity in India has been mainly by foreign R&D units (Mani 2009) and Indian firms have found their niche in a relatively subordinate position to the internationally dominant firms (D'Costa 2004).

In other sectors, Indian firms have circumvented their limited technology development capability in a variety of other ways such as sourcing technology from specialized technology suppliers, outsourcing to foreign firms, and wherever possible, through the older traditional routes of technological collaboration and joint ventures with multinational firms. The pattern of growth has also helped because in a number of services and construction activities, the role of self-development of technology in any case tends to be limited. Increased technological sophistication in these has been facilitated by technical equipment suppliers and software service providers. Even the foreign acquisitions by Indian firms, enabled mainly by their financial strength, have been perhaps attempts to acquire missing competitive strengths like innovative capacity (Nayyar 2008).

3.4.4 *Big Business and the State Under Liberalization: The New Economic Nationalism*

A close cooperation between the state and Indian big business has developed under liberalization through a mutually reinforcing, two-sided process. The state for its own imperatives has calibrated the liberalization process to safeguard national economic interests, particularly of Indian capital. At the same time, private capital's influence over policy making also increased with its larger and more dominant role in the economy.

Though there has been no ambiguity regarding its direction, liberalization has been a comparatively slow and gradual process in India. Instead of a one-shot adoption of free trade, protection levels were brought down in stages. Despite significant tariff reductions, the Indian market remains among the most protected in the world. India also leads the world in repeatedly taking recourse to anti-dumping measures to protect a range of domestic industries.[13] While it has signed numerous free-trade-agreements, India has been reluctant to do so with China, a major source of India's imports. Capital controls in general, and specifically the policy towards foreign investment, have also been liberalized progressively rather than at one go. Caps on foreign investment, some still existing and others gradually raised, have been used. In addition, some foreign exchange earning obligations were imposed in the earlier stages of liberalization. These, it has been argued, contributed to the development of automobile component exports from India (Kumar 2008).

Where liberalization measures resulted in a significant threat to Indian business from foreign capital, the state also showed a willingness to take countervailing measures. One prominent example of this is the virtual killing of the "market for corporate control" that was sought to be established in the initial flush of liberalization. Indian big business argued that it was unfair that while foreign firms were being allowed to hold large blocks of shares in companies, they were still subject to restrictions on inter-corporate investments. This made their companies apparently vulnerable to takeovers by big foreign firms. The state responded to big business lobbying and eased these restrictions and introduced other measures that would enable them to increase their stakes (Chalapati Rao and Guha 2006). As a result, incumbent managements of most large companies in India, domestic or foreign controlled, became virtually immune to hostile takeover.

The retreat from state monopoly in many key sectors has also been undertaken in a manner that has supported domestic capitalist development. In almost all the major sectors that have been de-reserved and/or opened up for increased participation of the private sector—telecom, power, mining, petroleum and gas, banking, insurance, airlines, and so on—the state has had to set up mechanisms to regulate them. The withdrawal of the state in one form has therefore necessitated its reappearance in another. While creation of new public enterprises has virtually completely ceased and some old ones have been privatized, a significant public sector survives in India today in many of these sectors. In most of these sectors there was virtually no Indian private sector presence before liberalization. A swift wholesale privatization of these sectors would most likely have handed over these sectors to MNCs. Instead, a high degree of national ownership has been maintained not only through public sector firms but also by enabling domestic private sector firms to set themselves up in these sectors. Each of these sectors now has important Indian (or part-Indian) private firms—for example Reliance and Essar in petroleum and gas, HDFC and ICICI in banking, and Bharti, Tata, and Idea (AV Birla) in telecommunication. This private sector development has been achieved in various ways. In the insurance sector, virtually every private firm is a joint venture between an international firm and a prominent Indian business group. A foreign investment cap in this sector has played a crucial role in creating this situation. In telecommunications, a combination of foreign investment caps, managed competition, an initially restricted licensing of private service providers that was gradually liberalized, and sale of a major state firm to an Indian group, achieved the result of creating Indian firms. In banking, while more foreign banks have been licensed than domestic private banks, regulations governing expansion of operations have favored the latter.

The gradual and in some respects restricted nature of Indian liberalization has checked foreign acquisition of Indian assets and facilitated the adaptation and adjustment of Indian big business to the new competitive context. Domestic capitalists have been able to leverage their strengths such as deep familiarity with local conditions because policy protected them. India's relatively limited success in attracting FDI, often attributed to insufficiently friendly policy, may therefore be interpreted as a success as much as a failure of Indian economic nationalism. The implied favoring of domestic capital has been critical for generating a rapid capitalist expansion in India that foreign capital could not have produced.

Even in the development of the private-sector-dominated and export-oriented IT sector, the state's role has been important (D'Costa 2009). It sponsored the development of software technology parks from 1991 and provided other infrastructural support to the sector. The software sector has been the greatest beneficiary of fiscal incentives, such as an extended tax holiday. The state has also politically supported the sector's efforts to gain and maintain international market access, including in the recurrent controversy over outsourcing. Above all, the critical need of the IT sector of a skilled workforce has been met to a great extent by public tertiary education institutions. Some of these institutions may be a legacy of the past, but they have been maintained along with efforts to expand their number.

Continued public sector presence in many spheres indicates that the old forms of state support to private capital have not entirely disappeared in India. Such support has also assumed new forms. For instance, public–private partnerships in infrastructure development have institutionalized state engagement with private capital in what was originally primarily the state's domain. Similarly, the state has sponsored infrastructure development by private capital through promotion of Special Economic Zones (SEZs) and the granting of numerous fiscal concessions. The state has also been actively involved in the process of private capital acquiring land on a vast scale for industrial projects, special economic zones, and real estate projects. Mining rights to private firms are granted by the state.

Liberalism has not eliminated the state as an important factor in the economy, but it has meant ceding of the commanding heights of the economy to private enterprise which has *structurally* increased its leverage with the state. Constrained in its ability to drive the economy's growth process through public investment, the state has had to induce the private sector to play that role. Policy has therefore had to be oriented towards encouraging private investment. In a liberal regime, this often has meant "concessions" and "incentives." In a federal system such as India's, the leverage of private capital over the state has been enhanced by the competition for investment between states that has resulted from liberalization. The ability of capital to extract tax concessions and other benefits, such as the provision of land at low cost, has been enhanced by liberalism. The implications of these measures for state revenues have further reinforced dependence on private capital. At the same time, large business firms that have established themselves in key sectors have increased their clout and thus influence on regulatory policy in many of these sectors.

Economic nationalism under globalization has also reinforced the power of Indian big business. Indian enterprises that can succeed and be players in the global economy have come to symbolize "successful" integration. Big Indian business firms have successfully set themselves up as the principal instruments of national economic achievement, champions of "national interest" and the symbols of national pride and success.[14] The tendency to view national success as something that coincides with *business* success has been actively promoted by Indian capital, and gained wide currency in the socially influential Indian middle class. This process first began perhaps with the success story of India's information technology sector but then became more widespread. The status enjoyed by corporate capital and its voice and influence over the policy making process have perhaps never been greater. Using this, Indian big business enterprises have been able to secure significant individual and collective benefits and dictate policy priorities.

Economic nationalism therefore survives in India after liberalization but in a form where it is more exclusively tied to advancing the interests of Indian big business. Directed towards strengthening the ability of Indian capital to compete at home and abroad it has also increased the stranglehold of capital over policy making. This has made it more difficult for the development of India's capitalists to be the means of a wider process of development. Indian capital has been proactively supported by the state and this has been crucial to its competitive strength and enabled it to lead a rapid process of capitalist expansion in India. However, the interests of other claimants to the state's attention—industrial labor, the urban and the rural poor, the agricultural and unorganized sectors—have consequently been hurt and remain at best addressed in a limited way.[15]

3.5 Conclusion

This chapter has argued that the shift in the outlook of Indian big business towards favoring India's increased integration into the global economy reflected the development and evolution of Indian capitalism under the older strategy of relatively autonomous development. This evolution had a dual character, the gaining of certain strengths even as weaknesses and dependence, particularly on the technology front, remained, which ensured that Indian capitalism had not graduated out of its low-income status. Yet Indian capitalists own interests in such circumstances, rather than the abandonment by the state of *Indian* capital, was an important factor underlying the durable shift in Indian economic policy from old-style economic nationalism. In fact, the state has continued to support Indian capital's growth and development in the new context in different ways. Economic nationalism in that sense has survived, but it is an inherently more exclusive form in which capitalist priorities press down harder on an already constrained state. Indian big business also has every reason to be happy with the outcomes of India's increased integration into the global economy. It has grown significantly, more rapidly than in the past, stepped onto the global stage, and can leverage the state more than before. In the process, since 1991 Indian big business has also changed: it is less industrial and more integrated into global production and financial systems. As the costs and gains of old-style economic nationalism become more unfavorable than before, Indian capital has tended to press for more rather than less liberalization.

Notes

1. However, until 2003–4, Indian growth rates after liberalization were not higher than in the 1980s.
2. Pedersen (2007) has highlighted this apparent paradox.
3. For one of the many media reports outlining the demands of this group, see "Manmohan to look into Bombay Club demands." *Business Standard*, November 11, 1993.
4. Javed Syed, "Tarun Das Breathes Fire on MNC Entrants One-Night Stand." *Economic Times*, March 20, 1996.
5. The private corporate sector in India is a subset of the private organized sector, but its dominant component.
6. In the pre-1991 reform period, MNCs entered India up to the mid-1960s and then later a few in the 1980s. Developments such as the nationalization of the oil industry eliminated MNC presence in that sector while domestic regulation in the 1970s induced some MNCs such as Coca Cola and IBM, to withdraw from India.
7. There was some foreign investment by Indian business firms in the 1970s, mainly in Southeast Asia and Africa, but the scale of internationalization remained limited.
8. See for instance, *Statement on Industrial Policy*, July 24, 1991, which announced many of the reform measures (reproduced in Government of India, Ministry of Commerce & Industry, Office of the Economic Adviser, *Handbook of Industrial Policy and Statistics*, 1999 and other years).
9. All figures in this subsection, unless otherwise mentioned, are from the Central Statistical Organisation (CSO), National Accounts Statistics of the Government of India.
10. Government of India, Economic Survey 2009–10.
11. Government of India, Receipts Budget 2008–09, Annex-12.
12. Even in automobile components trade India has a deficit, and imports have been growing faster than exports (Automotive Components Manufacturers' Association, India Auto Component Industry Performance Review 2009–10, http://www.acmainfo.com).
13. World Trade Organization, Statistics on Anti-Dumping. http://www.wto.org
14. The reactions to major acquisitions abroad by Indian companies serve to corroborate and underline this, including the public sector State Bank of India proudly

declaring that it cleared in a mere five minutes the loan of US$1 billion to the Tata group to finance the acquisition of Corus. See D'Costa 2009.

15. It is this reality that evoked the following conclusion:
"It is, then, plausible to suggest that this latest phase of an independent India is characterized by an intensification of conflict in the economy, in the polity, and in the interaction between economy and polity. There can be no doubt that the need for conflict resolution is much greater than ever before. But the task has become more difficult. And the effort is much less" (Nayyar 1998: 3129).

References

Alam, G. (1985). "India's Technology Policy and Its Influence on Technology Imports and Technology Development." *Economic and Political Weekly*, 20 (45–7): 2073–80.

Athukorala, P. (2009). "Outward Foreign Direct Investment from India." *Asian Development Review*, 26 (2): 125–53.

Bagchi, A.K. (1980). *Private Investment in India: 1900–1939* (reprint of 1975 Indian edn.). New Delhi: Orient Longman.

Basant, R. (2000)."Corporate Response to Economic Reforms." *Economic and Political Weekly*, 35 (10): 813–22.

Central Statistical Organisation (CSO). (various years). Ministry of Statistics and Programme Implementation, Government of India, *National Accounts Statistics*, various issues.

Centre for Monitoring the Indian Economy (CMIE). (n.d.). *Prowess Database.*

Chalapati Rao, K.S. and Guha, A. (2006). "Ownership Pattern of the Indian Corporate Sector: Implications for Corporate Governance." Working Paper No: 2006/09. New Delhi: Institute for Studies in Industrial Development.

Chandrasekhar, C.P. and Ghosh, J. (2002). *The Market That Failed: Neoliberal Economic Reforms in India* (2nd edn). New Delhi: Left Word Books.

Chaudhuri, S. (2008). "Ranbaxy Sell-out: Reversal of Fortunes." *Economic and Political Weekly*, 43 (29): 11–13.

Chibber, V. (2004). *Locked in Place: State Building and Late Industrialization in India*. New Delhi: Tulika Books.

D'Costa, A.P. (ed.) (2010). *A New India? Critical Reflections in the Long Twentieth Century*. London: Anthem Press.

D'Costa, A.P. (2005). *The Long March to Capitalism: Embourgeoisment, Internationalization, and Industrial Transformation in India*. Basingtoke: Palgrave Macmillan.

D'Costa, A.P. (2009). "Economic Nationalism in Motion: Steel, Auto, and Software Industries in India." *Review of International Political Economy*, 16 (4): 620–48.

D'Costa, A.P. (2004). "The Indian Software Industry in the Global Division of Labor," in A.P. D'Costa and E. Sridharan (eds.), *India in the Global Software Industry: Innovation, Firm Strategies and Development*, 1–26. Basingtoke: Palgrave Macmillan.

Encarnation, D.J. (1989). *Dislodging Multinationals: India's Strategy in Comparative Perspective*. Ithaca: Cornell University Press.

Helleiner, E. (2002). "Economic Nationalism as a Challenge to Economic Liberalism? Lessons from the 19th Century." *International Studies Quarterly*, 46 (3): 307–29.

Jha, R. (2007). "Options for Indian Pharmaceutical Industry in the Changing Environment." *Economic and Political Weekly*, 42 (39): 3958–67.

Kohli, A. (2009). "Politics of Economic Growth in India, 1980–2005, Part II: The 1990s and Beyond," in A. Kohli (ed.), *Democracy and Development in India, From Socialism to Pro-Business*, 164–85. New Delhi: Oxford University Press.

Kumar, N. (2008). "FDI and Economic Development: Indian Experience in a Global Comparative Perspective," in S.R. Hashim, K.S. Chalapati Rao, K.V.K. Ranganathan, and M.R. Murthy (eds.), *Industrial Development and Globalisation*, 409–28. New Delhi: Academic Foundation.

Mani, S. (2009). "Is India Becoming More Innovative Since 1991? Some Disquieting Features." *Economic and Political Weekly*, 44 (46): 41–51.

Mazumdar, S. (2006). "Business Groups and Concentration in the Private Corporate Sector in India." Unpublished thesis, Jawaharlal Nehru University, New Delhi.

Mazumdar, S. (2008). "Investment and Growth in India under Liberalization: Asymmetries and Instabilities." *Economic and Political Weekly*, 43 (49): 68–77.

Mazumdar, S. (2010). "Industry and Services in Growth and Structural Change in India." Working Paper No: 2010/02. New Delhi: Institute for Studies in Industrial Development.

Misra, S. (1993). *India's Textile Sector: A Policy Analysis*. New Delhi, Newbury Park, and London: Sage Publications.

Nagaraj, R. (2003). "Foreign Direct Investment in India in the 1990s." *Economic and Political Weekly*, 38 (17): 1701–12.

Nayyar, D. (1998). "Economic Development and Political Democracy: Interaction of Economics and Politics in Independent India." *Economic and Political Weekly*, 33 (49): 3121–31.

Nayyar, D. (2008). "The Internationalization of Firms from India: Investment, Mergers and Acquisitions." *Oxford Development Studies*, 36 (1): 111–31.

Patnaik, P. (1992)."A Note on the Political Economy of the 'Retreat of the 'State'." *Social Scientist*, 20 (11): 44–57.

Pedersen, J.D. (2007). "The Transformation of Indian Business: From Passive Resisters to Active Promoters of Globalization." Paper prepared for Sixth Pan-European Conference on International Relations, University of Turin, Italy, September 12–15.

Pickel, A. (2003). "Explaining, and Explaining With, Economic Nationalism." *Nations and Nationalism*, 9 (1):105–27.

Rajeevan, M., Subramanian, M., Beligere, P., and Williams, R. (2007). "Research Study of Captives in India and China: A Majority of Parent Organizations also Rely on Third-Party Relationships." Infosys White Paper, June. http://www.infosys.com/global-sourcing/white-papers/captives-research-study.pdf [Accessed January 25, 2012].

Ray, R.K. (1985). *Industrialisation in India, Growth and Conflict in the Private Corporate Sector: 1914–47* (paperback edn, 2nd impression). Delhi: Oxford University Press.

Reserve Bank of India (2009). "Flow of Funds Accounts of the Indian Economy, 2001–02 to 2007–08." *RBI Bulletin*, October Supplement: 1–86.

Sengupta, A., Kannan, K.P., and Raveendran, G. (2008). "India's Common People: Who Are They, How Many Are They and How Do They Live?" *Economic and Political Weekly*, 43 (11): 49–63.

Shulman, S. (2000). "National Sources of International Economic Integration." *International Studies Quarterly*, 44 (3): 365–90.

Sivasubramonian, S. (2000). *The National Income of India in the Twentieth Century*. New Delhi: Oxford University Press.

Tyabji, N. (2000). *Industrialisation and Innovation: The Indian Experience*. New Delhi: Sage Publications.

United Nations Industrial Development Organization (UNIDO). *Industrial Country Statistics*, www.unido.org [Accessed January 25, 2012].

Wood, E.M. (1999). "Unhappy Families: Global Capitalism in a World of Nation-States." *Monthly Review*, 51 (3): 1–12.

4

From defensive to aggressive strategies: the evolution of economic nationalism in China

Yongnian Zheng and Rongfang Pan

4.1 Introduction

One fundamental aspect of China's domestic transformation and opening to the outside world over the past three decades relates to changes in the relationship between national identity and economic activities. While liberalism seems to have dominated the relationship, economic nationalism continues to play a significant role in China's integration into the world economy. China's ascent has also raised concerns about the potential impact of China's increasingly observable economic nationalism on its economic partners. China will have to take measures to cope with the rising controversies over trade and investment with its foreign counterparts and diffuse tensions surrounding China's economic nationalism. What policy measures China will take—more liberalism or nationalism—will further influence the world economy. Therefore, understanding the evolutionary ideology and practices of economic nationalism in China is indispensible to make sense of the country's changing pattern of international economic relations.

This chapter attempts to explore the role of economic nationalism in shaping China's international political economy by focusing on the relations between economic nationalism and policy changes in different time periods. Varying themes and emphases of the reform process and open door policy in different periods highlight the Chinese state's active and delicate responses to the challenges posed by globalization. In general, the fine tuning of commercial, financial, and technological policies over the past three decades reflects a gradual transition of economic nationalism from the conventional "defensive" one by shielding the domestic market from foreign competition to the present "aggressive" one by venturing into the global market. In the process, the Chinese state has managed to rebuild the state by continuously making proactive adjustments to the institutions. This strategic move is partly due to encroached state autonomy resulting from deepening globalization, whereby traditional protective policies and blatant violations of international economic rules are tolerated less in the international community today. On the other hand, China's economic achievement in the past three decades has earned it more leeway to resort to alternative practices that are less defensive or even more aggressive than before.

These changing techniques made possible China's integration into the world economy while maintaining the government's control over socioeconomic activities. In other words, China's conscious restructuring of institutions in response to globalization helps maintain equilibrium between the interlocking and complementary goals of strengthening national power and economic prosperity. However, such a fundamental shift in the forms of economic nationalism is by no means a complete negation of the past, but rather careful weighing and balancing, taking practices and policies that are viable in a neoliberal era and rejecting the others. These seemingly well-orchestrated efforts are in fact outcomes of a constantly evolving process of political contentions, intellectual discourse, and institutional changes. Since changes were difficult when meeting with resistance within the state, the weighing between what should be preserved and what should be changed is a vivid expression of the seesaw games between reformists and conservatives among Chinese top leaders, intellectuals, and other social and political groups.

We adopt a phase-wise approach to feature the dynamic process. While economic nationalism has remained in existence throughout China's economic modernization, its origins, forms of presentation, and themes have differed in different periods. Broadly speaking, since the late 1970s, economic nationalism has undergone three distinctive phases, which are in line with the three waves of liberal reforms during the same period. These three phases of economic nationalism share the common aim of making China a strong and prosperous country, but they are different from each other. In each of the three distinct phases economic nationalism is conceptually and empirically examined: economic nationalism as an ideology of the state, as industrial policies on the part of the government, and as industrial practices of individual firms.

Table 4.1 summarizes the different features of the three phases. The first phase covers the 15 years from China's opening-up in 1978 to Deng Xiaoping's Southern Tour in 1992. Just as its name implies, "Inviting-in" (*qing jin lai*) refers to the introduction of foreign capitalism, which was alien to the Chinese economy at that time. Traditional types of economic nationalism

Table 4.1. The evolution of economic nationalism in China

		Phase I	Phase II	Phase III
Manifestations	Actors	"Inviting In" (1978–91)	"Gearing with the World" (1992–2001)	"Going Out" (2002–Present)
Ideology	State	Learning from the West; "Crossing the river by feeling the stones"; Gradualism; Economic security; Nature: Defensive	Accepting international rules and norms; Nature: Defensive on the retreat; aggressive on the rise	"Harmonious World"; "Scientific Development Concept" Nature: Aggressive
Industrial Policies	Government	ISI Strategies; Tariffs; Non-tariff barriers; A dual foreign exchange system; Export retention quota; Export tax rebates; Credit loans to exporters; The special economic zones (SEZs); Government controls on the right to engage in foreign trade	Promotion of inward FDI; Trading market access for technology; Support of national brands; Protection of infant industries and strategic industries; Tariff reduction; Elimination of import quotas and licensing controls; Abolishment of export subsidies; The end of export retention	Promotion of domestic enterprises going overseas; "Culture going out"; "Media going out"; Selective inward FDI; Anti-Monopoly Law; Neo-techno-nationalism; "Indigenous Innovation"; Monetary nationalism; Protection of strategic industries
Industrial Practices	Firms	Foreign participation mainly through joint ventures; Monopoly of state-owned foreign trade firms; Small and medium-sized projects in the SEZs	Decentralization of SOEs in foreign business; Over 450 of the Fortune Global 500 invested in China	National oil companies searching for energy supply; Sovereign Wealth Fund; Mergers and acquisitions; Anti-takeovers of national brands

focusing on the import substitution industrialization (ISI) strategy characterize this stage. The second phase, "Gearing with the world" (*yu guo ji jie gui*), is characterized by China's efforts to be geared to international practices and the global market before its entry into the World Trade Organization (WTO) in 2001. In this period, China made pragmatic adaptations to international standards so that conventional economic nationalism was on the retreat while newly created measures came on the scene. In addition, opposition from the conservatives caused policy oscillations at this stage. From 2002 onwards, "Going-out" (*zou chu qu*), representing China's vigorous exploration of overseas markets, becomes the major theme of the third phase. Economic nationalism at this stage took on a new look, characterized by aggressively extracting economic benefits from the global economy by leveraging domestic and international resources. In the meantime, economic nationalism also exists in other forms, such as neo-techno-nationalism, with commitments for more international cooperation and monetary nationalism in pursuit of a significant role in the international financial system.

The chapter is divided into five sections. Sections 4.2, 4.3, and 4.4 examine the development of China's economic nationalism in the three phases respectively, with an emphasis on the most recent or third phase. The concluding section spells out implications of the changing relationship between the state and market for the future of Chinese economic nationalism in an increasingly borderless world.

4.2 Phase I (1978–91): Inviting In

After Deng Xiaoping initiated China's economic reform in 1978, the economy experienced a dramatic transition from a self-sufficient autarkic system to progressive opening to the outside world. At the initial stage of this transformation, foreign trade and export-oriented foreign direct investment (FDI) were for the first time invited to boost national economic development.[1] Against the backdrop of nationwide destitution resulting from the Maoist class struggles in the pre-reform era, the Chinese leadership under the Chinese Communist Party (CCP) recognized that economic development was the only solution to long-term backwardness, and such a goal could only be achieved by integrating the country into the global economy. This notion is based on the observation that the capitalist countries were actually more advanced than socialist China in almost every aspect. The mind-set of building China into a "rich nation with strong army" (*fu guo qiang bing*) transformed the anti-foreign nationalism in the Mao era to liberal nationalism, a non-xenophobic form of nationalism characterized by a desire to "learn from the West" throughout the 1980s.

However, this initial attempt is a far cry from being fully integrated into the free trade system. Although the reform coalition could generally agree on the need for economic modernization, members within the coalition disagreed with each other regarding to what extent deviations from the basic socialist institutions could be tolerated (Baum 1994). While middle-aged intellectuals and technocrats preferred relatively bold, aggressive structural reforms, members of the older generation of Marxist revolutionaries generally proved more cautious and conservative.[2] At the end of the debates, Deng Xiaoping sought to balance the two groups by adopting a gradualist approach to the reform. Guided by a mind-set of "crossing the river by feeling the stones," the leadership decided to take tentative and meticulous steps when wading into the capitalist world.[3] Deng (1993: 174) noted, as there was neither grand blueprint nor existing experience for the reform, "we are engaged in an experiment. For us, this is something new, and we have to feel our way." As the term "experiment" indicates, the reform was not meant to be carried out in a radical manner, though it might have seemed to be a dramatic one at that time. This is normally referred to as the key feature of China's reform: "gradualism" or "incrementalism," which has carried through to the present.[4]

Plans and policies made at this stage were mainly directed to protect the domestic market and avoid unforeseeable risks accompanying opening-up. Tariffs and non-tariff barriers (NTBs) were used extensively to avoid trade deficits and increase customs revenue. According to the International Monetary Fund (IMF), the unweighted average tariff rates of China were as high as 55.6% in 1982. They were later reduced to 43% in 1985 and remained almost unchanged until 1992 (Rumbaugh and Blancher 2004: 10). In addition to tariffs, the government expanded restrictions on foreign trade in a wide range of commodities by import licenses and quotas. By the end of the 1980s, nearly half of Chinese imports were subject to these restrictions (Lardy 2002: 39). Controls on the right to engage in foreign trade were the most important type of NTBs imposed by the government. Despite an increased number of companies granted trading rights, state-owned foreign trade firms were de facto monopolies, which effectively insulated the domestic market from foreign competition (Yu 2008: 6).

To encourage export and foreign exchange earnings, the government adopted a variety of export subsidies and retention quotas under a dual exchange system. Between 1986 and 1993, China maintained a dual exchange regime where a periodically adjusted official rate and a market-determined rate coexisted. Under such a dual system, foreign trading companies were required to surrender their export revenues at the official rates but were entitled to keep a proportion of the earnings, which could be traded in foreign currency swap centers or for import payment. The proportion of the retention quotas was significantly increased over the course of 1980s and the Foreign Exchange Adjustment Centers gradually became an important instrument to promote exports.[5] In the meantime, the Chinese renminbi was depreciated from the unrealistic overvalued level of 1.5 yuan per US dollar in 1980 to 5.2 in 1990.[6] Other export incentives such as export tax rebates and credit loans were also important approaches to enhance the competitiveness of exported commodities.

By establishing Special Economic Zones (SEZs), the government extended legislated advantages to firms engaged in export processing and granted duty-free imports for the production of exports. In contrast, domestic-oriented enterprises were completely excluded from such privileges. Branstetter and Lardy (2008: 637) argued that the "dualistic trade regime" put some Chinese domestic enterprises at a disadvantage while a large segment of the Chinese economy was effectively closed off to foreign competition. At this stage, FDI was restricted to export-oriented operations and its presence was only allowed in the form of joint ventures with Chinese companies. At the industry level, FDI was mainly channeled into small and medium-sized projects located in the SEZs. On one hand, it was beneficial to export processing firms to receive capital and technologies that they did not have compared to foreign invested enterprises (FIEs). On the other, domestic firms did not have to face competition from FIEs as they were only involved in the production of finished goods for export. So export promotion and protection were simultaneously pursued for China-based firms.

Due to the protective strategies taken by the government and a lack of rules and regulations, China's utilization of foreign capital and foreign access to the domestic market only saw moderate growth at this inchoate stage. China remained one of the most heavily protected economies in the world, with all foreign trade subject to formal government approval. On the whole, classic mercantilism characterized by the ISI strategy is the political doctrine of this phase, which was translated into policies maintaining infant industry protection, tariffs, non-tariff barriers, a rigid exchange rate regime, and capital account control.[7] In the pre-reform era under central planning, the international trade system was completely controlled by the 12 state-owned companies. Over time, substantial progress was made towards a freer economic regime, particularly in terms of foreign trade and investment. A static assessment of this phase may reveal a stereotypical form of economic nationalism, but when pre-reform practices are taken into account, the phase turns out to be a relatively liberal one. In other words, conventional economic nationalism persisted in relatively liberal forms at this stage.

4.3 Phase II (1992–2001): Gearing with the World

Entering the 1990s, China witnessed unprecedented economic growth. The 1989 crackdown on the pro-democracy movement resulted in unfavorable domestic and international sentiments for China's economic globalization. There were frequent debates over the direction of the reforms within the central leadership. The conservative elements in the party, especially the ideologues, were on the ascendancy (Zheng 2004: 3). They openly challenged the ideological implications of the pro-Western reforms in the 1980s, which they believed finally caused the "anarchism" (e.g., the pro-democracy movement). To them, it was the opening-door policy that opened the door to dangerous foes (the spread of capitalism as an idea and as a practice) (Sun 1995). Nevertheless, the Deng leadership managed to lead the intense political conflicts back on the reform course by pointing to the enormous benefits and achievements that the country had gained from the previous stage (ibid). It was the positive experience with opening up and an optimistic expectation for the future that facilitated China's determined move toward deeper integration with the world economy. In 1992, Deng (1993) made a high-profile southern tour to rally support for a new round of reform initiatives and advocated the transformation of the partially reformed planned economy to a market-oriented one. During the 14th Congress of the CCP (1992), the leadership incorporated the market economy into the Party Constitution, thus bringing the official debates on reforms to a close.

But soon after this there was a rise of scholarly debate over globalization. The New Left emerged against the backdrop of reform failure in the former Soviet Union and consequent financial meltdown sweeping Latin America, Eastern Europe, and East Asia successively during the decade. While new liberals contend that it is to the advantage of China to accept the existing international rules and norms, new leftists believe that the rules derived from Western "best practices" will not help promote China's national interests but may lead to the loss of national sovereignty instead.[8] The left favors independence and is against an export-led development strategy (see Liu 1994). The debates between the two contesting schools also include different interpretations of the East Asian economic miracle. In contrast to the comparative advantage discourse, the leftists argue for a "planned rationality" by the governments in these economies (Cheng Ming 1994; Cheng Fengjun 1996). These contending visions of the role of the state represent the interests of a wide range of social and economic groups. Notwithstanding the ideological conflict, both schools have the same concern: in what ways to shape China's socio-economic development in an integrating world economy. In this respect, scholarly controversies have had some influence on policy making.

The net result of political, intellectual, and ideological disagreements has been nationalism accompanied by a liberal export-led development strategy, aimed at merging with the global capitalist system. At this stage, the Chinese leaders were able to reconcile nationalism and globalism by selectively accepting international standards and practices (literally, "gearing with the world," *yu guoji jiegui*) (Zheng 2004: 39–59). A quest for enhanced legitimacy, particularly in the international arena, has become the primary goal of the Chinese state (Jacobson and Oksenberg 1991; Pearson 1999). Since China applied for re-entry into the General Agreement on Tariffs and Trade (GATT) in 1986, it has dramatically reconstructed the existing institutions and created new ones to make its way into the free-trade regime. Compared to the spontaneous nature of the first phase of reform, transformation at this stage was to some extent promoted by coping with external pressures when adapting to the international economic system. As tariffs and NTBs are in direct conflict with the free-trade regime, the government had no other choice but to gradually give up the practices of restraining imports and regulating exports. Its endeavors to gain access to the GATT and later to the World Trade Organization (WTO) resulted in a general retreat of economic nationalism, albeit only in the traditional sense.

As part of China's WTO accession efforts, the central government implemented several rounds of liberalization reforms to make China into a level playing field for international trade. It reduced the average tariff level from 40% in 1992 to 14% in 2001 and eliminated import quotas as well as licensing controls for nearly 1,000 commodities.[9] One of the noteworthy moves made was to abolish export subsidies in 1991, and most of the bold moves were initiated in the mid-1990s. These included the implementation of freely convertible renminbi under the current account, the end of the export retention requirement, and the revocation of the dual exchange system.

The government also held a very active stance in promoting and facilitating FDI into the country by improving the regulatory framework and offering tax incentives (Shirk 1994). It managed to turn China into one of the world's most attractive investment destinations. This resulted in the rapidly growing presence of multinational corporations (MNCs) during the decade. By the end of 2001, over 450 of the Fortune Global 500 invested in China (Jiang 2008: 72). Inward FDI stock saw a phenomenal growth from US$36.1 billion in 1992 to US$203.1 billion in 2001, and its percentage of gross domestic product (GDP) also increased from 5.9% to 15.4% in the period under question.

However, this does not mean that economic nationalism completely gave way to liberalism. On the contrary, it survived as a more laissez-faire variant in a more liberalized economic environment. While the defensive nature of protecting domestic business from foreign competition became outdated, fostering domestic firms' competitiveness in the global arena came into vogue. In other words, economic nationalism is harnessed to serve the goals of international competition. As Helleiner and Pickel (2005: 220) note, economic nationalism and globalization are mutually reinforcing, and nationalism can be associated with liberal economic policies. This "liberal economic nationalism" challenges the conventional view that economic nationalism is always a "protectionist" ideology backing non-liberal economic policies (Helleiner and Pickel 2005: 224).

During this decade, the Chinese government sought to make use of international resources to enhance national competitiveness while placing curbs on these resources. Such tactics are best known as the forced transfer of technology, with technology as a performance requirement for the MNCs operating in China. At this stage, FDI and industrial policies included explicit and implicit provisions for technology transfer, which was phrased by Yang and Su (2000: 43) as "trading market access for technology" (*shi chang huan ji shu*). According to Yang and Su, the Chinese government has enjoyed a bargaining position vis-à-vis MNCs and succeeded in getting them to infuse advanced technologies into China. In this way, the Chinese state effectively harnessed international resources for its benefit by combining liberalization with state intervention. Aside from this new form of economic nationalism, traditional forms such as support of national brands and protection of infant industries still persisted at this stage. Up to the 1990s, China protected its automobile industry by imposing high tariffs on imports of automobiles.

Economic nationalism gained ground in the mid-1990s. The influx of FDI brought fierce competition to domestic enterprises and gave rise to opposition to rapid liberalization. Consequently, these competing interests evolved into political struggles over industry protection versus liberalization at all levels of government. Opponents of foreign investment argued against the preferential tax treatment for FDI, claiming that policies discriminating against domestic enterprises should be amended to create a fair environment for competition. On the other hand, supporters of globalization contended that competition from MNCs could expedite the process of technological upgrading among national industries. In the end, the Chinese government decided to tighten control over foreign investment in 1995. Most significantly, the tax exemption system for foreign investors to import capital equipment was abolished to protect domestic equipment manufacturers. Accordingly, inward FDI has played a less important role in the Chinese economy since the mid-1990s. As Figure 4.1 shows, the annual FDI inflows as a percentage of gross fixed capital formation saw a dramatic rise to the peak of 17% in 1994, followed by a precipitous decline to 10% in 2001.

Facing the shock of the 1997 Asian financial crisis and deteriorating international economic environment, the Chinese government had to loosen the tight controls on foreign capital. At the end of 1997, the government took further steps in the reduction of tariffs and resumed tax exemptions selectively. However, this time the criteria were not set to discriminate against domestic or foreign investment, but rather to encourage the import of advanced technologies and equipment. This compromised version extended tax exemptions to both domestic and foreign enterprises, thus easing the objections from both sides. In the foreign trade arena, China also eliminated the export license system and quotas on 27 categories of commodities, representing 20% of China's total exports (Yang and Su 2000: 42).

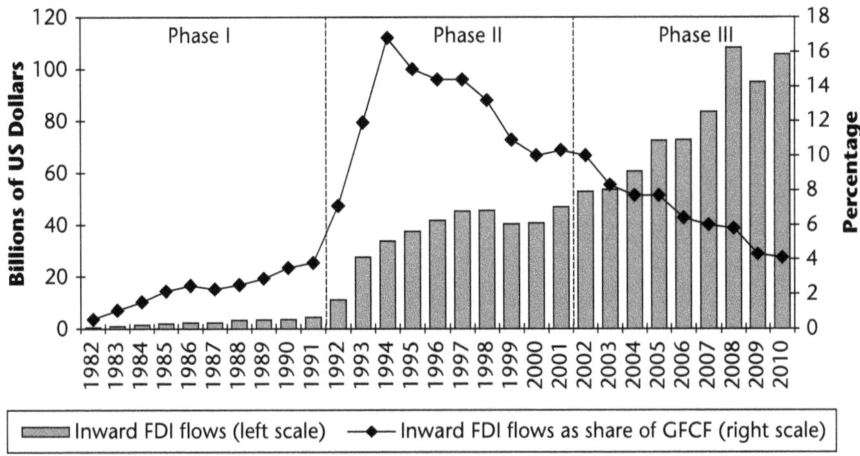

Figure 4.1. Inward FDI flows to China (1982–2010).

Notes: GFCF = Gross Fixed Capital Formation.

Source: United Nations Conference on Trade and Development (UNCTAD), http://www.unctad.org/Templates/Page.asp?intItemID=5823&lang=1 [Accessed January 25, 2012].

Accordingly, worries about the negative impact of globalization, though less pronounced than in the previous round of economic nationalism, were still a significant influence at the end of the century. The New Left discourse argued that the benefits of globalization were uncertain but the costs were real, and infant industries needed to be protected from foreign competition (Fewsmith 2008: 222). China's WTO entry was deemed a walk right into the trap, "a broader web of institutions designed to enhance the control of Western capitalist states, particularly the United States, over the developing world" (Fewsmith 2008: 223). In addition, criticisms of foreign investment abounded in China at the turn of the new millennium.[10] However, due to reformist dominance in the top leadership and tight control of the mass media, the opposing views were mostly limited to intellectual and professional debates. In addition, those within the opposition group were far from unanimous among themselves and were not organized to influence policy making (Feng 2006: 87).

On the whole, Chinese opening up and integration into the global economy at this stage was characterized by a tug of war between economic liberalism and economic nationalism. While a rapid liberalization took place in China's foreign economic relations over the first half of the decade, a major bout of economic nationalism came back at high pitch in 1996, and a moderated version of liberalism followed. To be accepted by the international community, the Chinese state had made concessions by opening its door wider, but it managed to exchange market access for other benefits, especially high technologies of MNCs.

4.4 Phase III (2002–Present): Going Out

The third phase of economic nationalism is better understood based on the "peaceful development" and "harmonious world" conceptions developed under the Hu Jintao leadership. After two decades of continuous growth, the West started to view the increasingly powerful China with uncertainty and anxiety. In particular, China's growing participation in international political and economic activities gave rise to the "China threat" argument beginning in the 1990s.[11] When Hu took over the helm in 2002, China was perceived to be strategically contained and criticized for its economic nationalism. The CCP found that the policy decisions of the previous phase to keep a low profile were becoming increasingly untenable. In response to the situation, Hu introduced in 2005 the concept of building a "harmonious world" based on the "peaceful rise" and "peaceful development" concepts developed in the early twenty-first century.[12] The "harmonious world" concept provides guidelines and principles for Chinese foreign policy and its overall international strategy.

In the economic sphere, the "harmonious world" concept underscores the role of economic globalization in world peace and development.[13] While promising continued and active participation in economic globalization and regional cooperation, China also emphasizes promotion of mutual benefit with other countries while encouraging self-reliance on the other.[14] These ideological changes, on the one hand, were in a large part due to the agreements that China was committed to within international institutions particularly after its accession to the WTO, and on the other hand, reflected China's growing confidence in its domestic development and its capability to compete in the global arena. The "harmonious world" concept also serves as the ideological base of China's "going out" strategy.

4.4.1 *The "Going Out" Strategy*

In accord with the CCP ideology, economic nationalism at this stage takes on a brand new look. As the first two stages of opening up are respectively "inviting" foreign participation in domestic development and bringing itself on a par with the rest of the world by "gearing with the world," economic nationalism in the first two decades is by nature a defensive one. In comparison, the primary form of economic nationalism in the current stage is an aggressive one, featured by the proactive overseas ventures of domestic capital. The "going out" policy doctrine was first initiated by Jiang Zemin in 1999 and officially confirmed at the 16th National Congress of the CCP in 2002. As a new form of opening up, the strategy was implemented to explore foreign markets and optimize the allocation of resources. To breed a number of strong

MNCs and brand names, it was explicitly stated that competitive firms were encouraged to invest abroad.

The "going out" initiative became possible because of the accelerated build-up of China's foreign exchange reserves, which was in turn determined by the surging surpluses under both current and capital accounts. As Figure 4.2 shows, China witnessed a surging current account surplus from US$35 billion in 2002 to US$436 billion in 2008, which was followed by a drop because of the global financial crisis. At the same time, the foreign exchange reserves in China increased eightfold from US$297.7 billion in 2002 to US$2.45 trillion by the end of 2009. According to Wu and Seah (2008: 46), the huge foreign exchange reserves that China has accumulated have far exceeded the amount needed to defend its currency against volatility or shield itself from external shocks. Moreover, the volume of inward foreign investment seems large enough for future development. In this context, China can afford large investments overseas and not be as desperate to attract foreign investment as it was in the early 1990s. Its strategy of foreign investment utilization thus experienced a shift from the focus on quantity to the quest for quality. On the other hand, Chinese-owned enterprises, especially large state-owned enterprises (SOEs), are playing an increasingly important role in global markets to gain new advantages for China in international economic cooperation.

Even though China began its outward foreign direct investment (OFDI) in the early 1980s, it was not until 2004 that the volume began to grow sharply. As shown in Figure 4.3, OFDI remained insignificant—below US$1.0 billion in the first phase and experienced fluctuations in the second, followed by a slight

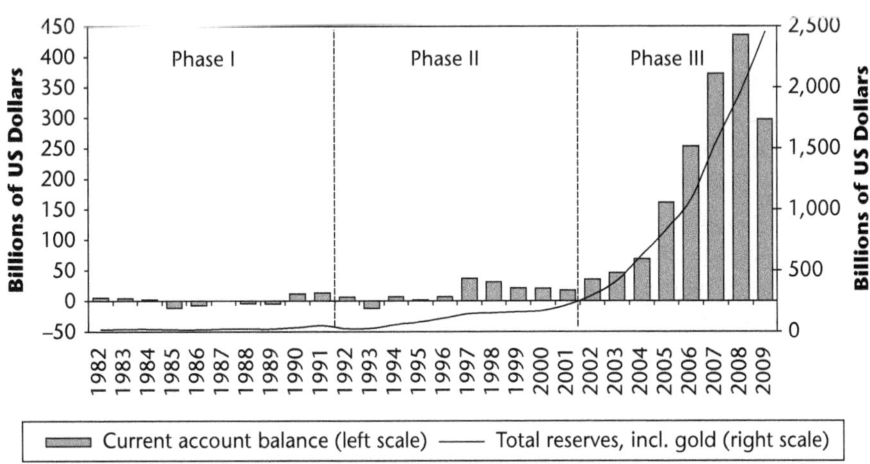

Figure 4.2. Current account balance and total reserves (1982–2009).

Source: World Development Indicators Online (WDI), http://data.worldbank.org/indicator [Accessed January 25, 2012].

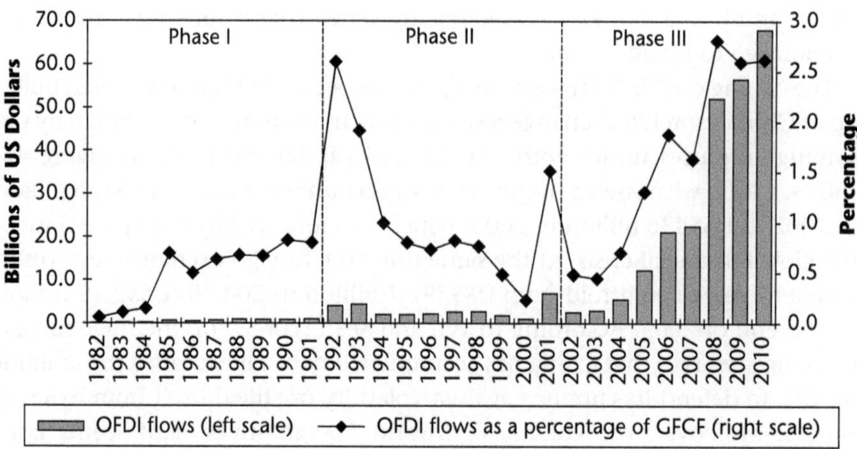

Figure 4.3. Outward FDI flows and percentage of fixed capital formation (1982–2010).
Notes: OFDI = outward foreign direct investments; GFCF = Gross Fixed Capital Formation.
Source: United Nations Conference on Trade and Development, (UNCTAD). http://www.unctad.org/Templates/Page.asp?intItemID=5823&lang=1 [Accessed January 25, 2012].

dip to as low as US$2.5 billion before increasing sharply to US$68 billion in 2010. One of the most reported motivations for the surging OFDI is China's growing appetite for natural resources to fuel its accelerating economic growth. Since China's self-sufficiency in oil production ended in 1993, the government had no other choice but to opt for tapping into global energy resources to secure reliable supplies. Oil imports have increased dramatically to fill the gap between stagnant production and fast-growing consumption over the past 15 years. In 2009, China's crude oil imports reached an alarming level of 204 million tons and exceeded 52% of total consumption, which passed the 50% energy security alert level (Wang Qian 2010). To reduce overdependence on oil imports, China embarked on a quest for energy security in the late 1990s.

China has aggressively sought to secure supplies of energy by investing in equity stakes to obtain control of overseas energy assets, particularly crude oil. While the governments in the West usually take a relatively hands-off approach to oil companies' investment and purchasing decisions, the Chinese government intervenes in the operations to secure ownership of foreign upstream production assets by Chinese national oil companies (NOCs) (Eurasia Group 2006). These large NOCs, namely the China National Petroleum Corporation (CNPC), the China Petrochemical Corporation (Sinopec), and the China National Offshore Oil Corporation (CNOOC), were the most influential ones in the process. A study by FACTS Global Energy reveals that

China's equity (net) oil production from its overseas operations accounted for 25% of China's total crude oil imports, 23% of domestic oil production, and 12.5% of oil consumption (Dittrick 2010: 20). It is estimated that by 2020 the overseas equity volume could account for half of China's domestic oil production (Dittrick 2010: 20). In 2007, the "going global" (a variant of "going out") strategy was reiterated by Hu Jintao at the 17th Party Congress of the CCP, stressing the mutual benefit of international cooperation, particularly in energy and resources.

With the accelerating pace of "going global," China's aggressive efforts are now facing the charge of Chinese "neocolonialism" in the West. Concerns arise over China's "mercantilist energy-security strategy," saying that China is trying to "lock up" the world's natural resources, gain "preferential access" to available output, and extend "control" over the world's extractive industries (Silk and Malish 2006). In response, Chinese officials and analysts argue that the government aims at providing economic assistance to less developed countries, nurturing a mutually beneficial and win-win situation, and promoting its new foreign policy goal of creating a "harmonious world" (Wang 2008: 31). China is also taking concrete steps to show its goodwill to the host countries. Through official bilateral agreements, China financed infrastructure and natural resource development projects in these countries with a mix of development aid, concessional loans, technical assistance, and state-sponsored investments. As these projects are government sponsored and carried out by government agencies or state enterprises on favorable terms to promote economic growth in recipient countries, some regard these economic activities and investments as foreign aid (Lum 2009: 1). Owing to these projects, China has bolstered its diplomatic presence and economic influence in the developing world, particularly in Africa, Southeast Asia, and Latin America. This strategy is widely known as China's "new frontier" diplomacy. Using "soft power," China was able to combine the exploration of natural resources with the goal of deepening multifaceted ties with developing countries. As Wang (2008: 34) notes, the "new frontier" diplomacy indicates a transition in China's role from a regional power to a genuine global player, through which China "began to find its own true identity."

Another aggressive "going out" step taken by China was the official launch of the China Investment Corporation (CIC) in 2007. The sovereign wealth fund (SWF) was established to expand the use of China's foreign exchange reserves and facilitate the balance of international payment. The fund has over US$200 billion under management, making it the newest and the fifth-largest SWF in the world. Through government-directed vehicles, China is looking for higher returns by aggressively investing in foreign assets.[15] A range of government-backed entities also began to massively expand their overseas loan portfolios.[16]

While leading SOEs and government investment funds are after natural resources, private companies are launching aggressive merger and acquisition (M&A) programs to acquire advanced technologies and expertise from foreign enterprises. The acquisition of IBM's global PC business by China's largest computer manufacturer Lenovo in 2004 is the best case in point. Over the past decade, the Chinese state has collaborated with private businesses in global ventures. To facilitate OFDI, the government issued several policies to ease and decentralize regulatory procedures for outbound investments and provided a wide range of incentives offering priority access to financing, foreign exchange, tax concessions, and preferential customs treatment for investments in preferred destinations.[17] Moreover, broadening financing channels, including low-interest loans from state-controlled banks, were also used by the government to support firms with overseas ambitions. Due to growing political support and preferential policies, OFDI has kept increasing over the past few years. Chinese enterprises concluded 38 overseas M&A deals in 2009 with a combined value of more than US$16 billion, an increase of 90% compared to 2008 (Hu 2010). Entering 2010, Chinese firms initiated a new "shopping spree," with the Geely-Volvo deal as the most eye-catching case (*Nikkei Weekly* 2010).

In addition, China is now planning to energetically boost "culture going out" and "media going out" as part of its efforts to enhance its soft power and global influence, namely "harmonious culture." With regard to the export of cultural products and services, favorable policies facilitating market expansion, technical innovation, and customs clearance will be put into place. These policies are meant to help create national brands and promote the Chinese image across the world. In the meantime, domestic cultural enterprises providing products and services such as music, exhibitions, acrobatic and dance shows, radio and TV programs, publications, and cartoons are also encouraged to establish their overseas business by setting up branches, M&A, and partnerships (Wang Yan 2010). Separately, a US$6.6 billion government program will finance international ventures undertaken by state media (including CCTV and Xinhua news agency), namely "overseas propaganda" (*waixuan gongzuo*) (Lam 2009). This combination of economic and cultural prowess may become a major force of China's surging economic nationalism in the post-crisis era.

4.4.2 *Selective FDI and Anti-takeover*

While China is aggressively transforming itself from a foreign investment destination into a generous global investor, it has become increasingly selective in terms of inward foreign investment. Abandoning a mind-set of "the more the better," China issued regulations to make a distinction between "good" and "bad" FDIs. In the 11th Five-Year Plan, the government made a strategic shift in the utilization of foreign investments, which stresses a fundamental change of focus from making up for the shortage of capital and foreign currencies to bringing in technologies, expertise, and talent. Certain restrictions related to environmental protection and energy conservation are also taken into consideration: FDI is forbidden to flow into industries with high pollution or high energy consumption.

In the meantime, the government has also tightened regulations on takeovers of Chinese firms by foreign companies. For instance, the world's largest beverage maker, Coca-Cola, failed to acquire China's largest beverage firm, Huiyuan, in 2009. The failed acquisition is the first prohibition decision adopted under the Chinese Anti-Monopoly Law, which took effect in August 2008. The decision aroused concerns about a resurgence in China's economic nationalism, exerting a negative effect on foreign investment looking for other transactions in China. In the Western media and think tanks, nationalism and industry policy are regarded as the major factors in China's antitrust review under the Anti-Monopoly Law. It is reported that the decision was an outcome of the nationalist outcry in the Chinese media, and "at least partly presented as a necessary measure to protect a prominent domestic brand from foreign ownership" (Anderlini and Cookson 2010). Ng argues that protectionism in the guise of antitrust might be the dark side of Chinese nationalism (2009).

Due to the changing policies and anti-takeovers of national brands, there has been a rising concern about a "worsening investment environment in China" in the West, accusing China of protectionism and manipulation of industrial policies. According to Bradsher (2010), China's bias toward local companies has been driven by a powerful combination of economic nationalism and an evolving blend of capitalism and socialism. In response, Chinese officials and experts have refuted the allegations and promised that China will stick to its opening-up policy and strive to create a more open investment environment while taking other issues like environment-friendly policies and fair competition into consideration. With these official statements, China means to deliver a message to the world that it will actively promote a more balanced process in economic globalization.

4.4.3 *Neo-techno-nationalism*

Techno-nationalism as a commitment to use political means to secure technological progress is not new; China and other countries have long tended to pursue technological strategies in the interest of national defense and economic advantage. While Chinese techno-nationalism in the first two phases existed in traditional forms, the third phase featuring new ideologies deserves examination here. Under the Hu-Wen leadership, the "scientific development concept" (*kexue fazhan guan*) became the guiding ideology of the CCP and reinforced the role of technology and innovation in the development of the Chinese economy. Accordingly, a new form of economic nationalism, namely neo-techno-nationalism, has become clearly evident in China's research, technology, and industrial policies.[18]

Entering the new millennium, China has been vigorously developing new technology policies to promote its own technical standards. China's promotion of indigenously developed technologies as industry standards was seen by many foreign observers as a barrier to international trade and investment and in conflict with international standards. However, Suttmeier and Yao (2004: 43) found that China's model of neo-techno-nationalism is compatible with the globalizing world: China is using standard strategies to advance national interests by leveraging globalization.[19] Unlike traditional forms of techno-nationalism, China pays attention to international commitments, cooperation with foreign partners, and public–private partnerships. Another special report also shows that Chinese policy stances range from techno-nationalist to relatively open techno-globalist orientations.[20] As McKay (2007) notes, China's positive attitude towards FDI in technology industries has fostered a more liberal approach to technological autonomy. Literally, "China is pursuing a more laissez-faire variant of techno-nationalism" (Commander 2005).

A controversial issue related to neo-techno-nationalism is the "indigenous innovation" officially unveiled in the National Medium- and Long-Term Plan for the Development of Science and Technology (2006–2020) in 2006.[21] The plan encourages "indigenous innovation" based on the assimilation and absorption of imported technologies through co-innovation and re-innovation. Aside from the major rules and regulations labeled techno-nationalism, some other mandates are also questioned by foreign countries. These include exclusion of foreign technology in such core infrastructure as banking and telecommunications, government procurement policies favoring domestic products, and Chinese industrial and technology standards different from international norms.

To China, "indigenous innovation" is a strategic step to carry the course of reform and opening forward as it encourages all enterprises, domestic or foreign, to carry out innovative activities, increase investment in R&D, and gain indigenous intellectual property rights. However, in the West the innovation campaign is increasingly perceived as "anti-foreign and regressive" (McGregor 2010). China faced a storm of criticism, especially after its announcement of computer security rules in 2008 requiring disclosure of key encryption information to be eligible for sales in China. The regulatory policy triggered suspicion from abroad as promotion of domestic innovation at the expense of foreign competitors (*Wall Street Journal* 2010). Overall,

China's industrial policies and national standards remain as sources of trade disputes in the international community. As McGregor (2010) noted in his report to the US Chamber of Commerce, "it is very clear that China has switched from defense to offense."

4.4.4 *Monetary Nationalism*

Along with China's rapid economic ascent and global integration, there has been growing speculation on the future role of its currency, the renminbi (RMB).[22] In the aftermath of the 2008 global financial turmoil, the Chinese government adopted a variety of new currency policy initiatives to mitigate the negative impact of a weakening US dollar. These aggressive moves include bilateral currency-swap agreements with other emerging economies, the pilot scheme of offshore trade settlement in RMB, and an ambitious plan to build Shanghai into an international financial center by 2020. It was generally believed that China was working toward a global currency that relies less on the dollar and thus influences the dollar-dominated international financial system.

Some argue that the future RMB internationalization will serve China's broader goal of international integration (Ye 2010). However, most research shows that the RMB will not be able to replace the dollar to become a global currency any time soon as it is not freely convertible under the capital account (see Cohen 2009; Eichengreen 2009). Other studies found that the RMB is only likely to evolve into a regional currency in the medium term and RMB regionalization is an "inevitable step" towards RMB internationalization (see Gao and Yu 2009; Wu, Pan, and Wang 2010). Another report, by the Center for Strategic and International Studies, concurs with these findings but argues that even though the long-term impact remains to be seen, the geopolitical impact may be felt more immediately: the Chinese government is now striving to "use its economic weight, financial resources, and growing geopolitical influence" to ensure a larger voice in future international financial and economic system (Murphy and Wen 2009).

In addition to the "going global" of the RMB, China's foreign exchange regime has long been in the limelight of political rhetoric by the rest of the world. The peg of China's currency to the US dollar has come under criticism since 2003 because of the RMB depreciation along with the dollar, which made Chinese exports less expensive relative to others. Malpass (2005) regarded China as a clear example of "exchange rate protectionism," with a neomercantilist emphasis on the promotion of exports through the pursuit of currency depreciation policies. Three years after the implementation of a managed float system (2005–8), China met with similar pressure again when a de facto currency peg to the dollar was put into place in response to the global financial crisis. US officials and experts threatened to label China as a "currency manipulator" as it managed to keep the value of its currency artificially low to give its exports a competitive edge in foreign markets, which led to China's trade surplus and global trade imbalances.

In brief, traditional forms of economic nationalism have been frequently challenged by the international capitalist community and are gradually being replaced by new ones at the third stage. Accordingly, policies have experienced a shift from the use of protective measures with a defensive posture to the use of strategies with an aggressive posture. These strategies include encouragement of outward FDI and overseas M&A, tightening controls on inward FDI, active promotion of indigenous innovation, and pursuit of a bigger role in the future international financial system. For China, the international economic community now has declining concerns over blatant violations of international norms but increasing disputes over issues where there were no internationally agreed rules or principles (Kennedy 2008).

4.5 Conclusion

Since 1978, China has experienced three distinctive periods of opening markets and reform towards globalization. In tandem with the process, China's economic nationalism has also undergone three similar phases. In each of the three phases, the relationships between the state and the market, and between national identity and economic activities have been constantly changing. As a result of political and intellectual contentions at different times, globalization and economic nationalism have had distinct themes in each phase. In terms of globalization, China has moved from "inviting" the outside world to participate in its economic development, to "gearing with the world" in an effort to bring itself on a par with the rest of the world. Further, the current "going out" strategy reveals an increasingly confident China seeking to participate in international economic activities and undertake greater responsibilities in international affairs (Zheng and Tok 2007).

With the aim of fending off destabilizing factors associated with neoliberalism, China's economic nationalism has gone through several transformations in response to the changing themes of its international integration. When China first opened its door, economic security was its top priority. The leadership took a conservative and gradualist approach preferring to learn as they went. At this stage, economic nationalism generally took up a defensive posture and China remained one of the most heavily protected economies in the world. In the second phase, traditional forms of nationalism gradually gave way to aggressive measures to gain economic benefits from globalization. Entering the current phase, economic nationalism shifted from defensive protection to vigorous participation in overseas economic activities while stressing the "harmonious world" and "scientific development" concepts. China's outbound investments have reached commercially and geo-economically significant levels and begun to challenge international investment norms and affect international relations (Rosen and Hanemann 2009). In general, China has been searching for the best way to deal with the relationship between the state and the market in terms of foreign economic activities, while at the same time minimizing possible debilitating effects on its integration into the global economy.

However, the whole course is not as smooth as delineated here. There have been seesaw games between economic nationalism and economic liberalism in China's globalization. Strategy reversals and policy oscillations were particularly evident from the middle to the end of the 1990s when China faced challenges both from within and without. Aside from political conflict, scholarly debates and social movements also contributed to the vicissitudes. In the process, the Chinese state managed to leverage domestic and international resources for economic and political gains oriented towards autonomy and independence. This was achieved mainly through innovation of alternative institutions to harness economic liberalization and globalization.

By looking at the ever-changing economic dimensions of nationalism in a globalizing China, one can see how it has managed to survive, adapt to, and maybe outperform the liberal international order. As China plays an increasingly significant role in the global economy, its economic nationalism is destined to keep on changing, but the commitment to globalization is likely to remain unchanged in the coming decades. Going forward, China is expected to follow its current lead and expand its investment overseas through its national champions, but more discreetly than before. In addition, due to rising concerns such as energy savings and environmental protection, the Chinese government may become more selective in approving foreign investment. Most importantly, as China has long been at the low end of the international production chain due to limited technological capability and a lack of innovation, it is very likely to put much emphasis on the promotion of indigenous innovation in the long term because this is the key to industrial upgrading and sustainable development. China may continue to loosen its control on the exchange rate regime as one of its pragmatic choices. Therefore, a mixed pattern of changes is likely to develop, but in general, traditional and defensive economic nationalism will be gradually replaced by a new and aggressive one.

Notes

1. In the past, foreign trade monopoly by the state was mainly to regulate supply and demand.
2. Baum (1994) provided a detailed discussion about the debates. Middle-aged intellectuals and technocrats include China's new premier, Zhao Ziyang, and the new CCP chief, Hu Yaobang. Members of the older generation of Marxist revolutionaries include such notables as Peng Zhen, Chen Yun, Wang Zhen, Bo Yibo, and Hu Qiaomu.
3. This was first raised by Chen Yun in the central working conference speech on December 16, 1980. Chen is one of the most influential leaders and one of the top leaders of the CCP for almost its entire history.
4. For a discussion of China's gradualist or incremental approach to economic reform, see Fewsmith (1994) and Walder (1996).
5. More details about the swap market were described in Khor (1994).
6. *China Statistical Yearbook* (various issues).
7. China still maintains a tight control on capital account up to now while it gradually reduces the use of tariffs, non-tariff barriers, and a rigid exchange rate regime in the two recent phases.
8. For example, typical liberal discourse on globalization includes Li Shenzhi (1994a, 1994b); Lin Yifu, Cai Fang, and Li Zhou (1994); and Lin Yifu (1996). For the new left discourse, see Shi Zhong (1995).
9. *China Customs Statistics Yearbook* (various years).
10. For a summary of the negative impact of FDI, see Chen Bingcai, Wang Yunguan, and Yao Shumei (1998).
11. For discussions on the China threat theory, see Roy (1996); Gertz (2000); Broomfield (2003); Al-Rodhan (2007).
12. The phrase "harmonious world" was brought out by Chinese President Hu Jintao in the speech given at the Asia Pacific Economic Cooperation CEO Summit on November 17, 2005. For a discussion on "peaceful rise," see Suettinger (2004) and Guo Sujian (2006).
13. Tang Jiaxuan expounded economic elements of the "harmonious world" concept during a speech at an international seminar on "China's Peaceful Development and a Harmonious World" in 2007.
14. For the notion of self-reliance, see Wen Jiabao's speech at Harvard University in 2003.
15. However, CIC was met with public admonition and popular accusations of incompetence after the poor performance of several investments. Consequently, CIC went through an internal reorganization, diversified its overseas portfolio, and made a strategic shift from the financial sector to the real economy.
16. For example, the National Social Security Fund (NSSF), China Development Bank (CDB), and the China Export-Import Bank (Exim).
17. These include the circulars issued by the State Administration of Foreign Exchange (SAFE) in 2003, and by the Ministry of Commerce (MOFCOM) and the Ministry of Foreign Affairs (MFA) in 2004 and 2009.

18. According to Yamada (2000), neo-techno-nationalism has four main characteristics in comparison to traditional techno-nationalism: expanded state commitments to promote technical innovation domestically; more reliance on the private initiative and the public–private partnerships; more openness toward foreign R&D entities; and more commitments for international rule-making and policy coordination.
19. The model was developed by Yamada (2000: 7).
20. Suttmeier, Yao, and Tan (2006). This *NBR Special Report* is a follow-on work to an earlier NBR publication, drawn from a January 2006 workshop that NBR organized at Tsinghua University (Beijing, China).
21. This ambitious plan intends to make China a technology powerhouse by 2020 and a global leader in science and technology by 2050.
22. For literature on RMB internationalization before the 2008 global financial crisis, see Hu (2008); Liu and Li (2008); and Dobson and Masson (2009).

References

Al-Rodhan, K.R. (2007). "A Critique of the China Threat Theory: A Systematic Analysis." *Asian Perspective*, 31 (3): 41–66.

Anderlini, J. and Cookson, R. (2010). "Huiyuan Juice Shares Suspended on Loan Fears." *Financial Times*, September 10.

Baum, R. (1994). *Burying Mao: Chinese Politics in the Age of Deng Xiaoping*. Princeton, N.J.: Princeton University Press.

Bradsher, K. (2010). "Business in China, Never Easy, Gets Harder." *International Herald Tribune*, May 17.

Branstetter, L. and Lardy, N. (2008). "China's Embrace of Globalization," in L. Brandt and T.G. Rawski (eds.), *China's Great Economic Transformation*, 21–38. New York: Cambridge University.

Broomfield, E.V. (2003). "Perceptions of Danger: The China Threat Theory." *Journal of Contemporary China*, 12 (35): 265–84.

Chen, B., Wang, Y., and Yao, S. (1998). "Waizi neng bu neng dakua neizi?" (Can Foreign Investment Defeat Domestic Investment?). *Zhongguo gaige bao* (China reform news), April 13: 8; April 20: 8.

Cheng, F. (1996). "Lun dongya chenggong de zonghe yaosu: donya jingji minzu zhuyi" (A Comprehensive Factor of East Asian Miracle: East Asian Economic Nationalism). *Zhongguo shehui kexue jikan*, 15.

Cheng, M. (1994). "Dongya moshi de meili" (The Glamour of the East Asian Model). *Zhanlue yu guanli*, 2.

Cohen, B. (2009). "The Future of Reserve Currencies." *Finance & Development*, 46 (3): 26–9.

Commander, S. (2005). *The Software Industry in Emerging Markets*. Cheltenham, UK: Edward Elgar.

Deng, X. (1993). *Deng Xiaoping wen xuan* (Selected Works of Deng Xiaoping), 3. Beijing: Ren min chu ban she.

Dittrick, P. (2010). "Chinese Oil Companies Invest Heavily Abroad." *Oil and Gas Journal*, 108 (5) (8 February): 20.

Dobson, W. and Masson, P.R. (2009). "Will the Renminbi Become a World Currency?" *China Economic Review*, 20 (1): 124–35.

Eichengreen, B. (2009). "The Dollar Dilemma." *Foreign Affairs*, 88 (September–October), 53–68.

Eurasia Group (2006). "China's Overseas Investment in Oil and Gas Production." Prepared for the US–China Economic and Security Review Commission, October 16.

Feng, H. (2006). *The Politics of China's Accession to the World Trade Organization—The Dragon Goes Global*. New York: Routledge.

Fewsmith, J. (2008). *China since Tiananmen: From Deng Xiaoping to Hu Jintao*. New York: Cambridge University Press.

Fewsmith, J. (1994). *Dilemmas of Reform in China: Political Conflict and Economic Debate*. Armonk, N.Y.: M.E. Sharpe.

Gao, H. and Yu, Y. (2009). "Internationalization of the Renminbi." Paper submitted to the BoK-BIS Seminar in Seoul, March 19–20.

Gertz, B. (2000). *The China Threat: How the People's Republic Targets America*. Washington, DC: Regnery.

Guo, S. (2006). *China's "Peaceful Rise" in the 21st Century: Domestic and International Conditions*. Burlington, Vt.: Ashgate.

Helleiner, E. and Pickel, A. (eds.) (2005). *Economic Nationalism in a Globalizing World*. Ithaca: Cornell University Press.

Hu, F. (2008). "The Role of the Renminbi in the World Economy." *Cato Journal*, 28 (2): 219–24.

Hu, Y. (2010). "M&A Mania." *Beijing Review*, February 11. www.bjreview.com.cn/business/txt/2010-02/05/content_245409.htm [Accessed January 25, 2012].

Jacobson, H.K. and Oksenberg, M. (1991). *China's Participation in the IMF, World Bank and GATT: Toward a Global Economic Order*. Ann Arbor, Mich.: University of Michigan Press.

Jiang, X. (2008). *"Zhongguo kaifang 30 nian: Zengzhang, jiegou yu tizhi bianqian"* (30 years of opening-up in China: Growth, Structure, and Institutional Changes). Ren min chu ban she.

Kennedy, S. (2008). "Chinese Economic Nationalism: The Effect of Interests and Institutions." *National Committee on US–China Relations*, Background Paper for the conference "China, the United States and the Emerging Global Agenda," July 13–15, 2008 at the Wye River Conference Center.

Khor, H.E. (1994). "China's Foreign Currency Swap Market." *IMF Papers on Policy Analysis and Assessment No. 94/1*. Washington, DC: International Monetary Fund.

Lam, W. (2009). "Chinese State Media Goes Global." *Asia Times Online*, January 30. www.atimes.com/atimes/China/KA30Ad01.html [Accessed January 25, 2012].

Lardy, N. (2002). *Integrating China into the Global Economy*. Washington, DC: Brookings Institution.

Li, S. (1994a). "Quanqiuhua shidai zhongguoren de shiming" (Chinese Mission in an Age of Globalization). *Dong Fang* (The Orient), 5.

Li, S. (1994b). "Cong quanqiuhua shidian kan Zhongguo de xiandaihua wenti" (Understanding the Problems of China's Modernization from the Perspective of Globalization). *Zhanlue yu guanli* (Strategy and Management), 1.

Lin, Y. (1996). "Ziyuan jiegou shengji: ganchao zhanlue de wuqu—dui 'biaojiao youshi zhanlue' piping de jidian huiying" (Upgrading the Resource Structure: Misunderstanding the Catching-up and Surpassing Strategy—Some Responses to Criticism on the "Comparative Advantage Strategy"). *Zhanlue yu guanli*, 1.

Lin, Y., Cai, F., and Li, Z. (1994). *"Zhongguo de qiji: fazhan zhanlue he jingji gaige"* (China's Miracle: Development Strategy and Economic Reform). Shanghai: Sanlian shudian.

Liu, L. (1994). "Chukou daoxiang xing jingji fazhan moshi bu shihe Zhongguo guoqing" (An Export-Led Model of Economic Development is Not Suitable for China's National Conditions). *Zhanlue yu guanli*, 2.

Liu, L. and Li, D. D. (2008). "RMB Internationalization: An Empirical and Policy Analysis." 19th CEA (UK) Annual Conference paper, April.

Lum, T. (2009). "China's Assistance and Government-Sponsored Investment Activities in Africa, Latin America, and Southeast Asia." Congressional Research Service (CRS), November 25.

Malpass, D. (2005). "Exchange Rate Protectionism: A Harmful Diversion for Trade and Development Policy." *Cato Journal*, 25 (1): 107–10.

McGregor, J. (2010). "China's Drive for 'Indigenous Innovation': A Web of Industrial Policies." US Chamber of Commerce Reports and Studies, July 28.

McKay, E. (2007). "Chinese Techno-Nationalism and the Three-Note Chord." Paper presented at the annual meeting of the Midwest Political Science Association, Chicago, April 12.

Murphy, M. and Wen, J.Y. (2009). "Is China Ready to Challenge the Dollar? Internationalization of the Renminbi and Its Implications for the United States." Report of the CSIS Freeman Chair in China Studies, Center for Strategic & International Studies, October.

Ng, G. (2009). "Coca-Cola's Bid for China Firm Sparks Juicy Debates." *The Straits Times*, March 22.

Nikkei Weekly (2010). "China Firms See World As Their Oyster." April 26.

Pearson, M.M. (1999). "China's Integration into the International Trade and Investment Regime," in E. Economy and M. Oksenberg (eds.), *China Joins the World: Progress and Prospects*, 177–221. New York: Council on Foreign Relations Press.

Rosen, D.H. and Hanemann, T. (2009). "China's Changing Outbound Foreign Direct Investment Profile: Drivers and Policy Implications." *Policy Brief* No. PB09–14, Washington, DC: Peterson Institute for International Economics.

Roy, D. (1996). "The 'China Threat' Issue: Major Arguments." *Asian Survey*, 36 (8): 758–71.

Rumbaugh, T. and Blancher, N. (2004). "International Trade and the Challenges of WTO Accession," in E. Prasad (ed.), *China's Growth and Integration into The World Economy: Prospects and Challenges*. Washington, DC: International Monetary Fund, 633–83.

Shi, Z. (1995). "Bu ying ba bijiao youshi de luoji tuixiang jiduan" (The Logic of Comparative Advantages Should not Be Pushed to Extremes). *Zhanlue yu guanli*, 3.

Shirk, S. (1994). *How China Opened its Doors: The Political Success of the PRC's Foreign Trade and Investment Reforms*. Washington, DC: The Brookings Institution.

Silk, M. and Malish, R. (2006). "Are Chinese Companies Taking Over the World?" *Chicago Journal of International Law*, 7: 105–32.

Suettinger, R.L. (2004). "The Rise and Descent of Peaceful Rise." *China Leadership Monitor*, 12. http://media.hoover.org/sites/default/files/documents/clm12_rs.pdf [Accessed March 22, 2012].

Sun, Y. (1995). *The Chinese Reassessment of Socialism, 1976–1992*. Princeton, N.J.: Princeton University Press.

Suttmeier, R.P. and Yao, X. (2004). "China's Post-WTO Technology Policy: Standards, Software, and the Changing Nature of Techno-Nationalism, Special Report." National Bureau of Asian Research, No. 7, May 2004.

Suttmeier, R.P., Yao, X., and Tan, A.Z. (2006). "Standards of Power? Technology, Institutions, and Politics in the Development of China's National Standards Strategy." National Bureau of Asian Research, Seattle, WA, http://www.nbr.org/publications/issue.aspx?id=2c5aea9e-ad6c-4a9e-a448-6f471fd22384 [Accessed January 25, 2012].

Walder, A.G. (1996). *China's Transitional Economy*. Oxford: Oxford University Press.

Wall Street Journal (2010). "China to Implement Encryption Rules." April 29: 4.

Wang, J. (2008). "China's New Frontier Diplomacy," in S. Guo and J.M.F. Blanchard (eds.), *"Harmonious World" and China's New Foreign Policy*, 15–21. Lanham: Lexington Books.

Wang, Q. (2010). "Oil Imports Hit Alarming Level in China: Study." *China Daily*, January 14.

Wang, Y. (2010). "Chinese Media and Culture Heading Abroad." *China Daily*, Hong Kong Edition, April 29.

Wu, F., Pan, R., and Wang, D. (2010). "The Chinese Renminbi (yuan): A New Global Currency in the Making?" *World Economics*, 11 (1): 147–79.

Wu, F. and Seah, A. (2008). "The Rise of China Investment Corporation: A New Member of the Sovereign Wealth Club," *World Economics*, 9 (2): 46.

Yamada, A. (2000). "Neo-Techno-Nationalism: How and Why it Grows." *Columbia International Affairs Online*, March. www.cias.kyoto-u.ac.jp/jcas/nc/yamada.pdf [Accessed January 25, 2012].

Yang, D. and Su, F. (2000). "Taming the Market: China and the Forces of Globalization," in A. Prakash and J.A. Hart (eds.), *Responding to Globalization*, 33–64. New York: Routledge.

Ye, X. (2010). "Renminbi guoji hua de zhanlue xuanze" (The Strategic Choice of of Renminbi Internationalization). *Jingji Daokan* (Economic Herald), 6: 8–9.

Yu, M. (2008). "Zhong gou dui wai mao yi san shi nian (1978–2008)," China Center for Economic Research Working Paper Series No. C2008007, Peking University.

Zheng, Y. (2004). *Globalization and State Transformation in China*. New York: Cambridge University Press.

Zheng, Y. and Tok, S. K. (2007). "'Harmonious Society' and 'Harmonious World': China's Policy Discourse under Hu Jintao." Briefing Series—Issue 26, University of Nottingham, China Policy Institute.

5

Globalization, finance, and economic nationalism: the changing role of the state in Japan

Takaaki Suzuki

5.1 Introduction: Economic Nationalism and Japan

In this era of globalization, the fate of economic nationalism appears uncertain. For many, economic interdependence has made national borders more porous and states less willing and able to adopt social and economic policies designed to achieve nationalist goals. The dramatic rise in both the speed and volume of global capital has given large asset holders of mobile capital greater voice and power to discipline the state and weaken the state's ability to adopt developmental policies or address the widening gap in democratic legitimation (Cerny 1996; Habermas 1999; Sassen 2006). Moreover, a more porous border has purportedly made it more difficult to make the ontological distinction between the "national" and the "foreign," and the question of "who is us" has become difficult to answer in nationalist terms (Reich 1990). Still further, there has also been a discernable paradigmatic shift marked by the ascendency of neoliberalism as the dominant global paradigm. Whereas the import substitution model of Latin America, the export promotion model of East Asia, or even the Keynesian welfare state model of the West were all seen as viable national economic models in the early decades of the postwar period, all these models were discredited by the early 1980s in favor of a conservative neoliberal model that stressed privatization, liberalization, and a small government.[1]

In contrast, there are others who maintain that these changes do not mark the death knell of economic nationalism (Crane 1998; Shulman 2000; Helleiner and Pickel 2005). Proponents of this position readily accept the fact that economic policies traditionally associated with economic nationalism have declined. Trade barriers such as tariffs and quotas, government subsidies for infant industries, and regulatory barriers for foreign investments and exchange are far less prevalent today than they were in the past. But the measurement of economic nationalism, according to this perspective, should not be based on the presence or absence of a particular set of protectionist policies, but rather in terms of the economic goals that states pursue. Economic nationalism is not about what states do, but why. Economic conditions change, and states must alter their policies accordingly. But provided that these policy changes can be demonstrated to be based on nationalist motivations, arguments about the decline of economic nationalism are seen to be misplaced, even in instances where economic policies traditionally associated with economic nationalism are abandoned.

In light of these two contrasting positions, in this chapter, I seek to contribute to this volume's general question about how economic nationalism in Asia has changed in the last 30 years and where it might be heading in the future by focusing specifically on the case of Japan. Viewed from a comparative perspective, Japan is arguably the single most important country in any discussion about the efficacy of economic nationalism. During the early decades of the postwar era, Japan stood at the forefront of what would later be known as the "East Asian developmental state model" (Deyo 1987; Amsden 1989; Haggard 1990). Drawing on the institutional legacies of the Meiji and wartime eras, the model was predicated on the assumption that a strong and autonomous state pursuing developmental goals and working in close collaboration with large private corporations could achieve better economic results than states guided by laissez-faire principles.[2] In the first four decades of the postwar period, this model delivered on its promises. Buoyed by double-digit gross domestic product (GDP) growth in real terms during the 1950s and 1960s, Japan's GDP rose rapidly and surpassed that of West Germany in 1968 to become the second largest free market economy in the world. In the subsequent two decades, Japan's economy continued to grow at a rate faster than those of other advanced industrial democracies while maintaining a relatively low level of unemployment and a high level of income equality.

In the early 1980s, however, adulation over Japan's brand of economic nationalism began to erode, and a new economic paradigm was embraced by Japan's long-standing political party in power, the Liberal Democratic Party (LDP). Just as Great Britain and the United States ushered in a new economic neoliberal regime under Thatcher and Reagan, the Japanese government, under the leadership of LDP prime minister Nakasone Yasuhiro (1982–7), embraced a neoliberal ideology that eschewed Keynesianism in favor of monetarism and stressed the primacy of privatization, liberalization, and a small government (Otake 1987). This neoliberal strategy delivered on its promises, but not without consequences. An expansionary monetary policy helped generate one of the longest periods of sustained economic growth in the postwar era at the time, and the enormous budget deficit that the Nakasone administration inherited was eliminated by 1990.[3] But with ready access to cheap money, the stock and real estate markets in Japan rose spectacularly in the second half of the 1980s, only to have these markets come crashing down in the early 1990s. In turn, as assets plummeted and borrowers defaulted on their loans, some of Japan's largest financial institutions over the next decade and a half declared bankruptcy, while others, struggling to resolve their staggering levels of non-performing loans, cut back on the creation of new loans. The result has been a prolonged period of economic stagnation that has come to be known as Japan's "lost decade."

Interestingly, while the Nakasone administration was credited with ushering in a prolonged period of economic growth throughout the 1980s, the economic philosophy that underpinned it was not blamed for the economic collapse that followed. Instead, the neoliberal ideology that Nakasone embraced grew stronger as the economy weakened, finding its greatest proponent in the figure of LDP prime minister Koizumi Junichiro (2001–6) and key members of his cabinet, such as economic minister Takenaka Heizo. During the Koizumi administration, both the cause and cure of Japan's malaise came to be based on neoliberal premises. According to this view, the cause was the continued legacy of a strong and activist state inherited from Japan's developmental state model. The cure, therefore, was to conduct neoliberal structural reform and scale back the state so that the market could efficiently decide how to allocate scarce resources.[4] Hence, even in the case of Japan, the economic institutions and policies that were traditionally associated with Japan's distinct brand of economic nationalism were discredited as neoliberalism became the orthodoxy.

This transition in Japan provides an excellent opportunity to examine the interplay of globalization, neoliberalism, and economic nationalism. In doing so, one key objective of this study is to challenge the neoliberal interpretation of Japan on both empirical and theoretical grounds. My general argument is that this orthodox neoliberal perspective offers at best only an incomplete picture of the relationship between the state and the market that serves to obscure both the state's ongoing involvement in the economy, as well as the potential range and realm of agency the state possesses. This picture is incomplete because a market based on laissez-faire principles still needs the state both for its creation and its maintenance. Just as the seminal work of Karl Polanyi has demonstrated that the road to the classical liberal market in the nineteenth century was paved by the strong hand of the state, efforts to recreate and maintain a more liberalized market in the current era have entailed more, rather than less, state activity in many key areas of the economy (Polanyi 1957).

This is not to suggest that the role of the state has simply expanded in accordance with the requisites of a more liberalized market. Rather, in the process of transitioning to a more liberalized market, past activities of the state have been cut back and discredited while new ones have been created. What this has meant specifically in the case of Japan is that the political party in power has scaled back the role of the state in many economic regulatory and welfare-related areas that were associated with the developmental state model, as advocated by proponents of neoliberalism. However, the party in power has also expanded the role of the state in areas that help promote and preserve the stability of a more liberalized and financialized market, a point that clearly contradicts the anti-statist tenets of neoliberalism. In short, the rise of neoliberal globalization has been accompanied by the erosion of Japan's developmental state model, but not the role of the state per se.

In the following section, I seek to illustrate this point empirically by focusing primarily on Japan's financial and macroeconomic policies since the early 1980s. I demonstrate that economic globalization and greater financial liberalization was accompanied not simply by "more rules," but by the creation of several powerful state-backed institutions entrusted with substantial financial resources and a wide range of regulatory authorities that go well beyond what is deemed "prudential regulatory" safeguards. Instead, when many banks and other financial institutions recorded high levels of non-performing loans, the Diet passed key legislation that would allow the state to use huge sums of money to protect depositors of failed banks, recover bad loans, liquidate and temporarily nationalize failed banks, and strengthen the capital-adequacy ratio of solvent banks. Moreover, when these measures proved inadequate, a newly independent Bank of Japan would aggressively adopt both conventional and unconventional monetary policy measures in an effort to restore financial stability. Consequently, the role of the state as lender, depositor, guarantor, and investor rose during this period, and the overall size of the state as a percentage of GDP grew significantly.

In the third and final section, I discuss the theoretical implications of my findings to the broader question concerning liberalism, globalization, and economic nationalism in contemporary Japan. Contemporary scholars of economic nationalism have rightly argued that economic nationalism should not be measured by the presence or absence of a particular set of protectionist policies because it is not about what states do, but why. Accordingly, while the early postwar mercantilist policies associated with Japan's developmental state model have been discredited in favor of neoliberal reform, the state has continued to play a prominent role in the management of the economy in the process of this transition. Despite emphasizing different policies, both periods share in common the presence of a far more activist state than one that is generally recognized by proponents of neoliberalism who extol the virtues of a minimalist state.

By the same token, however, treating economic nationalism as synonymous with economic liberalism is equally problematic because there are still important and useful distinctions that should be made between a neoliberal state and an economic nationalist state. In particular, a neoliberal state is one that is committed to creating and maintaining the stability of a more liberalized market. Who the actual players are in the liberal economic system (i.e., whether they are purportedly national by some measure) is less relevant than the issue of creating, fostering, and stabilizing the particular requirements of that system. At times the neoliberal state may serve the interests of distinct national entities, but at other times the liberal economic reforms it adopts may come at the expense of national entities, or erode the very distinctiveness of what constitutes the national through foreign direct investments and partnerships. In light of this caveat, I offer several theoretical suggestions to assess further the relationship between neoliberal globalization and economic nationalism for future research.

5.2 Globalization, Liberalism, and the Japanese Model in Transition

In the contemporary era marked by economic globalization, conventional wisdom suggests that national differences will disappear as states that have hitherto pursued different economic models and strategies will be compelled to converge toward the "best practices" of a liberal market system. Nowhere is this argument more forcefully stated than in the two broad policy areas examined in this paper. In the realm of macroeconomic policy, the neoliberal position argues that the dramatic globalization of the international capital market will restrict the government's ability to adopt Keynesian fiscal policies because mobile asset holders at home are now more capable of exercising their "exit" threat on governments that fail to minimize the size of the state and adopt more "market friendly" measures. Moreover, since international financial investors deem governments with large budget deficits to be less creditworthy that those that have their fiscal house in order, the competition to attract global capital encourages governments to retrench and adopt more stringent budgets.[5]

A similar argument is made in the realm of financial policy. In both popular and scholarly accounts, many portray the dramatic globalization of the international financial market as a force that has eroded the authority and autonomy of sovereign states. According to this view, regulatory barriers to international capital are increasingly costly to erect, both politically and economically. Greater capital mobility, transnational linkages, and the growth of international market structures are seen to introduce a competitive system whereby transnational actors not only exercise more power over states by utilizing greater "exit" threats, but where states often undermine their own regulatory powers willingly in order to attract "footloose" capital flows (Cerny 1996). Hence, even in the case of East Asia, where the developmental state model had posed a serious challenge to classical liberal orthodoxy, the financial crisis that plagued this region in the 1990s is now seen as evidence of the need to withdraw the visible hand of the state and adopt greater free market reforms (Mallaby 1998: 13; Laurence 2001).

These two arguments about macroeconomic and financial policies have a direct and important bearing on the issue of how globalization affects economic nationalism in the case of Japan. As noted at the outset, Japan in the early postwar period stood at the forefront of what would later be known as the East Asian "developmental state" model. Given Japan's economic success during this period, scholars have written and debated extensively about the chief characteristics of Japan's economic model, and these studies in turn have informed the extensive comparative literature on the "varieties of capitalism" found among advanced industrial democracies (Crouch and Streeck 1997; Hollingsworth and Boyer 1997; Hall and Soskice 2001). Although it is not within the scope of this chapter to cover all the various aspects of the Japanese model in detail, there are two broad institutional features that are worth noting at the outset given their centrality in the literature.

The first and most widely cited feature entails the distinct pattern in which state and business relations were organized in the early postwar era. From a comparative standpoint, Japan's economic ministries, in particular the Ministry of International Trade and Industry (MITI) and the Ministry of Finance (MOF), represented a classic case of an embedded autonomous state (Evans 1989).[6] Staffed by an elite corps of career bureaucrats recruited primarily from Japan's most prestigious academic institution (Faculty of Law at the University of Tokyo), these two central ministries were accorded a high degree of prestige and organizational autonomy. Senior officials were selected almost exclusively from among their pool of career officials who advanced from within the rank and file. The bureaucratic system of recruitment, career advancement, and retirement also fostered strong networks between these economic ministries and key public and private institutions (Johnson 1978; Blumenthal 1985). The basic aim of these ministries was defined in developmental, rather than regulatory terms, and the model was predicated on the assumption that a strong and autonomous state pursuing developmental goals and working in close collaboration with large private corporations could achieve better economic results than states guided by laissez-faire principles (Johnson 1982).

The second important institutional feature is the manner in which partisan politics was shaped in Japan's postwar democratic polity. From a comparative perspective, Japan represented a classic example of a conservative one party dominant system. Only three years after the end of the Occupation (1945–52), the fluidity and uncertainty that marked the first ten years of partisan politics in Japan in the immediate aftermath of World War II came to a close. Spurred in part by the perceived threat of a newly unified Socialist Party (formed on October 13, 1955), the Liberal and Democratic Parties—under strong pressure from big business leaders—united on November 15 to form the Liberal Democratic Party (LDP) (Masumi 1988: 73–174). The combined strength of these two parties insured the LDP a legislative majority in the Diet, and the social basis of LDP support meant that the new party in power would be a conservative one. Relying heavily on the financial support of big business, the voting strength of farmers, and the technical expertise of central economic ministries, the LDP began its long-term dominance by adopting a conservative economic strategy designed to maximize economic growth while minimizing the size of the public sector.

Both financial policy and macroeconomic policy played an important role within these institutions. In terms of financial policy, private financial institutions were heavily regulated, compartmentalized, and protected by the MOF under a "convoy system" in order to prevent bank failures and to ensure a steady and stable supply of funds from the private household sector to the corporate sector, with depositors receiving below-market rates for their savings. Capital inflows and outflows were also restricted, giving banks a profitable spread between the low rates they charged to corporate borrowers and the even lower rate they paid to household depositors. As a cornerstone of MITI's industrial policy, funds from the household sector to the corporate sector were channeled through the Fiscal Investment and Loan Program (FILP). In terms of macroeconomic policy, the use of fiscal policy as an instrument of economic stimulus was limited; in general, the government budget was balanced and kept small as a percentage of gross national product (GNP) during the first decade and a half of LDP rule (1955–70). Moreover, with exchange rates fixed under the Bretton Woods system, monetary policy was constrained by Japan's balance of payments; as a general pattern, peaks in the business cycle were accompanied by current account deficits, and the government responded by adopting contractionary monetary policies (Ackley and Ishi 1976; Noguchi 1987; Hamada and Patrick 1988).[7]

This institutional setup would begin to undergo significant change within the next two decades. With the economy posting roughly a double-digit rate of average annual growth in real terms, this economic strategy proved highly successful in keeping the LDP in power during the 1960s. By the following decade, however, the very success of this strategy helped create a setting that would undermine it. Rapid economic growth produced a demographic shift that significantly reduced the relative voting strength of farmers while increasing the electoral clout of white-collar, middle-class voters. This latter group began to throw their weight behind progressive candidates in key local elections who campaigned and won under a platform that called for an expanded government role in welfare-related programs. Economic success also meant that internationally competitive businesses could finance a larger portion of their investments through retained earnings or the Euromarket, rather than through domestic financial markets that were tightly regulated by the MOF, or through FILP, administered by MITI. In order to remain the party in power, therefore, the LDP from the 1970s onward needed to adapt to these changes and adopt an economic strategy that would expand its constituent base and transform the party from one that relied primarily on farmers and big business into one that scholars of comparative politics term a "near catch-all party."[8]

The initial change emerged in the realm of macroeconomic policy, where the LDP had both the opportunity and the incentive to abandon its policy of fiscal stringency in favor of fiscal expansion throughout the 1970s. With internationally competitive businesses now able to secure funds elsewhere, a greater share of private household savings could be used to finance the public sector debt accrued by the use of fiscal stimulus, and the government bonds issued to cover the budget shortfall would be purchased by an underwriting syndicate led by the main city banks. Predictably, the two budget categories that received the lion's share of the increase in government spending were those that would help bolster and expand the party's constituent base, namely social welfare-related expenditures and public works projects. The former drew the support of white-collar, middle-class voters, while the latter benefited both the construction industry and big business.[9] Moreover, FILP lending to small and medium-sized businesses rose dramatically during this period, but not for purposes of industrial policy; instead FILP funds were used as an instrument of political exchange in an effort to draw small and medium-sized business support away from the Japanese Communist Party (JCP) (Hirose 1981; Calder 1988).

This transition toward a Keynesian welfare state, however, proved short-lived. Although boosting the level of social welfare spending and public works projects was highly effective in keeping the LDP in power throughout the 1970s, it produced by the end of the decade a budget deficit that was spiraling out of control. Japan started the decade with a balanced budget, but by 1980 Japan's central government financial balance stood at 8.6% of nominal GDP, a rate considerably higher than that of all other G-5 nations at the time. In the absence of any substantive policy changes related to government taxes or expenditures, government debt was projected to rise at an even higher rate because large volumes of government bonds would mature and propel the share of the budget devoted to debt repayment to a level higher than any other category of government expenditure.[10]

This in turn had a direct impact on Japan's financial market. By the end of the 1970s, the tightly regulated financial market came under strain as banks were no longer willing to continue purchasing rapidly rising levels of government bonds, by then at below-market rates, without the ability to sell them back in the secondary market (Rosenbluth 1989: 44–5). Furthermore, the financial liberalization adopted in May 1975 by the USA, and then by London in the 1980s, meant that Japanese borrowers could secure better rates than in the heavily regulated Japanese financial market. Overseas financing by Japanese corporations rose from a mere 15 billion yen in 1973 to 421 billion in 1975, and by 1982 the total reached 1.4 trillion (Rosenbluth 1989: 165; Laurence 2001: 121).

It is against this backdrop that the Japanese government began to embrace the neoliberal reform measures described in the previous section. In the realm of macroeconomic policy, the LDP repudiated Keynesianism in favor of monetarism. Reducing the level of deficit financing became the main priority, and no new taxes were to be introduced to achieve this goal. In stark contrast to the profligate spending patterns of the 1970s, the government throughout the 1980s adopted "zero ceiling" and "minus ceiling" policies whereby the major domestic spending items in Japan's General Account Budget were first frozen from one year to the next, then cut in subsequent years.[11] To offset this contractionary fiscal policy stance, monetary policy became the chief instrument to promote economic growth. The official discount rate (ODR) set by the Bank of Japan was lowered from 7.25% in 1980 to 2.5% by 1987.[12]

In the case of financial policy, a market that was compartmentalized and heavily restricted under the convoy system gradually gave way to a more liberalized market. In response to Japanese corporate borrowers increasingly utilizing the Euromarket for funds, the government began to liberalize the domestic bond market, easing the ability of Japanese corporations to issue straight bonds and convertible bonds in the Japanese financial market without the heavy collateral restrictions that had been in place since the prewar period. In exchange, banks received greater entry into the private placement market. The latter led to the first major break in Article 65 of the Securities Exchange Act, the Japanese equivalent of the Glass-Steagall Act enacted in 1948 under the US Occupation.[13] International political pressures also contributed to the liberalization process. Amid growing US concerns over its mounting bilateral trade imbalance with Japan, Japanese government officials negotiating with their US counterparts struck an agreement in May 1984 to liberalize the Euroyen market in several key areas.[14] US pressures also helped foreign firms gain entry into the Tokyo Stock Exchange (TSE) in 1985. In turn, the presence of foreign securities companies in the TSE allowed large Japanese institutional investors with foreign offices to circumvent the high and fixed commission rates charged in the TSE by placing their orders through their foreign offices (Rosenbluth 1989: 50–95; Laurence 2001: 103–144).

This trend toward neoliberal reform strengthened, rather than declined, despite the collapse of the real estate and stock markets at the end of the 1980s and the long period of economic stagnation that followed. Amid mounting concerns that the Tokyo financial market would increasingly lose market shares to other international financial centers, the Hashimoto administration (1996–8) in November 1996 launched the "Japanese Big Bang." With the aim of making the Tokyo financial market comparable in scale to those of London and New York, the plan called for sweeping financial reforms that would transform Japan's financial market into one that was "free, fair, and global" by the year 2001 (Dekle 1998: 237).[15] The Hashimoto administration also threw a cold damper on efforts to stimulate the economy through Keynesian fiscal policy. Instead, it adopted a stringent budget for the 1997 fiscal year and phased in a scheduled consumption tax increase from 3 to 5% in an effort to reduce the sizable budget deficit incurred in the first half of the decade. This effectively stopped the modest recovery underway. After posting a real GDP growth of 1.5% in 1995 and 3.9% in 1996, the economy slid back into a serious recession, in no small part as a result of the contractionary impact of the Hashimoto administration's macroeconomic policy (Posen 1998).

In the following decade, the neoliberal structural reform movement would find an even greater advocate in the figure of Prime Minister Koizumi, even as the economy slid back into a period of stagnation. Throughout his long and influential tenure as Prime Minister (2001–6), Koizumi stood by the principle that there could be no economic recovery without neoliberal structural reform, and he vowed to dismantle the traditional institutional basis of LDP support that stood in the way. What this meant in the realm of financial policy was a divisive internal fight within the LDP over the privatization of Japan's postal savings system, the world's largest deposit-taking institution and a crucial source of electoral support for LDP factional members opposed to Koizumi's reforms (Maclachlan 2006). FILP lending, one of the chief instruments of Japan's developmental model, also dropped sharply during this period. In the area of macroeconomic policy, Koizumi eschewed the use of Keynesian fiscal policy to jump-start the economy and instead vowed to reduce Japan's budget deficit through expenditure cuts, often in areas that had served as a key instrument of political exchange as well as the "functional equivalent" of social welfare.[16] As an alternative means to stimulate the economy, the government relied on the aggressive use of monetary policy, including the zero interest rate policy (ZIRP) and quantitative easing.

Admittedly, all these changes noted above are consistent with the neoliberal claim that economic globalization will compel states that have hitherto embraced different economic models to converge toward the "best practices" of a liberal market system. As neoliberal reform progressed in Japan, the state's traditional role in both developmental and welfare-related functions has declined significantly. Predictably, these changes have been accompanied by the "worst practices" of a liberal market system: income inequality and the level of poverty in Japan have risen sharply since the early 1980s (Tachibanaki 2006; Fukawa and Oshio 2007).

But this represents only part of the picture of how the relationship between the state and the market has changed in Japan. In the process of making the transition to a more liberalized market, past activities of the state were cut back and discredited while new ones were created. What this has meant specifically in the case of Japan is that the political party in power has scaled back the role of the state in many economic regulatory and welfare-related areas that were associated with the developmental state model, but it has expanded the role of the state in areas that help preserve the stability of a more liberalized market. In short, the rise of neoliberal globalization has been accompanied by the erosion of Japan's developmental state model, but not the role of the state per se.

For example, one insightful comparative study, which includes the case of Japan up to the mid-1990s, reveals how financial globalization has meant "freer markets" *and* "more rules": the Japanese state opened the financial market to more competition by liberalizing interest rates and commercial activities across financial sectors, but it also introduced new regulations and reorganized its control of private sector behavior (Vogel 1996). The evidence, moreover, becomes even more compelling in the second half of the 1990s when many financial institutions suffered from high levels of non-performing loans. Greater financial liberalization was accompanied not simply by "more rules," but by the creation of several powerful state-backed institutions entrusted with substantial financial resources and a wide range of regulatory authority that went well beyond what were deemed "prudential regulatory" safeguards. Instead, when many banks and other financial institutions recorded high levels of non-performing loans, the Diet passed key legislation that would allow the state to use huge sums of money to protect depositors of failed banks, recover bad loans, liquidate and temporarily nationalize failed banks, and strengthen the capital-adequacy ratio of solvent banks. Consequently, the role of the state as lender, depositor, guarantor, and investor rose dramatically during this period.

A clear example of this can be seen in the significantly increasing extent to which the state has adopted the role of private financial institutions in terms of both providing loans and collecting savings deposits since 1989. Although private financial institutions faced fewer market restrictions in terms of the financial commodities and services they could offer, private banks retrenched and reduced their volume of lending throughout the 1990s. Consequently, the state filled in the gap, providing both loans and credit guarantees.[17] As can be seen in Table 5.1, public sector lending in 1989 amounted to 278 trillion yen, or 22.3% of total lending. Ten years later, public sector lending had climbed to 552 trillion yen, representing 35.4% of total lending (Bank of Japan 2008).

The state's role in the deposit-taking side is equally telling. Despite the fact that financial liberalization allowed commercial banks to offer depositors more competitive rates, the state-run postal savings system continued to play a prominent role in taking in deposits throughout the 1990s. Indeed, postal savings deposits increased significantly during this period as depositors lost confidence in private banks given the banks' large accumulation of non-performing loans. As illustrated in Table 5.2, total deposits in postal savings were already quite high in 1989, amounting to 135 trillion yen, or 15.2% of total deposits. In ten years, postal savings deposits almost doubled in real terms, totaling 261 trillion yen (Bank of Japan 2008). The irony here is that despite the repudiation of the developmental model, the state was relying increasingly on one of the model's chief institutions (i.e., FILP) to raise the level of public sector lending and deposit-taking (Johnson 1982).

Another example of how the role of the state expanded during this period can be seen in terms of how the state dealt with private financial institutions. While economic minister Heizo Takenaka succinctly summarized the neoliberal position when he stated that "no bank was too big to fail," the state did not simply let market forces winnow out weak financial institutions. Instead,

Table 5.1. Public sector lending as a percentage of total loans

Year	Total loans	Loans by public finance	Loans by PF/total loans
1989	12,462,307	2,783,583	22.34%
1990	13,281,081	3,029,823	22.81%
1991	13,829,940	3,293,929	23.82%
1992	14,279,510	3,606,892	25.26%
1993	14,548,020	4,035,608	27.74%
1994	14,788,899	4,432,990	29.98%
1995	15,207,314	4,591,725	30.19%
1996	15,262,123	4,867,451	31.89%
1997	16,211,710	5,079,253	31.33%
1998	15,830,802	5,281,621	33.36%
1999	15,612,060	5,529,142	35.42%
2000	15,728,689	5,535,660	35.19%
2001	15,066,044	5,372,353	35.66%
2002	14,533,678	5,168,915	35.57%

Note: In 100 million yen.
Source: Bank of Japan, Flow of Funds Data, www.boj.or.jp/en/stat/sj/sj.htm [Accessed March 17, 2008].

Table 5.2. Postal savings deposits

Year	Total deposits	Postal savings deposits	Postal s. share/total dep.
1989	8,869,442	1,350,876	15.23%
1990	9,135,078	1,366,391	14.96%
1991	9,424,026	1,559,939	16.55%
1992	9,656,511	1,709,971	17.71%
1993	9,989,764	1,844,519	18.46%
1994	10,246,516	1,985,509	19.38%
1995	10,621,183	2,140,276	20.15%
1996	10,843,232	2,262,506	20.87%
1997	11,141,090	2,419,668	21.72%
1998	11,342,902	2,541,769	22.41%
1999	11,842,778	2,616,989	22.10%
2000	11,928,225	2,512,333	21.06%
2001	12,186,355	2,411,949	19.79%
2002	12,279,025	2,377,006	19.36%

Note: In 100 million Japanese yen.
Source: All figures taken from Flow of Funds Data, Bank of Japan, www.boj.or.jp/en/stat/sj/sj.htm [Accessed March 17, 2008].

when many banks and other financial institutions recorded high levels of non-performing loans, in 1998 the Diet passed a package of bills that provided roughly 60 trillion yen (12% of nominal GDP) of public funds to be supervised by a newly created Financial Reconstruction Commission (FRC, *Kinyu Saisei Iinkai*). The new law gave FRC the mandate to protect depositors of failed banks, recover bad loans, liquidate and temporarily nationalize failed banks, and strengthen the capital-adequacy ratio of solvent banks.[18] With these new laws in place, the government took immediate action, nationalizing two major banks (Long-Term Credit Bank and Nippon Credit Bank) and injecting 7.7 trillion yen of public funds into the banking system, primarily by purchasing the banks' preferred stock or bonds. Over time, as the government continued to inject public funds into commercial banks, the state in essence purchased a significant share of the stock ownership of private banks in exchange for the banks' ability to continue conducting business.[19]

The state has also played a prominent role in managing the government bond market. While neoliberal observers are quick to point out the extensive amount of deficit-financing bonds the government has issued in its effort to cover the shortfall between tax revenues and public expenditures, what often goes unmentioned is the extensive role the state has played in purchasing the debt that it creates. In fact, over half the total amount of government bonds outstanding is currently held by the state itself, with the lion's share in the hands of the Trust Fund Bureau (a bureau within the MOF) and the Bank of Japan (BOJ).[20] Although this has kept the cost of both borrowing and debt repayment low, it has not produced the smaller state that neoliberals promised. While the government has scaled back its commitment to welfare and developmental-related expenditures, the size of the public sector as a share of the total economy has grown significantly since the early 1980s as a result of its management of the hidden debt. The hidden debt refers to the practice of reducing the size of the general account budget (Japan's main central government budget) by simply postponing various obligatory payments from the central government budget by borrowing funds from other government accounts (for details, see Suzuki 1999: 195).

This overall trend can be seen in Table 5.3, which details the pattern of change in Japan's various public sector accounts from 1960 to 2009. While it is not within the scope of this chapter to explain in detail the intricacies of Japan's public financial system, it is important to note several basic features for the purposes of clarification. In broad brushstrokes, Japan's public sector accounts can be divided into four separate budget categories: the General Account, Special Accounts, Government Affiliated Agencies, and Local Government Accounts. Given its centrality in Diet deliberations over public policy, the General Account Budget is often referred to as Japan's main budget, and it is often used in cross-national comparative analysis of public policy. Revenues are collected primarily from taxes and bond issues, and the expenditures are divided into three basic categories: general expenditures, transfer to local governments, and debt repayment. The general expenditures in the General Account Budget are classified by major government programs, such as social security, public works, national defense, economic cooperation, education and science, and energy measures. In contrast, the public sector account for Government Affiliated Agencies refers to specially designated public sector corporations that were created primarily to serve as the cornerstone of Japan's Fiscal Investment and Loan Program and industrial policy.

Taken together, these two public sector accounts make up the backbone of the developmental and welfare component of the state. The figures presented in Table 5.3 reveal that the size of the General Account Budget, as a percentage of GDP, rose from 9.4% in 1960 to 17.1% in 1980, but then leveled out from this period to the present. Expenditures for Government Affiliated Agencies were as high as 9.2% of GDP in 1965 but fell sharply after 1980. In 2008, expenditures dropped to as low as 0.4% of GDP. In contrast, the net size of the public sector taken as a whole (figures represented in the last row of Table 5.3, labeled net total/gdp) not only rose from 18.8% in 1960 to 44.7% in 1980, but continued to rise thereafter, reaching a peak of 58.1% in 2005. What this clearly indicates is that the net size of the state has increased since the early 1908s, even as the developmental and welfare function of the state has declined or remained flat. The General Account Budget was not the main contributor in the rise of the public sector as a whole from the 1980s onward.

In sum, the measures adopted by the state since the early 1980s refute the simple notion of a regulatory race to the bottom, and they go well beyond the neoliberal prescription for the state to create and enforce prudential

Table 5.3. Public sector expenditures from general, special, government-affiliated and local accounts, 1960–2009 (in billion yen and percentage of GDP)

	1960	1965	1970	1975	1980	1985	1990	1995	2000	2005	2009
General account	1,570	3,658	7,950	21,289	42,589	52,500	66,237	70,987	84,987	82,183	88,548
%GDP	9.4	10.8	10.6	14.0	17.1	15.9	14.7	14.3	16.9	16.3	16.9
Special accounts	3,549	6,708	16,988	36,412	89,771	119,531	175,486	241,718	318,689	411,944	354,915
%GDP	21.3	19.9	22.6	23.9	36.1	36.2	38.9	48.6	63.2	81.9	67.6
Government affiliated	1,383	3,090	5,808	12,234	20,438	13,307	5,523	8,086	7,661	4,678	2,126
%GDP	8.3	9.2	7.7	8.0	8.2	4.0	1.2	1.6	1.5	0.9	0.4
Local accounts	1,538	3,612	7,898	21,559	41,643	50,527	67,140	82,509	88,930	83,769	82,556
%GDP	9.2	10.7	10.5	14.1	16.8	15.3	14.9	16.6	17.6	16.6	15.7
Net total	4,803	10,340	21,807	54,008	110,924	132,425	161,992	211,213	262,616	292,395	261,634
GDP	16,681	33,765	75,299	152,362	248,376	330,397	451,683	497,740	504,119	503,187	524,867
Net total/GDP (%)	28.8	30.6	29.0	35.4	44.7	40.1	35.9	42.4	52.1	58.1	49.8

Source: Figures are from Ministry of Finance, Zaisei Kinyu Tokei Geppo, various editions, http://www.mof.go.jp/pri/publication/zaikin_geppo [Accessed January 25, 2012].

regulations so that the market mechanism can operate with greater efficiency and transparency. Instead, in the case of Japan, financial liberalization has been accompanied by active Diet deliberations that culminated in the creation of new public institutions with substantial financial resources and regulatory powers. While measures such as the Big Bang were indeed significant in liberalizing the Japanese financial market, the government also became a more direct and active participant in the financial market by staking out an ownership position in all the major banks, temporarily nationalizing major banks, expanding its role as both a lending and deposit-taking institution, and controlling more than half the entire government bond market. All told, the net size of the state has increased as a result of these activities that seek to preserve the stability of a more liberalized financial system even as the developmental and welfare function of the Japanese state has waned.

5.3 Theoretical Implications for Economic Nationalism in Japan

What do these findings suggest about the impact of neoliberal globalization on economic nationalism in Japan? As demonstrated in the previous section, Japan's political party in power began in the early 1980s to move away from the developmental state model in favor of a neoliberal ideology that eschewed Keynesianism in favor of monetarism and stressed the primacy of privatization, liberalization, and a small government. Over the course of the next three decades, support for this neoliberal ideology would grow stronger as the economy weakened, finding its greatest proponent in Prime Minister Koizumi Junichiro and his chief economic cabinet members, such as Economic Minister Takenaka Heizo. What this transition has meant in tangible economic policy terms is that the party in power would scale back the role of the state in many economic regulatory and welfare-related areas, but the state would also take on a much greater though often hidden role in areas that helped preserve the stability of a more liberalized and financialized market. Hence, while many past policies that were associated with the developmental state model have been discredited and curtailed, the actual size and role of the state has expanded nonetheless. Consequently, in the case of Japan, the rise of neoliberal globalization has been accompanied by the erosion of the developmental state model, as neoliberal proponents advocate, but not the role of the state per se, a point that clearly contradicts the basic anti-statist tenet of neoliberalism.

How then do we evaluate this transition in terms of economic nationalism in Japan? Does the repudiation of the developmental state model in favor of neoliberal economic reform signal the end of economic nationalism in Japan? Or, does the fact that the Japanese state still plays a significant role in managing the economy indicate the continuation of economic nationalism under a different guise? To a large extent, the answer depends on the definition and criteria that we use for economic nationalism. From a historical standpoint, economic nationalism was viewed as the antithesis of economic liberalism. While economic liberals drew their inspiration from Adam Smith, economic nationalists were informed by the views of thinkers such as Hamilton and List who were generally more concerned during their lifetime about the dangers of laissez-faire than about the dangers of government intervention. Whereas economic liberals advocated the principles of free trade to enhance the wealth of nations, economic nationalists advocated the use of protectionist policies to achieve mercantilist goals (Gilpin 1987). If this is the definition and criteria that we apply, then economic nationalism in Japan has clearly eroded since the early 1970s. Overt forms of protectionist policies such as import quotas, selective tariffs, and subsidies to infant industries were pervasive practices in the first two decades of the postwar era. But by the end of the Kennedy and Tokyo rounds of GATT, these policies were largely abandoned.[21]

Relying on this definition and criteria of economic nationalism, however, is problematic. As Gerschenkron (1962) and others have noted, historical timing matters. While protectionist policies may be deemed consistent with economic nationalism in one instance (i.e., a late industrializing nation seeking to catch up to early industrializers), free trade policies may be consistent with economic nationalism in another (i.e., late industrializers who are now competitive and stand to gain from a free market). Moreover, as Cameron demonstrated, economic liberalization does not necessarily come at the expense of the state's social policy commitments, or the state's policy space more broadly defined (Cameron 1978). This latter point is clearly confirmed by one of the central findings of this study, namely that the net size of the Japanese state expanded in the process of adopting neoliberal reforms even as its developmental and welfare functions waned. In short, economic liberalism and economic nationalism need not be mutually exclusive.

By the same token, however, treating economic nationalism as synonymous with economic liberalism is equally problematic. Conceptual stretching of the term can only go so far before it is rendered meaningless, and there are important and useful distinctions that should be made between a neoliberal state and an economic nationalist state. As Polanyi rightly noted, the neoliberal state is not a minimalist state. Rather it is an active and interventionist state that seeks to create and preserve a certain kind of economic system, namely one based on neoliberal principles. Issues such as who the actual players are in the liberal economic system, or who the winners and losers are under this system, are less relevant than the issue of creating, fostering, and stabilizing the particular requirements of that system. At times it may serve the interests of distinct national entities, but at other times it may come at the expense of national entities, or the nation as a whole. It may even erode the very distinctiveness of what constitutes the national through foreign direct investments and partnerships. In the contemporary context, this later point was already being discussed and debated almost two decades ago when Robert Reich asked the basic ontological question, "who is us?" Subsequent scholars have followed suit to make the broader historical point that if the nation is a modern phenomenon, then economic globalization and interdependence may be ushering in a postmodern, and hence post-national phenomenon, with the creation of the EU as a precursor.[22]

Given this impasse, one plausible solution is to define economic nationalism not in terms of specific sets of policies, such as protectionism and infant industry promotion, but rather in terms of the goals that states pursue and the outcomes they produce. This is in fact the analytic turn made by some current scholars of economic nationalism, and they have redefined economic nationalism to refer to economic policies that seek to enhance the power and prestige of the nation. Central to this project has been an effort to "bring the nation back in" to the analysis of economic nationalism (Crane 1998; Helleiner and Pickel 2005).

To be sure, this reconceptualization of economic nationalism potentially provides a better alternative to the conventional definition. At the same time, however, efforts to "bring the nation back in" pose their own set of challenges given the fact that there are multiple and competing theoretical conceptions of nationalism. Some treat the nation in instrumental or functional terms while others view it in discursive or constitutive terms (Hobsbawm 1990; Anderson 1991). There is also the contested question of "when is a nation." While "primordialists" view the nation as a phenomenon that has existed since the dawn of history, others treat the nation as a modern phenomenon (Ichijo and Uzelac 2005). The point here is not to catalog all the various theories of nationalism, but rather to indicate how these recent efforts to "bring the nation back in" to the study of economic nationalism poses its own set of challenges. I identify below two such challenges and the implications for assessing economic nationalism in contemporary Japan.

First, any serious attempt to bring the nation back in must clearly distinguish the ontological difference between the nation and the state. Although the definitions of both vary considerably, the former generally refers to a collectivity of people who see themselves as one people on the basis of factors such as common ancestry, history, society, institutions, ideology, language, and territory. In contrast, a state is commonly defined as a political system that possesses a monopoly on the legitimate use of violence. Unlike a state, a nation does not require a central military-political bureaucracy to exist. Indeed, in many instances, nationalism takes the form of a nation seeking its own state.[23] This is simply another way of making the broader point that there are often many nations within a territorial sovereign state. Given this distinction, it is important to provide analytically clear criteria that can be used to distinguish economic goals that serve the state's interest versus those that serve the interests of the nation. Enhancing the power and prestige of the state is not the same as enhancing the power and prestige of the nation. In fact, in the field of international relations, the former is generally treated as a function emanating from an anarchic international system where unit-level characteristics, such as the nation, are meaningless (Waltz 1979).

Second and relatedly, it is important to establish clear criteria for what counts as economic nationalism and what does not. Although recent scholars such as Helleiner and Pickel have stressed the importance of identifying the manner in which economic policies are legitimized,[24] rhetorical justifications that merely evoke the sentiment of nationalism in support of a given economic policy is not enough. For example, there are many instances where the call to adopt a certain economic policy may be evoked in the name of national interest, but in reality the policy may merely serve the narrow interest of a specific industry or class, and come at the expense of others within the nation or the nation as a whole. In other instances, nationalist appeals made by state leaders in support of a given economic policy may simply mask inter-party or intra-party rivalry. These circumstances clearly contradict Helleiner and Pickel's own claim about the basic ontological characteristic of economic nationalism that is purportedly constituted by the "horizontal comradeship" of the nation's members (Helleiner and Pickel 2005: 222–5).[25]

A similar concern applies in cases where even genuine nationalist intentions yield bad nationalist outcomes. If certain economic policies weaken national power, or erode the very distinctiveness of what constitutes the national, it is hard to justify such economic policies as an example of economic nationalism regardless of genuine intent. This is another way of stating that the content of economic policy, as well as its outcome, matter in establishing criteria for what counts as economic nationalism, and more importantly, what does not. Regrettably, this is a point that is recognized, but not adequately examined, by Helleiner and Pickel. As part of their effort to demonstrate that what counts as economic nationalism is far broader than traditional forms of protectionism, they start from the basic premise that the policy content of economic nationalism is "best seen as ambiguous," and that in theory "its policy content can be 'everything'." The one caveat that they do identify is that economic nationalism must be "associated with core nationalist values such as a commitment to national sovereignty," but beyond this brief and basic point, the issue is not explored further (Helleiner and Pickel 2005: 225). Examining the outcomes and effects of economy policy decisions are thus crucial in avoiding unfalsifiable claims about economic nationalism.

What this suggests, then, is that one must go well beyond the rhetorical justifications made by state leaders in support of Japan's transition from a developmental to a neoliberal state and examine critically both the operating logic of the neoliberal state and the various effects that it produces. On this score, evaluating the impact of economic globalization and neoliberal reform on economic nationalism in Japan becomes more ambiguous. To be sure, neoliberal proponents such as Prime Minister Koizumi and Economic Minister Takenaka repeatedly embraced nationalist rhetoric in their pursuit of neoliberal reform, and they were able to achieve some tangible results in restoring economic growth during their tenure in office. But the overall picture of Japan's economic performance in terms of economic growth and productivity since the early 1990s has been dismal. More significantly, as neoliberal reform progressed in Japan, it was accompanied by the "worst practices" of a liberal market system, with income inequality, employment instability, and the level of poverty in Japan all rising sharply since the early 1980s (Tachibanaki 2006). Taken together, these outcomes suggest that despite the nationalist rhetoric employed by political leaders who have adopted neoliberal reforms in Japan, their ability to deliver on their promises of promoting economic nationalism remains unfilled.

Notes

1. On the ideational change from Keynesianism to Monetarism, see Hall (1989). For a comparative examination of this transition, see Gourevitch (1986). For the case of Japan, see Suzuki (2002).
2. The landmark study is Johnson (1982). For economic institutional continuities between the prewar and postwar period, see also Noguchi (1998).
3. In comparative terms, Japan's budget deficit at the start of the 1980s was higher than the other G-5 nations. For details of the measures that were adopted to eliminate the deficit by 1990, see Suzuki (1999).
4. Critics of the Japanese model argued that while other advanced industrial economies, such as Sweden, suffered a similar financial meltdown, they were able to recover faster because they allowed Schumpeter's logic of creative destruction to take place. In contrast, critics argued that the Japanese model gave the state greater capacity to postpone necessary changes, while the state's close institutional ties with the corporate sector, together with Japan's weak social safety net, created the incentive for the state to do so. Consequently, firms that had gone out of business often had a higher level of total factor productivity than zombie companies that survived through state assistance. The aggregate effect of this "reverse Darwinism" was seen as a chief reason for why Japan's economy suffered a prolonged period of economic stagnation, and the strong and interventionist state was blamed for creating it. See for example Katz (2008).

5. For some notable examples of this literature, see Scharpf (1991), Kurzer (1993), Martin (1994), Schwartz (1994), Cerny (1996), Keohane and Milner (1996). For the economic model, see Mundell (1968), Mussa (1979), Frenkel and Razin (1985). For an excellent review of this literature, see Cohen (1996).
6. In 2001, MITI was reorganized into METI (Ministry of Economy, Trade, and Industry), and the MOF was reorganized and its Japanese name was changed from *Okurasho* to *Zaimusho*. The MOF's English name has remained the same.
7. Predictably, the incentive to adjust was weaker when running a balance of payments surplus.
8. The term was originally coined by Giovanni Sartori (1976) and defined as a party system in which one party repeatedly wins a majority of seats in parliaments. In the case of Japan, the important exception was labor, which remained divided and less organized than in other advanced industrial democracies.
9. With the slowdown in the economy in the second half of the 1970s, big business leaders became one of the most vocal proponents of fiscal expansion. For an in-depth treatment, see Suzuki (2000).
10. The share of the budget devoted to debt repayment was already quite large by 1980, with only social security expenditures and public works occupying a larger share. By 1985, the share of the budget devoted debt repayment exceeded that of social security expenditures in 1985, making it the single largest expenditure item on the budget.
11. The government also postponed various obligatory payments from the General Account Budget by using funds from other public accounts.
12. For an in-depth treatment of the international and domestic politics of Japanese macroeconomic policy during this period, see Suzuki (2000): 135–203.
13. With the passage of the 1982 Banking Law, banks were allowed to enter into the retailing and dealing of government bonds, thereby breaking the firewall that had hitherto separated the banking and securities industry.
14. Restrictions on Japanese corporate access to the Euroyen bond market were eased; foreign governments and non-Japanese private corporations were authorized to issue unsecured bonds in the Euroyen market; and the foreign exchange market in both forward transactions and currency swaps were liberalized for both residents and non-residents.
15. The targeted areas for reform covered the banking, securities, and insurance industries as well as accounting and foreign exchange. The key components of the "big bang" measures included: liberalization of international capital transactions; product liberalization in securities, investment trust, derivatives, loan securitization; deregulation of cross-entry among financial industries; removal of the ban on financial holding companies; liberalization of fixed brokerage commissions; and stricter accounting standards and disclosure rules for banks and securities.
16. For an analysis of the LDP's key instruments of political exchange, see Calder (1988). For an extended analysis about the functional equivalent of welfare, see Estévez-Abe (2008).
17. In addition to the public financial corporations that traditionally formed the core of FILP lending activities, the Bank of Japan became increasingly involved in this

activity, purchasing commercial papers from corporations unable to raise funds from private financial institutions. Commercial papers are negotiable, short-term, unsecured promissory notes issued in bearer form, usually on a discount basis, by a corporation to raise working capital for any term normally up to 180 days. At the end of September 1998, BOJ had purchased 5.6 trillion yen worth of commercial paper, or 39% of the total outstanding. Figures are from Ostrom (1998): 1–3.

18. The two major bills passed were the "Law Concerning Emergency Measures for the Reconstruction of the Functions of the Financial System" and the "Financial Function Early Strengthening Law": 17 trillion yen was allocated for the purpose of refunding depositors of failed banks, 18 trillion yen for state-run bridge banks or other forms of public control, and 25 trillion yen for capital injection into solvent banks.
19. By 2005, the amount of public funds used to stabilize the financial system totaled 35.8 trillion yen (Ikeo and Goto 2006: 106).
20. At the end of fiscal year 1999, the total amount of government bonds outstanding held by financial institutions was 360.6 trillion yen, of which 187.3 trillion were held by the public sector. The Trust Fund Bureau held 79.9 trillion yen, while the Bank of Japan held 49.8 trillion. Figures are from Bank of Japan (BOJ) (2000) chart 15.
21. For an overview of Japanese trade policy, see Komiya and Itoh (1988). It is worth noting, however, that the issue of non-tariff barriers remained an important point of contention well into the 1980s. On this point, see Johnson 1995: 69–95.
22. For an intriguing discussion on this point, see Ruggie (1993). For an excellent analysis on the denationalization of the state, see Sassen (2006). The term "denationalization" is also used in a similar vein by Ruggie (1995): 508.
23. For an interesting account of how minority nations pursue free trade policies against the state as a form of economic nationalism, see Shulman (2000).
24. As Helleiner and Pickel note: "In our view, the conception of economic nationalism need not be restricted to specific policy doctrines, but rather should be viewed more generically. That is, the global significance of the national, as culture and rhetoric, suggests that whatever the specific content of such doctrines, their conception and legitimation always (and in most cases primarily) occur in a national context. The most important implication of this conceptual shift is that it allows us to treat economic liberalism as a particular form of economic nationalism" (2005: 12).
25. This ontological claim about economic nationalism is made more forcefully by Nakano: "Economic nationalists prefer to mobilize the resources of the nation as a whole and spread the benefits beyond the boundaries of class. In other words, they avoid economic policies which may undermine the unity of the nation. This is one of the distinctive features of economic nationalism in comparison with economic liberalism and Marxism" (2004: 222).

References

Ackley, G. and Ishi, H. (1976). "Fiscal, Monetary, and Related Policies," in H.T. Patrick and H. Rosovsky (eds.), *Asia's New Giant: How the Japanese Economy Works*, 153–247. Washington, DC: Brookings Institution.

Amsden, A.H. (1989). *Asia's Next Giant: South Korea and Late Industrialization*. New York: Oxford University Press.

Anderson, B. (1991). *Imagined Communities: Reflections on the Origin and Spread of Nationalism*. London: Verso Books.

Bank of Japan. "Flow of Funds Data." www.boj.or.jp/en/stat/exp/data/exsj01.pdf [Accessed March 17, 2008].

Bank of Japan. (2000). "Japan's Financial Structure—In View of the Flow of Funds Accounts." www.boj.or.jp/en/research/brp/ron_2000/data/ron0012a.pdf [Accessed January 25, 2012].

Blumenthal, T. (1985). "The Practice of Amakudari within the Japanese Employment System." *Asian Survey*, 25 (3): 310–21.

Calder, K.E. (1988). *Crisis and Compensation: Public Policy and Political Stability in Japan, 1949–1986*. Princeton: Princeton University Press.

Cameron, D. (1978). "The Expansion of the Public Economy: A Comparative Analysis." *The American Political Science Review*, 72 (4): 1243–61.

Cerny, P.G. (1996). "International Finance and the Erosion of State Policy Capacity," in Philip Gummett (ed.), *Globalization and Public Policy*, 83–104. Cheltenham: Edward Elgar.

Cohen, B.J. (1996). "Phoenix Risen: The Resurrection of Global Finance." *World Politics*, 48 (2): 268–96.

Crane, G. (1998). "Economic Nationalism: Bringing the Nation Back in." *Millennium—Journal of International Studies*, 27 (1): 55–75.

Crouch, C. and Streeck, W. (eds.) (1997). *Political Economy of Modern Capitalism: Mapping Convergence and Diversity*. London: Sage.

Dekle, R. (1998). "The Japanese 'Big Bang' Financial Reforms and Market Implications." *Journal of Asian Economics*, 9 (2): 237–49.

Deyo, F.C. (1987). *The Political Economy of the New Asian Industrialism*. Ithaca: Cornell University Press.

Estévez-Abe, M. (2008). *Welfare and Capitalism in Postwar Japan*. Cambridge and New York: Cambridge University Press.

Evans, P.B. (1989). "Predatory, Developmental, and Other Apparatuses: A Comparative Political Economy Perspective on the Third World State." *Sociological Forum*, 4 (4): 561–87.

Frenkel, J.A. and Razin, A. (1985). "Government Spending, Debt, and International Economic Interdependence," *Economic Journal*, 95 (379): 619–36.

Fukawa, T. and Oshio, T. (2007). "Income Inequality Trends and their Challenges to Redistribution Policies in Japan." *Journal of Income Distribution*, 16 (3/4): 9–30.

Gerschenkron, A. (1962). *Economic Backwardness in Historical Perspective*. Cambridge, Mass.: Harvard University Press.

Gilpin, R. (1987). *The Political Economy of International Relations*. Princeton: Princeton University Press.

Gourevitch, P. (1986). *Politics in Hard Times: Comparative Responses to International Economic Crises*. Ithaca: Cornell University Press.

Habermas, J. (1999). "The European Nation-State and the Pressures for Globalization." *New Left Review*, 234 (May/June): 46–59.

Haggard, S. (1990). *Pathways from the Periphery: The Politics of Growth in the Newly Industrializing Countries*. Ithaca: Cornell University Press.

Hall, P.A. (1989). *The Political Power of Economic Ideas: Keynesianism across Nations*. Princeton: Princeton University Press.

Hall, P.A. and Soskice, D.W. (2001). *Varieties of Capitalism: The Institutional Foundations of Comparative Advantage*. Oxford: Oxford University Press.

Hamada, K. and Patrick, H.T. (1988). "Japan and the International Monetary Regime," in D. Okimoto and T. Inoguchi (eds.), *The Political Economy of Japan Volume 2: The Changing International Context*, 108–37. Stanford: Stanford University Press.

Helleiner, E. and Pickel, A. (2005). *Economic Nationalism in a Globalizing World*. Ithaca: Cornell University Press.

Hirose, M. (1981). *Hojokin to Seikento*. Tokyo: Asahi Shinbunsha.

Hobsbawm, E.J. (1990). *Nations and Nationalism since 1780: Programme, Myth, Reality*. Cambridge: Cambridge University Press.

Hollingsworth, J.R. and Boyer, R. (1997). *Contemporary Capitalism: The Embeddedness of Institutions*. Cambridge: Cambridge University Press.

Ichijo, A. and Uzelac, G. (2005). *When is the Nation: Towards an Understanding of Theories of Nationalism*. London: Routledge.

Ikeo, K. and Goto, Y. (2006). "The Government and the Financial System: An Overview." *Public Policy Review*, 2 (1): 97–140.

Johnson, C. (1995). *Japan, Who Governs? The Rise of the Developmental State*. New York: Norton.

Johnson, C. (1982). *MITI and the Japanese Miracle: The Growth of Industrial Policy, 1925–1975*. Stanford: Stanford University Press.

Johnson, C. (1978). *Japan's Public Policy Companies*. Washington, DC: American Enterprise Institute.

Katz, R. (2008). "A Nordic Mirror: Why Structural Reform has Proceeded Faster in Scandinavia than in Japan." Working Paper Series, Center on Japanese Economy and Business.

Keohane, R. and Milner, H. (1996). *Internationalization and Domestic Politics*. Cambridge: Cambridge University Press.

Komiya, R. and Itoh, M. (1988). "Japan's International Trade and Trade Policy, 1955–1984." *The Political Economy of Japan*, Vol. 2, 173–224. Stanford: Stanford University Press.

Kurzer, P. (1993). *Business and Banking: Political Change and Economic Integration in Western Europe*. Ithaca: Cornell University Press.

Laurence, H. (2001). *Money Rules: The New Politics of Finance in Britain and Japan*. Ithaca: Cornell University Press.

Maclachlan, P.L. (2006). "Storming the Castle: The Battle for Postal Reform in Japan." *Social Science Japan Journal*, 9 (1): 1–18.

Mallaby, S. (1998). "In Asia's Mirror." *The National Interest*, 52: 13–22.

Martin, A. (1994). "Labour, the Keynesian Welfare State, and the Changing International Political Economy," in R. Stubbs and G.R.D. Underhill (eds.), *Political Economy and the Changing Global Order*, 60–74. New York: St. Martin's Press.

Masumi, J. (1988). *Gendai Seiji: Volume* 1. Tokyo: University of Tokyo Press.

Mundell, R.A. (1968). *International Economics*. New York: Macmillan.

Mussa, M. (1979) "Macroeconomic Interdependence and the Exchange Rate Regime," in R. Dornbusch and J.A. Frenkel (eds.), *International Economic Policy: Theory and Evidence*, 160–99. Baltimore: Johns Hopkins University Press.

Nakano, T. (2004). "Theorising Economic Nationalism." *Nations and Nationalism*, 10 (3): 211–29.

Noguchi, Y. (1987). "Public Finance," in K. Yamamura and Y. Yasuba (eds.), *The Political Economy of Japan. Volume 1, The Domestic Transformation*, 186–222. Stanford: Stanford University Press.

Noguchi, Y. (1998). "The 1940 System: Japan under the Wartime Economy." *The American Economic Review*, 88 (2): 404–7.

Ostrom, D. (1998). "Central Banks Adjust Monetary Policy to Global Turmoil." *JEI Report*, 1: 1–3.

Otake, H. (1987). "Nakasone Seiji no Ideorogii to Sono Kokunai Seijiteki Haikei" (The Ideology of Nakasone's Politics and their Domestic Political Background). *Revaiasan*, 1: 73–91.

Polanyi, K. (1957). *The Great Transformation*. Boston: Beacon Press.

Posen, A. (1998). *Restoring Japan's Economic Growth*. Washington, DC: Institute for International Economics.

Reich, R. (1990). "Who Is US?" *Harvard Business Review*, January/February: 53–64.

Rosenbluth, F.M. (1989). *Financial Politics in Contemporary Japan*. Ithaca: Cornell University Press.

Ruggie, J. (1993). "Territoriality and Beyond: Problematizing Modernity in International Relations." *International Organization*, 47 (1): 139–74.

Ruggie, J. (1995). "At Home Abroad, Abroad at Home," *Millennium*, 24 (3): 507–26.

Sartori, G. (1976). *Parties and Party Systems: A Framework for Analysis*. Cambridge: Cambridge University Press.

Sassen, S. (2006). *Territory, Authority Rights: From Medieval to Global Assemblages*. Princeton: Princeton University Press.

Scharpf, F.W. (1991). *Crisis and Choice in European Social Democracy*. Ithaca: Cornell University Press.

Schwartz, H. (1994). "Small States in Big Trouble: State Reorganization in Australia, Denmark, New Zealand, and Sweden in the 1980s." *World Politics*, 46 (4): 527–55.

Shulman, S. (2000). "Nationalist Sources of International Economic Integration." *International Studies Quarterly*, 44 (3): 365–90.

Suzuki, T. (1999). "Administrative Reform and the Politics of Budgetary Retrenchment in Japan." *Social Science Japan Journal*, 2 (2): 195–213.

Suzuki, T. (2000). *Japan's Budget Politics: Balancing Domestic and International Interests*. Boulder: Lynne Rienner Publishers.

Suzuki, T. (2002). "Keynesianism, Monetarism, and the Contradiction of Japan's Modern Welfare State." *The Japanese Economy*, 30 (2): 42–78.

Tachibanaki, T. (2006). "Inequality and Poverty in Japan." *The Japanese Economic Review*, 57 (1): 1–27.

Vogel, S.K. (1996). *Freer Markets, More Rules: Regulatory Reform in Advanced Industrial Countries*. Ithaca: Cornell University Press.

Waltz, K. (1979). *Theory of International Politics*. New York: McGraw-Hill.

6

Open trade, closed industry: the Japanese aerospace industry in the evolution of economic nationalism and implications for globalization

Toshiya Ozaki

6.1 Introduction

Can a mature and advanced industrial economy pursue economic nationalism as we enter the twenty-first century and as we witness the evolution of economic globalization? Or should it commit itself to the liberal multilateralism that has been the foundation of the postwar international economic system? Should it also make every effort to encourage others, especially emerging economies, to embrace liberalism and multilateralism rather than narrow nationalistic policies?

Nationalism is an easy-to-use but difficult-to-analyze terminology. John Breuilly is probably one of the best known scholars who articulately defined nationalism as: "political movements seeking or exercising state power and justifying such actions with nationalist arguments" (Breuilly 1995: 3). He then highlighted the three basic assertions upon which any "nationalist arguments" may be developed:

1. There exists a nation with an explicit and peculiar character;
2. The interests and values of this nation take priority over all other interests and values; and
3. The nation must be as independent as possible (Breuilly 1995: 3).

Applying this observation to economic activities, one may define economic nationalism as a political movement, usually developing and implementing an economic policy. Such policy embodies an explicit national character, pursues national economic interests and values that take priority over all others, and promotes national independence. It is with this understanding that this chapter shares the common definition of economic nationalism defined in Chapter 1, in which economic nationalism is understood to be a set of state practices, policies, and strategies to protect and promote national economic interests. More specifically, economic nationalism may aim to foster international competitiveness of certain industrial sectors or even particular firms, induce growth and structural change, promote particular national champions (firms), sectors (such as information technology, aerospace), and products (national brands) vis-à-vis foreign nationals or foreigners. In achieving these goals of economic nationalism, policy makers frequently work in concert with industry representatives and labor groups.

Economic nationalism, thus, may be at odds with liberal multilateralism, the guiding principle of the postwar economic system. It posits that laissez-faire pursuit of profit maximization still requires a state to cooperate with other states in providing a liberal and nondiscriminatory infrastructure of economic exchange for market participants.

As such, a nationalist economic policy seems to present a major dilemma to a mature and advanced industrial economy of the twenty-first century with competing issues. On the one hand, there is a steady demand by firms in mature and advanced economies for governmental help in accessing foreign markets. There is wide recognition among firms and policy makers of advanced economies that the postwar international economic system has been beneficial to them. It allows firms to access foreign resources, technologies, capital, and markets, and for economies to sustain growth. They thus want to make sure that the system will be sustained and expanded by covering more products and countries, and by having stronger rules and enforcement mechanisms to curb tariffs, non-tariff barriers and other nationalist economic policies. On the other hand, there is a growing demand by firms in mature and advanced economies for help in maintaining their traditional industrial competitiveness or creating new competitive industries against their foreign rivals, especially those of emerging economies. Furthermore, they are facing heightened difficulty in cooperating with other states to sustain and improve the international economic system. Following the end of the Cold War, the world has become far more fragmented. The international economic system may no longer be sustained by the coordination of just a small number of advanced economies, especially the USA, the EU, and Japan. The failure of the Doha round of the World Trade Organization (WTO) negotiation in 2008 highlighted both the widened conflicts of economic interests among the member economies, especially between the advanced and emerging economies, and the declining American leadership in mobilizing support for the liberal multilateral economic system.

In this chapter, I would like to use the Japanese case to demonstrate these difficult challenges. A particular focus will be on Japanese manufacturing firms that influence and are influenced by national economic policies. Japan has been known as a country of close government–industry cooperation and policy activism in markets. If there are growing demands by mature and advanced industrial economies to pursue a nationalist economic policy and there are growing difficulties for them to cooperate in curbing such domestic demands to sustain the international economic system based on multilateralism, it may be worthwhile to closely examine how Japan is trying to cope with these challenges. Many Japanese firms, once hailed as global champions, are struggling as the globalization of business has dramatically reduced protective barriers and heightened competition. Is there a chance for mature manufacturing firms of Japan to remain competitive against current and future rivals, many of which are predominantly from emerging economies? Where do firms look for opportunities to create and strengthen competitiveness? Should the Japanese government lend support?

These challenges are not unique to Japan. Facing similar intense competition, many large-scale manufacturing firms in mature economies of Europe and North America are fast "modularizing" their production processes and "offshoring" them to overseas locations, most of which are in newly industrialized and emerging economies. By doing so, they are trying to optimize resource allocation across borders. Some firms go even further, giving up their own manufacturing capabilities by outsourcing production altogether to firms of emerging economies. Will there be a chance for a manufacturing firm of a mature economy to successfully compete, let alone survive, if it has to enter into a new market segment in which dominant rivals may be from emerging economies?

In the rest of the chapter, I will examine the Japanese search for answers to cope with these challenges by conducting a case study surrounding the development of both industrial policy and trade policy. I will explore the intense debate between the Japanese government and its counterparts in the civil aircraft manufacturing industry sector as they search for a new source for their future industrial competitiveness. Japan's quest to regain manufacturing competitiveness forced the government and firms to redefine economic nationalism so that they would develop nationalist industry policies while simultaneously embracing the liberal trade regime of the WTO. What this study uncovers is the process by which the Japanese government took the initiative to develop a shared view with its industrial counterparts to re-establish the industrial competitiveness of Japanese firms. They have come to a mutual understanding that the liberal international economic system may not force national economies to be alike or uniform; removing tariff and non-tariff barriers may not result in a level playing field across countries. Rather, it must lead to exposing firms more directly to national differences that were once obscured by these barriers. By recognizing this fact, the Japanese policy makers and their industry counterparts started appreciating that national differences were indeed a source of both opportunities and challenges for firms to compete globally. They then began applying this understanding to the Japanese social and institutional context to perform more efficiently and effectively and hence to develop competitiveness against their foreign rivals. In other words, the Japanese policy makers and business executives developed a consensus that firms are embedded in national institutions and hence nationality continues to matter substantially for firms to compete in the age of globalization.

This chapter makes a number of contributions to the unsettled question of economic nationalism under globalization. One is the re-examination of the Japanese economic model in the dramatically changing international context as one of the key steps toward the understanding of economic nationalism of East Asia in the early twenty-first century. Japan's policy developments reflect the broader developments that are taking place in East Asia. A second contribution is theoretical. Although the present study is not aimed at building or testing a theory, it demonstrates the significance of an institutional approach to international business studies. Pertaining to theory, scholars of Japan have found that Japanese policy makers relied extensively on an institutional framework as proposed by Aoki (2000, 2001; see also Aoki and Dore 1994; Aoki, Kim and Okuno 1997; and Aoki, Jackson and Miyajima 2007); Dore (2000); and Fujimoto (2007), among others. They identified convincingly the strong link between competitive advantage of an industry and institutional arrangements of a society.

This chapter also highlights several reasons for the substantial transformation of Japan's economic nationalism over the last three decades for several reasons. First, the main players of the economy, Japanese multinational enterprises (MNEs), have become far more globalized, with their policy preferences becoming diverse and complex, and often in contrast to the government. Second and related, these Japanese MNEs, especially in the manufacturing sector, which has been the engine of Japan's rapid growth and development, face increasingly intense international competition from firms in emerging economies. Third, Japan's national economic goals have changed from "catching up" to "staying afloat" as Japan has transformed itself from a marginal developing economy to a large and mature developed economy. Finally, the end of the Cold War and the establishment of the WTO have dramatically changed the global institutional landscape in which Japan may devise and implement its policies. In the next section, I will examine the relevant literature. I will then present a case of the Japanese policy process in which a new consensus between the government and the industry is emerging. The chapter concludes by offering suggestions for further study.

6.2 Making Sense of Japanese National Economic Uniqueness

Japanese economic policy and its impact upon Japan's postwar development have been well studied. Johnson (1982) once argued that much of Japan's "miracle" in the postwar industrial development was attributed to aggressive intervention by the government in prioritizing strategic industries, accelerating adjustments by subsidizing them while making side payments to those industries with comparative disadvantages, and promoting research and development. He focused on comprehensive industry policies by Japan's Ministry of International Trade and Industry (MITI) during the first two decades after the end of World War II and the multilayered institutional arrangements for government-industry cooperation during the period that effectively resulted in the implementation of these industrial policies. Dore (1973) and Vogel (1979) illustrated a broader set of Japanese social contexts in which such policy activism was legitimatized by major stakeholders and market participants. Japan's aggressive policy intervention in economic activities was often considered to represent an alternative approach to a textbook economic development model of liberal economics that consists of free markets, disciplined fiscal policy, and open trade. As Amsden (1992) highlighted in her examination of South Korea, many elements of the Japan model were closely followed and adopted by other Asian economies, leading to what Wade (1990) summarized as "the East Asian model" of national economic development. While there is a considerable variety in the breadth and the depth of their policy activism, these East Asian governments share a common view that, domestically, a government has a much wider responsibility than liberal economists posit to make a market function. The responsibility not only includes a set of effective rules for commercial exchanges, but also involves everything from curbing domestic consumption and providing education to maintaining a favorable exchange rate and selecting a strategic industry. They also share a view that, internationally, their growth and development is closely interconnected with that of their neighbors. They thus recognize a responsibility to sustain this regional development pattern, as referred to by Akamatsu Kaname as the "flying geese model" (Kojima 2000).

These observations about Japan, however, stirred considerable controversy. During the 1980s and 1990s, the Japanese approach was repeatedly condemned by American politicians, journalists, and scholars as too parochial and nationalistic (Prestowitz 1993; Fallows 1994). The Japanese economic rise was interpreted in the USA as "a threat," not only to American firms but more importantly to liberal multilateralism, which is the guiding principle of the postwar international economic system as institutionalized by the General Agreement on Tariffs and Trade (GATT) and the International Monetary Fund (IMF). According to them, the Japanese approach was aimed at its own economic welfare gain at the cost of other economies, including the USA, by protecting and promoting its own industries and restricting foreign access to its markets. The result was that Japan was "free riding" the liberal, multilateral, international economic system, which the USA, along with other advanced economies, had been collectively assuming a dominant role in designing and sustaining (Gilpin 1987). Japan, with its nationalist policy to develop its own industries while curbing foreign—especially US—firms from entering the Japanese market, was seen as engaging in unfair trade practices. Japan was perceived as violating the basic tenet of the liberal trade and investment regime.

Once the Cold War ended in the early 1990s, the world witnessed intensification of globalization of business. Three interesting developments surrounding Japan made the Japanese nationalist actions less relevant. One was Japan's own economic difficulties. As Dore (2000), Lincoln (2001), and Vogel (2006) highlighted, the bursting of the economic bubble not only hit Japanese firms and the Japanese economy hard but also revealed inherent problems of many of the firms' management practices, ranging from lifetime employment to the deeply integrated long-term supply chain known as *keiretsu*. These admittedly were once hailed as the source of Japanese economic success, which paradoxically also contributed to the social and political difficulties in making the necessary adjustments. The second development was the rise of new global players. Past research on East Asian development (Wade 1990; Amsden 1992) highlighted the well-established pipeline of emerging economies that dramatically changed the landscape of the global economy. The third development is globalization itself. Friedman (1999), Ohmae (1999), and many others highlighted a qualitative change in the integration of economic activities across borders and concluded that the globalization process would make states less relevant and the world would become flat. With these three developments Japan becomes passé.

The stalling of the Japanese economy in the mid-1990s, followed by the collapse of South Korea, Thailand, and other Southeast Asian economies during the Asian financial crisis in 1997, seemed to be the final blow to the Japanese model. In Japan, the supposedly strong and effective government was unable to turn its economy around. In the rest of Asia, the governments were forced to transform their traditional developmental models as a condition for the IMF to bail them out and help them restructure their economies. But what replaced the Japan model? In the decade since the 1997 crisis, many Asian economies, including Japan, seem to have finally abandoned their state-led economic model and begun embracing the liberal economic principle. The trend continues with the rise of China and India, both of which also seem to have embraced the liberal market mechanism and freer trade. Japan's downfall was also attributed to its difficulty in continuing its nationalistic economic policies due to increased pressures from the USA, and its inability to adjust to a more liberal economic model. During the last two decades, economic nationalism in Japan and throughout Asia seemed to have lost its clout.

However, more evidence has been accumulated that points to the persistent significance of national differences and the durability of underlying national institutions. For example, as Ghemawat (2003a, 2003b) well highlighted, firms such as ABB and Coca Cola that pursued "globalized" strategies based on the assumption that the world would become flatter were spectacular failures as their intentional neglect of national differences led to serious strategic and operational difficulties. Some scholars have recognized that states still matter as they respond to globalization differently (Berger and Dore 1996; Hall and Soskice 2001). States are founded on a set of distinct social and cultural norms that are institutionalized by a complex web of formal laws, rules, and regulations. As a result, states have been transforming themselves at a much slower speed and in a far more limited scope than globalist observers had been anticipating. These observations reveal three interesting points. First, there is considerable durability of formal political, economic, and legal institutions of a state as well as of cultural, ethnic, religious, and other informal social institutional mechanisms of a society, even in the age of globalization (Ikenberry 2005). Second, there are large differences among governments around the world in their responses to globalization. Different national responses may reflect a number of factors ranging from institutional constraints and the ability of a government to analyze challenges and develop policy options, to different policy preferences by the political and industrial leaders and the electorate to similar challenges. Finally, states remain different even after their transformation in their responses to the globalization of business.

By studying international business and political economy, one may start to appreciate the diverse responses of states to the globalization process that may reveal a number of significant implications for business. First, both home and host countries are examined in the institutional context in which firms exist and undertake business. As Jackson and Deeg (2008) pointed out, institutions define the players, provide the payoff structure of business, and offer possible sets of strategies. In doing so, institutions are no longer seen as intervening variables, which the traditional international business studies have understood in terms of additional costs and constraints, or of distances from normalcy. Instead they are understood to give a set of overarching meanings and identities to firms and their interests, especially in terms of coordination, coherence, legitimacy, and governance. Using this framework, which is dubbed the "comparative capitalism" (CC) framework, empirical research has been carried out to highlight the diversity of global business and opportunities for firms to learn as well as to arbitrage.

An interesting application of the comparative capitalism framework to the architecture of industrial organization was developed by a group of Japanese scholars. Their arguments were twofold. The first step was drawn from the application of the industrial architecture perspective to the traditional resource-based view (RBV). Building upon the landmark contribution by Baldwin and Clark (1997, 2000) on the shift of industrial architecture from vertical integration to modularity, especially in the information technology industry, Fujimoto and his colleagues (1998, 2001) highlighted significant differences among major industrial economies in the architecture of industrial organization as their firms respond to globalization pressure. Fujimoto, who is widely recognized by the Japanese policy makers as an authoritative figure, began developing his insights into industrial architecture to account for underlying dynamics of the competitiveness of the Japanese manufacturing industry. He compared the auto industry of Japan and the USA (Clark and Fujimoto 1991) as an early member of the International Motor Vehicle Program (IMVP) of Massachusetts Institute of Technology (MIT).

Fujimoto and his colleagues introduced the two-dimensional product architecture framework. One dimension categorizes products in terms of the interdependence of parts design. Modular architecture allows components to interact entirely through a clear-cut interface. It allows for off-the-shelf commodity components. Integral architecture, on the other hand, requires components to "interact organically in complex ways," which Fujimoto described as "rubbing things together." Components are usually designed and developed specifically for a certain product but not other products (Fujimoto 2007). The other dimension categorizes openness of interface specification (see Table 6.1). Modular products, such as a personal computer (PC), can be open, with industry standards defining interface information, or closed, such as a mainframe computer, with firm-specific proprietary information on the interface specifications of modular parts. Naturally, in integral architecture, parts are designed with closely held information on specification. Integrating this architectural framework into the RBV, they highlighted the fact that many Japanese manufacturing firms have competitive advantage in manufacturing closed and integral products, such as passenger cars, motorcycles, and small electrical appliances, while they have a disadvantage in manufacturing open and modular products, such as personal computers and multipurpose package software. What they tried to highlight was startling.

Once this first step highlighting the variety of industrial architecture was developed, the next step was to link it to the variety of markets, as examined

Table 6.1. Product architecture

		Interdependence of parts design	
		Integral	Modular
Openness	Closed (firm-specific)	Closed integral Examples: • Small cars • Motorcycles • Game software • Consumer electronics	Closed modular Examples: • Mainframe computer • Machine tools • LEGO blocks (toys)
	Open (industry standard)		Open modular examples • Personal computers • Multipurpose packaged software • Financial products • Bicycles

Source: Adapted from "Figure 2–3 Closed/Open, Integral/Modular Architecture," Fujimoto (2007: 36).

by the comparative capitalism scholars. Manufacturing processes may be functional and economic. Yet they may be socially embedded. National differences may no longer be "additional costs or constraints" but may be recognized as underlying forces that give different meanings to social activities. It is with these insights into national institutional differences that one may start appreciating why it may be much more difficult for a firm to employ a simple "best practice" strategy by exporting a management practice that appears to be efficient in one country to the rest of the world, or a simple "adaptation" strategy to foreign institutions. This perspective uncovers why the globalization of business may not lead to a flat world, and hence why it may expose firms to national differences even more. It is here that a government on the one hand, and industries on the other, may have a common ground on which firms may seek to establish their competitiveness based on arbitrage of national differences, and especially on country-specific strengths that may be shaped in the institutional context.

6.3 Looking for the Right Manufacturing Sector

In May 2003, Japan's Ministry of Economy, Trade, and Industry (METI, a successor to MITI following the ministerial reorganization in 2001) started the "Environmentally Friendly High Performance Small Aircraft Project." It is a direct eight-year Research and Development (R&D) grant project administered by METI's New Energy and Industry Technology Development Organization (NEDO) (NEDO 2007). The first phase of the project would last for five years up to the development of a test plane, followed by a second phase covering the initial production of a commercial plane. The initial project would assist the development of a quiet and fuel efficient regional jet carrying 30 to 50 passengers. It would also assist in the research of process technologies that would enhance speed to market. Better fuel economy through weight and drag reduction were to be achieved by the development of material-related technologies including composite materials and enhanced computational fluid dynamics to speed up the design process (NEDO 2007). If successful, Japan would see the first "made in Japan" commercial jetliner in its history.

Why should the Japanese government take a lead in creating a new industry? This is a major empirical question about the economic nationalism of a mature and advanced economy. As we observed, the Japanese government made clear during the 1990s that it would embrace the liberal economic principle by domestically promoting liberalization and deregulation and internationally committing itself to the WTO. This policy position was supported by the Japanese industry as they benefited from these policies with their global expansion. If so, does the newly proposed aircraft project contradict Japan's economic policy position? Why is it important for the government of a mature and advanced economy to be actively involved in a strategically important industrial sector if its firms are no longer "infant?" Furthermore, even if the Japanese government identified the civil aviation industry as a strategic sector and developed a convincing reason to support it, there is another question. Will the government have a legitimate and effective policy tool to help the mature Japanese manufacturing industry successfully enter the market, which is already dominated by Canada's Bombardier and Brazil's Embraer, and worse, which will be further crowded by the two emerging market players from China and Russia that are committed to play major roles in the market?

6.3.1 *Japan's Aerospace Industry*

Japan, which has been known for the auto industry and a host of other competitive manufacturing industries, does not have a fully-fledged aerospace industry of its own. This is partly historical. For eight years from 1945, the USA banned any Japanese firms from manufacturing aircraft. Once the ban was lifted, it did encourage the development of some indigenous aerospace capability. The sector's commercial and technological development fell under the aegis of the Ministry of International Trade and Industry (MITI), a predecessor to METI. The Aerospace and Defense Industries Division (ADID) of the Manufacturing Industries Bureau at MITI had a responsibility to promote both the civil and defense aviation industries. Beginning in the 1960s, Japan attempted to develop a civil airliner program designed to act as a technology driver in much the same way as policies had done for other sectors such as memory chips or supercomputing (Fong 1998).

The resulting program, the YS-11, was a commercial failure. The MITI-led consortium, incorporated in 1959 as Nihon Aircraft Manufacturing Corporation (NAMC), was successful in designing and building a 60-seat turbo-propeller aircraft. In 1962, the first YS-11 had a maiden flight. It obtained the "type" (airworthiness) certificate in 1964. However, it was unable to secure large orders, especially in foreign markets, to keep the plane commercially viable. The aerospace industry is characterized by an economy of scale with a large initial investment in research and development. It also needs substantial investment to develop an extensive after-market service network for maintenance. Without securing enough orders, the YS-11 quickly accumulated losses and the government was forced to give up the project in 1973 with the total production of only 182 aircraft.

Since then, the attention of the Japanese aerospace industry has shifted toward coproduction agreements with foreign—mainly US—partners, and the industry has pursued two strategies. One plan was for Japanese industry to become key subcontractors of Boeing in the area of civil aircraft. The other was for Japanese firms to manufacture military aircraft under license with Lockheed for the Japanese self-defense force. Subsequently, the Japanese aerospace industry has never become a serious global player comparable to its counterparts in the automobile industry or the electronics industry. The partnership with Boeing started with the 767 project in 1977 with 15% of the initial R&D cost covered by the Japanese consortium. The partnership continued with the 777 and the 787 projects, which turned out to be commercially successful. Yet, the Japanese participation in developing a civil aircraft remained that of a secondary player. Japan's military side was even more marginal. Its constitutional constraints never allowed the massive, military-led subsidies enjoyed by US firms during the Cold War. The constitution also banned exports of military products. Unlike the US industry, Japan has few specialist aerospace firms; the three key firms, namely Mitsubishi, Fuji, and Ishikawajima Heavy Industries, are all integrated manufacturers with a wide portfolio of business areas.

6.3.2 *Aerospace and Japan's Industrial Future*

Developments in the aerospace sector cannot be understood outside a more general review of Japan's competitive position. Japan's economy performed poorly during the 1990s. Following the burst of the economic bubble in 1991, both the government and companies were slow to cope with the mounting challenges. Japan's stalemate contrasted with the dramatic rise of China and other emerging economies, creating additional pressure on Japanese manufacturing firms. There was a serious debate regarding the future of the Japanese manufacturing sector. It was against this background that METI embarked on a review of both the long-term technological outlook and its role for Japanese firms to develop their capabilities.[1] The sector accounted for less than a quarter of gross national product (GNP), but it was still the export engine of the Japanese economy. The Japanese services sector was considered to be less competitive (METI 2005). METI's review led to a white paper in 2001 titled "Focus 21," which became a new policy direction for its R&D initiatives. The emergent consensus among the policy makers and business leaders was:

1) Japanese industries have several areas of competitive strength. Of these, the following four areas are identified as having potential for future growth: bio-technologies, information and communication technologies, environmental technologies, and nano-technologies.
2) While the auto industry may lead the manufacturing industry for some time, other manufacturing sectors must develop innovative technologies to sustain their global competitiveness.
3) The traditional budgetary distribution before the Koizumi government was inefficient with grants to too many projects. It was replaced by a more focused approach with two criteria: (i) New initiatives must fall under the four priority areas, as spelled out above, and (ii) R&D efforts must lead to commercial success in a relatively short period (METI 2001).

One of the highlights of Focus 21 was the civil aircraft sector. Under Focus 21, ADID developed a series of policies in close consultation with the Aircraft Committee (Kokuki Iinkai) of the Industry Structure Council (Sangyo Kozo Shingikai). The committee was formally launched in September 2001 and generally embraces ADID's policies. It also provided valuable insights into the latest industry developments. Since its launch, the committee has met at least ten times: once a year in 2001 and 2002, and then twice a year since 2003 (METI 2004). At its eighth meeting on February 4, 2005, the committee decided to set up a special task force called the Development Project Promotion Special Committee (Kaihatsu Jigyo Suishin Senmon Iinkai) with the express purpose of overseeing the regional jet project. It hosted the first meeting on March 17, 2005 (METI 2005).

ADID operates in a manner strikingly consistent with the classic Japanese model of coordination among firms and METI. ADID has three main tools to achieve its policy objectives: information gathering, analysis, and sharing; indirect intervention; and direct intervention through subsidies. However, Japan's budgetary situation has had an impact on the manner in which METI supports industrial policies across sectors. Tight budgets placed an emphasis on the ability of sectors to "sell" their ideas in competition with other programs. The new emphasis on aerospace technologies and their importance to Japan can be seen in the development of the Mitsubishi Regional Jet (MRJ) project, which is considered to be ADID's concrete response to Focus 21. It is no secret that METI and the Japanese manufacturers shared a strong and long-lasting desire to develop a civil aircraft manufacturing industry. The sector was considered to have a very large positive externality with its technological intensity. It also involves a large number of subcontractors manufacturing a large number of parts. A commercial aircraft typically involves roughly 200,000 parts, ten times more than a car, which involves 20,000 parts. This industrial characteristic highlights the significance of effective coordination for closed-integral interface among the industry participants.

By the early 2000s, a number of developments changed the landscape. During the 1990s, the regional jet market grew rapidly and was dominated by two manufacturers, Bombardier and Embraer (Goldstein and McGuire 2004). It was seen as particularly promising to a new entrant given that the market was still growing while Boeing and Airbus were absent. At the same time, there were potential new entrants, namely China with its ARJ21 project and Russia with the Sukhoi RRJ100 project. Domestic considerations also played their part; a new market for smaller jets was anticipated with the expansion of Tokyo's congested Haneda airport. For the first time, there was a chance for regional jets to serve the capital by linking it to secondary cities.

The decision to develop a new regional airliner was assisted by concerns that the Japanese manufacturers relying on Boeing for subcontracting work were hostage to Boeing's product planning processes. In the early 2000s, Boeing's next project was also unclear. The dramatic slowdown in international jet orders after September 11, 2001 also served to remind the industry of its overreliance on its American partners for business. Though pleased with their status on the Boeing 787 program, Mitsubishi managers were nonetheless concerned that there would be no new Boeing programs that would enable the company to develop its capabilities in design and composite manufacturing processes. The regional jet project was a way to develop Mitsubishi's capabilities, without offering a product to compete with Boeing. The decision also reflected the emerging consensus that was shaped between the government policy makers and the industry policy participants that Japan would continue to rest on the manufacturing sector for its economic prosperity. There was a long and intense discussion not only within ADID but across METI and the policy participants at the Industry Structure Council about the future of Japanese manufacturing. The discussion touched upon a broad range of issues, including the strength of Japanese industries. They assessed it not only on a firm's capability and global positioning, but also on the institutional context.

The discussion involved many Japanese scholars. As examined in the preceding section, their arguments were twofold. The first argument was developed upon the industrial architecture framework over the modular-integral and open-close matrix. They argued that the Japanese manufacturing firms consistently demonstrate competitive strength in closed-integral products. They found a causal linkage between manufacturing high-quality, closed-integral products by a Japanese firm and intense flow of information and close collaboration across firms. This observation led to the second argument by the Japanese policy participants that Japanese manufacturing excellence in closed-modular products has reasons beyond their firm specific capabilities. They argued that such characteristics as intense flow of information and close collaboration across firms, as institutionalized in their supply chain, were made possible within a broader Japanese social institutional context based on long-term, iterated-game relations. In short, not only Japanese firms, but also a significant part of their value chains, are socially embedded. Their understanding of the Japanese institution runs parallel with the recent studies on the diversity of institutions, the "comparative capitalism" (CC) framework (Jackson and Deeg 2008). Several strands exist within the CC framework, resting their theoretical foundations on broad academic disciplines ranging from sociology (as represented by Dore), political science (by Hall and Soskice), to economics (by North, Williamson, and Aoki, among others) (Hall and Soskice 2001). They all share, as Jackson and Deeg summarized, that "institutions exist in distinct national configurations or types that generate a particular systemic logic of economic action and competitive advantages related to complementarities among those institutions" (Jackson and Deeg 2008: 541). Applying this perspective to the Japanese manufacturing industry, Japanese government policy makers and industry policy participants started looking at the locked-in relationship between Japanese institutional characteristics and the industrial competitiveness of a manufacturing sector that has not been modularized. The sector thus requires intense interaction and coordination for successful management of closed-integral interface among parts and component manufacturers on the one hand and the assemblers on the other. The institutional characteristics of the aerospace industry here look very similar to those of the Japanese auto industry. Tariff and non-tariff barriers are no longer important because "institutional fit" between social and industrial institutional characteristics and product architectures may provide an industry with a distinctive competitive advantage. Different institutional arrangements are understood to have "distinct strengths and weaknesses for different kinds of economic activity" (Ghemawat 2003a; Jackson and Deeg 2008: 541).

It is important to note that these scholarly findings have been closely followed by the Japanese policy community. For example, METI has been commissioning studies on Japanese industrial competitiveness from the institutional perspective at its own research arm, the Research Institute of International Trade and Industry (RIITI), which was reorganized in 2001 as the Research Institute of Economy, Trade and Industry (RIETI). Its interests in the CC perspective culminated when it appointed Masahiko Aoki as its president in 1997, a position he held until 2004. Under his directorship, the institute hosted conferences, commissioned studies, and published discussion papers focusing on institutional foundations of Japanese industrial competitiveness. Applying the CC framework to the Japanese manufacturing industry, they started to recognize certain causal linkages between such social institutions as lifetime employment, the *keiretsu* inter-firm relationship, the main-bank financial system and the main-bank-led corporate governance structure on the one hand, and the ability of a firm to maintain competitive advantage in closed-integral products on the other. Closed and integral products require a continuous flow of proprietary information not only between the R&D, engineering, and manufacturing divisions within a firm but also with its suppliers. The lifetime employment system encourages employees to collaborate with others and accumulate knowledge as a part of their career development within the firm. The *keiretsu* relationship encourages firms to collaborate based on a long-term trust relationship rather than an opportunistic short-term market transaction. The main-bank system, with its corporate governance structure, shields firms from the short-term pressure of capital markets. They have access to longer term financing by "main banks" and their managers are encouraged to develop and implement a longer term strategy in product planning, research and development, and human capital development.

Aoki, Fujimoto, and many other scholars who uncovered the significant linkage between institutional arrangements and industrial competitiveness, helped them explore institutional implications for Japan's industrial competitiveness. In short, they argued that the competitiveness of Japanese manufacturing firms was not a firm-level phenomenon, but was deeply rooted in Japanese social institutions. It is in this context that the Japanese aerospace industry in general and Mitsubishi in particular argued that the aerospace industry would allow Japan a chance to establish its competitiveness. Here, a new role for government is recognized in promoting national competitiveness through the state's ability to design and sustain social institutions in particular ways. Designing institutional arrangements to promote national competitiveness is economic nationalism in action.

Aoki, Fujimoto and others argued that the proposed regional jet would be developed on a closed-integrated, not an open-modular, architecture incorporating advanced technologies, an architectural model similar to the auto industry. They also argued that, similar to the Japanese industrial institutions that helped strengthen the competitive advantage of the auto industry, these industrial institutions should help strengthen the competitiveness of the regional jet.

6.3.3 *MRJ Project*

The "Environmentally Friendly High Performance Small Aircraft Project" of METI, which began in 2003, was supposed to be an open and transparent R&D grant project. NEDO provided public notice and invited proposals. Only Mitsubishi applied, and was granted the development money. Mitsubishi formed a consortium with Fuji Heavy Industry, Japan Aircraft Development Corp (JADC 2008), and Japan Aerospace Exploratory Agency (JAXA). METI will subsidize up to 50 percent of the R&D cost. The total development cost was reportedly initially estimated at 50 billion yen.

Mitsubishi proposed a major revision of the plan in 2005 by shifting the target from a 30–50 seat plane to a 70–90 seat plane. The change was based on the latest market research conducted by JADC and by the strong pressure of the two Japanese airlines, JAL and ANA, the potential customers. The importance that Mitsubishi assigned to the project was evidenced in its reorganization in 2007, which enhanced the position of the aerospace division within the corporate structure.

METI officials confirmed that their immediate goal for the MRJ project was not directly aimed at maximizing Japan's national security but to promote the aerospace industry as a key industry. They insisted that having a world-class aircraft manufacturing industry is by itself important to the national interest. However, they also pointed out that promoting the industry should be a critical and integral part of the foundation of Japan's national security, and they anticipated that the plane would be bought by Japan's military and coast guard.

6.4 Globalization and Economic Nationalism

In retrospect, the MRJ project was one of the first strategically targeted Japanese industry policies since WTO was launched and since Japan openly and firmly embraced liberal multilateralism. Since the late 1980s, METI had not introduced an industry policy openly aimed at helping Japanese firms achieve their globally competitive position (Elder 2003). This was partly because of the bilateral trade friction between the USA and Japan, but more importantly because of Japan's policy shift. The formal launch of WTO in 1994 and METI's policy shift to fully embrace liberal multilateralism and more actively use a market mechanism reduced the role of the traditional industrial policy (Dore 2000; Vogel 2006).

ADID's decision was therefore a major puzzle. It clearly set a policy goal to help the Japanese aircraft industry achieve commercial competitiveness in the global market and it was determined to walk a tightrope under the WTO rule, positioning the project as promoting environmental technologies, one of the few exceptions that developed economy governments may pursue under the free trade rule. In this respect, the project may be regarded as a classic industrial policy to pursue economic nationalism.

Yet, the policy debate leading to the MRJ project highlights a new dimension of economic nationalism. Traditionally, economic nationalism was at odds with economic liberalism. It was aimed at benefiting its own economy at the cost of others. The Japanese policy debate, however, was not over nationalism versus liberalism, but about their integration. A consensus was developed by the Japanese policy makers and policy participants from the manufacturing industry that liberal markets were not created equal. Social institutions shape liberal markets of labor, capital, and goods and services substantially differently from one country to another.

Equally important, another consensus was developed that the Japanese manufacturing competitiveness in incremental innovation based on their closed and integral architecture was closely linked with uniquely Japanese social institutional arrangements, especially in labor relations, capital markets, supply chains, and corporate governance. Mitsubishi had positioned itself to take advantage of this policy context. The company had developed the skills essential for any new foray into aircraft manufacturing. Foremost, it had developed capabilities in the design and manufacture of load-bearing composite materials. As noted, this capability was developed during its work on the F-2 fighter and Boeing's 787. Also, the aircraft industry is capital-intensive and customer expectations of after-sales support are crucial elements of the marketing of the aircraft. Mitsubishi was effectively the only diversified manufacturer with sufficient resources, including capital and market credibility, to make a sustained assault on the regional aircraft market.

Opportunities exist for a government to design and sustain social institutions in particular ways so that they may promote international competitiveness of a targeted industry. This new institutional approach is an obvious, even if subtle and indirect, expression of economic nationalism. ADID successfully developed a consensus among the policy participants that the future of the Japanese manufacturing sectors would continue to rest on the closed-integral architecture of the manufacturing industry that would fit with Japan's socio-economic institutions and would offer a unique institutional context for competitiveness. Once it developed this consensus, the rest (i.e., executing a state R&D subsidy for environmental technologies as approved under the WTO rule) was a less complicated administrative process.

In this respect, the policy process leading to the MRJ project represented a new chapter of economic nationalism. It reflected the assessment by the Japanese policy participants of the future of the Japanese manufacturing sector against the increasingly difficult global competition. As discussed here, their assessment was based on the examination of the institutional strength of the Japanese economy. They concluded that the aerospace industry, more than any other, would present a bright spot in the institutional context for the future of the Japanese manufacturing industry. It would allow the Japanese economy, and especially Mitsubishi, a chance to prove that the manufacturing industry would continue to lead the Japanese economy with its global competitiveness by exploiting the institutional fit with the closed-integral architecture of products. They concluded that the Japanese manufacturing industry should be able to compete effectively if they carefully identified an industrial segment that capitalizes on their institutional strengths, and if government would sustain and strengthen them.

6.5 Conclusion

As of this writing (July 2011), the MRJ project is seemingly on track. In September 2010, Mitsubishi announced that it had entered the production drawing phase for MRJ (Mitsubishi 2010). In April 2011, it announced the commencement of its assembly work (Mitsubishi Aircraft Corporation 2011a). And in June of the same year, it announced an order from its third customer, ANI Group, making the initial orders total 125 planes including options from the three firms (Mitsubishi Aircraft Corporation 2011b).

Changes in Japanese policies for the aerospace industry have emerged from a complex interplay of factors, some external to Japan, others internally generated. Concern about Japan's slippage in international manufacturing, combined with concerns about the increased technological capabilities in many countries, allowed METI to catalyze a new, stronger technological orientation to industrial support policies. The process analyzed here suggests strong elements of continuity with past practice. For example, METI continues to be keenly interested in manufacturing, perhaps still neglecting innovation in services. The bureaucracy is also active in developing policy and overseeing its implementation. Again, these characteristics are well known to observers of the Japanese developmental state.

However, changes are also noteworthy. The close involvement of Mitsubishi in the early phases of the project and its dominance of the development phase are strikingly unlike earlier Japanese efforts in aerospace. METI's more competitive internal processes seem to have resulted in a "selecting out" of less-well-resourced and capable firms at an earlier stage. With less money to devote to a project, METI led the industry policy participants to evaluate chances and risks to the future of the Japanese manufacturing industry in a far broader context. They concluded that the Japanese manufacturing industry should be able to compete effectively only if they would carefully identify an industrial segment that would capitalize on their institutional strengths. Also, the policy participants were acutely aware of the overall Japanese government commitment to the liberal economic principle in the domestic market and in WTO, both of which METI itself was responsible for.

Clearly, Mitsubishi was well placed to both facilitate and benefit from this policy shift. METI's renewed interest in aerospace as a technology driver coincided with a re-evaluation within the firm of its prospects in the sector. The firm has developed considerable technical expertise in composite construction thanks to its involvement with Boeing and with military procurement, as well as its acknowledged program management skills acquired across a range of sectors. These capabilities emerged over many years, but global concerns about fuel efficiency in aircraft have provided the firm with a key competitive capability. The project also throws some doubt on bald statements concerning the inability of large Japanese firms to develop new capabilities. Aerospace is entering a period of change, as the dominance of Western firms erodes as new markets and new technologies evolve.

What does this case tell us about change in Japan's economy? This chapter outlines a situation where Japan seeks to adapt and evolve to economic and technological change. But it also reveals the role of institutions that Jackson and Deeg (2008) identified in generating a particular systemic logic of economic action and competitive advantages. Institutional arrangements provide "distinct strengths and weaknesses for different kinds of economic activity." The consensus on the regional jet project that the industry and the government developed clearly reflects their understanding of the "social embeddedness of firms" and their implications for the comparative advantage of a nation and the competitive advantage of a firm. Even if they were aware that the market would become crowded with new entrants from China and Russia, they came to conclude that the regional jet project would let Mitsubishi develop a plane with a significant competitive edge over rivals. Their confidence was based on their belief that Japan would continue to maintain its competitive advantage in a closed-integrated, rather than open-modular, production architecture incorporating advanced technologies that firmly rest on Japan's institutional arrangements. They also saw that the Japanese industry would continue to retain a competitive advantage in environmental technologies in general, and their application to the aerospace industry in particular. In short, they decided to take advantage of the arbitrage opportunity that they believed was presented to the aerospace industry by the institutional characteristics of Japan.

Together, they came to conclude that the aerospace industry in general and regional jets in particular would represent a strategically important segment for Japan's future. Clearly a single case study cannot provide a complete answer, but the analysis of the policy process leading to the MRJ project reveals an advanced and sophisticated analysis of industrial competitiveness in the age of globalization. The globalization of business does not mean that the world becomes uniform, but rather it offers new opportunities for firms to establish competitive advantages that may be firmly based on their national institutional foundations. Consequently, governments may have important roles to play in carefully designing and sustaining social institutions that define labor practices, capital flows, supply chains, and corporate governance as it tries to encourage firms to strengthen competitive advantages even under the liberal trade regime. Economic nationalism today certainly looks different from that in the past. It is far more subtle, indirect, and complex. Yet, there seems to be significant room for firms to arbitrage national differences and for governments to help them take advantage of the differences as one of their national policy priorities in the age of globalization. The implication to the neighboring Asian governments and their firms is obvious: that globalization offers new opportunities, which the state could seize favorably for national development.

Note

1. Interviews with METI officials and Mitsubishi executives were conducted in Tokyo, Japan, intermittently between December 2007 and June 2008.

References

Amsden, A.H. (1992). *Asia's Next Giant: South Korea and Late Industrialization.* Oxford: Oxford University Press.

Aoki, M. (2000). *Information, Corporate Governance, and Institutional Diversity: Competitiveness in Japan, the USA, and the Transitional Economies.* Oxford: Oxford University Press.

Aoki, M. (2001). *Towards a Comparative Institutional Analysis.* Cambridge, Mass.: MIT Press.

Aoki, M. and Dore, R. (1994). *The Japanese Firm: The Sources of Competitive Strength.* Oxford: Oxford University Press.

Aoki, M., Jackson, G., and Miyajima, H. (2007). *Corporate Governance in Japan: Institutional Change and Organizational Diversity.* Oxford: Oxford University Press.

Aoki, M., Kim, H., and Okuno, M. (eds.) (1997). *The Role of Government in East Asian Economic Development: Comparative Institutional Analysis*. Oxford: Oxford University Press.

Baldwin, C.Y. and Clark, K. (1997). "Managing in the Age of Modularity." *Harvard Business Review*, 75 (5): 84–93.

Baldwin, C.Y. and Clark, K. (2000). *Design Rules*. Cambridge, Mass.: MIT Press.

Berger, S. and Dore, R. (eds.) (1996). *National Diversity and Global Capitalism*. Ithaca: Cornell University Press.

Breuilly, J. (1995). *Nationalism and the State*. Manchester: Manchester University Press.

Clark, K. and Fujimoto, T. (1991). *Product Development Performance: Strategy, Organization, and Management in the World Auto Industry*. Boston: Harvard Business School Press.

Dore, R. (1973). *British Factory, Japanese Factory: The Origins of National Diversity in Industrial Relations*. Berkeley: University of California Press.

Dore, R. (2000). *Stock Market Capitalism: Welfare Capitalism: Japan and Germany versus the Anglo-Saxons*. Oxford: Oxford University Press.

Elder, M. (2003). "METI and Industrial Policy in Japan: Change and Continuity," in U. Schaede and W. Grimes (eds.), *Japan's Managed Globalisation*, 159–90. London: M.E. Sharpe.

Fallows, J. (1994). *Looking at the Sun: The Rise of the New East Asian Economic and Political System*. New York: Vintage.

Fong, G. (1998). "Follower at the Frontier: International Competition and Japanese Industrial Policy." *International Studies Quarterly*, 42 (2): 339–66.

Friedman, T. (1999). *The Lexus and the Olive Tree: Understanding Globalization*. New York: Farrar Straus Giroux.

Fujimoto, T. (2007). *Competing to be Really, Really Good: The Behind-the-scenes Drama of Capability-Building in the Automobile Industry*. Tokyo: I-House Press.

Fujimoto, T., Nishiguchi, T., and Ito, H. (eds.) (1998). *Readings: Supplier System* (in Japanese). Tokyo: Yuhikaku.

Fujimoto, T., Takeishi, A., and Aoshima, Y. (2001). *Business Architecture* (in Japanese). Tokyo: Yuhikaku.

Ghemawat, P. (2003a). "The Forgotten Strategy." *Harvard Business Review*, 81 (11): 76–84.

Ghemawat, P. (2003b). "Semiglobalization and International Business Strategy." *Journal of International Business Studies*, 34 (2): 138–52.

Gilpin, R. (1987). *The Political Economy of International Relations*. Princeton: Princeton University Press.

Goldstein, A. and McGuire, S. (2004). "The Political Economy of Strategic Trade Policy and the Brazil–Canada Subsidies Saga." *World Economy*, 27 (4): 541–66.

Hall, P. and Soskice, D. (eds.) (2001). *Varieties of Capitalism*. Oxford: Oxford University Press.

Ikenberry, J. (2005). *American Foreign Policy*. Boston: Houghton Mifflin.

Jackson, G. and Deeg, R. (2008). "Comparing Capitalisms: Understanding Institutional Diversity and its Implications for International Business." *Journal of International Business Studies*, 39 (4): 540–61.

JADC. (2008). *Minkan Kokuki Nikansuru Chosa Kenkyu* (Research on Commercial Aircrafts; in Japanese). Tokyo: JADC.

Johnson, C. (1982). *MITI and the Japanese Miracle*. Stanford: Stanford University Press.

Kojima, K. (2000). "The 'Flying Geese' Model of Asian Economic Development: Origin, Theoretical Extensions, and Regional Policy Implications." *Journal of Asian Economics*, 11 (4): 375–401.

Lincoln, E. (2001). *Arthritic Japan: The Slow Pace of Economic Reform*. Washington, DC: Brookings Institute Publishing.

METI (1998, 1999, 2000, 2001, 2003, 2004, and 2005). *Abridged Minutes, Sangyo Kozo Shingikai Kokuki Iinkai* (in Japanese; Aircraft Committee, Industry Structure Council).

METI (2004) *Abridged Minutes, Kogata Ryokakuki Kaihatsu Jigyo Suishin Senmon Iinkai, Sangyo Kozo Shingikai Kokuki Iinkai* (in Japanese; Development Project Promotion Special Committee, Aircraft Committee, Industry Structure Council).

Mitsubishi Aircraft Corporation (2010). "Mitsubishi Aircraft Proceeds with MRJ Manufacturing Phase." Press Release No. 016. www.mrj-japan.com/press_releases/news_100915.html [Accessed January 25, 2012].

Mitsubishi Aircraft Corporation (2011a). "MHI Commences Mitsubishi Regional Jet Assembly Work." *Press Release*. www.mrj-japan.com/press_releases/news_110405.html [Accessed January 25, 2012].

Mitsubishi Aircraft Corporation (2011b). "ANI Group Holdings Ltd. Signs MOU with Mitsubishi Aircraft for Purchase of 5 MRJ Aircraft: A New Step in Cultivating the Asian Market." Press Release No. 19. www.mrj-japan.com/press_releases/news_110616.html [Accessed January 25, 2012].

New Energy and Industry Technology Development Organization (NEDO). (2007). *Annual Report Fiscal Year 2006–2007*, 34–6. (in Japanese). Tokyo: NEDO.

Ohmae, K. (1999). *The Borderless World: Power and Strategy in the Interlinked Economy*. New York: Harper.

Prestowitz, C. (1993). *Trading Places: How We Are Giving Our Future to Japan and How to Reclaim It*. New York: Basic Books.

Vogel, E. (1979). *Japan as Number One: Lessons for America*. Cambridge, Mass.: Harvard University Press.

Vogel, S. (2006). *Japan Remodeled: How Government and Industry Are Reforming Japanese Capitalism*. Ithaca: Cornell University Press.

Wade, R. (1990). *Governing the Market*. Princeton, N.J.: Princeton University Press.

7

South Korea's globalization in the late twentieth century: an end to economic nationalism?

You-il Lee[1]

7.1 Introduction

South Korea's (hereafter Korea) industrial capitalism since its liberation from Japan in 1945 has had a long history of nationalism, especially towards foreign economic policies (Dent 2000). The Korean state's authoritarian and corporatist structures underpinned the developmental state. State-allocated monopolies and the reliance on the international economy for foreign capital in the form of aid and loans pushed Korea's growth trajectory in a highly neo-mercantilist direction. Other peculiar characteristics of Korea's development trajectory include the long-running developmentalist alliance between the state and big business, the *chaebol*, groups of mostly family-owned and managed conglomerates in Korea such as Samsung, Hyundai, SK, Daewoo, and LG, and authoritarian labor control (Deyo 1987; Luedde-Neurath 1988; Bello and Rosenfeld 1990; Kong 2000). However, the outbreak of the 1997 Asian financial crisis, which had serious impacts on Korea, loosened the state-driven market and industrial policies and a strong nationalist policy towards foreign investment. For the first time in modern Korean capitalism, the Korean state under Kim Dae-jung (1998–2003) attempted to move the economy towards a neoliberal paradigm of economic growth. This move implied the functional demise of the state as a response to new economic conditions triggered by the financial crisis. However, as I show below, the Korean state continues to pursue a nationalist agenda despite its seeming embrace of globalization.

Korea did shift its policies when it comes to foreign direct investment. Between 1962 and 1995, 8,269 companies invested in Korea. Between 1996 and 2004 another 21,045 companies made investments (KABC 2004: 16). During the four-year period after the crisis (1998 to 2001), Korea attracted around US$52 billion in inward foreign direct investment (FDI), double the entire amount of the previous four decades. This shows, on the surface, the Korean state's stark change in foreign economic policies, departing from decades-old adherence to economic principles oriented towards a neo-mercantilist and developmental statist growth model (*Korea Inc.)* of state-capital collusion, to one more consistent with the neoliberal formula of economic globalization embedded in pro-inward FDI policies.[2]

The chapter examines the process by which economic nationalism was challenged in Korea in the post-World War II era of globalization and questions whether globalization and internationalism signal that we can expect all vestiges of the collectivist nature of late capitalist development to disappear. A closer look at the evolution of the Korean political economy since its first adoption of industrial capitalism reveals that despite some recent efforts by the Korean government to further an economic globalization agenda, a strong and extensive tradition of economic nationalism,[3] where the state plays a key role in planning and implementing economic change, is still evident in Korea (Dent 2003; Lim 2010). This chapter argues that the economic trajectory has not shifted with Korea's neoliberal globalization reforms, also known as *Segyehwa* (globalization) in Korean. Anchored around outward FDI, Kim Young-sam's regime (1993–98) launched the Korean version of globalization in 1994. Alternate plans of subsequent Korean regimes (Kim Dae-jung, 1998–2003, and Roh Moo-hyun, 2003–8) to embrace neoliberal globalization principles, including active encouragement of inward FDI, have not reversed the traditional nationalist development trajectory. Rather, the process has strengthened the state's capacity. The neoliberal "economic activities in the previous regimes are still subordinate to the goal of state building and the interests of the state" (Hall 2004: 84). According to Lee and Hewison, "deepening globalization has become a state mantra for moving beyond crisis, developmentalist state models and lower-technology and lower-labour cost technologies to a modernized, globalized, market-driven and mass-consumption economy" (Lee and Hewison 2010: 184).

This chapter is divided into five sections. The next section provides an overview of the Korean political economy in which the relationship between economic nationalism and state policy is examined. This is followed in the third section by a critical examination of the different phases of the Korean state's economic globalization efforts through inward FDI-led economic integration conducted over the last three regimes (1993–2008).[4] Section 7.4 looks at the impacts of the legacy of state-led development (economic nationalism) on Korea's newly adopted inward FDI-led globalization drive. The final section critically examines whether the 1997 economic shock and the implications that flowed from this were responsible for changing the Korean development trajectory from a neo-mercantilist to a neoliberal model.

7.2 Korea's Economic Nationalism: An Engine of Growth?

Over the last three decades, Korea has experienced a period of sustained rapid economic growth. Between 1962 and 1991, real economic growth exceeded 9% per year. The Korean government has implemented major economic reforms, such as the adoption of more realistic exchange rates to boost domestic production and maintain a comfortable balance of payments position, the centralization of import controls, and the introduction of export incentives. The government has also encouraged industries to look to global markets and to develop the country's comparative advantage in the export of light and labor-intensive manufactures. One critical element in facilitating export-oriented industrialization (EOI) has been low production costs including, until the early 1980s, a relatively compliant and disciplined workforce able to work long hours intensely. Consequently, between 1965 and 1984, agriculture's contribution to gross domestic product (GDP) dropped from 38% to 14% and the share of manufacturing increased from 25% to 40%. The portion of trade in the gross national product (GNP) soared from 12% in 1957 to 56% in 1991 (Yoon 1995: 13). These elements have converted the image of Korea from that of a primarily agrarian country to that of a newly industrializing country (NIC) based on manufacturing and services.

In Korea, the legacy of state dirigisme and the state's tight connection with *chaebol* in the domestic economy had their origins in the Park Chung-hee era (1961–79). The Park regime's strong emphasis on social and economic independence from foreign forces, state arbitration in the socio-political and economic spheres, and the heavy protection of indigenous business (*chaebol*) under the policy of "nation-building through exports," saw state control in all aspects of the Korean economy, including trade, agriculture, steel, shipbuilding, and cement industries.

Considerable debate about Korea's developmental capitalism over three decades (1960s–80s) occurred among neoliberal economists who attributed the country's rapid economic growth to the pursuit of export-oriented industrialization (EOI) along with policies that favored a market orientation and minimal state intervention (Westphal 1978, 1990; Krueger 1982, 1990; Little 1982; Riedel 1988). Political economists focused on domestic political processes and the role of the state in Korea (Kuznets 1985; Amsden 1987a, 1987b, 1992, 1994; Moon 1988; Wade 1988a, 1988b, 1992, 1998; White and Wade 1988; Chu 1989; Haggard and Moon 1990; Woo 1991; Streeten 1993; Weiss 1998, 2003; Haggard 2000; Woo-Cumings 2003). In spite of this considerable debate, the consensus has been that the Korean state has intervened in the market as the *primum mobile* of socio-economic and cultural progress. In other words, Korea's economic success, and its place at the top of the economic hierarchy among developing countries, is a product not of culture, geography, or uninhibited market forces, but of the actions and institutions of a developmental state (Hart-Landsberg, Jeong, and Westra 2007: 1). Robert Gilpin's neo-realist approach (neo-mercantilism to economic nationalism) well captures the Korean case in which "economic activities are and should be subordinate to the goal of state-building and the interests of the state" (quoted in Crane 1998: 57). In Haggard and Moon's words, "Korean economic development is best understood in terms of a statist model in which the state is conceived as having the relative autonomy in its ability to define developmental goals and the power to build the social coalitions to support them" (Haggard and Moon 1983: 140). Sakong and Jones take a firmer stand on the statist model:

> The Korean State (Park Chung-hee) has in no sense pursued a laissez-faire strategy towards the economy: rather it has been heavily interventionist in attempting to influence the micro-economic decisions of productive units either through stimulating, forcing, or cajoling private enterprises; these intervention efforts have been effective in actually altering private decisions, resource allocation and economic outcomes. (Jones and Sakong 1980: 288)

The Korean state's active and intensive intervention in economic affairs had become the central pillar of the Park Chung-hee regime's growth strategy (Kong 2000: 38). Park's address in 1962 reflects this view:

> The economic, social and political goals we set after the revolution are: promotion of the public welfare, freedom from exploitation, and fair distribution of income among the people. It is obvious that these goals cannot be reached overnight. They are, nevertheless, the fundamental aims of the economic order towards which we must move. Before these goals can be achieved, we must see to it that after more than a decade of stagnation, our poor economic power is greatly strengthened and that the heretofore underdeveloped power of productivity is fully utilised. We must take a great leap forward toward economic growth.... It is urgently necessary to have an economic plan or a long-range development program through which reasonable allocation of all our resources is feasible. (quoted in Amsden 1987a: 49)

The above statement clearly confirms that, for Park, the state must lead and protect the economy for the sake of the nation's survival. As such, economic nationalism is closely bound up with the imperative of political survival. The Park regime continued throughout the 1960s and 1970s to exercise control over the entire economic growth process. Korea's strong and extensive economic nationalist tradition can be found in the state's "developmental alliance" forged with the *chaebol* (Dent 2000: 280–2). The state set industrial targets, directed lending, protection, and subsidies for a small number of big firms, and controlled foreign exchange to allow the state to select investment projects for the *chaebol* (D'Costa 1994: 55; Hall 2004: 79). The state also regulated financial capital flows through complete control over banks. Between 1961 and 1980, the state owned most of the important banks, including the Bank of Korea, five nationwide commercial banks, six special banks, and the two development banks (Korean Development Bank and Export-Import Bank) (Luedde-Neurath 1988: 76). State involvement in the financial sector in this period was all embracing, ranging from low-level personnel policy, salary reviews, and budgets, to setting ceilings for individual banks and controlling their operating funds and interest rates. Further, the Korean state controlled the financial system and monetary policy through the Ministry of Finance, which supervised the Bank of Korea through the Monetary Board, appointed all senior bank officials, and cleared major credit allocations (Eckert 1993: 107). In other words, the Korean state's autonomy and control over the economy embedded in its economic nationalism strategy was central to the nation's economic success that was achieved in a relatively short period of time.

Korea's economic nationalism during the high-growth decades (1960s and 1970s) can be found in the state's tight grip on the business sector. Using the corporate sector (*chaebol*) as the engine of rapid economic growth, the Park regime provided a variety of incentives to assist in the rapid expansion of national champions spearheaded by the *chaebol*. These incentives included cheap credit, suppression of labor unions, and the exclusion of foreign companies and imports that directly competed with domestic products (Kong 2000: 38–9). In the initial period of Korea's modern economic growth during the 1960s, the inflow of foreign capital was encouraged to make up for the shortage of domestic savings and foreign reserves. Song Byung-nak, a former technocrat under the Park Chung-hee regime, provides a succinct summary of the nature of *Chungkyung Yuchak* (state-*chaebol* tight coalition):

> Under the government export promotion strategy, "survival of the fittest" among competing firms was not determined in the marketplace, but through discretionary government actions. "Fitness" was judged in terms of the ability to expand exports, rather than based on profitability. If determined "unfit," firms were likely to face bankruptcy. Such firms were under constant threat of tax investigations and other punitive sanctions. On the other hand, firms that efficiently used their government-backed loans to expand exports were implicitly considered fit and favoured with even further support. (quoted in Hart-Landsberg, Jeong, and Westra 2007: 4)

Kim Woo-choong, former chairman of Daewoo group, reflects well the *chaebol* attitude: "The government tells you it is your duty and you have to do it, even if there is no profit" (quoted in Harris 1987: 151). However, the Korean state preferred foreign borrowing over inward FDI, which brought foreign resources under its control. The general fear of Korean industries being dominated by foreign entities, which was deeply rooted in Korea's recent history of Japanese colonization from 1910 to 1945, was too widespread inside Korea for the state to accommodate foreign companies. This fear of domination occurred despite Japanese economic nationalism being a role model for Korea (Hall 2004) and Korea relying on the use of Japanese technology, as in the steel industry (D'Costa 1994: 56–7).

A stock of hard-working, low-cost, and disciplined labor, reliance on foreign capital, the creation of *chaebol*, and the Korean state's nationalist economic policies have all contributed to Korea's remarkable export performance and state-led capital accumulation. Furthermore, lacking a significant division of labor, traditional Korean society was largely static, where communication and the flow of information were not extensive. Consequently, it was relatively easy for the central state to control the individual, and this, in turn, provided fertile ground for the maintenance of an authoritarian political system, which lasted for more than three decades. This notion of *Korea Inc.* continued to exist and even strengthen in the 1980s and 1990s. The Korean state has been relatively free from dominant social constituencies and has played a central role in the process of capital accumulation. The state took the position of both investor and financier from the beginning of the military-led Park Chung-hee regime in the early 1960s. This economic trajectory was facilitated by those who had vested interests in the continuation of a nationalist regime. These interests were provided with monopolies and other contracts and patronage. The Park regime furthered its objectives by securing national ownership, controlling strategic resources, and building an integrated industrial base such as steel and shipbuilding industries (D'Costa 1999; Shin and Ciccantell 2009). These industries were never intended to act as primary exporters of goods as an end in itself, but as a means of underpinning the ideological commitment to a self-sufficient national economy.

Thus, the Korean case departs from the dependency perspective, which argues that the state operates as an instrument of the bourgeoisie or its factions and represents their interests. The role of socio-political and institutional processes of capital accumulation and state intervention provide rather more plausible insights into the development of Korea's postwar industrial capitalism. Indeed, the notion and structure of *Korea Inc.* has been hailed by many neighboring Asian countries, such as Indonesia, Malaysia, and Thailand. As discussed below, however, such a statist regime was also one of the main triggering factors behind the Asian financial crisis in the late twentieth century (Krugman 1998).

7.3 *Segyehwa* (Globalization): A New Form of Economic Nationalism (1992–8)

With progressive Korean industrialization, the limits of industrial policy based on low labor costs have been brought into sharp relief. Other factors, such as labor and land costs, impeded export-led economic growth and brought about a strong tendency for Korean firms to become excessively dependent on Japan and the USA for their supply of critical components. For example, during the 1980s, Korean firms depended on Japanese corporations for 40–60% of their machines, 60% of their parts, and 50% of their licensed technology (Hart-Landsberg, Jeong, and Westra 2007: 9). Korea's lack of technological competitiveness is an inheritance from Korea's industrialization strategy of the 1960s and 1970s. Then, Korea's EOI policies (state-*chaebol* tight coalition) offered business conglomerates tax breaks and other financial incentives. Therefore privileges were granted to export industries in proportion to gross exports rather than being tied to value added. Export incentives were quite lucrative so there were natural tendencies for Korean firms to import parts then assemble them for re-export. In the 1970s, especially, there was little incentive for Korean businesses to develop products of their own.

This is the backdrop that helps explain why Korea experienced such difficulty in developing its own technology-intensive industries. But at the same time, because of the lack of local investment in research and development (R&D), outward FDI in low-labor-cost regions became the most attractive option for Korean firms. This strategy has enabled the maintenance of its comparative advantage and export market shares. These factors have been pivotal in developing a consensus in Korea that it ought to expand production in knowledge-intensive industries such as computers, pharmaceuticals, and atomic power, and reduce the importance of pollution-prone and labor-intensive industries such as chemicals and textiles. A consequence of this can be seen in the frequent and progressive relaxation of foreign exchange control and deregulation towards foreign investment laws since the early 1990s. This has been accelerated by President Kim Young-sam's globalization drive (*Segyehwa*), which puts a strong emphasis on introducing new technologies, which Korean companies are so far only able to procure from other countries. The Korean government's ambitious blueprint, issued in 1992, aimed to see Korea become one of the top seven technological powers in the world by 2000. To achieve this goal, the government had invested US$15.4 billion in high-tech industries by the end of 1996. Kim Young-sam's statement made at the 1995 New Year's press conference depicts the strong nationalist sentiment even when pursuing globalization:

> Globalization is the quickest way to build the Republic into a first-rate nation in the coming century. This is why I outlined a concept of *Segyehwa* last November (1994) and why the administration is now concentrating all its energies on this task with the aim of globalizing political, diplomatic, economic, social, educational, cultural, athletic and all other fields. Our perspective, attitude, institutions, and practices must all be elevated to global standard. Globalization cannot be achieved overnight, however. It will require hard work, great endurance and true courage. It is the only way for us to go. There is no other choice. Therefore, I set globalization as the foremost national goal for this year. (quoted in Park, Jang, and Lee 2007: 342)

Similar to Park Chung-hee's motto, "nation building through exports," Kim Young-sam's new growth strategy, "Segyehwa," is a state-enhancing, top-down strategic plan and, perhaps more importantly, a governing ideology which is the pinnacle of state-driven developmental nationalism. The 1993 "100 Day Plan for the New Economy" initiated by the Kim administration was regarded as revolutionary. Its main goal was to liberalize the restricted business areas such as agriculture, government procurement, retail financial services, and capital markets, in an effort to meet the membership criteria for joining the Organization for Economic Cooperation and Development, which Korea joined in October 1996. The plan was to initially increase the percentage of the domestic market open to foreign investment from 83% in 1993 to 93% in 1997, and then to 99.5% in 2000 (Cha 1994: 515–23). But it should be noted that keeping the basic national philosophy (i.e., socio-economic and political independence from foreign forces) unchanged, new growth strategies were only adjusted when structural problems in the economy—international and domestic—required the state to adopt more outward-looking policies in the name of economic pragmatism. This was designed to acquire technological know-how and investment from private and foreign capital. Such was the case when Kim Young-sam faced internal and external challenges. Of necessity, he opened the economy to foreign capitalists and followed policies towards a more market-oriented philosophy.

Does this new strategy oriented towards a neoliberal doctrine mean an end to economic nationalism? The Kim Young-sam regime made only limited progress with economic liberalization, aimed at dismantling the underpinning structure of the Korean political economy—"a network of power relationships that centre on the state-*Chaebol* nexus" (Dent 2000: 281). Instead, as Park, Jang, and Lee (2007) stated in their examination of how the Korean government had submissively managed economic globalization under the 1997 financial crisis, Korea's first experience of a globalization campaign accommodating principles of neoliberal global capitalism was largely resisted by the *chaebol* (Dent 2000: 275–302; 2003: 261–6). Samuel Kim calls Kim Young-sam's *Segyehwa* "a status drive and an easy and cheap way of projecting a new Korean identity" (Kim 2000: 3). More importantly, the *Chungkyung Yuchak,* which is the center of Korea's economic trajectory and economic nationalism, has proven difficult to relinquish. Barry Gills points out that Kim Young-sam's

> initial anti-*chaebol* (big deal) measures and attempts to dismantle vested interests and root out corrupt practices made part of the middle classes uneasy, reviving a conservative backlash against reform. More fundamentally, Kim Young-sam concluded that he could not conduct his economic policy without the cooperation of the *chaebol,* and thus turned away from the idea of a decisive break in the government-*chaebol* reliance. (quoted in Dent 2000: 281)

Some of the most conspicuous evidence of the continuing existence of economic nationalism can be found in Korea's move towards outward FDI (OFDI). One of the top-down and command-and-control reforms administered by Kim Young-sam's globalization drive was the frequent and progressive relaxation of foreign exchange controls and deregulation of OFDI laws from the early 1990s. Korean *chaebol* responded to those initiatives. In terms of cumulative total investment, Korean OFDI, particularly in the Asian developing countries, increased from US$5.4 billion involving 2,726 projects at the end of 1993 to US$10.22 billion with 5,327 projects at the end of 1995 (Bank of Korea 1993: 31; Bank of Korea 1996). In most Southeast Asian countries, since the early 1990s, Korea has been among the top ten investors. To the Korean state (the Kim Young-sam regime), "globalization" meant increasing exports and booming OFDI (Sachwald 2001). From the late 1980s onward there was a vast relocation of the export manufacturing base to avoid trade friction with trading partners caused by Korea's balance of payments surplus. Furthermore, because wages had risen so rapidly since the 1980s, Korean firms had invested overseas to better their competitive position. In particular, there has been an especially strong increase of Korean OFDI in labor-intensive industries, including textile, garments, and assembly of electronic products. From 1986 to 1991, there had been a rapid increase in OFDI because the Korean won was appreciating, trade pressures and friction were on the rise, and labor costs had jumped. Korean OFDI climbed to US$3,059 million in 1995, 27 times greater than the US$113 million in 1985. In particular, in 1995 Korean OFDI hit an all-time high of US$4,913 billion divided among 1,560 projects, a rise of 37% in volume and a 19.9% decline in the number of projects approved compared to 1994. On the basis of the cumulative total from 1968 to 1995, Korean OFDI worldwide stood at US$10,243 billion spread over 5,327 projects (*The Korea Times,* February 3, 1996). On the other hand, the total amount of FDI inflows accumulated over the previous 35-year period of 1962–96 was US$24.6 billion (Min 2006: 11). In other words, the term "Segyehwa" is not meant to be international "integration" but "Koreanization" of the international economy. However, this process of state-led *chaebol-based* "Koreanization" or "transnationalization of *Chaebol*" as a part of *Segyehwa* (Dent 2003: 263) became a major triggering factor behind Korea's unprecedented financial crisis in 1997 (Cho 2008: 83). Firstly, the *chaebol* and their subsidiaries had been major players in Korea's OFDI activities. By 1996, the top 30 *chaebol* owned 668 subsidiaries ranging across almost every industrial sector, from consumer goods, automobiles, finance, machinery, electronics, engineering, construction, and cosmetics, to insurance and securities. Among these 668 subsidiaries, 55 were controlled by Samsung, 46 by Hyundai, and 48 by LG (New Industry Management Academy 1997). A critical point is that the legacy of economic nationalism, or *Korea Inc.*, through state-capital collusion, was still prevalent during the Kim Young-sam era using the control of finance as a key policy tool. This enabled the state to have control over politics and led to the practice of favoring people and companies in regard to economic policies. A number of *chaebol* groups benefited from this tight alliance, especially when they needed financial help in expanding their industries overseas, including in European countries. Barry Gills' view on the Kim Young-sam's twin "Segyehwa" policy sums up the alliance:

> The imperative of supporting *Chaebol* global strategies proved stronger than that of economic liberalization, and that replacing statist, neo-mercantalist forms with 'competitive capitalism' in Korea's political economy was generally unworkable. (quoted in Dent 2000: 283)

On the other hand, the Korean state continuously showed xenophobic restriction on inflows of foreign direct investment. It is no wonder that in 1997, most of the top 30 *chaebol* were found to have piled up debts averaging about 4.5 times more than their assets. The debt-to-equity ratio averaged 449.4% in 1997. The top 30 industrial conglomerates accumulated a total debt of 249.67 trillion won (US$177 billion) (Gong 1999). It was inevitable that this debt problem would spill over into the banking and financial sectors and become one of the triggers behind the 1997 financial crisis.

Krugman (1998) argues that the financial crisis may have been only incidentally about currencies but was mainly about bad banking and its consequences. He further asserts that a pattern of close state–business–bank interactions gave birth to an intrusive government that encouraged business conglomerates to rely on debt financing through the government's system of preferential policy loans. Krugman has labeled this type of interplay a form of "crony capitalism" (Krugman 1998: 62–78). Weiss and Hobson (1998) argue that the 1997 meltdown of Asian currencies was fundamentally rooted in the vulnerability of state capacity to the strong winds of global finance. In other words, state power is the most critical variable in explaining both the sources of the crisis and its ensuing severity. Chang (1998) and Chang and Yoo (2000), in their study on the deep causes of the Korean financial crisis, show how the transitional (rather weakening) state capacity, especially the Kim Young-sam regime and its relationship with business and institutions, led to the crisis. Haggard, Pinkston, and Seo (1999) also argue that despite Korea's political tradition of strong presidents, the inconsistency between the government and the policy-making process under the Kim Young-sam administration led to the depth of the crisis. Chang (1998) saw the solution to the crisis, contrary to the International Monetary Fund's (IMF) bailout packages that break crony capitalism and reduce state power, in strengthening, not weakening, the "coordinating function" of the state. Lee and Kim (1998) provided a similar view, that cessation of state involvement in the Korean economy could hardly occur, even in the IMF-era brought about by the 1997 financial crisis.

7.4 The 1997 Financial Crisis: An End to Economic Nationalism?

When Kim Dae-jung took office as the head of state on February 25, 1998, the new administration inherited an economy that was shattered by currency attacks. The 1997 Asian financial crisis had brought dramatic changes to the Korean political economy. The new administration was also pressured to carry out massive structural reforms and economic liberalization as a condition of the US$58.4 billion financing package provided by the IMF. The conditions of the rescue package (a three-year standby agreement with the IMF approved on December 4, 1997) imposed by the IMF certainly demanded a fundamental and major overhaul of the state-driven Korean political economy. Korea was expected to move away from its industrial policies, its strong nationalist policy towards inflow of foreign capital, and weaken the dominance of the market by a tight cabal of *chaebols*. In other words, the IMF conditions were to uproot the tradition of Korea's economic trajectory embedded in economic nationalism. The Kim Dae-jung administration, "In keeping with the established ritual of newly incumbent Korean presidents, has shown a strong commitment in establishing neo-liberal governance by restructuring financial sectors, mostly banks and decoupling the state–*chaebol* nexus" (Dent 2003: 263). As Ha and Lee noted:

> The primary objective of government reform was to transform the state-led economic system into a market-friendly system. To this end, the administration undertook financial liberalization, corporate restructuring, labour market flexibility, and privatization. (Ha and Lee 2007: 896)

Ironically, this financial crisis prompting externally driven pressures by IMF rescue packages offered opportunities to implement major reforms, including hostile mergers and acquisitions (M&A), full opening of the domestic market to foreign products, and massive restructuring of financial institutions and the *chaebols*. Only after teetering on the brink of default in late December 1997 during the currency crisis did Korea realize that short-term borrowing carried substantial hazards and that FDI inflows could act as an important stabilizer against the risk of financial panic. The Korean government's adoption of sweeping measures to actively promote FDI can be best summed up with the enactment of the Foreign Investment Promotion Act (FIPA) of 1998. This landmark piece of legislation guarantees international remittances by foreign investors, legally and unconditionally, even under certain circumstances of exogenous shocks such as natural disasters and wars (Article 3). As Christopher Dent pointed out, the new government intended to "change the calculus of the state's relationship with transnational capital, essentially switching priorities from promoting *Chaebol* transnationalization to domestic economy transnationalization" (Dent 2003: 264). In other words, the aim of the reforms was to change the engine of the Korean economy from *chaebol* expansion to inward FDI. In contrast to the dwindling OFDI, FDI inflows began to surge from 1997 and maintained strong growth until 2002. FDI inflows in 1997 were valued at US$7 billion, more than double the previous year's figure. FDI inflows peaked in 1999 and 2000, reaching US$15.5 billion (11% of exports) and US$15.2 billion (8.8% of exports), respectively (Min 2006: 11). Of a total of 1,148 possible sectors for inward FDI, 1,117 sectors were completely opened and 18 sectors were partially opened to foreign investors at the end of 1998 (Min 2006: 9). This stark change was a direct consequence of the state's curtailment of the Kim Young-sam administration's OFDI strategy (Dent 2003: 264).

This new growth strategy based on inward FDI-led globalization does not mean an end to Korea's rapid economic trajectory embedded in strong economic nationalism. The sweeping and sudden departure from the previous Kim Young-sam regime's OFDI-led globalization strategy may be seen as the retreat of the state. One would also expect the result of the financial crisis-driven reforms to be the eventual disintegration of the state and its inevitable declining capacity. However, the new Kim Dae-jung government's "big deals," such as restructuring of banking sectors and of major conglomerates, were carried out under state leadership. As Samuel Kim writes, "President Kim Dae-jung's espousal of participatory democracy and a liberal market economy were top-down, command-and-control reform plans. Instead of using market principles, the government resorted to command-and-control-style arm-twisting to get the top 5 *Chaebol* to follow state guidelines" (Kim 2000: 3). In their study of the political economy of financial liberalization in Korea during the financial crisis, Kalinowski and Cho (2009) show that the stabilization of the Korean financial sector during the financial crisis could not be attributed to financial liberalization but was accomplished by "massive state intervention" (Kalinowski and Cho 2009: 229). Even the neoliberal "economic activities are still subordinate to the goal of state building and the interests of the state" (Hall 2004: 84). As Shin correctly addresses, the state-driven economic nationalism should not be treated as a constraint or paradox but as a motivation and paradigm of the Korean political economy (Shin 2003). Kim Dae-jung's "liberal motivation for liberalization," as was the case (*Segyehwa*) for the Kim Young-sam regime, had been instrumental, led by developmental and neo-mercantilist policies.

As Cho points out, "although the government followed the free market principles recommended by the IMF, it (the state) still held its initiative in a new coordination role, such as coordinating relations between new economic actors, making a new regulatory rule and channeling certain economic actors to new areas" (Cho 2008: 84). Woo-Cumings (2003) writes that this type of process of reform, or strong "administrative guidance," is another form of top-down state intervention. Moon and Lim (2003) see this as "managerial globalization," and the state's conscious strategic response to external stimuli (Moon and Lim 2003: 63). Weiss also calls it a "transformative capacity of the state," which means the "ability (power) of the state to coordinate industrial change to meet the changing context of international competition" (Weiss 1998: 7; 2003: 293–317). Korea's new inward FDI-led globalization strategy was not meant to influence the Korean state's traditional role in which "[it] still plays a strategic role in taming domestic and international market forces and harnessing them to a national economic interest" (White and Wade 1988: 1). Rather, it meant the creation of a "neo-developmental" paradigm "under which the relationship of business and the government became a collaborative symbiosis featuring a greater privatization of state-owned enterprises" (Cho 2008: 84).

7.5 Back to Nationalism as a "Hegemonic Ideology" (2003–8)

The Roh Moo-hyun administration (February 2003–February 2008) inherited Kim Dae-jung's achievements on the external front. At the beginning, it offered a glimpse of what Korea could do better externally through his "globalization efforts." It aimed at transforming the nation into an information and knowledge superpower, a process that was initiated by his predecessor, with an emphasis on regionalism. For example, Korea was envisioned as an international logistics, financial, and research and development hub of Northeast Asia. In his inaugural address on February 23, 2003, Roh states:

> In this new age, our future can no longer be confined to the Korean peninsula. The Age of Northeast Asia is fast approaching. Northeast Asia, which used to be on the periphery of the modern world, is now emerging as a new source of energy in the global economy. Korea is being equipped with all the basic requirements necessary to lead the Age of Northeast Asia in the 21st century. Korea is well poised to emerge as an international logistics and financial hub in Northeast Asia. (quoted in Kim 2007: 20)

Roh's predecessors all had political slogans such as Park Chung-hee's "nation building through exports," Kim Young-sam's "Segyehwa," and Kim Dae-jung's "information and knowledge superpower." Roh adopted the slogan, "logistical and financial hub of Northeast Asia" as a governing nationalistic ideology. As Samuel Kim correctly views it, all these presidents saw "no contradictions between (instrumental) nationalism and (instrumental) globalization; rather they all viewed globalization as the most expeditious way of developing a national identity of Korea as an advanced world-class nation state" (Kim 2007: 25).

The Roh Moo-hyun regime, which came into power leaning towards egalitarianism, often defied the market dictates and was lukewarm about extending the potential benefits of globalization. However, the Roh regime paid more attention to distributional targets than to the efficiency gains that a vibrant and dynamic economy needs so much. Furthermore, under the Roh administration, the National Assembly, the judiciary, the tax authority, several interest groups, and the Korean media added fuel to the rise of traditional doctrines of economic nationalism by showing fear of the growing foreign presence in Korea. In fact, there were a number of foreign business grievance cases, which cast serious doubts on the Roh regime's announced commitment to inward FDI liberalization and its adherence to sustained globalization (Fairclough 2005; Graham 2005). Equally important, the Korean mentality and consciousness towards foreign countries and economic globalization needs to be noted. Despite its remarkable economic transformation in the late twentieth century, from a predominantly agricultural society into an industrial one, a corresponding change in people's consciousness and perception is yet to materialize. The recent increase in Korea's sentiment against foreign capital can be attributed to the growing presence of foreign-controlled banks, the entry of foreign equity funds, and a series of anti-globalization/liberalism protests in 2009 against a free trade agreement with the USA and imports of US beef. These lead to the question of whether Korea is reverting to the Korea of old, that is, to a country dictated by isolationism, self-sufficiency, and a closed mind-set (Fairclough 2005; Noland 2005). In this sense, Korea's stance toward foreign investment is "at best ambivalent" (Klingner and Kim 2007: 7). A comment by an official from the Korean Ministry of Foreign Affairs and Trade reflects this sentiment: "selling Daewoo to Ford, GM or any other foreign companies to many Koreans equates to selling your country" (quoted in Dent 2003: 265).

There is, however, a more fundamental issue to be addressed, that being the concept of globalization as perceived by the three previous regimes of Kim Young-sam, Kim Dae-jung, and Roh Moo-hyun. The Kim Young-sam regime never had a neoliberal globalization strategy, though it created and initiated the term *Segyehwa*. The Kim Dae-jung administration encouraged FDI inflows only to rescue an ailing economy. In addition, Kim's external reforms—aimed at attracting foreign capital by guaranteeing market predictability, financial transparency, and a flexible labor market—were mandated by the IMF, and were not of his own initiative (Cho 2008: 84). So he did not have a consciously drawn neoliberal globalization strategy. Roh had, at most, globalization efforts taking the form of a vision of a Northeast Asia hub, but he failed to push it forward along the road to globalization. This is because, as indicated earlier, Korea's economic policies used to be state driven and nationalistic, and Korea, like Japan, has long spurned and minimized foreign competition in the local market. Hence Korea's industrialization strategy has worked only in favor of the *chaebol*.

7.6 Conclusion

This chapter conducted a survey of Korea's political economy through the four different regimes of the Park Chung-hee to the Roh Moo-hyun administrations. An important point emerges from this survey. The significant increase of foreign capital in Korea from the late 1980s has been closely related to the Korean state's shift in economic policies, particularly towards foreign capital. Various structural changes domestically and internationally resulted in changes in the Korean regimes' economic policy (e.g., Kim Young-sam's *Segyehwa* and Kim Dae-jung's inward FDI-led globalization) from one that was strongly nationalist to one more open to foreign investment, which might seem to be an erosion of structural power of the state. This should, however, be understood as a form of restructuring to retain state power and control over international capital flows with an eye to strengthening financial capitalists.

The above observation presents an important insight into different sets of dynamics in decision making. It also suggests that without a political and institutional analysis of the evolution in the changing nature of a state's economic policies, there is no way of understanding the current pattern of foreign investment in Korea. This suggests a very different—indeed a much more appealing—consideration from theories of neoclassical economics, which emphasize factor endowments. The Korean case clearly shows that structural and institutional factors such as state–capital relationships affected by internal and external factors in the course of capitalist industrialization did not seem to influence Korea's development trajectory but served to strengthen state capacity and its pursuit of economic nationalism. Various economic activities adopted over the process of capitalist industrialization, whether neoliberal or neo-mercantilist, have been found to be subordinate to the goal of state building and the interests of the state. This study revealed that the Korean regimes' motivation to free the economy was directed and promoted by developmental and neo-mercantilist policies. The neoliberal nature of globalization entailing an open and expanding market in Korea in the late twentieth century has not yet brought about political, institutional, and sociocultural transformations corresponding to the shift in Korea's developmental growth paradigm nor has it weakened the state-driven economic trajectory. The Korean state still continues to manage the economy as part of a nationalist project. The Korean regimes' "liberal motivation for liberalization" in the late twentieth century has been directed and promoted by developmental and neo-mercantilist policies. Thus, vestiges of the collectivist nature of economic nationalism have not disappeared and hence Korean development should be interpreted as a political phenomenon rather than simply an anti-neoliberalism stance.

Notes

1. The author thanks the International Graduate School of Business, Centre for Asian Business, and Division of Business at the University of South Australia, and Korea Foundation for research support. The author would also like to thank Anthony D'Costa for his constructive comments on earlier drafts of the chapter.
2. Choi's definition of "authoritarian developmentalism" provides a useful tool to understand the notion of *Korea Inc*. It features the following characteristics: "consolidation of a stable political base through coercive force; accelerated industrialization through tightly staged authoritarian planning with a heavy reliance on foreign capital; and the creation of a political of civilian bureaucrats, technocrats, and industrialists centred on military elites" (Choi 1993: 26).
3. A good conceptual and theoretical discussion on economic nationalism can be found in Baughn and Yaprak (1996: 759–78); Crane (1998: 55–75); Dent (2000: 275–302); Pickel (2003: 105–27); and Hall (2004: 79–99). We follow Dent's interpretation of the term, "economic nationalism" as the "proclivity of the state, firms and individuals for economic actions, decisions or alliance-formation that seek to advance the nation's international position at the potential expense of foreign national or international interests" (Dent 2000: 282). Korean economic nationalism, as Cho Younghan correctly states, underscores "national growth and modernization, processes in which the nation-state plays a central role in allocating economic

elements to maximize their efficiency; it particularly highlights the increasing amounts of export/trade and the progress of industrialization" (Cho 2008: 85).

4. The chapter adopts Held's definition of globalization as "a process (or set of processes) which embodies a transformation in the spatial organization of social relations and transactions—assessed in terms of their extensity, intensity, velocity and impact—generating transcontinental or interregional flows and networks of activity, interaction, and the exercise of power" (quoted in Beeson 2000: 337).

References

Amsden, A.H. (1987a). *Asia's Next Giant: South Korea and Late Industrialization*. New York: Oxford University Press.

Amsden, A.H. (1987b). *Republic of Korea—Country Study*. Helsinki: World Institute for Development Economics Research of the United Nations University.

Amsden, A.H. (1992). "A Theory of Government Intervention in Late Industrialization," in L. Putterman and D. Rueschemeyer (eds.), *State and Market in Development: Synergy or Rivalry?*, 53–84. Boulder and London: Lynne Rienner Publishers.

Amsden, A.H. (1994). "Why Isn't the Whole World Experimenting with the East Asian Model to Develop? Review of The East Asian Miracle." *World Development*, 22 (4): 627–33.

Bank of Korea. (1993). *The Current Development of Korean FDI by Year*. Seoul: Bank of Korea.

Bank of Korea. (1996). *Economic Statistics Yearbook 1996*. Seoul: Bank of Korea.

Baughn, C. and Yaprak, A. (1996). "Economic Nationalism: Conceptual and Empirical Development." *Political Psychology*, 17 (4): 759–78.

Beeson, M. (2000). "Mahathir and the Markets: Globalization and the Pursuit of Economic Autonomy in Malaysia." *Pacific Affairs*, 73 (3): 335–51.

Bello, W. and Rosenfeld, S. (1990). *Dragons in Distress: Asia's Miracle Economies in Crisis*. San Francisco: Institute for Food and Development Policy.

Cha, D.-S. (1994). "Korea's New Economy Plan and Recent Economic Reform." *Journal of Asian Economics*, 5 (4): 515–23.

Chang, H. (1998). "South Korea: The Misunderstood Crisis," in K.S. Jomo (ed.), *Tigers in Trouble*, 223–31. London: Zed Books.

Chang, H. and Yoo, C. (2000). "The Triumph of the Rentiers?" *Challenge*, 43 (1): 105–24.

Cho, Y. (2008). "The National Crisis and De/Reconstructing Nationalism in South Korea during the IMF Intervention." *Inter-Asia Cultural Studies*, 9 (1): 82–96.

Choi, J. (1993). *Political Cleavages in South Korea*. Ithaca: Cornell University Press.

Chu, Y.-H. (1989). "State Structure and Economic Adjustment of the East Asian Newly Industrializing Countries." *International Organization*, 43 (4): 647–72.

Crane, G. T. (1998). "Economic Nationalism: Bringing the Nation Back in." *Millennium: Journal of International Studies*, 27 (1): 55–75.

D'Costa, A.P. (1999). *The Global Restructuring of the Steel Industry: Innovations, Institutions and Industrial Change*. London: Routledge.

D'Costa, A.P. (1994). "State, Steel and Strength: Structural Competitiveness and Development in South Korea." *The Journal of Development Studies*, 31 (1): 44–81.

Dent, C.M. (2000). "What Difference a Crisis? Continuity and Change in South Korea's Foreign Economic Policy." *Journal of the Asia Pacific Economy*, 5 (3): 275–302.

Dent, C.M. (2003). "Transnational Capital, the State and Foreign Economic Policy: Singapore, South Korea and Taiwan." *Review of International Political Economy*, 10 (2): 246–77.

Deyo, F.C. (1987). *The Political Economy of the New Asian Industrialism*. Ithaca: Cornell University Press.

Eckert, C.J. (1993). "The South Korean Bourgeoisie: A Class in Search of Hegemony," in H. Koo (ed.), *State and Society in Contemporary Korea*, 95–130. Ithaca and London: Cornell University Press.

Fairclough, G. (2005). "Free-market Push Divides Korea." *The Wall Street Journal*, November 24.

Gong, B.H. (1999). "The *Chaebol*—Myth and Reality." *Business Korea*, 16 (10): 34–8.

Graham, E. (2005). "South Korea Must End Its Corporate Xenophobia." *Financial Times*, August 4.

Ha, Y.-C. and Lee, W.H. (2007). "The Politics of Economic Reform in South Korea: Crony Capitalism after Ten Years." *Asian Survey*, 47 (6): 894–914.

Haggard, S. (2000). *The Political Economy of the Asian Financial Crisis*. Washington, DC: Institute for International Economics.

Haggard, S. and Moon, C. (1990). "Institutions and Economic Policy: Theory and a Korean Case Study." *World Politics*, 42 (2): 210–35.

Haggard, S. and Moon, C.-I. (1983). "The South Korean State in the International Economy: Liberal, Dependent, or Mercantile?" in J.J. Ruggie (ed.), *The Antinomies of Interdependence*, 131–90. New York: Columbia University Press.

Haggard, S., Pinkston, D., and Seo, J. (1999). "Reforming Korea Inc.: The Politics of Structural Adjustment under Kim Dae Jung." *Asian Perspective*, 23 (3): 201–35.

Hall, D. (2004). "Japanese Spirit, Western Economics: The Continuing Salience of Economic Nationalism in Japan." *New Political Economy*, 9 (1): 79–99.

Harris, N. (1987). *The End of the Third World: Newly Industrializing Countries and the Decline of an Ideology*. London: I. B. Tauris.

Hart-Landsberg, M., Jeong, S., and Westra, R. (2007). *Marxist Perspectives on South Korea in the Global Economy*. Aldershot, UK: Ashgate.

Jones, L. and Sakong I. (1980). *Government, Business, and Entrepreneurship in Economic Development: the Korean Case*. Cambridge, Mass.: Harvard University Council on East Asian Studies.

KABC (Korea Associates Business Consultancy). (2004). *Profitability of Foreign Companies in Korea: Another Reason to Invest*. Seoul: Korea Associates Business Consultancy.

Kalinowski, T. and Cho, H. (2009). "The Political Economy of Financial Liberalization in South Korea: State, Big Business, and Foreign Investors." *Asian Survey*, 49 (2): 221–42.

Kim, S.S. (2000). "Korea and Globalization (*Segyehwa*): A Framework for Analysis," in S.S. Kim (ed.), *Korea's Globalization*, 1–28. Cambridge and New York: Cambridge University Press.

Kim, S.S. (2007). "Nationalism and Globalization in South Korea's Foreign Policy," *New Asia*, 14 (3): 5–48.

Klingner, B. and Kim, B. (2007). "Economic Lethargy: South Korea Needs a Second Wave of Reforms." *Backgrounder*, 2090: 1–13.

Kong, T.Y. (2000). *The Politics of Economic Reform in South Korea: Fragile Miracle*. London and New York: Routledge.

Krueger, A. (1982). "Newly Industrializing Economies." *Economic Impact*, 40 (4): 26–32.

Krueger, A. (1990). "Government Failures in Development." *Journal of Economic Perspectives*, 4 (3): 9–23.

Krugman, P. (1998). "Saving Asia: It's Time to Get Radical." *Fortune*, 7 (September): 75–80.

Kuznets, P. (1985). "Government and Economic Strategy in Contemporary South Korea," *Pacific Affairs*, 58 (1): 44–67.

Lee, S. and Hewison, K. (2010). "Introduction: South Korea and the Antinomies of Neo-Liberal Globalisation." *Journal of Contemporary Asia*, 40 (2): 181–7.

Lee, Y. and Kim, H. (1998). "The Dilemma of Liberalization: Financial Crisis and the Transformation of Capitalism in South Korea." Conference "From Miracle to Meltdown: the End of Asian Capitalism," Perth, Australia, August 20–22.

Lim, H. (2010). "The Transformation of the Developmental State and Economic Reform in Korea." *Journal of Contemporary Asia*, 40 (2): 188–210.

Little, I. (1982). *Economic Development: Theory, Policy and International Relations*. New York: Basic Books.

Luedde-Neurath, R. (1988). "State Intervention and Export-Oriented Development in South Korea," in G. White (ed.), *Developmental States in East Asia*, 68–112. London: Macmillan Press.

Min, B.S. (2006). "Trade and Foreign Direct Investment Patterns in the Republic of Korea in the Aftermath of the 1997 Asian Financial Crisis." *Asia-Pacific Trade and Investment Review*, 2 (1): 3–24.

Moon, C.-I. (1988). "The Demise of a Developmentalist State? Neoconservative Reforms and Political Consequences in South Korea." *Journal of Developing Societies*, 4: 67–84.

Moon, C.-I. and Lim, S.H. (2003). "Weaving Through Paradoxes: Democratization, Globalization, and Environment Politics in South Korea." *East Asia Review*, 15 (2): 43–70.

New Industry Management Academy (NIMA). (1997). *The Analysis of Financial Affairs of the Top Thirty* Chaebol. Seoul: NIMA.

Noland, M. (2005). "Foreign Investors are a Progressive Force." *Korea Times*, September 22.

Park, G., Jang, Y., and Lee, H. (2007). "The Interplay between Globalness and Localness: Korea's Globalization Revisited." *International Journal of Comparative Sociology*, 48 (4): 337–53.

Pickel, A. (2003). "Explaining, and Explaining with, Economic Nationalism." *Nations and Nationalism*, 9 (1): 105–27.

Riedel, J. (1988). "Economic Development in East Asia: Doing What Comes Naturally?" in H. Hughes (ed.), *Achieving Industrialization in East Asia*, 1–38. Cambridge: Cambridge University Press.

Sachwald, F. (ed.) (2001). *Going Multinational: The Korean Experience of Direct Investment.* London: Routledge.

Shin, G. (2003). *The Paradox of Korean Globalization.* Stanford: The Asia-Pacific Research Center, Stanford University.

Shin, K. and Ciccantell, P.S. (2009). "The Steel and Shipbuilding Industries of South Korea: Rising East Asia and Globalization." *Journal of World-System Research,* 15 (2): 167–92.

Streeten, P. (1993). "Markets and States: Against Minimalism." *World Development,* 21 (8): 1281–98.

Wade, R. (1992). "Review Article: East Asia's Economic Success–Conflicting Perspectives, Partial Insights, Shaky Evidence." *World Politics,* 44 (2): 270–320.

Wade, R. (1998). "The Asian Debt-and-Development Crisis of 1997–? Causes and Consequences." *World Development,* 26 (8): 1535–53.

Wade, R. (1988a). "State Intervention in Outward-Oriented Development: Neo-Classical Theory and Taiwanese Practice," in G. White (ed.), *Developmental States in East Asia,* 30–67. London: Macmillan Press.

Wade, R. (1988b). "The Role of Government in Overcoming Market Failure: Taiwan, Republic of Korea and Japan," in H. Hughes (ed.), *Achieving Industrialization in East Asia,* 129–63. Cambridge: Cambridge University Press.

Weiss, L. (2003). "Is the State Being 'Transformed' by Globalization?" in L. Weiss (ed.), *States in the Global Economy: Bringing Domestic Institutions Back In,* 293–317. Cambridge: Cambridge University Press.

Weiss, L. (1998). *The Myth of the Powerless State.* Ithaca: Cornell University Press and Cambridge: Polity Press.

Weiss, L. and Hobson, J. (1998). "State Power and Economic Strength: Revisited: What's so Special about the Asian Crisis?" Conference "From Miracle to Meltdown: the End of Asian Capitalism," Perth, Australia, August 20–22.

Westphal, L. (1990). "Industrial Policy in an Export-Propelled Economy: Lessons from South Korea's Experience." *Journal of Economic Perspectives,* 4 (3): 41–59.

Westphal, L. (1978). "The Republic of Korea's Experience with Export-Led Industrial Development." *World Development,* 6 (3): 347–82.

White, G. and Wade, R. (1988). "Developmental States and Markets in East Asia: An Introduction," in G. White (ed.), *Developmental States in East Asia,* 1–29. London: Macmillan Press.

Woo, J. (1991). *Race to the Swift: State and Finance in Korean Industrialization.* New York: Columbia University Press.

Woo-Cumings, M. (2003). "Diverse Paths Towards 'The Right Institutions': Law, the State, and Economic Reform in East Asia," in L. Weiss (ed.), *States in the Global Economy: Bringing Domestic Institutions Back In,* 200–24. Cambridge: Cambridge University Press.

Yoon, Y. (1995). "Globalization: Toward a New Nationalism in Korea." *Korea Focus,* 3 (1): 13–28.

8

Disciplining globalization for local purposes? The peculiarity of contending Singaporean economic nationalisms

Alan Chong

8.1 Introduction

It is almost axiomatic in the mainstream literature on capitalism that economic nationalism is undesirable on the grounds of advancing scientific, sustainable, wealth-generating policy. Market forces are thought to weed out inefficiencies in production and consumption as if by the force of nature. The Singaporean experience, like that of so many late-developing states, sought hybrid responses to the theoretical challenges posed by such statements of free enterprise orthodoxy.[1] Independent Singapore's first finance minister, Goh Keng Swee, was mindful of the imputed laws of capitalist markets when he articulated the view that while foreign enterprises would generate "surplus value," in the Marxist sense,

> ... it would be wrong to conclude that the whole benefit of these activities accrued to foreigners, though they were undoubtedly the principal beneficiaries. Apart from workers engaged in these enterprises, there was often a substantial spill over to local entrepreneurs and others who engaged in similar activities. For instance, rubber estates in Malaysia were introduced by foreign enterprises. In the course of time, local residents entered the field; these were not all capitalists. The peasant population also benefited, growing rubber in smallholdings as a supplement to their traditional activity. (Goh 1995a: 6)

Although this statement was made in 1971 at the height of the Cold War and under the extended drama of decolonization, there was no opprobrium attached to mixing capitalist and Marxist terminology to sketch a unique position. Interestingly, right from its inception, the ruling People's Action Party (PAP) government placed tremendous faith in human ingenuity in imitating success and exploiting ancillary opportunities that might open up alongside the mainstream patterns of dependency between developing and developed economies. Singaporean economic nationalism has been enunciated *officially* as the pragmatic blending of social, political, and economic inspirations for the purpose of building a sustainable globalized economy in order to achieve Singaporean socio-political purposes as defined by its ruling government. In operational terms, economic nationalism meant disciplining labor attitudes to aid the purpose of collective economic improvement. However, in the early 2000s, an *unofficial* version of Singaporean economic nationalism sprouted from the grassroots sentiments of ordinary citizens. This has manifested through mild expressions of xenophobia and complaints about eroding welfare when foreigners appear to claim the larger share of benefits accruing from the openness of the Singaporean economy.

The author of a recent volume treating economic nationalism points out that extra-economic factors are of marginal relevance in the hitherto dominant "'economistic' conception of economic nationalism" (Pickel 2005: 3–4). For economists trained in rational choice approaches, nationalism belongs to the historical, political, and cultural realms that lie beyond their discipline's worldview. Studies of the role of government in economics have suggested that ideology motivates the governing of economic policy but can also serve as an oppressive tool contrary to the public interest (Samuels 1989). Furthermore, nationalism allied to economic matters precipitates inefficiencies that distort the operation of market prices. During the Asian financial crisis of 1997–8, the International Monetary Fund (IMF) and World Bank indirectly fingered nationalism as the legitimizing cloak for nepotistic banking and corporate practices. At another extreme, economic nationalism is contrasted to economic liberalism. For their part, scholars of nationalism rarely are interested in the economy as an extension of the explanation of the origins and manifestation of the "we-feeling" animating nation-building (Pickel 2005: 3–4). There are of course notable exceptions in the works of Ernest Gellner (1997) and Eric Hobsbawm (1997) where nationalism and capitalist economic systems theoretically developed a mutually reinforcing existence. In some ways, some might venture that the initial parts of Karl Marx's call for worker revolutions everywhere represented a clear parallel between nationalistic awakening and the augmentation of productive material power. Yet, in many developing regions, national governments have been trying to defy these dimensions of disconnection between nationalism and economic policy (Ohlin 1992). One might recall Mao Zedong's famous admonition to communist cadres everywhere: politics is always in command.

This chapter argues that official politics is attempting to only minimally command but always serve borderless capitalism in a joint mission with foreign investors of furthering the local citizens' prosperity at home and abroad. As a result, Singapore is incurring some painfully ironic consequences in the form of local antagonisms over living space, the socio-economic maladjustments from foreign workers' presence, the compulsion to host major economic conferences, which are perceived to be examples of trouble-free globalization, and the "revanchist economic nationalism" abroad plaguing Singapore's sovereign wealth funds and government-linked companies as they invest abroad. These outcomes can be termed the four stresses of globalization upon Singapore's economy. Before a critical scrutiny of both official and unofficial Singaporean economic nationalism can begin, Singapore's chameleon-like developmental discourse anchored around the idea of a self-synthesized developmental state needs to be appreciated. The first section will survey official Singaporean economic thought on the subject of rendering hospitality to capitalist globalization, given the hegemonic features of the dominant party democracy in the domestic realm. Singapore has been governed continuously by the PAP since independence. Its electoral mandates have regularly ranged between 60% and 84% of the popular vote and the past 52 years in power have allowed the Party's tight-knit leadership to plan and budget for long-term policy stability and feedback. This "single dominant party" outcome of Singaporean politics has been sufficiently entrenched for most outside observers to argue that macroeconomic policies can be said to have been husbanded by a small elite at the summit of a pyramidal political system with negligible opposition political parties. The second section will then examine how globalization brought in its train significant economic challenges with social and political fallout. These are the issues stemming from citizen and governmental experiences with the borderless economy mentioned above. These are the foundations of the unofficial economic nationalism, which is skeptical of untrammeled globalization. The final section will conclude with a restatement of the peculiarity of Singaporean economic nationalism in terms of a contested celebration of mercantilism with a globalist face.

8.2 Singapore's Chameleon-like Developmental Discourse

The Singaporean case is worthy of study for its distinctiveness in bending globalization to the service of official economic nationalism.[2] It is also worthy of study for its affliction by the ills of embracing globalization, such as the uncertainties that plague relations with foreign capital, the social fallout from allowing the mass entry of foreign labor of varying skill levels, the political costs of competition between locals and foreigners in the housing market, the nationalist agendas of its "globalizing" government-linked companies, and the local costs involved in demonstrating globalist credentials in hosting international conferences with neoliberal agendas. If there is any remaining statistical doubt about the value of Singapore as a poster child for the good and bad of globalization, it should be noted that A.T. Kearney and *Foreign Policy* magazine have consistently ranked Singapore amongst the top five most globalized nation-states in their Globalization Index between 2001 and 2007. In their final ranking in 2007, Singapore remained at number one on the basis of its high scores in the "four key components of global integration, incorporating measures such as trade and investment flows, movement of people across borders, volume of international telephone calls, internet usage, and participation in international organizations."[3] One could contest the legitimacy of these measures in their minutiae, but these are broadly relevant in reflecting the globalizing reality facing national economies today. In 2011, Singapore was rated by the World Bank as the world's easiest place to do business, while other economic intelligence agencies rated the Republic the best in labor–employer relations, and seventh in the world—and third in Asia—for possessing the most motivated workforce (Economic Development Board 2011).

The PAP strategy has been to frame objectives within socialist discourse while implementing a holistic economic strategy hospitable to foreign companies. On the occasion of the PAP's 25th anniversary in 1979, the then minister for trade and industry, Goh Chok Tong, explained the social objectives of the Party in the period 1959–65 in typical nationalistic fashion: the PAP wished to guarantee all citizens their right to employment and correspondingly prevent them from suffering "the privations and degradations that go with unemployment"; additionally, the Party would provide for the sick and those disabled through industrial injuries. There was no philosophy of primarily engaging external investors as a definite article of faith. The focus was "systematic industrialization" to alleviate unemployment. To a large extent this meant "import substitution was used as a device to attract investment, and pioneer tax incentives were given to encourage the establishment of industries new to Singapore" (Goh 1979: 65). The operating principle in those first five years of independence seemed to be "whatever works" to reduce unemployment. Even the prime minister at the time, Lee Kuan Yew, admitted scrambling for all sorts of quick solutions for an initially two-million-strong domestic market afflicted by high unemployment:

> ... we protected locally assembled cars, refrigerators, air-conditioners, radios, television sets and tape-recorders, in the hope that they would be partly manufactured locally. We encouraged our own businessmen who set up small factories to

> manufacture vegetable oils, cosmetics, mosquito coils, hair cream, joss paper and even mothballs! And we were able to attract Hong Kong and Taiwanese investors to build factories for toys, textiles and garments... It was an unpromising start. The Jurong industrial estate in the west of Singapore was empty in spite of the vast sums we had spent on infrastructure. (Lee 2000: 68)

The impending loss of the British naval and air bases following London's "East of Suez" strategic withdrawal between 1968 and 1971 heightened economic anxiety. Furthermore, neighboring Indonesia and Malaysia pursued nationalistic policies of diverting trade from Singapore's ports and were ostensibly trying to develop those very industries Singapore was angling for. Singapore's ejection from its brief and troubled federation with Malaysia between 1963 and 1965 complicated its import substitution industrialization (ISI) strategy.

Between 1961 and 1967, a switch towards globalization-friendly economic nationalism was inspired by two intellectual sources. The first was the influence of Dutch economic adviser, Albert Winsemius, who headed the UN Development Programme (UNDP) mission to Singapore during several visits in the early 1960s. According to Lee's account, Winsemius made an impression on the PAP leaders by encouraging them to defy communist solutions to Singapore's economic woes even when the mood of national liberation throughout the developing world encouraged it. More importantly, Winsemius persuaded Lee and his colleagues to retain the statue of Singapore's British colonial founder, Sir Thomas Stamford Raffles, for symbolic purposes. It would signal a warm welcome for technical, managerial, and entrepreneurial expertise from the primarily Western, developed states. In Lee's words, "investors wanted to see what a new socialist government in Singapore was going to do to the statue of Raffles. Letting it remain would be a symbol of public acceptance of the British heritage and could have a positive effect" (Lee 2000: 67). Lee went on to reflect personally upon what scholars would today term the human flows of globalization: "I had not looked at it that way, but was quite happy to leave this monument because he was the founder of modern Singapore. If Raffles had not come here in 1819 to establish a trading post, my great-grandfather would not have migrated to Singapore from *Dapu* county in Guangdong province, southeast China" (Lee 2000: 67). For the then finance minister, Goh Keng Swee, Winsemius left a deeply positive impression for having proposed an investment promotion agency for the dedicated purpose of attracting industrial investors to Singapore. "Singapore Inc." was to be marketed by the new Economic Development Board as a can-do site for foreign businessmen scouting for the equivalent of greenfield opportunities in Asia (Tan 2007: 90–2).

The other main influence came during Lee Kuan Yew's "sabbatical" at the Kennedy School of Government in Harvard University in the autumn of 1968.

On this occasion, Lee met with one of the leading scholars in political economy, Raymond Vernon. According to his account, Vernon educated him on the factors affecting profitability in any industry. Technology, industry, and wage-associated costs were significant in determining investment receptivity and corporate decision-making on locating factories. Lee figured out that Hong Kong, Taiwanese, and South Korean entrepreneurs were successful in responding to market shifts by changing product lines in the textile and garment industry in tune with the tastes of buyers in New York and other First World cities. Under Vernon's tutelage, Lee developed an appreciation that "reliable and cheap air and sea transport made it possible to move industries into new countries, provided their people were disciplined and trained to work the machines, and there was a stable and efficient government to facilitate the process for foreign entrepreneurs" (Lee 2000: 74).

Since the mid-1960s, the government of Singapore has systematically rolled out the red carpet for the wealthy foreign investor. It reflected the belief that foreign capital would make Singapore a thriving economic engine linked integrally to the world. To the PAP, it was never a case of placing the economy in the tow of foreign businesses within a purely capitalist frame. It was a courtship of foreign capital under the logic of a modern, rational, and open competitive system. Goh Keng Swee spelled it out clearly in a speech to the Singapore International Chamber of Commerce in 1968 where he noted that his country's economic nationalism divorced political anti-British sentiment from pragmatic hospitality to investments from all ideological directions (Goh 1995b: 115–16). Singapore would fashion itself as an iconic global city connected by telecommunications and transportation technologies to its world hinterland (Rajaratnam 1987; Goh 1995b: 230).

Furthermore, academic proponents of capitalist globalization such as Michael Porter and Joseph Nye have also been officially co-opted into the discourse of various ministries and government-linked institutes. A course conducted in 2005 by the International Trade Institute of Singapore for foreign participants under the ongoing collaboration protocols of the Singapore-Commonwealth Third Country Training Programme is, for instance, titled "Small and Medium Enterprises Cluster Initiatives to Enhance Competitiveness in the Commonwealth Countries." Its course content amplifies the technicalities of dependent capitalist strategy developed by Harvard University's Michael Porter in co-locating compatible business firms in a geographical cluster (Singapore Cooperation Programme 2011). In 2003, a government minister openly lauded Porter for providing the vision of "microeconomic competitiveness": "Wealth is created at the microeconomic level—in the ability of companies to identify new opportunities, create value and capture these values in innovative ways."[4] Joseph Nye's pronouncements upon globalization's potential quagmire following the 2008 US sub-prime crisis and the healthy economic trajectories of China and India have been taken very seriously by in-house analysts at the government-linked Civil Service College in recent years; their prognoses have predictably been to cleave to some version of a trend-anticipating, open, competitive system arbitrated by the PAP government in the domestic arena (Tang and Yuen 2010).

Domestically, official economic nationalism meant instilling discipline, skills, and an investor-friendly work ethic into the populace. The typical Singaporean National Day Rally speech,[5] which is equivalent to the US president's State of the Union address, consistently exhorts Singaporeans to maintain cohesion in the face of uncertain currents in the world economy. These portentous harms could manifest in an oil crisis, Wall Street scandals and bankruptcies, American and Eurozone national budget deficits, speculative attacks on Asian and European currencies, and credit crunches in major trading economies. The newest addition to that list is the 9/11 attacks by Al Qaeda terrorists on New York and Washington DC that have rattled world markets and employment figures far beyond the numbers of casualties at ground zero. Moreover, India and China are regularly forecast to be both threats and opportunities for Singaporean firms and workers.

The only defence in the face of such borderless threats was to "secure" the economic home front. Lifelong learning, high quality education, and avoidance of the culture of overwhelming dependence upon state-provided welfare had to be pursued on both familial and individual levels. Moreover, workers ought not to strike even if constitutional provisions allow for it. Employers' and employees' federations were cajoled by charismatic PAP leaders to participate in institutionalized closed-door forums mediating wage adjustments when dire economic winds threatened the growth of the national income pie. This concept of tripartite consultation created a whole new vocabulary—tripartism—in Singaporean parlance to supersede the politically charged and hackneyed "corporatism" label popular in parts of Africa, Latin America, central, and northern Europe. In this regard, the official version of Singapore Inc. possesses two faces as a shorthand for a developmental state: on one side, it preaches the disciplining of the population to render the Republic a hospitable landing site for globally circulating capital flows; on the other side, global flows of capital, technology, and trends can be reoriented through attraction to Singapore to serve the government and its people's needs by delivering jobs, fostering demand for ancillary services, and other positive spillover outcomes.

In theory, the Singaporean developmental state ought to be the poster child of an indigenously synthesized pro-globalization disciplinary state. But there are tensions in practicing this ideal in the face of globalization's inherent contradictions. The current prime minister, Lee Hsien Loong, has tried to reconcile the disciplinary aspects of globalization and Singaporean society, in "information age" discourse, which nicely sets the stage for the ensuing dissection of globalization's stresses upon Singapore's political economy. He has repeatedly emphasized the need for societal openness in trying new ideas as well as equipping Singaporeans with "the right knowledge and skills, so that everyone can play a part in creating value and growing the economic pie."[6] In a single statement, he was trying to apprehend the advantages of globalization's borderless flows, while at the same time, he was pronouncing in developmentalist fashion that one ought to think in terms of appropriate knowledge and skills. Lee concluded awkwardly that his government was under pressure to transform developmentalist mentalities but sounded unsure of mediating the rigid frame of the developmental state and the need for cohesion, *à la* a disciplined nationalistic workforce: "Singapore society is based on meritocracy, but this does not mean pigeonholing people into rigid categories. Instead we aim to offer many alternative paths to success, and many different ways of succeeding...."[7] If, following the critical literature on globalization (see, for example, Dasgupta and Kiely 2006), navigating globalization means making compromises to treat policy contradictions euphemistically, then it might be said that Singaporean globalization policy has grown politically chameleon-like without jettisoning discipline. Official economic nationalism was burnished with the promise of globalization rather than its downside. As the rest of the chapter will show, this official economic nationalism has revealed its own slippage within the first decade of the 2000s. Unsurprisingly, Lee Kuan Yew's sequel to his memoirs revealed his residual pessimism towards the existing strategy of manipulating globalization. While lamenting that Singapore possessed insufficient ballast of capable entrepreneurs and inventors, he observed that "we try [to generate indigenous initiatives], but unless we have enough people with the brainpower to run these companies, it can't be done. You look at all the successful companies, what is the key? Their brainpower. The thinker, good management, good innovators" (quoted in Han et al. 2011: 160). This is nonetheless introspection from the *summit* of official nationalism.

8.3 Globalization's Stresses: Four Cases

Capitalist globalization, under its assorted monikers ranging from market liberalization to the free flow of goods and services, theoretically connotes a felicitous cosmopolitan marketplace for the embryonic global citizen of the twenty-first century. But this exists, for the common man, in the abstract. He perceives globalization from the view on the street where he lives with his family and his friends. He may surf the internet or travel on business and vacation, but his referential lenses are honed in on the horizons of his housing district, the mass rapid transit systems he boards for work, the car he drives on local roads, national newspapers, and localized television channels. According to the new approach of reading "everyday politics" into political economy, non-elites affect elite-driven capitalism through bottom-up practices of defiance, qualified acceptance of the elite's designs, pure subversion of top-down economic decisions, or a mixture of all three (Widmaier 2009). The same analysis might well apply to the Singaporean who increasingly lives at a disconnected distance from the official rhetoric of strategically exploiting globalization in the national interest. In terms of the "rightness" of economic nationalism meshed with globalization, this chapter will demonstrate four strains that have appeared following the patterns predicted by the critical globalization literature (Falk 1999; Veltmeyer 2004; Amoore 2005). These pertain to conflicts over living space, the misfit of foreign workers in Singaporean society, the compulsion to host major economic conferences presumed to be trouble free, and "reverse nationalism" emanating from other countries against Singapore's sovereign wealth funds.

8.3.1 *Labor Needs Fulfilled, to the Extent of Creating Housing Market "Xenophobia"*

It is an article of faith amongst proponents of globalization that labor ought to be induced to migrate to the most efficient production centers that would optimize their contribution. In this way, the territories that mobile labor depart from ought to improve their efficiency and reward systems to match competing localities around the globe, contributing to an evening out of competitive pressures and stemming the loss of workers. Singaporeans have lived comfortably with this paradoxical logic for some time, since even in the first decade of independence, 1965–75, the rates of population increase and natural replacement rates mostly coincided (APMRN 2011). By about the mid-1980s, when Singapore's newly industrializing economy status was minted, population growth gradually outstripped natural growth. In May 1996, the government announced that up to 25,000 immigrants had been granted permanent residency annually even though it was not stated when this increased intake started. Nonetheless, the signs were ominous in various National Day Rally speeches in the mid-1980s by erstwhile prime minister Lee Kuan Yew, who declared that Singaporeans were not reproducing themselves in sufficient numbers to man the economy and the conscription-based armed forces. These comments presaged a controversial but short-lived policy of offering incentives for the population to fall in line with an embrace of eugenics.

Nonetheless, the official worry that the Singaporean workforce would be hollowed out by competition and emigration remained. An official report published in 1991 suggested that the rates of admission of foreigners into permanent residency in 1986 stood at 5,000 (Cheung 1991). It did not help that official statistics on the intake of foreigners as citizens or permanent residents were not made directly available for public access. One could, however, infer partially from the listing of the demographic breakdown between citizens, permanent residents, and non-residents. In 1990, within a population of 3.05 million, there were 112,100 permanent residents. Between 2000, which was a census year, and 2009, the number of permanent residents rose from 287,500 out of a total population of 4.03 million to 533,000 out of a total population size of 4.99 million (Government of Singapore 2010). Certainly, the figures do imply a significant increase in population density in the small island state. There was a twofold jump in the number of permanent residents between 1990 and 2000, and another one between 2000 and 2009. If one looks at the category of "non-residents" working and living in Singapore, the leap in numbers is even more startling: 311,300 in 1990 to 1,253,700 in 2009 out of a total population of 4.99 million (Government of Singapore 2010). In short, one out of every five people living in Singapore is most definitely a person of foreign origin without permanent residency. If one includes the 533,000 permanent residents under an even broader category of foreigners defined simply as "non-citizens," then nearly two out of every five people living in Singapore in 2009 would be a foreigner. In September 2010, another update by the government was released to the press indicating that "permanent residents" had increased to 541,000 and "foreigners" (i.e., non-residents) to 1,305,000 (Census Highlights 2010). This same news report noted that a Gallup poll published in August 2010 indicated that Singapore remained a top destination for migrants to the extent that, if everyone who wanted to move there were allowed to, the island's population would triple. The years 2009–10 could potentially be viewed as a demographic watershed or the brink of a political precipice. This is clearly population creep arising from borderless globalization. While there is no detailed time-series data produced by the Singaporean government, due probably to the political sensitivity of this trend, the following statistical snapshot (Table 8.1), revealing overall population growth overtaking growth in "Singapore residents" between 1980 and 2010, is indicative of the problem.

Correspondingly, the visibility of foreigners in the housing market has triggered some xenophobia that has been attributable to an unscientific combination of perception and a sense of nationalistic displacement. In this regard, this is not a problem of "objectivity"; it is a political problem of representing and perceiving one's benefit from the globalization gravy train that has been convincingly sold to Singaporeans by their government since 1965. Given the fact that Singapore has one of the world's highest home ownership rates at 95%, any rise or plunge in housing prices is a source of

Table 8.1. Population and growth rate 1980–2010

	Population and growth rate			
	Total population	Singapore residents	Total population growth	Singapore residents growth
	Thousand		Percent	
Census				
1980	2,413.9	2,282.1	1.5	1.3
1990	3,047.1	2,735.9	2.3	1.7
2000	4,027.9	3,273.4	2.8	1.8
Mid-year estimates				
2008	4,839.4	3,642.7	5.5	1.7
2009	4,987.6	3,733.9	3.1	2.5
2010 (Census)	5,076.7	3,771.7	1.8	1.0

Notes: Total population comprises Singapore residents and non-residents. Singapore resident population comprises Singapore citizens and permanent residents.

Source: "Population: Population and Growth Rate" in Department of Statistics Singapore, *Singapore in Figures 2011* (Singapore: Government of Singapore, 2011), http://www.singstat.gov.sg/pubn/reference/sif2011.pdf [Accessed January 25, 2012].

great public consternation. Things appeared to have come to a boil between 2007 and 2011 when property prices in Singapore defied the US sub-prime and Eurozone budget deficit crises, even though questions of housing availability and affordability have come to the fore before every general election in the 1990s. These are issues arising from situations of plenty and of quality, in contrast to the straightforward questions of physical availability that bedeviled the Republic's Housing and Development Board (HDB) and Urban Redevelopment Authority (URA) from the 1960s through 1970s. As the pro-government *Straits Times* newspaper observed, a situation of steadily rising prices ought to have provoked significant satisfaction in both the private and government-subsidized housing markets.[8] It should have logically been interpreted as a solid sign of asset appreciation and an endorsement of Singapore's economic health.

Yet Singaporeans have expressed fears of being priced out of the housing market. For those eyeing an upgrade from government-built and subsidized HDB flats to private property, rising prices have rendered an important component of the "Singapore Dream" out of reach. Those already within the private property category fear that even if they sold their existing properties for a tidy profit, the escalation in prices would eliminate their prospects of acquiring a comparable or higher-value property; the alternative would be to save the profits and downgrade to cheaper private property or enter the HDB market. HDB residents and property owners would also experience comparable downgrading and profit-undermining pressures when the private sector price hikes exert a spillover effect on HDB housing prices. How then do foreigners appear culpable in all this? In politically correct fashion, the main government-owned newspaper, the *Straits Times*, described the problem as the diminishing certainty that the children of today's Singaporean homeowners will be able to afford their own; and that it is the investor and speculator who benefit from a runaway housing market.[9]

Within the private sector, there is every visible sign that foreigners are buying up property in Singapore in increasing numbers even if the precise impact on Singaporean aspirations for housing upgrades remains unclear in 2010–11. In September 2007, the *New York Times* reported a 132% increase between 2005 and 2006 in the number of South Korean citizens buying private property on the island. It also noted that before 2005 drew the curtain on a host of transnational crises afflicting the Singapore economy, such as the SARS epidemic and regional economic difficulties, foreign homebuyers notched up no more than 20% of all central city purchases; by the middle of 2007, this figure had risen to 29%.[10] The same report also noted a simultaneously widening base of foreign buyers. In 2006, topping the list of foreign homebuyers were Indonesians and Malaysians, with each accounting for 19.6%, the Indians were coming in at 10.7%, and Britons at 8.7%. This was in contrast to the 2003 rankings of 28% Malaysians, 23% Indonesians, and 4% Indians.[11] A 2010 report by property company Knight Frank revealed that, between 2006 and 2009, the total percentage of foreigners buying property in Singapore stabilized between 22.6 and 24%. By the fourth quarter of 2009, Malaysians ranked first at 26%; Indonesians at 19%; Chinese nationals at 15%; Indians at 12%; "others" at 16%; and Britons at 4%. The prominence of Chinese (People's Republic of China, PRC) buyers can probably be attributed to the fact that PRC nationals had gained confidence in investing overseas in tandem with an investment spree by Beijing's sovereign wealth funds. Additionally, given Singapore's ethnic Chinese majority population, it was a safer investment destination than the rest of Southeast Asia. By March 2011, the PRC buyers had displaced Malaysians as the largest group of foreign property buyers at 24% and 21% respectively.[12]

Contrary to public perceptions, the Knight Frank report observed that "meanwhile, the share of Singaporean buyers increased by 4.9 percentage-points, from 71.7% in 2008, to 76.6% in 2009. Companies reduced their share, from 4.7% in 2008 to 1.6% in 2009, of overall private residential transactions."[13] In October 2010, Mah Bow Tan, Minister for National Development, sought to allay citizens' fears further following a slew of urgent measures taken to dampen property speculation. He claimed that the majority of private homebuyers were citizens while permanent residents comprised 13% and foreigners 12% according to statistics for the second quarter of 2010.[14] Mah reminded Singaporeans that it was part and parcel of a cosmopolitan city that foreigners had to live among them. By January 2011, Mah mollified private homebuyers further by imposing severe limits on loan availability for individual and institutional (e.g., company, trust) purchasers of second homes who intend to re-sell the latter for short-term profit.[15]

In contrast, the market for HDB flats is considered a protected preserve for Singaporeans and permanent residents given the strict nationalistic eligibility criteria. Nonetheless, citizens wishing to make a case for the complaint of "globalization as foreign intrusion into heartland territory" would point to the fact that permanent residents are not on the same footing as citizens. Following Parliamentary questions concerning the presence of permanent residents in HDB estates, where 80% of Singaporeans live, Minister for National Development Mah Bow Tan, revealed that permanent residents constituted 14% of the population living in HDB flats. He was also quoted as saying that "PR [permanent resident] families own only 5% of HDB flats; however there are western and northern towns where this proportion is slightly higher than the 5% average."[16] Furthermore, Minister Mah pointed out that permanent residents are not drivers of the surge in HDB property prices in either the re-sale or rental markets. Moreover, HDB housing already regulates ethnic quotas for residents in HDB blocks as part of multiracial nation-building policies introduced in 1989. To further calm public consternation about foreigners driving up property prices and disrupting social cohesion, the Minister took the opportunity to announce that a 5% limit would be imposed on permanent residents wishing to live in HDB "neighborhoods" and a cap of 8% per HDB block. Additionally, permanent residents would have to comply with existing ethnic residency quotas.[17] It was equally reassuring for the government and those pro-globalization sections of the Singaporean public that a 2008 public housing survey of residents' well being and social capital revealed that 77% of respondents island-wide indicated that they shared extensive interactions with neighbors of other ethnicities and nationalities (HDB 2010: 42–3). These interactions took the form of exchanging food, social visits, and casual conversation.

The remaining 23% of respondents revealed, however, some degree of alienation:

> For the 23% of residents who did not interact with neighbours of other ethnic groups or nationalities, more of them comprised younger residents aged below 35 years or those 65 years or older. As to why residents did not interact with neighbours of other ethnic groups or nationalities even if they had such neighbours, the younger residents explained that they had little or no time to interact. Elderly residents who could not interact with neighbours of a different ethnicity or nationality often mentioned language difficulties. In general, reasons for residents not interacting with neighbours of other ethnic groups or nationalities were the absence of such neighbours nearby for the largest ethnic group and presence of language barriers for older residents. (HDB 2010: 43)

This minority of respondents that bucked the trend of statistically-affirmed harmony in relation to the human flows of globalization need not be worrying if it were not close to the 25% mark. This means that nearly one in four Singaporean HDB residents experienced or asserted palpable social distance towards foreigners. This speaks volumes of that sizable minority among the 80% of the Singaporeans who live in HDB housing. This minority still believes that globalization is introducing a harsh "foreignness" into what they perceive should be a financially and socially protected housing market.

8.3.2 *Socio-economic Maladjustments from Foreign Workers' Presence*

In contrast to the controversy surrounding housing xenophobia, foreign residents who have bought or rented property on the island have lauded the island's attractiveness as a "global city" in some very conventional ways that have proven the PAP government's globalization-friendly nationalism a theoretical success. Foreign expatriates at every level of the skill ladder are, in turn, approved in official pronouncements as a highly positive injection for the Republic's economic growth. However, the gap between public perception and governmental optimism has emerged as an inconvenient truth about globalization.

Referring to the PAP's initiatives from 2000 onwards to host Formula One motor racing and two casino-based integrated resort complexes, the head of consulting and research of the global real estate company DTZ, tellingly commented that foreigners hold the opinion that Singapore as a global city "is no longer just seen as a place to work, but also as a place to have fun."[18] With this tone, comparisons immediately come to mind, regardless of accuracy, of New York, London, Monte Carlo, Tokyo, Seoul, Las Vegas, or Los Angeles. A Korean professional who had been living in Singapore for seven years described the island as a nascent miniature Seoul:

> There are definitely more Koreans living here in the last few years. Everywhere I go, I hear Korean... Now in every major food court, there is one Korean food stall; there are several Korean supermarkets and I know of at least two Korean rice cake shops here. Those are so specialized you'd really need a sizable Korean community to support them.[19]

These anecdotal impressions do not compose an accurate picture of globalized Singapore but they suggest that becoming a global lifestyle hub implies ostentatious displays and accoutrements of opulence. Perhaps this was a major draw, for even philanthropist-cum-*kungfu* film star Jet Li and his wife, who acquired Singaporean citizenship, purchased a S$20 million bungalow in the prestigious part of Singapore's Bukit Timah district in 2009. Likewise, Li's fellow action movie star, Jackie Chan, acquired properties in Singapore's prime districts in 2007 and 2010. Chan's friend and Hong Kong pop singer, Emil Chau, joined Chan in buying a unit in the upmarket Centennia Suites earlier in 2010. For the Singaporeans more accustomed to nation-building rhetoric uttered on every National Day and in the various national education classes in primary and secondary schooling channels, the actual consequences of living in a global city may be too much to bear, compounded in no small part by a deep misunderstanding of the sociological implications of globalization. Getting used to the idea of becoming a playground for Asia's rich and famous might mean accepting the price pressures exerted by "star quality" residents who perform symbolic labor in a global entertainment industry. At the other extreme, there is public discomfort over overcrowding on public transport, triggered by the presence of low-skilled foreign workers.

On a broader scale, the officially embraced entry of foreign workers into the labor force was intended to highlight the PAP's pragmatism in sustaining economic growth in the face of a declining birth rate and ageing population, as well as intensifying competition from China, India, and Southeast Asia in the higher value-added industries. Foreign workers enter the Singaporean workplace at both high- and low-skill levels and this has contributed to complaints on civil society blogs and in Parliament that the disciplinary developmental state is failing its citizens. The then minister for finance, Tharman Shanmugaratnam, repeated the standard neoliberal response to charges that the entry of foreign workers willing to work at low wages was driving down the incomes of "Singaporeans at the lower end of the income ladder."[20] He argued that despite the global knock-on effects of the dot-com bust in 2000, the 9/11 terrorist attacks in 2001, and the impact of the SARS epidemic in 2003, Singapore managed to sustain comfortable growth rates from 2004 to 2010 due to liberalizing policies that were pro-business and pro-globalization. Letting in foreign workers to propel business expansion almost overnight and fulfill factory orders placed from abroad meant that wages actually rose once the labor market tightened. This in turn benefited Singaporean low-wage earners from 2006 to 2008. He produced statistics showing that as foreign workers' presence increased beyond 25% to more than 30% in 2009, unemployment dropped below 4% and remained below that. Furthermore, the Minister asserted that foreign workers had speeded up public works projects such as the expansion of the Mass Rapid Transit network, "ease[d] supply bottlenecks" in the private property market, and staffed public hospitals and nursing homes. While foreign workers were a quick booster, this was unsustainable in the long run since it might discourage productivity training in companies and "run up against the social and physical limits" that an ever-increasing foreign worker population would bring.[21] Even then Minister Mentor Lee Kuan Yew, the elder statesman, has acknowledged the loud grumblings of Singaporeans and suggested that the Republic's globalized economy faced a catch-22 situation: it could reduce overcrowding on the buses and mass rapid transit system by restricting the entry of foreign workers, but this would also stymie infrastructure building, cool the economy, and reduce incomes along with it.[22]

These issues came to a head in October 2008 when residents of the overwhelmingly middle-class Serangoon Gardens housing district established online petitions and organized their own citizens' forums to protest plans to set up a dormitory for up to 1,000 foreign workers working in nearby factories. Residents feared the low-skilled foreigners would generate traffic jams, soil their streets, undermine the value of their properties, and potentially take liberties with women and children. The Member of Parliament for the area placated the residents by getting the Ministry for National Development to re-zone the traffic access routes to the dormitory and to run regular police and citizen patrols in the affected areas. The PAP government could not back down completely since the protest signified an unofficial nationalism grating against its globalization formula. A local news editorial tactfully explained that the lesson to be drawn ought to be sensitivity training in handling a foreign-labor-induced public ruckus.[23] This formulation might as well have applied to how the authorities tried in 2008–9 to dampen the rifts in Singapore's economic image at other times; for example, when the occasional group of foreign workers staged mass sit-ins at the Ministry of Manpower over unpaid wages from local companies; when the government raided crammed and unsanitary worker dormitories; and over Singaporean complaints about Chinese service counter staff who insisted on speaking Mandarin to non-Chinese Singaporeans.

8.3.3 *Validating Official Nationalism Via Globalization-friendly Conferencing*

As part of the PAP government's relentless efforts to stay engaged with a global economy, it has actively fostered the Republic's reputation as a meetings, incentive travel, conventions, and exhibitions (MICE) hub in the Asia-Pacific, and where possible, the world at large. This business of hosting events related to the flow of neoliberal capitalism involves providing physical and transport infrastructure support, coupled to digital connectivity. The point is to demonstrate to the world that the island is an important node of global flows of important people and ideas, and at the same time earn both tourism-related receipts and a cumulative reputation as a reliable supporter of the *right* sort of globalization. The logistics and manpower requirements of hosting meetings suited the original disciplinary characteristics of the Singaporean developmental state in coordinating the operation of an award-winning international airport with land transport highways and seaport connectivity, along with staff trained in the drudgery of setting up conference props and the service culture of "attentiveness with a smile." All this, packaged for a competitive price with add-on sightseeing possibilities for international delegates in Singapore and neighboring Southeast Asia, is intended to be a conference organizer's dream come true. Akin to setting in motion a mass display at an Olympic ceremony, Singaporean planners have honed conference hosting to a fine art. It has been estimated that the Republic has hosted close to 6,000 business events annually over the past few years. In 2008, Singapore reportedly accounted for one-fourth of all the business events held in Asia, and confirmed bookings for 2011 through 2012 appear to portend rich earnings for the MICE industry.[24] The two casino-cum-integrated resorts, Resorts World Sentosa and Marina Bay Sands, were completed in 2009–10 with the MICE strategy in mind.

This is arguably irrelevant to the study of economic nationalism if one observes it only for its quantitative contribution to the Singaporean economy, which has been estimated to be some 40% of tourism receipts in 2008. But this desire for global validation of Singapore's globalized status connotes also the relentless need to socially engineer one's citizens, as well as permanent residents, into a culture of tolerating the constant reinvention of Singapore's physical and socio-cultural landscape to host an endless stream of events such as MICE, the Formula One night race, the World Trade Organization (WTO), World Bank and International Monetary Fund (IMF) ministerial meetings, the APEC summit, and most recently the inaugural Youth Olympic Games. Motorists often have to put up with traffic redirections and selected road closures in the center of the commercial district, school children have to be mobilized for ceremonial displays, and undesirable sections of the nascent global civil society screened for terrorist and subversive activity for preemptive purposes.

The PAP government learned from the strengthening pattern of raucous civil society protests that had gained momentum from the WTO's Seattle Round in 1999. In 2006, when both the World Bank and IMF held their annual meetings back-to-back in Singapore, Singapore blacklisted 28 of approximately 500 civil society activists that both organizations had invited for "engagement" with the two aid-giving organizations. Furthermore, a few strictly circumscribed protest zones were made available in the conference venue and the authorities drew attention to their tough internal security laws dealing with assemblies without prior permit. The loud protests of some of those groups whose members were on the blacklist prompted the erstwhile World Bank president, Paul Wolfowitz, to scold the Singaporean authorities for "authoritarian" measures that violated their hosting agreement. The Singaporeans responded by allowing 22 of the 28 on the blacklist to enter Singapore, but this gesture was spurned as too little and too late by Oxfam and Greenpeace.[25] Having been accustomed to the tranquillity of domestic law and order implemented by the PAP government, the majority of Singaporean public opinion appeared supportive of their government's stance on policing the IMF–World Bank meetings, convinced in all probability by the highly securitized discourse of post-9/11 terrorist threats and other subversion. Once again, it appears that discipline is understood to mesh with "good globalization."

8.3.4 *Singapore's Sovereign Wealth Funds and Government-linked Companies: Economic Nationalism Encounters Obstacles Abroad*

According to the much-cited US Treasury Department's definition, a sovereign wealth fund (SWF) is a "government investment vehicle which is funded by foreign exchange assets, and which manages those assets separately from the official reserves of the monetary authorities (the Central Bank and reserve-related functions of the Finance Ministry)" (US Treasury Department 2007). The report went on to cite the Abu Dhabi Investment Authority (ADIA) and the Government of Singapore Investment Corporation (GIC) as examples. In domestic parlance, SWFs are more generically described as government-linked companies (GLCs). These have been established for the purpose of developing the national economy and serve to connect "Singapore Inc." with the world's investor networks and industrial markets. GLCs obviously cover a wide swath of government-involved businesses, ranging from investment companies of the GIC type; to oil rig manufacturers like SembCorp Marine; the operator of the public subway system, Singapore Mass Rapid Transit Corporation; Singapore Airlines; SingTel, the corporatized former national telecommunications monopoly; and the holding company Temasek Holdings, which maintains stakes in most of these companies. There are also degrees to which one can define government shareholder stakes in all of these companies, with the exception of GIC and Temasek which are wholly owned by the Singaporean government. Often, the jointness of investment priorities between Temasek Holdings and its many subsidiaries has been construed as the visible hand of the Singaporean government. This may occasionally count against GLCs when foreign governments scrutinize their investments overseas.

The operating vision behind GLCs has in fact adhered to traditional interventionist approaches to economic management, although this has evolved in the last decade towards "externalizing" the Singapore economy through overseas investments that occupy approximately 70–90% of their portfolios. This figure uses Temasek and GIC investments as a gauge. Given the weakness of domestic capital at the onset of independence, the government of Singapore had to start up many industries and plant the confidence factor that private entrepreneurs at home and abroad were unwilling to supply. Such was the origin of Temasek and its subsidiaries. Research over the past decade has estimated their contribution to Singaporean GDP to range between 13 and 60% depending on one's preferred accounting criteria. In 2010, Temasek and its companies were reported to manage a portfolio worth S$186 billion, while the corresponding figure for GIC has been publicly mentioned as exceeding S$141 billion (US$100 billion).[26] The size of the stakes are matched by the fact that former cabinet ministers and directors from the other GLCs chair and sit on the board of directors of Temasek, whereas for the GIC, serving ministers sit on the board of directors. Minister Mentor Lee himself chaired GIC from its inception until mid-2011, when the current prime minister, Lee Hsien Loong, succeeded him. Also sitting on the board of directors are the two deputy prime ministers, who simultaneously hold the appointments of three ministries Finance, Manpower, and Home Affairs, the Minister for Education, the Minister for Trade and Industry, the Chairman of the Singapore Stock Exchange, the Chairman of Sembcorp Industries (an important GLC in the field of oil rig construction, marine services, and shipbuilding), two former ministers holding the portfolios of Finance, Transport, and Foreign Affairs, and Lee Kuan Yew, currently a "Senior Advisor."[27] Since the GIC is a traditional SWF, its main mission is to manage the population's employment-derived and government-administered Central Provident Fund pool of compulsory savings along with other government surpluses.

Although the profit motive drives Singaporean SWFs and GLCs, it is often also an understated national interest that motivates their overseas investments. Temasek tends to invest in overseas infrastructure companies, banks and telecommunications firms. GIC favors banks and real estate. This is where mercantilist considerations operate under the covering logic of globalization in Singapore's government-spawned "transnational corporations." This sort of logic runs the political risk of triggering emotional public opinion and reactive nationalism in the nation-states Singaporean SWFs and GLCs operate in. In many instances, GLCs had to beat a retreat when confronted with hostile public and corporate opinion. In the 1990s, ventures involving Singapore Airlines and the Tata Corporation to establish an additional Indian airline foundered on bureaucratic resistance. In 2003, Singapore Technologies Telemedia's bid to acquire bankrupt US telecommunications firm Global Crossing required personal interventions between then Prime Minister Goh and President Bush himself to override the Pentagon's national security reservations over the sale. SingTel has likewise had to assuage Australian security sensitivities arising from its purchase of the local Optus corporation, while in Indonesia SingTel has occasionally riled local patronage networks in its drive to capture market share through a local mobile telecommunications subsidiary. Temasek Holdings itself provoked a political backlash among anti-Thaksin political movements in Thailand in 2006–7 when it acquired a controlling stake in Shin Corporation for US$1.9 billion. It also sparked some concern in Europe and the USA when it invested in Merrill Lynch and Barclays during the US sub-prime mortgage crisis in 2008–9, causing its portfolio value to shed 31% when stocks in those two banks slid under market turbulence and other loan difficulties. GIC also invested in UBS and Citigroup during the same period, stirring criticism of its misjudged investments. Although Temasek had recouped its losses by late 2009, GIC faced a mixed picture as its annual report admitted that its portfolio "suffered a loss of more than 20% in Singapore dollar terms in the financial year to 31 March 2009."[28] In February 2010, GIC was reported to have resigned itself to a "paper loss" of 70% of its original purchase of its UBS stake given the Swiss financier's continued weaknesses.[29]

Leaving aside the emotive charge of investor folly, these risky investments may be interpreted in part as an attempt to either forge a long-term portfolio or to assist in stabilizing the world economy by supporting key Western financial institutions through signalling confidence in their value. Lee Kuan Yew's memoirs provided an insight into this psychology when he argued that it was vital to acknowledge the centrality of Americans and Europeans in setting the rules in a globalized economy, hence it would be useful to support their pillars even in the name of economic nationalism (Lee 2000: 389–91). While there is some truth in Western criticisms of the culture of secrecy in Temasek and GIC, these criticisms do not acknowledge the fact that both the GLC and SWF have made attempts since 2004 to accommodate the increased demands for corporate transparency as they evolve as global players. Both have published annual reports on their websites, although Temasek's is slightly more detailed than GIC's. But GIC must also be assessed as a very traditional nationalistic financial vehicle that manages Singaporeans' government-supervised retirement savings that are also liable to speculative attack along with GIC's image as the people's "insurer of last resort" (Clark and Monk 2010). This aspect of GIC may be regarded as a throwback to an orthodox version of rearguard economic nationalism, in which the state and its financial minions bail out both its corporate and non-corporate citizens when the national economy is headed for bankruptcy. In 2009, Temasek's short-lived attempt to engage the services of the American Charles Goodyear as a replacement for its Singaporean CEO, Ho Ching, demonstrated once again the embeddedness of traditional economic nationalism within the mission of Temasek. Charles Goodyear's four-month probationary stint as CEO-designate was described by the finance minister Tharman Shanmugaratnam as having run aground due to "strategic differences" between Goodyear and his Singaporean colleagues.[30] Nonetheless, Temasek is basking in the nationalistic glow of a sharp rebound in its profit for the financial year that ended on March 31, 2011: net profit was S$13 billion compared with S$5 billion the year before, due to its large portfolio of 77% exposure to a booming Asia.[31]

As the preceding four dimensions of frictions arising from embracing globalization have shown, Singaporeans have learned that an open border does not guarantee the comprehensiveness of welfare for citizens. The existence of an open economy coexists with externally originated competition for jobs and housing space, along with the official emphases on promoting neoliberal functions as an economic hub and cross-border investments, in a very complex equation. Upon close inspection, these issues tend to boggle the undiscerning public mind. They may even appear to generate a crisis of confidence in the strategizing of globalization by the PAP state. Yet, there is a silver lining in the very rhetoric of official economic nationalism that is tautologically comforting. The PAP state has earned in the past an almost sterling record of stewardship of the economy, and there is little deep-seated reason why the electorate would not want to vote to retain the existing dominant party democracy if it responds to public expectations that it rectify the negative consequences of globalization. Prime Minister Lee Hsien Loong candidly admitted during a CNN-hosted event in October 2010 that had he known "how quickly the pace of change would accelerate and how much our people would be under pressure from globalization . . . we would have put even more resources in" and started the emphasis on skill-upgrading and retraining five to ten years earlier.[32] In this way, official economic nationalism tries to be a deep envelope that purports to protect local welfare while also straining to remain globalization-friendly.

8.4 Conclusion

The official Singaporean attempt to discipline globalization for local purposes is certainly a bold experiment for even a developed economy. What makes it even more remarkable is its soft authoritarian political system that promotes a particular reading of globalization as a necessary extension of a paternalistic state. Citizens might thus understand that globalization will work for them so long as the "chameleon-like" political communication from the PAP government, which has ruled the island state since independence, can reconcile the positive realities of globalization with the less-positive ones in public discourse. On the other hand, globalization has evidently precipitated physical stresses on the ground, which have compelled Singaporeans to differentiate citizens from permanent residents and other transient foreign workers. This unofficial reactionary nationalism manifests in contestations over the price of housing, the real and imagined social costs of sharing space with foreigners on a crowded island, the strictures of controlled behavior demanded of globalization-trained Singaporeans in hosting showcase conferences, and the frictions between locally-grown SWFs and GLCs and overseas expectations of their nationalistic agendas. While much more work needs to be done to investigate these "inconvenient" aspects of the official version of "good globalization," it should be evident that globalization is indeed straining the capitalist aspirations of the Singaporean nation-state by provoking its nationalistic sensitivities. One might argue that the "inner globalization" of having large numbers of foreign labor in one's midst, and other externally originated scrutiny in the public face, is not unique to Singapore. But it does draw attention to the ironies confronting a shrewdly hybridized globalization-friendly economic nationalism. The PAP's economic thought will at some point have to transcend Premier Lee's retrospective moment of candour about the harsh accelerated impact of globalization's pressures. The general elections of May 2011 have witnessed a clash between the official and unofficial nationalism. Voters incensed over the consequences of overcrowding and competition for jobs and housing turned against a slate of prominent PAP incumbents to elect the biggest group of opposition parliamentarians since independence. Interestingly, the PAP managed to retain a significant mandate of 60.1% of the popular vote, which indicated that a sizable majority desires to stretch nationalism to both protect local interests while keeping faith in globalization. This is just the beginning of a serious reckoning between two areas of Singaporean economic nationalism that will be acting out a peculiar public contestation under the umbrella of "Singapore Inc."

Notes

1. The Singaporean approach predates Peter Evans's argument about the developmental state's "embedded autonomy" in structuring long-term development even though the Singaporean logic mirrors his argument. See Evans (1995), chapter 1.
2. This line of argument follows up on my earlier survey of the nature of Singapore's foreign economic policy in Chong (2007).
3. Kearney (2007a). See also the linked report at Kearney (2007b).
4. "Managing in an Uncertain World: The New Normal." Speech by Cedric Foo, Minister of State for Defence and Chairman, SPRING. Singapore, August 1, 2003 at the International Management Action Award (IMAA) 2003 Presentation, Ritz-Carlton Millenia, Singapore. http://stars.nhb.gov.sg/stars/public/viewHTML.jsp?pdfno=2003080105
5. It usually takes place a week after Singaporean National Day (the equivalent of Independence, Revolutionary, Republic, or Founder's Day) on August 9.
6. "ICT and the Knowledge-Based Economy." Speech by Prime Minister Lee Hsien Loong at the APEC CEO Summit, November 17, 2005, in Busan, South Korea. http://stars.nhb.gov.sg/stars/public/viewDocx.jsp?stid=34532&lochref=viewHTML.jsp?pdfno=2005111701&keyword=economy
7. Lee Hsien Loong, "ICT and the Knowledge-Based Economy."

8. Fiona Chan, "Who Really Gains from Runaway Property Prices?" *The Straits Times* (Singapore), May 8, 2010. http://www.asiaone.com/Business/My+Money/Property/Story/A1Story20100507-214798.html
9. Chan, "Who Really Gains from Runaway Property Prices?"
10. Sonia Kolesnikov-Jessop, "Singapore Drawing More Foreign Investors." *The New York Times*, September 27, 2007.
11. Kolesnikov-Jessop, "Singapore Drawing More Foreign Investors."
12. "Chinese Top Foreign Buyers of Singapore Homes: Report." *Agence France Presse*, May 25, 2011. http://sg.finance.yahoo.com/news/Chinese-top-foreign-buyers-afpsg-3189377410.html?x=0
13. Knight Frank (2010). *Real Estate Market Highlights, October–December 2009/Fourth Quarter*, pp. 2–3. Singapore: Knight Frank. www.kf.sg/images/publication/pdf/KF_Real_Estate_Highlights_4th_Quarter_2009.pdf
14. Jessica Cheam, "S'poreans driving property market, says Mah." *Straits Times* (Singapore), October 19, 2010.
15. Esther Teo, "New Property Measures to Curb Property Speculation." *Straits Times* (Singapore), January 14, 2011.
16. Jessica Cheam, "New Limits on Sale of Flats to PRs." *Straits Times* (Singapore), March 6, 2010.
17. Cheam, "New Limits on Sale of Flats to PRs."
18. Kolesnikov-Jessop, "Singapore Drawing More Foreign Investors."
19. Kolesnikov-Jessop, "Singapore Drawing More Foreign Investors."
20. Tharman Shanmugaratnam, "Economic Growth Benefits All Citizens. Singapore's Low Income Families." *Straits Times* (Singapore), March 6, 2010.
21. Shanmugaratnam, "Economic Growth Benefits All Citizens."
22. Clarissa Oon, "Citizen–PR distinction has sharpened: MM." *Straits Times* (Singapore), February 19, 2010.
23. Hui Yee Tan, "Wake-up Call from Dorm Issue." *Straits Times* (Singapore), October 17, 2008.
24. "Singapore's MICE Industry Gathers Momentum." Report authored by Janus Corporate Solutions, Singapore, July 7, 2010. www.guidemesingapore.com/blog-post/singapore-business/singapore-mice-industry-gathers-momentum
25. Wayne Arnold, "Singapore Blocks IMOxChapML.dtdF Protesters." *International Herald Tribune*, September 18, 2006.
26. Temasek Holdings, "Our Portfolio Value Since Inception." www.temasekreport.com/2010/portfolio/inception.html GIC, "Overview." www.gic.com.sg/aboutus.htm
27. GIC, "About Us—Board of Directors." www.gic.com.sg/about/gic-board-of-directors
28. GIC, "Report on the Management of the Government's Portfolio for the Year 2008/09." 10 www.gic.com.sg/PDF/GIC_Report_2009.pdf
29. Gabriel Chen, "GIC may have 70 percent paper loss on UBS." *Straits Times* (Singapore), February 12, 2010.
30. U-Wen Lee, "No Timetable to Name New Temasek CEO." *Business Times* (Singapore), August 19, 2009.

31. Bernice Han, "Temasek Profit Doubles to $10 bn." *Agence France Presse*, July 7, 2011.
32. Xueying Li and Cassandra Chew, "What PM Lee Would Have Done Differently." *The Straits Times* (Singapore), October 21, 2010.

References

Amoore, L. (ed.) (2005). *The Global Resistance Reader*. London: Routledge.

Asia Pacific Migration Research Network (APMRN). (2011). "Issues Paper from Singapore." Available at http://www.unesco.org/most/apmrnw13.htm [Accessed January 25, 2011].

Census Highlights 2010. (2010). "Census Highlights—Advance Estimates from the 2010 Census have thrown up some interesting facts." *The Straits Times* (Singapore), September 1.

Cheung, P.P.L. (1991). "Social and Economic Implications of Singapore's Immigration and Emigration Patterns." Paper for International Conference on Migration, Centre for Advanced Studies, National University of Singapore, February 7–9. Cited from Asia Pacific Migration Research Network (APMRN) "Issues paper from Singapore." http://www.unesco.org/most/apmrnw13.htm [Accessed January 25, 2012].

Chong, A. (2007). "Singapore's Political Economy, 1997–2007: Strategizing Economic Assurance for Globalization." *Asian Survey*, 47 (6): 952–76.

Clark, G.L. and Monk, A. (2010). "Government of Singapore Investment Corporation (GIC): Insurer of Last Resort and Bulwark of Nation-State Legitimacy." *The Pacific Review*, 23 (4): 429–51.

Dasgupta, S. and Kiely, R. (eds.) (2006). *Globalization and After*. New Delhi: Sage.

Economic Development Board, Government of Singapore. (2011). "Why Singapore—Singapore Rankings—Singapore Economic Development Board." www.edb.gov.sg/edb/sg/en_uk/index/why_singapore/singapore_rankings.html#rank_chart [Accessed January 25, 2012].

Evans, P.B. (1995). *Embedded Autonomy: States and Industrial Transformation*. Princeton: Princeton University Press.

Falk, R. (1999). *Predatory Globalization*. Oxford: Polity Press.

Gellner, E. (1997). *Nations and Nationalism*. Oxford: Blackwell. (Reprinted from the 1983 edn.)

Goh C.T. (1979). "The Singapore Economy: Looking Back and Looking Forward," in *People's Action Party 1954–1979*. PETIR 25th Anniversary Issue, 64–71. Singapore: Central Executive Committee People's Action Party.

Goh, K.S. (1995a). "The Economics of Modernization," in K.S. Goh (ed.), *The Economics of Modernization*, 1–15. (2nd edn). Singapore: Federal Publications. (First published 1979).

Goh, K.S. (1995b). "Foreign Big Business in Singapore," in K.S. Goh, *The Economics of Modernization*, 115–16. (2nd edn). Singapore: Federal Publications.

Government of Singapore. (2010). *"Yearbook of Statistics 2010."* Singapore: Government of Singapore. http://www.singstat.gov.sg/pubn/reference/yos10/statsT-demography.pdf [Accessed July 14, 2010].

Government of Singapore, Department of Statistics. (2011). "Population: Population and Growth Rate," in *Singapore in Figures 2011*. Singapore: Government of Singapore. http://www.singstat.gov.sg/pubn/reference/sif2011.pdf [Accessed January 25, 2012].

Han, F.K. et al. (eds.) (2011). *Lee Kuan Yew: Hard Truths to Keep Singapore Going*. Singapore: The Straits Times Press.

HDB (Housing Development Board). (2010). "*Public Housing in Singapore: Well-Being of Communities, Families and the Elderly. HDB Sample Household Survey 2008.*" Singapore: Housing and Development Board. www.hdb.gov.sg/fi10/fi10297p.nsf/ImageView/Survey2008/$file/Monogram+2+Lores_R1.pdf [Accessed January 25, 2012].

Hobsbawm, E. (1997). *The Age of Capital 1848–1875*. London: Weidenfeld and Nicolson.

Kearney, A.T. (2007a). "Globalization Index 2007 Methodology." www.atkearney.com/index.php/Publications/globalization-index-data-2007.html [Accessed January 25, 2012].

Kearney, A.T. (2007b). "Hong Kong, Jordan, and Estonia Debut Among the Top 10 in Expanded Ranking of the World's Most Globalized Countries." www.atkearney.com/index.php/News-media/hong-kong-jordan-and-estonia-debut-among-the-top-10-in-expanded-ranking-of-the-worlds-most-globalized-countries.html [Accessed January 25, 2012].

Lee, K.Y. (2000). *From Third World to First: The Singapore Story 1965–2000*. Singapore: Times Editions.

Ohlin, G. (1992). "Varieties of Policy in the Third World," in L. Putterman and D. Rueschemeyer (eds.), *State and Market in Development—Synergy or Rivalry?*, 9–14 Boulder: Lynne Rienner.

Pickel, A. (2005). "Introduction: False Oppositions. Reconceptualizing Economic Nationalism in a Globalizing World," in E. Helleiner and A. Pickel (eds.), *Economic Nationalism in a Globalizing World*, 1–20. Ithaca: Cornell University Press.

Rajaratnam, S. (1987). "3.5 (c) Singapore, Global City (1972)," in C.H. Chee and U. Obaid (eds.), *The Prophetic and the Political. Selected Speeches and Writings of S. Rajaratnam*, 225–7. Singapore: Graham Brash.

Samuels, W.J. (ed.) (1989). *Fundamentals of the Economic Role of Government*. Westport: Greenwood Press.

"Singapore Cooperation Programme—Training Courses." (2011). http://app.scp.gov.sg/disp_courseinfo_new.asp?crseid=457 [Accessed January 25, 2012].

Tan, S.S. (2007). *Goh Keng Swee: A Portrait*. Singapore: Editions Didier Millet.

Tang, G. and Yuen, V. (2010). "Rethinking Recovery: Possible Discontinuities and Implications for Singapore." *Ethos*, 7 (January). www.cscollege.gov.sg/cgl/pub_ethos_10h1.htm [Accessed January 25, 2012].

US Department of the Treasury. (2007). "Appendix 3: Sovereign Wealth Funds." US Department of the Treasury Semiannual Report on International Economic and Exchange Rate Policies from June 2007. www.ustreas.gov/offices/international-affairs/economic-exchange-rates/pdf/2007_Appendix-3.pdf [Accessed January 25, 2012].

Veltmeyer, H. (2004). *Globalization and Antiglobalization: Dynamics of Change in the New World Order*. Aldershot: Ashgate Publishing.

Widmaier, W. (2009). "Economics are too Important to Leave to Economists: The Everyday—and Emotional—Dimensions of International Political Economy." *Review of International Political Economy*, 16 (5): 945–7.

9

A new "brand" of Chinese economic nationalism: from China made to China managed

Karl Gerth

Since the early 1990s, economic nationalism in China has evolved away from orthodox economic nationalist concerns about protecting the home market from foreign products, services, and direct investment via tariffs and non-tariff barriers and the implementation of trade policies designed to restrict foreign business activities aside from export industries. Economic nationalism in China now has shifted dramatically toward owning and managing domestically and internationally competitive brands. This transition is not accidental but is an explicit goal of current Chinese state policy. Since Beijing decided to join the World Trade Organization (WTO) in the early 1990s, the country has had to comply with new trade rules liberalizing its markets for goods and services. WTO membership was often heralded as the quintessential symbol of the demise of economic nationalism, something that would create a "flat world" wherein borders and nationalities finally surrendered to competitive advantage. Ironically, though, the obligations of WTO membership have actually helped push China toward a newer, more sophisticated form of economic nationalism. This newer form stresses the control of the higher value portions of the value chain, especially branding, rather than simply economic nationalism focused on production with the use of local labor and capital.

Contemporary production typically involves many steps of vertical and horizontal integration of manufacturing and services—from sourcing raw materials, their transformation into finished and semi-finished goods, and their distribution, marketing, and retailing. Branding products is part of marketing but under intense capitalist competition for capturing global markets, branding has taken on a whole new meaning. Product design, both technical and aesthetic, is a high-value input into marketing and branding. Branding is normally associated with firms. However, under globalization states have become important players in their own right, promoting the nation's particular attributes as "brands" or supporting national firms to create and market their own brands. Thus, "champagne" is a brand associated with France and the French government ensures that such a national attribute is not misused by other companies or countries. Governments such as Singapore "brand" the entire nation as a well-functioning city, a destination for foreign direct investment with everything from world-class infrastructure to high-end shopping. Branding is thus a national economic concern. Successful companies with successful products lend their names to national brands. Boeing of the USA, Sony of Japan, Bang and Olufsen of Denmark, and Acer of Taiwan are illustrative examples. Thus China's economic rise is associated with Chinese business expansion, and while no assumption can be made about the emergence of Chinese brands, the high economic stakes, its capitalist drive from the low end of the value chain, and future ambitions, suggest the inevitability of the Chinese state to want to move up the chain with a national brand project.

Using a historical approach and national branding as a point of entry, this chapter examines China's branding in the recent past, identifies the contemporary shift toward creating national brands, and highlights the implications of this shift on the emergence of Chinese brands in the global economy. The chapter is divided into five sections. The first section examines the re-introduction of the most important element of branding, modern advertising; the second briefly explains how branding has become a new measure of national economic strength, leading to the third section, a brief history of economic nationalism in China since the early twentieth century; and a final section examines the difficulties facing Chinese efforts to realize these new goals of brand nationalism by building domestically and internationally competitive brands.

9.1 Advertising and the Revival of Branding

Branding relies on the creation and maintenance of a perception of value and advertising is the key to creating that perception. Unsurprisingly, image-based rather than straightforwardly descriptive advertising was suppressed during the Maoist era (1949–76). Thus this new emphasis on owning and managing brands parallels the re-emergence of consumerism, and especially advertising, in China since the start of the reform era under Deng Xiaoping in 1978. In the first decade of the reforms, China was an economy of shortages with few national brands and little advertising of any kind. When David Ogilvy, dubbed the Father of Advertising, visited China in the early 1980s, he was struck by the near-absence of advertising in Chinese life. He described the print advertisements he did see as looking like specification sheets, containing little more than detailed, technical information about a product and no evocative images, and the few commercials on Chinese television mostly featured industrial products such as electric motors rather than consumer goods. The few big billboards that appeared in major cities, far from displaying fast cars or fun drinks, proclaimed the latest in Communist propaganda. Ogilvy noted that the most important advertising medium in China was radio, "the communal speaker system reaching 75 percent of the population" that would broadcast ads, one right after another, twice a day (Ogilvy 2007: 187).

With market reforms came advertising. Overnight, a great variety of color replaced navy blue (the color of workers' clothing) and green (the color of soldiers' uniforms) as the unofficial colors of Maoist state socialism, in almost every corner of China. The transformation has been both dramatic and rapid. China's ad market has grown by 40% a year over the past two decades and is predicted to pass Germany as the world's third largest market in 2011.[1] In 2008, bolstered by spending for the Beijing Olympics, advertising spending in China grew to nearly US$70 billion, still under half of what the US spends but up 17% over 2007.[2] And there is no shortage of outlets for advertisements: China now has more than two thousand newspapers with a total circulation above a billion, the world's ten largest general-circulation magazines, and over a thousand satellite, cable, and broadcast television channels and three hundred radio stations with a wide audience across China, all providing a vast market for advertising. Nearly all Chinese have access to TVs—and advertising.[3] As China places greater reliance on markets, Beijing is forcing media outlets that once relied on state subsidies to support themselves, to do so via advertising. The results of this policy shift are visible with the presence of advertising seemingly everywhere.

The eventual omnipresence of advertising in China began with outdoor advertising, now a billion-dollar industry, which was the only media sector to allow foreign investment before China joined the WTO in 2001. Once allowed to do so, large foreign-based media companies quickly stepped in and took over, including the world's largest outdoor advertising company, Clear Media, which now manages a network of 27,000 bus stop panels in China. Clear Media introduced international "best practices" such as the use of vivid color, celebrity endorsements, catchy slogans, the frequent rotation of advertisements, and other eye-catching techniques. Indeed, China may even create new best practices that surpass those of the ad-saturated USA by finding new public places to put advertising. In addition to all the usual places—busses, bus stops, along roads, on buildings—advertisements have also popped up on little TV screens in taxis. Even elevators—both while waiting and while riding—sport flat-panel screens broadcasting ads.

Advertising in China is now a huge industry. With over 80,000 ad companies that employ over a million people it is a larger employer in China than in the USA.[4] This is a very large group of people now devoted to something very different from their Mao era counterparts: getting people to think about brand-specific products and identify with new lifestyles. A lot of energy and money is facilitating the introduction of global advertising techniques, all designed to remake Chinese consumer consciousness by getting consumers to desire specific products, to ask the equivalent of a question that defines modern consumerism: Pepsi or Coke? One cosmetics brand alone, Oil of Olay, spent 4.7 billion RMB in advertising in China in 2004.[5] Joining the WTO required China to open its advertising industry to foreign investors and to allow wholly owned foreign firms in by 2005, accelerating the introduction of the latest advertising practices and bringing with them a globally standardized visual culture. To compete, Chinese agencies have had to quickly emulate international practices as Chinese companies such as Haier, Huawei Technologies, Lenovo, and Li Ning sportswear spend billions of dollars on advertising to build their brands against foreign competitors.

The purpose of such advertising is not simply to provide information about available goods and services but to help create brands, which in turn help shape modern individual and collective identities. Brands are the fundamental building blocks of modern consumer cultures, shaping the way people develop their individual and collective identities. As expressed by one 30-something professional woman in Beijing, "Brand names are social status and quality of life. For example, when I was in the United States, I didn't pay much attention to brand names. Here it's a culture. Look at me now, I'm equipped with nothing but brand names, say, Gucci, Fendi, Armani, Versace and the like."[6] Brands, it's worth remembering, are symbolic embodiments of all the information and associations, real or imagined, connected with a product or service—such as thinking that driving an expensive Toyota Prius makes one an environmentalist. So brands incorporate not only information, but expectations. Branding, then, of which advertising is a key component, is not only the creation, management, and delivery of a product or service, it is also the creation of expectations and associations connected with such products and services.

9.2 Chinese Brands: The New Measure of National Strength

In China, branding is more overtly an issue of economic nationalism than in the USA and elsewhere. Most Americans associate the work of branding with companies and the marketplace, not with government officials and the state. Americans think it is Apple's job to make the iPod brand a household name, not the US government's. But in China, consumerism is not simply a product of "the free market," something that developed naturally once the Chinese state got out of the way. Rather, consumerism is a consequence of ongoing policy decisions by China's leaders, most notably to join the WTO and simultaneously to allow multinational companies much greater access to Chinese consumers and to build internationally competitive Chinese-based brands in the ways described below. As Chinese marketing expert Leng Zhenxing has argued, "Banknotes are just like votes. The more the foreign brands get, the less will be left for domestic products."[7] A useful measure of the shift from a few to a plethora of branded products in China is what has happened in trademark registration. In 1980, the Chinese government received 20,000 applications for trademark registrations, a number that by 1993 had reached 132,000 and continued to grow exponentially. By 2004, more than half of all the 2,240,000 registered trademarks had been registered since 2000, a quarter of them just that year. Although the number of foreign applications has also expanded dramatically during the Reform era, from only 20 countries with 5,130 trademarks to 129 countries with more than 400,000 trademarks, more than 80% of those applications have been made by Chinese companies (State Council Information Office 2005).

Yet most consumers outside China, despite being surrounded by goods made wholly or in part there, would probably find it difficult to name a famous Chinese product brand. But if China has its way, that will change dramatically in the coming years. It is hard to exaggerate China's current level of national anxiety over the competitiveness of Chinese brands. A historical analog might be the sense of urgency in the USA to win the Space Race after the Soviet Union launched Sputnik in 1957. Similarly, Chinese leaders believe they need to launch national brands or gain ownership of international ones before it is too late, and survival is seen as much too important to leave to "the market" or individual companies. Rather, building or buying brands is considered a matter of national economic security and, of course, of national pride—China wants its own international *brands* to reflect its commercial success and its new status as a first-rate power.

The success of Chinese brands depends, first of all, on convincing Chinese consumers to buy them—no easy task now that the country can no longer ensure consumer loyalty to domestic manufacturers the way it had since 1949: by protecting its markets, banning imports, limiting access to the foreign currency needed to buy imports, and levying tariffs so high that foreign goods became prohibitively expensive. These brands also have to be built in what is an unreliable marketplace saturated with fakes. No wonder a 2005 survey of 1,200 students in Shanghai and Beijing found that all of their favorite brands were foreign, led by Nike, Sony, Adidas, and BMW.[8] Chinese policy makers fear that if such trends continue across China and across product categories, China will be permanently stuck at the low end of the value-added chain, doing the hard manual labor and collecting low wages but owning precious little of the "value-added," the difference between the cost of making something and its sale price. For instance, the difference between the final assembly costs for the work done in China is estimated at US$4 in 2007 versus the US$299 price tag of a 30-gigabyte video iPod paid by US consumers.[9] Moreover, if foreign owners of favored brands, such as Nike, should decide to shift production to countries with even lower labor costs and weaker environmental protections, China would not even get the low value-added from manufacturing. In effect, then, the logic of China's economic development strategy is forcing it to urge state and private companies to spend billions building brands.

Beginning in the 1980s, Chinese government officials, business leaders, and academics began to urge domestic companies to climb the value-added chain—from simply manufacturing products for multinational brands to developing technology and managing and owning globally competitive brands. This form of economic nationalism is pragmatic. The brands do have to be born or developed in China. When they cannot build brands from scratch, they buy them. This pragmatism is well illustrated by the Chinese partially state-owned company Lenovo, which acquired IBM's personal computing division to create a new company, making it one of the world's largest personal computer manufacturers (Huang 2008).[10] Put another way, this is the difference between manufacturing Mickey Mouse toys and owning and managing Disney's creative operations. Chinese leaders argue that China's massive trade surplus is misleading: Chinese exports are primarily low value-added, meaning that the real value is collected not by China, which provides the physical labor, but by foreign multinationals, which manage and own the technology and brands. Again, a 30-gigabyte iPod has an export value of US$150, but the value added and collected by Chinese labor amounts to only US$4.[11] According to China's Ministry of Commerce, less than 20% of Chinese enterprises participating in foreign trade have their own brands, and less than half of those export them abroad.[12]

Despite short-term anxiety about China's ability to change this situation, Chinese officials hope to emulate the Japanese model of moving up the value-added chain, routinely pointing out that while products "Made in Japan" were considered inferior 40 years ago, they are now viewed as standards of excellence. According to Li Guangdou, a Chinese marketing expert, domestic enterprises can also learn from the success of South Korean firms: "South Korean products used to be synonymous with low-grade products. But when we look at the current situation, Samsung has become one of the world's 100 most valuable brands."[13] For the Chinese, matching these countries' success is a matter not only of national economic well being but of national pride.

That this government-directed movement has had some success in weaning Chinese consumers from a preference for international brands can be seen in the growing popular indignation at what is seen as the inferior treatment of Chinese consumers by foreign companies. As domestic product quality has improved and demand for higher-quality products and luxury goods has grown, so have expectations for brand performance. Consumers, no longer content with first-world market leftovers, have felt increasingly aggrieved, arguing that multinationals do not respect Chinese consumers, take market access for granted, cut corners on safety and quality, ignore Chinese laws, and dump their low-end products there. A popular sentiment about the sales strategy of Japanese companies, for instance, holds that they sell their highest-quality products in European and American markets, their second-best in their domestic market, and their lowest-grade products in the markets of developing countries such as China. One woman, for instance, told me that "Chinese consumers are definitely treated differently by foreign companies! The products they market in China are outmoded. Japan, for example, sends us mobile phones that couldn't make it in Japan, and their cosmetics often contain different ingredients."

The associations between China and inferior brands are bad for the China brand. And the Chinese media, sensitive to such slights and feelings, inevitably highlight the foreignness of a company when any consumer scandal related to imported goods breaks out. In 2003, stories circulated in the media about a Shanghai-based company that, after buying 50 computers from US-based Dell, claimed that the products had been overpriced by nearly US$100,000 and that customers with the same problem in other Asian countries had been treated better. A public campaign against Dell and other foreign companies forced Dell to backtrack. In 2005, quality problems and recalls undermined the reputation of several major international brands: KFC and Heinz were exposed for including the banned carcinogenic dye Sudan-1 in their food, Nikon had to recall defective batteries, Sony had to suspend distribution of six digital camera models with defects, and the level of iodine in Nestle's Golden Growing 3 Plus Baby Formula was found to exceed national standards. In 2005, General Mills' high-end ice cream brand Häagen-Dazs (widely known for its advertising slogan, "if you love her, treat her to Häagen-Dazs") was castigated for operating an "underground" ice-cream cake factory in Shenzhen without proper permits. One Chinese newspaper indignantly wrote, "Why did Häagen-Dazs dare flaunt this practice and what sort of pressure lay behind this illegal factory."[14]

According to Mao Shoulong, a professor at the People's University in Beijing, a rising number of complaints against foreign brands may be partially "due to nationalism because Chinese people feel they might be discriminated against by foreign firms," but he also suggests that foreign brands may be a victim of their own success: "Chinese consumers are more critical of multinational products, as foreign companies have a better image and local consumers have higher trust and higher expectations of foreign brands. That is why consumers gladly pay higher prices for foreign brands."[15] In contrast, powerful domestic brands are sometimes protected from similar consumer scandals. For instance, in 1997, the head of the Beijing *Youth Daily* was fired after publishing a report claiming that yoghurt drinks manufactured by the state-owned Hangzhou Wahaha Group had fatally poisoned several children.[16]

As China becomes increasingly inundated with new waves of products and brands, Chinese consumers demonstrate a deep ambivalence toward domestic brands, as reflected in consumer demands that the government protect Chinese brands against international rivals even as those consumers simultaneously buy foreign products. Photographs of anti-Japanese protests in the spring of 2005, for instance, ironically show many protesters holding Japanese cell phones and cameras. That same year, China's biggest private pollster found that despite popular anti-Japanese sentiments and protests, almost half of those surveyed said they would buy a Japanese car. Such mixed feelings were expressed by Lin Li, a 35-year-old woman shopping in Beijing's Japanese-owned Ito Yakado Shopping Centre, who, while putting a tube of Korean-conglomerate LG toothpaste into her basket, observed that "I like foreign brands because they ensure stable quality and good service. Of course, I hope there will be a day when I can no longer tell the difference between domestic and foreign brands."[17]

This ongoing tension over the seductive power of foreign names has led to some official policies to resist it. Paris of the East Plaza, French Gardens, and Ginza Office Tower are a few of the real estate developments forced to change their names by authorities in the southwestern city of Kunming. The city decided that the trend of attracting China's new middle class by giving new developments foreign-sounding names served to debase traditional culture and introduced rules against naming developments after foreign places, people, or companies. According to the Kunming Communist Party Secretary, "the fashion for foreign-sounding names on buildings is a loss to native culture and reflects poor taste."[18] Officials sometimes also take action against advertising that they find disrespectful to Chinese culture. In 2004, the government banned a Nike commercial featuring US basketball superstar LeBron James outwitting a kung-fu master, claiming that consumers had complained about the ad campaign's disrespectful use of the traditional symbol of dragons. Likewise, in 2003, Toyota created a controversy with an ad for a new Land Cruiser by showing stone lions, traditional symbols of authority, bowing to the vehicle. According to one ad industry executive, "The government sees itself as a guardian of people's dignity and, every so often, it picks a victim to attack in the interests of nationalism."[19]

Chinese companies sometimes take advantage of these sentiments to boost business, killing two birds with one stone as they build bigger businesses and create nationalistic-minded consumers at the same time. Take online gaming, where imports account for 90% of China's US$500 million-dollar market. This led a Chinese software company to collaborate with the China Youth Union, the Communist Party's youth division, and spend 50 million yuan to develop an online game called Anti-Japan War, set in the 1937–45 war between the two nations. Players begin as farmers or workers who aspire to become soldiers in the CCP's Eighth Route Army by rescuing anti-Japanese guerrillas and elderly citizens endangered by Japanese soldiers. The Beijing-based company Huagizixun similarly marketed a line of domestically developed and manufactured digital cameras by naming them after significant events in the war against Japan. The Patriot V (*Aiguo* V) series included models such as the V815, named after the date of the end of World War II (August 15). The company's president, Feng Jun, claimed his products were selling well and suggested that business competition with Japan was simply war by other means: "We're determined to take the offensive against Japan until its digital cameras, which the country considers Japanese brands' last stronghold in the electronic products market, fall to the ground."[20]

9.3 Economic Nationalism in China Since 1900

These national aspirations to create competitive Chinese brands have reintroduced a central theme in Chinese consumerism that was first created with the arrival of mass-produced branded imports in the late nineteenth century (Gerth 2004). The economic nationalism that figured prominently in Sino-foreign relations in the first third of the twentieth century has re-emerged as China has again joined global capitalist markets. In the early twentieth century, the rapid increase in imports and the desires they stimulated threatened powerful domestic interest groups. Among these, Chinese politicians worried about growing trade deficits, which became a new and prime symbol of national weakness. Educated elites, who had begun to read works on Western political economy, feared the loss of sovereignty implicit in the growing foreign dominance of the economy, and manufacturers struggled to produce products to compete against new imports. No one believed that the average Chinese housewife would automatically choose what they called Chinese "national products" over "foreign products"; indeed, they assumed she would intentionally choose foreign products, which were assumed by consumers to be lower priced, higher quality, and sometimes more fashionable.

These anxieties over consumers choosing price and quality over patriotism ultimately produced a multifaceted "Buy Chinese" campaign modeled on similar campaigns in countries such as the USA, India, and many other countries wherein advocates developed countless ways to exhort compatriots to consume their own national products.[21] These included skillfully using the same tools as their foreign rivals, such as advertisements, department stores, product exhibitions, and boycotts.

The formation of the People's Republic of China in 1949 soon ended the ease with which consumers could choose foreign products. Mao Zedong's regime aimed to turn cities known for their consumption into centers of production instead, emulating the Soviet Union's economic model with its emphasis on state-owned heavy industry over consumer goods, and gradually forced foreign multinationals to leave China and eliminated most foreign products from store shelves. After some initial hesitation, which allowed consumer lifestyles to persist into the mid-1950s, the state appropriated all private enterprises and consumer culture was virtually outlawed. Thirty years later, after the death of Chairman Mao in 1976, China dramatically changed course. With the start of Deng Xiaoping's economic reforms and the policy known as "opening to the outside world," or simply the Open Door Policy, China slowly began to permit the import of consumer goods. As with WTO membership decades later, allowing greater access for imports to domestic markets was a small price to pay to gain better access to foreign consumer markets for Chinese products.

But over the past three decades, as the range and volume of imports has grown, the tension between "Chinese products" and "foreign products" has periodically re-emerged in Chinese attitudes. One reason for this is that as China's WTO commitments have allowed easier market access for multinationals, this has rendered countless village-owned and state-owned enterprises uncompetitive and created millions of unemployed and angry workers. Chinese students continue to invoke the language of economic nationalism and to call for boycotts of foreign goods, as they did to protest the US bombing of the Chinese embassy in Belgrade in 1999, and more recently in a widespread boycott of the French retailing giant Carrefour in retaliation for the disruption of the 2008 Olympic torch relay in Paris. Chinese consumers also periodically call for boycotts of specific foreign products when they feel Chinese consumers collectively have been treated poorly or differently by multinational companies. Such actions demonstrate doubts among the Chinese about the wisdom of leaving the national well being to the "free market."

A hundred years ago, China struggled to catch up as a global *manufacturing* superpower. Mission accomplished. Now the Chinese recognize that in the "post-industrial" reign of "service economies," their country now needs to become a *branding* superpower. Chinese government and business leaders view domestic ownership of global brands and intellectual property as symbolic of national wealth and power, the economic equivalent of hosting the Olympics but much more permanent. China wants its own domestic companies to join the list of prominent global brands associated with powerful countries such as the USA (McDonald's, Microsoft, Apple, Boeing, Starbucks, Google), Germany (BMW), Japan (Honda, Nintendo, Sony), and Korea (LG, Samsung). Moreover, the government wants to develop competitive brands across the spectrum of consumer products and services, including high-tech consumer electronics (such as Midea headquartered in Shunde near Hong Kong), and to revive "established brands" in traditional areas such as medicine (Tongrentang). This push to create Chinese-owned brands also applies to the service sector, where the Ministry of Commerce has set ambitious targets, including developing 100 restaurant brands, 50 famous hotel brands, and prominent brands in the beauty, laundry, and home service industries.[22] To help accomplish these goals, state policies have promoted the creation of large-scale, horizontally integrated multinational corporations to compete against foreign multinationals. In the 1990s, the state selected a "national team" of 120 industrial groups to receive state assistance, and it promoted 925 top domestic brands. The conglomerates behind the brands include the energy giants Sinopec and CNPC, Sanjiu and Dongbei in pharmaceuticals, Dongfang in power equipment, Yiqi and Erqi in automobiles, Shougang and Baogang in steel, and Datong and Shenhua in coal mining.[23]

In 2002, the Chinese state further strengthened its control over large companies by creating the very powerful if infelicitously named State Assets Supervision and Administration Council (SASAC) (pronounced sah-sack). Given the power of this organization, this acronym is worth remembering; it may be the most important one in China after PLA (People's Liberation Army). SASAC owns and runs over 150 enormous corporations, including 8 of the 14 mainland Chinese enterprises listed on the Fortune 500. Where China once invited in foreign investors with its Open Door Policy, since the early 1990s it has also been laying the groundwork for these new Chinese conglomerates to exit through that door. For instance, the Chinese government has used SASAC to entice them to "go global" with favorable policies, including the abolition of foreign currency restrictions for overseas investment[24] (Bellabona and Spigarelli 2007). China intends to remake the perception of Chinese brands, and hence of China itself, around the globe through these new, internationally prominent brands. The effects of the Chinese government's pressure on the nation's biggest companies to sell more branded products abroad is most visible in developing markets, where the Chinese already sell branded appliances, consumer electronics, and even automobiles. One can find Chinese-made Geely cars even on the streets of Havana, where there are reports that Cuban Communist Party officials have switched their allegiance from solidly built, old Russian Ladas to new-model Geelys.[25]

These initiatives are simply a dry run for competition in developed markets. China's biggest appliance maker, Haier, already sells small refrigerators under its own name in the USA and plans to popularize its full-size refrigerators next. It's also aggressively trying to acquire established white goods brands, including a failed attempt to buy Maytag in 2005 and a subsequent effort to buy established brands, including GE's white goods division (Gao et al. 2003). In a country where after-sales service had disappeared under Mao, Haier has attempted to brand itself as a leader in customer service, differentiating itself from its rivals with its slogan, "Phone up for immediate repairs, 24 hours a day." They also have tried to extend this branding abroad, arguing that the company is a "local" in each country where it operates.

Although international pressure and its entry into the WTO forced China's leaders to remove formal barriers to foreign products, this hasn't stopped them from playing both a direct and an indirect role in promoting brand nationalism. For instance, in 2003 the former chief negotiator in China's efforts to join the WTO, Long Yongtu, claimed that encouraging Chinese consumers to purchase Chinese products "will violate neither the WTO rules nor the market economic rules." Chinese entrepreneurs routinely express a similar sentiment. According to underwear manufacturer Zhou Xiaoning of the Zhongke Group, domestic brand consciousness is critical to Chinese economic development: "Without the recognition of domestic consumers, how can China brands grow and mature?"[26] Likewise, in the summer of 2008, the national government even incorporated the establishment, protection, and management of national brands into its national strategy.[27]

Although accepting WTO restrictions ostensibly promises a level playing field for foreign products in China, Chinese leaders continue to use government policies to create non-tariff barriers to foreign trade. For example, the China National Tobacco Corp. (CNTC), a government monopoly, still controls 90% of the domestic cigarette market, helped by non-tariff barriers such as the regulations governing new cigarette factories, limits on the number of sales offices, and provincial-level quotas to preserve its market share. Successful foreign brands, most notably Philip Morris' Marlboro, are allowed to enter the market only by producing their branded cigarettes at CNTC-affiliated factories. These "partnerships" allow CNTC to limit competition, acquire new technology, leverage a high-profile international brand, and gain access to overseas markets.[28] And these barriers can also be erected at the local and provincial level. One county in China made international news for trying to raise revenue by requiring its officials to smoke only local brands or face fines. And each administrative unit was assigned a minimum number of cartons to consume.[29]

Government-sponsored promotion of Chinese brand consciousness has also included setting up new mechanisms to help domestic consumers identify Chinese products among the torrent of brands now available. In anticipation of stiff foreign competition after entry to the WTO, the State General Administration for Quality Supervision and Inspection and Quarantine, China's watchdog for product quality, set up a "China brand name strategy promotion commission" and awarded 57 brands from 45 enterprises the title of "China's Top Brand." The goal was to alert Chinese consumers to high-quality domestic brands.[30] In a move reminiscent of China's anti-imperialist economic nationalist campaigns of the early twentieth century, the government now organizes exhibitions for "established brands" (*laozihao*) to increase national brand awareness among consumers.

Another advantage Chinese companies have over their international competitors is that the huge and highly competitive Chinese market forces multinationals to adapt international brands to local tastes—what some have called "glocalization." This has become ever more essential as Chinese consumers, now confronting choice rather than scarcity, become pickier about what they buy. Of course, multinationals can and do overcome these obstacles. For international brands, one of the earliest and most basic localization efforts has been selecting a Chinese-language brand name that sounds felicitous and invokes the right images. Unlike alphabets based solely on sounds, most Chinese characters also have evocative meanings, making essentially meaningless brand names such as Xerox or Intel impossible in Chinese. When Coke first entered China in the 1920s, it rendered its name *kou ke kou la*, which meant "a thirsty mouth and a mouth of candle wax." Coke soon changed the translation to *ke kou ke le*, which instead translates as "a joyful taste and happiness" (Yan 1994). Laurent Philippe, the head of Procter & Gamble in China, recognized the importance of selecting Chinese names that "trigger meaningful visuals or associations with benefits," and thus it is no accident that the Chinese characters used for Pampers, the disposable baby diaper brand, carry much the same meaning as the English-language name: "helping baby's comfort"[31] (Penhirin 2004). The product's phenomenal success in China has become international marketing history.

A key "glocalizing" strategy is to recognize and reinforce consumer differences, and give consumers the perception, if not the reality, that their individual needs are being met. Companies have learned that they cannot target "the Chinese" as a homogenous market of largely identical consumers. The resulting move toward market segmentation—the recognition that subgroups within a market share common characteristics that set them apart—is forcing companies to expand their product offerings to accommodate regional, generational, class, and other preferences. To meet regional taste preferences, for instance, KFC sells "Old Peking Style Chicken Rolls" with sweet bean sauce and mushroom chicken porridge (Wang 2008). At the same time, the consumption of branded products also makes those segmentations possible. Consuming segment-specific branded products has become a way for Chinese consumers to manifest differences in wealth, education, and regional identity. If you are what you consume (say, a BMW), you are also what you do not consume (a Red Flag, Brilliance, or other Chinese-brand car).

Now that China's biggest cities have become major markets for both Chinese and international brands, marketers are increasingly turning their attention to capturing the hearts, minds, brand loyalties, and purchasing power of Chinese consumers outside the 100 million-plus Chinese living in a handful of big cities. After all, China has over 150 cities with populations of more than a million (compared to the USA, which has around ten). On the one hand, by creating nationally recognized chains and brands, companies are standardizing the shopping experience so that the majority of the population now recognizes hundreds, even thousands, of brands, and making these available across the country. But while producing brands intended for mass or even universal consumption, companies are also segmenting the market and expanding product offerings to accommodate varying preferences. For instance, in 2000 GM offered a limited number of car models in China, primarily large, high-end Buicks costing around US$40,000. Private ownership of cars had just begun, and GM's primary customers were government officials and entrepreneurs who wanted large sedans to transport top cadres. Just five years later, GM was marketing $75,000-plus Cadillac SRX sport-utility vehicles to the very rich; the popular $30,000 Buick Regal to cost-conscious entrepreneurs looking for a high-status car; the $15,000 to $20,000 Buick Excelle to mid-level managers; the $19,000 Chevrolet Epica sedan, the $10,000 to $12,000 Aveo hatchback, and the $5,700 Spark minicar to younger urbanites buying their first cars; and $4,000 to $6,500 minivans designed to carry seven passengers and their cargo to buyers in the countryside. To reach this broader market, it also expanded its distribution network to over a thousand outlets, up from just nine in 1998.

Chinese and foreign companies alike have also learned how to adapt quickly to the varying needs of the population. The appliance maker Haier sells dozens of washing-machine models in China, including a tiny one targeted at rural customers that costs only US$37. After a farmer in Sichuan Province supposedly broke his Haier washing machine by using it to scrub yams, the company decided to cater to this market by building new models designed to wash yams and shrimp (Wen 2007). Similarly, the Korean multinational Samsung discovered that customers living in the hot and humid southern province of Guangdong wanted larger refrigerators than those in the north.[32]

9.4 China's Branding Challenges

Despite government investments and policies that favor China's own products, Chinese companies face a number of challenges as they make the transition from the earlier fragmented, state-run, and production-oriented economy to one driven by creating consumer desires and meeting consumer demands. The first of these challenges is one China faced a century ago when Japan overtook it as the world's largest exporter of silk and the British in India took a commanding share of the global tea trade: the mass production of consistency. Chinese products have real and perceived problems with consistency—that is, with producing large quantities of identical, high-quality goods. This is especially true in the food industry, where foreign brands provide nearly identical products regardless of time or place. While there are, of course, efforts to localize international fast-food chains, consumers at a McDonald's or KFC in most of the world can expect their food to look and taste the same wherever they buy it (see Watson 2006). In contrast, the well-known Chinese fast food Yangzhou Fried Rice tastes different from restaurant to restaurant and even from chef to chef, though China has started to create successful fast-food chains like Kungfu, known for its steamed food, which aims to deliver orders within 80 seconds.

Under the productivist paradigm of the Maoist era, consistency was much less important than supply. Demand was assumed and, thanks to shortages, was assured. But with the country's re-integration into global capitalist markets, China's political and business leaders want to consolidate and standardize domestic products before foreign companies do. Take the tea industry, where one would assume China would have a competitive advantage. China has over 1,000 varieties of tea, many of which are renowned throughout the world. However, there are no national tea brands, far less international ones. Thanks to climate and soil conditions as well as traditional preferences, most Chinese tea brands are regional. Southern Chinese tend to prefer green tea and Northerners prefer jasmine-favored tea. Moreover, many teas are still produced by families, making it nearly impossible to ensure their quality. These problems, combined with a growing Chinese appetite for trustworthy branded products, have confirmed government fears: aggressive foreign expansion. The Anglo-Dutch Unilever Group has bought out a Chinese tea brand, Jinghua Tea, and expanded its Lipton black tea to Lipton green and jasmine tea. If Chinese companies can't create competitive tea brands, what hope is there for other products?

As noted, Chinese companies and officials trying to build Chinese brands also battle a legacy of the socialist economy's emphasis on managing shortages on the supply side rather than appealing to consumers on the demand side. That is, the Mao regime emphasized quantity, not quality, much less the product differentiation that is the foundation of branding. Quality, moreover, was often sacrificed in favor of simple availability.[33] But manufacturers who once had monopolies and could assume endless demand cannot do so anymore. Take, for example. Beijing's Daming Optical, established in 1937, which first built its reputation by selling high-quality foreign brands. It was the first commercial optician to sell foreign-made glasses and, after nationalization, was also permitted to sell to foreigners. However, market deregulation has given its domestic competitors access to foreign suppliers, ending Daming's monopoly. To compete, it has opened dozens of chain stores, launched advertising campaigns, renovated storefronts, and retrained employees to be more service oriented. To reinvent its "established brand" status, Daming, like many other brands that survived the Maoist era, has had to explore partnerships with better-capitalized foreign companies to survive.[34] As a young Chinese professional from Beijing noted, "Most 'established brands' are good and are well thought of by consumers. But these products are only good enough to attract Chinese consumers and not foreigners, so their continued existence cannot be easy."

Another legacy of the socialist era is the near absence of prominent domestic brands. Before the reforms, watches were one of the "three luxuries" for most Chinese, and China had several prominent domestic watch brands, such as Shanghai, Seagull, and Five Star. Perhaps they were "luxuries" not because of their price but because of their scarcity. In the early 1970s, when there were almost no imported rivals, although watches like the Shanghai cost the equivalent of four or five months' salary for most people, even at that price, Chinese willingly waited in long lines whenever supplies appeared. But this began to change in the early 1980s, when domestic brands began to lose the mid- and high-end watch market. At first, mid-level foreign brands such as Citizen and Seiko captured market share, and since then Rolex, Omega, and Cartier have become new status symbols. While Chinese manufacturers still control the low-end market for watches, the mid- and high-end markets are now controlled by foreign brands, which comprise a third of the 200 or so brands on the market. Chinese watch makers have attempted but failed to develop luxury watch brands and seem unable to overcome the public perception that domestic watches are inexpensive but inferior.[35]

Other Chinese companies have had a difficult time making the transition from state patronage and the prestige derived from a lack of access or monopoly to market competition and advertising. Take Maotai, the famous Chinese liquor distilled from fermented sorghum and manufactured exclusively in the southwest province of Guizhou (like "Champagne," Maotai is trademarked by place). Maotai was a favorite liquor of Chinese leaders Deng Xiaoping, Zhou Enlai, and Mao Zedong and used to toast at important state occasions, including ceremonies marking events from the founding of the People's Republic of China to its entry into the WTO. Because of its high profile and the fact that one needed written permission to obtain it, Maotai never needed to advertise. Although Maotai is now affordable, available, and heavily advertised, intense competition in the liquor industry has undermined its status and therefore the value of the brand.[36] Cognac is the liquor of choice today, thanks to its position as a status symbol among China's newly rich. Savvy producers have reinforced this image. In 1994, Seagram introduced a mid-priced cognac, Martell Noblige, aimed at middle-class Chinese consumers anxious to emulate elite lifestyles. At home and abroad, the Chinese now consume a fourth of the global cognac supply.[37]

Despite government efforts to help officially designated established brands compete, the companies behind these brands still often make basic mistakes of brand management based on socialist-era assumptions; indeed, "branding" itself is often considered a waste of money. In 1990, the former Ministry of Commerce awarded the title "old and famous brands" to 1,600 shops and enterprises in the clothing, medicine, and food and beverage industries. These nationalized holdovers from the pre-Maoist eras had never needed to turn a profit, and even household names like Quanjude's Peking duck, Tongrentang's traditional Chinese medicine, and Wuyutai's tea have faced difficult transitions. Of these designated famous brands, 20% have been operating at a loss for years and are nearly bankrupt, while another 70% are barely profitable. Thus, these former pillars of Chinese consumer consciousness have begun to disappear. In January 2003, for instance, Wangmazi Scissors, a Beijing institution founded in 1651, sparked a national debate on traditional brands by announcing its bankruptcy.[38]

Beyond the problem of profitability, established companies sometimes lost out to opportunistic newcomers in the race to register established brand names. A type of steamed bun from Hunan province, Deyuan baoyi, named after a famous provincial, was registered by a company from outside the province. A type of a famous stuffed steamed bun from Hunan province, Deyuan baozi, for instance, was registered by a company from outside the province. (Imagine if a Pittsburgh-based company owned the rights to Philly Cheese Steak.) It took the original company nearly 20 years to recover the rights. In other cases, foreign companies have registered the names of long-established Chinese brands in their own countries. By 2005, 180 Chinese brands were registered by foreign companies in Australia and at least 100 Chinese brands in Japan; a full 15% of Chinese brands that applied for registration abroad were embarrassed to learn that others had already beaten them to it (Xiang 2005). The most famous example was the huge computer manufacturer Lianxiang, now known in English as Lenovo, which had to change its name from Legend because of such trademark conflicts.

Lastly, the fact that China more often resembles a collection of diverse markets than a single, integrated market has slowed brand development in China. There are, for instance, 400 brands of cigarettes in China, the world's largest consumer, where about 60% of men smoke. Given regional tastes, China more closely resembles the historically fragmented European market than the relatively now homogeneous North American market. Because of a lack of distribution infrastructure, national brands must rely on local partnerships or acquisitions. In the 1990s, Tsingtao Brewery, for example, successfully built a national network by acquiring 22 local breweries stretching from Shenzhen in the far south to Beijing in the north. The less-expensive Beijing-based Yanjing Beer Company, China's largest brewer, also followed the same strategy. In contrast, foreign breweries like Anheuser-Busch constructed enormous production facilities that exceeded the capabilities of the logistical infrastructure, leading Anheuser-Busch ultimately to buy a fourth of Tsingtao to gain access to the Chinese beer market, now the world's largest, and making Tsingtao one of the country's most famous exported products.

9.5 Conclusion

For Chinese consumers, among the consequences of this national obsession with creating national brands is the increasing standardization of brands across the nation, a foundational element of a national consciousness through consumerism. One might view this as a Chinese McDonaldization or internal Coca-Colonization, as China, like the USA in the early twentieth century, goes from having countless local brands to having a handful of national and international ones. To win the battle of the brands in the marketplace, Chinese brands will have to do all the obvious things. They will have to provide value for whatever they charge, including making high-quality, innovative products. They will also have to make their brands household names with positive associations though advertising in all its wondrous forms, from the yeoman bus stop poster to the subtle product placement in popular movies and TV shows.

Since the late nineteenth century, China's leadership (if not necessarily its housewife-on-the-street consumers) has developed a strong sense of economic nationalism and demonstrated a willingness to make any sacrifice to develop world-class industries in the name of "national survival," including sacrificing the well being of China's workers and the health of its environment. In the current post-industrial world, Chinese leaders see ownership and control over world-class brands as the next battleground, the key to continued economic development.

And if China can't win the brand wars in the marketplace, it could choose to take other steps to control access to the market, regardless of its WTO obligations, such as further promoting the purchase of brands abroad. In at least some crucial sectors, Chinese companies can also make themselves not just the most attractive but the only brand by controlling resources and production. In the new field of green energy technology, for instance, China's willingness to mine without regard to environmental and human costs has made it the producer of over 90% of the world's rare earth metals, vital raw materials required to make all sorts of high-tech products, from Prius hybrid cars to wind turbines to missiles.[39] Although the WTO may have the final say, simply by imposing tighter restrictions on the sale and export of these natural resources, China has found a very easy way not only to compete with pioneering green companies in the rest of the world, but to ensure brand supremacy for things such as wind turbines and car batteries, some of the most important industries of the twenty-first century.

Notes

1. R. Bender, "China to Overtake Germany as No. 3 Ad Market in 2011," *Wall Street Journal*, December 5, 2010.
2. Xiao Y., "Ad Spending Rises 17 Percent in the First Quarter of 2008, with Steady Increases by Olympic Partners." *Zhongguo xinwen bao*, May 15, 2008.
3. Xie G., "A Report on the 2006 Chinese TV Ad Market." *Xinwen zhanxian*, March 2007.
4. "A Million Advertising Employees Face Assessment Examination." Zhongguo xinwen chuban wang, October 29, 2007. The USA employed about half a million in advertising and public relations in 2006. See US Bureau of Labor Statistics, "Advertising and Public Relations Services." http://www.bls.gov/oco/cg/cgs030.htm
5. Yang W., "Spending on Cosmetics Advertising is the Highest," *Xinjing bao*, February 28, 2005.
6. J. Borton, "Magazine Licensing Red-Hot in China." *Asia Times*, December 16, 2004.
7. "Official: Consumption of Chinese Products should be Encouraged." *China Daily*, September 19, 2003.
8. Xuan Yi, "Who Pays for Cool? A Survey of Consumer Sentiment among Current University Students." *Beijing chenbao*, April 30, 2004.
9. H. Varian, "An iPod Has Global Value. Ask the (Many) Countries That Make It." *New York Times*, June 28, 2007.
10. Yasheng Huang argues that the company is *not* "Chinese" and became successful through its access to foreign capital via Hong Kong. See his *Capitalism with Chinese Characteristics: Entrepreneurship and the State* (2008): 1–10. That said, the myth that it is a "Chinese company" is what matters here.
11. A. Wheatley, "China Starts to Protect Trademarks." *International Herald Tribune*, September 16, 2008.

12. Zhang Y., "Ministry of Commerce: only 20 percent of companies involved in international trade have their own brands." *Beijing chenbao*, February 28, 2007.
13. Wen B., "Chinese Enterprises Urgently Need to Improve Their Brand Competitiveness." *Zhishi chanquan bao*, January 16, 2004.
14. Wang Z., "The Business Logic Behind the Shenzhen Häagen-Dazs Incident." *Ershiyi shiji jingji baodao*, July 6, 2005.
15. Dai Y., "Great Expectations." *China Daily*, March 13, 2006.
16. "Consumer Rights—Buyers Bite Back." *China Economic Review*, January 23, 1999.
17. Liu W., "Consumers Have Their Say." *China Daily*, January 9, 2004.
18. Yu J., "Kunming Development Arouses Local Resentment," *Zhongguo qingnian bao*, August 8, 2005; "Kunming Bans Foreign-sounding Names." *China Daily*, September 14, 2005.
19. A. White, "Nike Faces China Ire over 'Fear' Ad." *Media Asia*, December 17, 2004.
20. "Chinese Companies Cashing in on Anti-Japanese Sentiment." *Yomiuri Shimbun*, September 29, 2005. For more on Feng Jun, see Fan Yinghua, "Feng Jun: A Patriot's Paranoia." *Xiaokang caizhi*, August 17, 2009.
21. For a good overview of the Indian case, see C.A. Bayly, "The Origins of Swadeshi (Home Industry): Cloth and Indian Society, 1700–1930" (1986) and Sumit Sarkar *The Swadeshi Movement in Bengal, 1903–1908* (1973). For a survey of similar efforts to link nationalism and consumption in America from the Boston Tea Party to the present, see Dana Frank, *Buy American: The Untold Story of Economic Nationalism* (1999). I briefly survey these and others in Gerth, "Introduction," *China Made*, (2004).
22. "China's Established Brands: Beijing Has the Most." *Beijing yule xinbao*, October 8, 2006.
23. An Li, "A Gathering for 925 Products," *Zhongguo zhiliang yu pinpai*, Issue 1, 2006. Cambridge University management professor Peter Nolan has written extensively on the subject of China's "national team." See, for instance, his *China and the Global Economy* (2001).
24. "SASAC Director Li Rongrong: Only the Best State-owned Enterprises Should Make Acquisitions in Europe and the United States."*Zhongguo zhengquan bao*, September 27, 2008.
25. E. Israel, "Sturdy Lada Faces a Rival for Cuban Affection." *International Herald Tribune*, September 30, 2009.
26. "Official: Consumption of Chinese Products should be Encouraged." *China Daily*, September 19, 2003.
27. "The Guiding Principle of National Intellectual Property strategy." http://baike.baidu.com/view/1736822.htm June 5, 2008.
28. M. Young, "Marlboro Country's Borderline with China." *Asia Times*, March 10, 2006.
29. C. Coonan, "Chinese Workers Urged to Puff Up Economy by Smoking." *Irish Times*, May 5, 2009; see also J. Wang, "Tobacco Monopoly Faces the Impact of International Competition." *Kaifang chao*, August 2003.
30. "45 Businesses Scoop Top Brand Gongs." *Xinhua*, September 3, 2001.
31. Shi Y., "An Analysis of Some Problems Translating Luxury Brand Names." *Jingji yu shehui fazhan*, April 2009.

32. D. Roberts and D. Rocks, "China: Let A Thousand Brands Bloom." *Business Week* Online, October 17, 2005.
33. J. Iyengar, "China Strives for its Own Global Mega-brands." *Asia Times*, October 5, 2004.
34. J. Liu, "Eye on Expansion." *China Daily*, August 22, 2005.
35. "Foreign Brands Replace Chinese Watches as Status Symbols." *People's Daily* Online, April 5, 2006; Luo Yaxian and Zou Qilin, "The Life and Death of the Chinese Watch Industry." *Qiye guanli*, July 2008.
36. "Maotai Liquor: From Drink of Officials to Drink of Ordinary People." *China Daily*, September 29, 2002.
37. J. Scarry, "Making the Consumer Connection: Heroes Can Mean Everything When Marketing in China." *The China Business Review*, April 24, 1997; L. Huang, "Declining Consumer Demand for Domestic Baijiu: Young People Think Drinking it is Unfashionable." *Changcheng wang*, November 26, 2009.
38. "Brands May Not Live Forever." *China Daily*, May 4, 2004; "Old Firms Need Brand Protection." *China Business Weekly*, August 9, 2004.
39. K. Bradsher, "China Tightens Grip on Rare Minerals." *New York Times*, August 31, 2009.

References

Bayly, C.A. (1986). "The Origins of Swadeshi (Home Industry): Cloth and Indian Society, 1700–1930," in A. Appadurai (ed.), *The Social Life of Things: Commodities in Cultural Perspective*, 285–321. Cambridge: Cambridge University Press.

Bellabona, P. and Spigarelli, F. (2007). "Moving from Open Door to Go Global: China Goes on the World Stage." *International Journal of Chinese Culture and Management*, 1: 93–108.

Frank, D. (1999). *Buy American: The Untold Story of Economic Nationalism*. Boston: Beacon Press.

Gao, P., Woetzel, J., and Wu, Y. (2003). "Can Chinese Brands Make it Abroad?" *The McKinsey Quarterly*, 4 (December): 54–65. Special Edition: Global Directions.

Gerth, K. (2004). *China Made: Consumer Culture and the Creation of the Nation*. Cambridge, Mass.: Harvard University Press.

Huang, Y. (2008). *Capitalism with Chinese Characteristics: Entrepreneurship and the State*. Cambridge: Cambridge University Press.

Nolan, P. (2001). *China and the Global Economy*. New York: Palgrave Macmillan.

Ogilvy, D. (2007). *Ogilvy on Advertising*. London: Carlton Publishing Group.

Penhirin, J. (2004). "Understanding the Chinese Consumer." *The McKinsey Quarterly*, 3 (July): 46–57.

Sarkar, S. (1973). *The Swadeshi Movement in Bengal, 1903–1908*. Cambridge: Cambridge University Press.

State Council Information Office. (2005). "New Progress on China's IPR Protection" (white paper). April 21.

Wang, J. (2008). *Brand New China: Advertising, Media, and Commercial Culture*. Cambridge, Mass.: Harvard University Press.

Watson, J. (ed.) (2006). *Golden Arches East: McDonald's in East Asia* (2nd edn). Stanford: Stanford University Press.

Wen, H. (2007). "A Confucian Capitalist Goes Global." *CommonWealth Magazine* (Taiwan), January 31.

Xiang J. (2005). "Reflection on the Promotion of Brand Strategy by Government—A Research on the Development of Commercial Brands in Huangpu District." Masters in Public Administration Thesis, Fudan University, Shanghai, November.

Yan, R. (1994). "To Reach China's Consumers, Adapt to Guo Qing." *Harvard Business Review*, 72 (5): 4–10 (September/October).

10

Chinese economic nationalism, Japanese enterprises, and localization: the growing importance of social engagement

Keikoh Ryu

10.1 Introduction

The long and complex history between China and Japan, and in particular the "negative heritage" of World War II, which has been exacerbated by recent territorial disputes involving the Senkaku Islands and the natural resources of the East China Sea,[1] has effectively alienated the two countries and led to a pervasive culture of anti-Japanese sentiment throughout China. Following the violent anti-Japanese demonstrations of 2005, China's hostility towards Japan has also had an effect on the economic prospects of Japanese corporations, creating apprehension over the future of Japanese corporate and trade relations in China. The widespread dissemination of anti-Japanese propaganda by the Chinese media has further contributed to this negative image of Japanese corporations. This pervasive climate of anti-Japanese sentiment has forced Japanese companies seeking to expand their businesses abroad to grapple with the unique challenges of navigating the highly politicized environment of Chinese economic nationalism. Although the Chinese mainland remains an important market for a variety of Japanese industries, these economic ties have formed against a historical backdrop characterized by complex and thorny political issues that cannot be resolved through compromise alone. Hence, despite Japan's continued support for China's economic and technological development, mutual misunderstandings and historical grudges are likely to dictate Sino-Japanese relations in both the public and private sector for some time to come.

Anti-Japanese sentiment aside, China is currently in the midst of a strategic crossroads in its development which begs a radical re-examination of the last 30 years of economic reform since the Cultural Revolution.[2] As the world's second largest economy, third largest trader, and the largest recipient of foreign direct investment with two trillion dollars in foreign reserves, China's status in the global economy is impressive. Yet its rapid growth is unbalanced and possibly unsustainable. In an effort to maintain a delicate equilibrium between continuous economic growth, environmental protection, and social stability, President Hu Jintao[3] and Premier Wen Jiabao[4] have developed political ideologies based on the prioritization of social issues rather than purely economic ones. This shift is at the heart of the notion of the "harmonious society," a national vision geared toward continuous, stable development and based on the recognition that social problems can only be addressed by paying greater attention to the impact of economic development on society at large.

All of this begs the question: how should Japanese corporations respond to Chinese economic nationalism in growing their business? The performance of Japanese enterprises in China has always been an important topic of study, though very few have directly addressed the effects of Chinese economic nationalism on the performance of Japanese corporations operating in China. Based on field research conducted between April 2006 and September 2009, this chapter begins with an analysis of the state of Sino–Japanese relations and the theoretical framework behind strategies for dealing with economic nationalism, and goes on to discuss economic nationalism in China and its impact on Japan's commercial prospects in terms of the growing importance of "business–society relations" in reversing this trend. The chapter concludes by recommending strategies for social engagement that deal effectively with these issues. Generally speaking, Japanese corporations attempting to make inroads into China must not only compete with domestic and multinational corporations, but also work to improve their public image by focusing on social issues of environmental protection and social stability.

10.2 The Sino–Japanese Predicament

10.2.1 *Politics and Economics of Sino–Japanese Relations*

This section focuses on the recent political and economic history of Sino–Japanese relations in order to identify the obstacles posed by the rise of Chinese economic nationalism and to place the competitive market faced by Japanese corporations in context.

Sino–Japanese relations are perhaps best described as both "near and far"—near in terms of geography, culture, and economics, yet far in terms of politics, customs, and ways of thinking. In particular, the "negative heritage" of World War II has effectively led to a history of hostility and alienation between the two countries that continues to this day.[5] Although relations have improved since Junichiro Koizumi stepped down as prime minister in 2006,[6] anti-Japanese sentiment in China continues to be informed by territorial disputes over the Senkaku Islands and the natural resources of the East China Sea, as well as the controversy over the visits of high-ranking officials to the Yasukuni Shrine, where the spirits of Japanese war criminals are honored.

On April 9, 2005, the lingering controversy over the Yasukuni Shrine, along with changes to Japanese history textbooks that whitewashed Japan's wartime behavior, and the proposal that Japan be granted a permanent seat on the United Nations Security Council, led to large-scale protests across China. Businesses with connections to Japan were vandalized by protesters, as were billboards advertising Japanese goods and stores stocking Japanese products. Begun in Beijing and quickly spreading to Shanghai, Tianjin, Xiamen, and Guangzhou, these demonstrations shocked many Japanese nationals living and working in China. More recently, in March 2009, Prime Minister Taro Aso sent a potted plant as an offering to the Yasukuni Shrine and referred to the Senkaku Islands as Japanese territory protected under the US–Japan Treaty of Mutual Cooperation and Security. And in September 2010, the Japanese Coast Guard's arrest of a Chinese trawler captain in disputed waters snowballed into a heated diplomatic standoff with severe repercussions for the two nations' economic and political ties.[7]

Yet while the history between the two countries has been characterized by complex and thorny political issues that have proven resistant to resolution through negotiation and compromise, the development of economic relations between China and Japan has been vigorous (Figure 10.1). Since as early as 2002, the growth of the Chinese economy has been instrumental to Japan's economic well being, and Japanese companies remain some of the most prominent supporters of China's economic and technological development. Through a combination of outsourcing and foreign direct investment,[8] Japanese multinational enterprises (MNEs) have fostered mutually beneficial relations with Chinese firms by gradually integrating them into their global production networks. While Japanese MNEs have utilized China's cheap and productive labor force to strengthen their global competitiveness, Chinese firms have used Japan's global marketing networks and world-renown brands to sell "made-in-China" products around the world.

Japanese corporations have increased their presence in China significantly over the past decade as China has developed into more than simply an inexpensive place for production. From 1990 to 2003, Japan was China's number one trading partner, and in 2007 it emerged as China's top export customer, with bilateral trade between the two countries reaching an

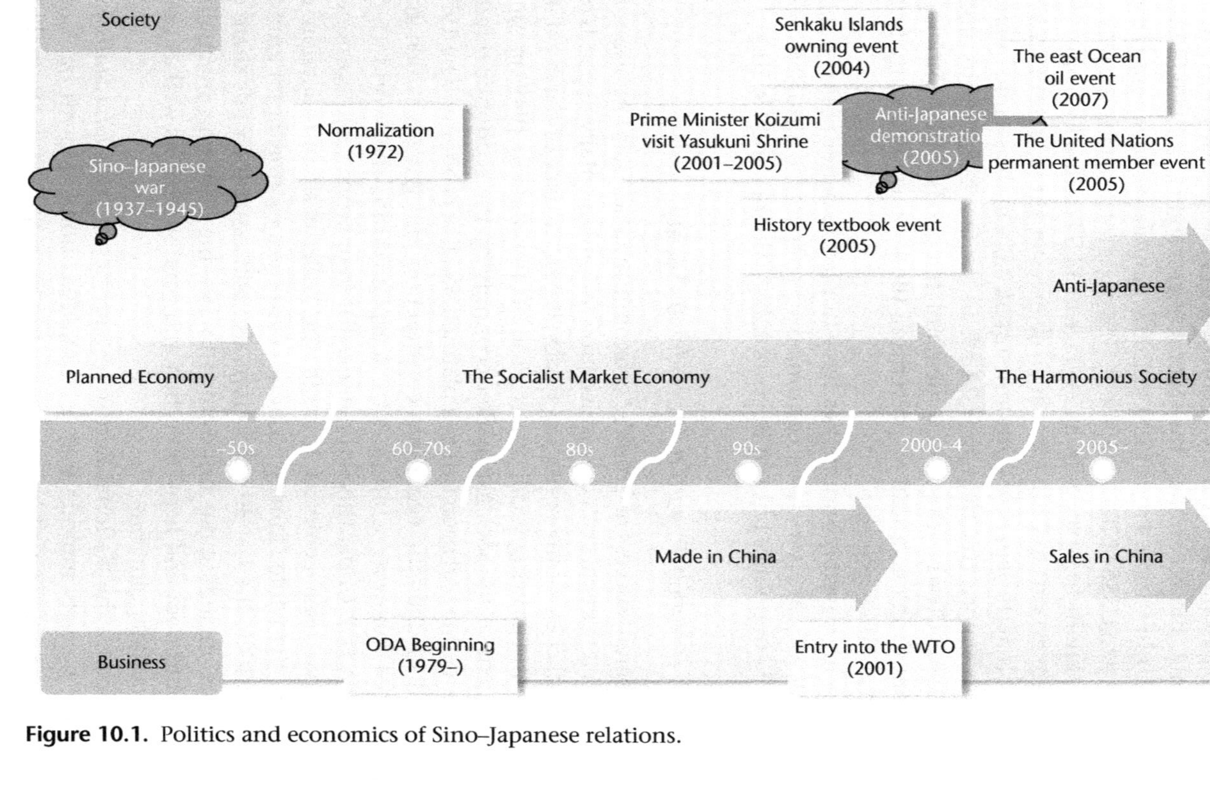

Figure 10.1. Politics and economics of Sino–Japanese relations.

estimated US$236.6 billion or 17.7% of total Japanese external trade. For the first time in history, Sino–Japanese bilateral trade has exceeded that of American–Japanese trade, though the size of China's economy remains less than a quarter of that of the USA (Xing 2008).[9]

Since 1989, Japan has also been extremely active in investing in China's nascent economy, and is currently the second largest source of foreign direct investment (FDI) in China. From 1990 to 2007, cumulative Japanese FDI in China amounted to US$64 billion, or about 10% of its total FDI for the period. While China's exports to Japan grew an average of 14.9% annually from 1990 to 2007, Japanese exports to China rose at an even faster annual rate of 18.5%. Despite the fact that the Japanese economy shrank 0.6% in the second quarter of 2008, Japan's exports to China grew 24.5% in the first five months alone (Xing 2008: 1–4). Clearly, the robust demand for goods and technology emanating from China is crucial to preventing the Japanese economy from slumping into another recession.

Nonetheless, improved economic ties have not led to better political relations, which is why analysts have continued to refer to the Sino–Japanese dynamic as "cold in politics but hot in economics" (Hughes and He 2006).

10.2.2 *China's Evolution Toward a "Harmonious Society"*

Despite the apparent success of China's "economic miracle," it is important to keep in mind that the country's continued growth fundamentally depends on whether its market economy continues to develop in the face of harsh political conditions and growing social unrest. From its founding in 1949 up until the establishment of the socialist market economy by the economic reform policy of 1978, China had been run as a planned socialist economy. The 1978 policy resulted in dramatic economic construction and growth which has only accelerated following China's 2001 acceptance into the World Trade Organization (WTO). Under this unique socialist framework, rapid economic development has been achieved through the widespread introduction of foreign capital. Yet while China's economy continues to grow at an annual rate of around 10%, the last 30 years have also witnessed their fair share of social problems, including but not limited to growing economic inequality between rich and poor and between urban and rural society, as well as rampant environmental pollution.

Data provided by the National Bureau of Statistics in the *China Statistical Yearbook* (2007) clearly indicate that such rapid economic growth has only increased the existing disparity of wealth among the populace. It also reflects the fact that the development of the eastern portion of the country has far surpassed that of the western regions. Furthermore, the wasteful and inefficient use of resources has led to a vicious cycle in which rapid growth is invariably followed by environmental destruction. In 2007, China's energy consumption per 10,000 RMB (Chinese yuan or renminbi) (US$1,292) of gross domestic product amounted to 1.21 tons of coal equivalent, which is about nine times as great as that of Japan and about six-and-a-half times that of Germany. China's total energy consumption in 2006 included 2.37 billion tons of coal, up 9.6% from the year before; 320 million tons of crude oil, up 7.1%; 55.6 billion cubic meters of natural gas, up 19.9%; 416.7 billion kilowatt-hours of hydropower, up 5%; and 54.3 billion kilowatt-hours of nuclear power, up 2.4%. Failure to pay salaries, hazardous working conditions, child labor, and human rights violations involving migrant workers are all well documented. More recently, there has been a series of scandals reflecting unprecedented levels of corporate depravity: babies sickened by tainted powdered milk in Fuyang,[10] patients dying from counterfeit medicine sold by pharmacies in Qiqihar,[11] workers trapped in a coal mine in Shanxi, and a young engineer dead from overwork at a major IT firm in Beijing.

Yet for all their severity, these scandals have also brought to the fore various social problems that have emerged as a direct result of rapid economic growth, bringing China to a crossroads in its development, which begs a radical reexamination of the last 30 years of economic reform since the Cultural Revolution. In recent years, this has prompted the government into action and led to the adoption of an ideology that prioritizes social issues in an effort to maintain a delicate balance between economic growth and social stability. This is why President Hu Jintao's regime has officially sought to promote "continuous stable growth"[12] through the creation of a "harmonious society" to inherit the strategy of "prioritized economic construction."[13] In its simplest form, the "harmonious society" envisioned by the Chinese Communist Party[14] refers to a national vision geared toward continuous stable development, as opposed to rapid and unrestrained growth. Underlying this ideology is the recognition that the social problems discussed above can only be addressed by paying greater attention to the impact of economic development on the society at large.

As evident in the various policies enacted in its "eleventh five-year plan" (2006–10), the Communist Party is also attempting to build an economy that values the environment by prioritizing energy-saving and recycling.[15] Rather than focusing exclusively on economic growth, such initiatives are meant to improve the general standard of living as well. This is why the government has shifted from establishing a definite benchmark for the gross domestic product (GDP) growth rate each year to promising a GDP growth rate per capita that is twice as high as it was in 2000—a policy that has met with a favorable response from the populace. Generally speaking, the notion of a "harmonious society" reflects a growing awareness of how social issues are inextricably linked to economic development.

10.3 A Theoretical Framework

In some respects, the difficulties facing Japanese corporations in China are emblematic of those facing all multinational enterprises (MNEs) seeking to take advantage of emerging markets. To the extent that their interests differ from the policies of the state in which they conduct business, MNEs often find themselves in conflict with local government, with which they must learn to collaborate as both a means of fostering economic development and as a strategy for corporate survival. Because mutual misunderstandings and historical grudges are difficult to eradicate, however, anti-Japanese sentiment is likely to dictate Sino–Japanese relations in both the public and private sector for some time to come. This begs the question: what sort of localization strategies should Japanese corporations adopt in a country fraught with cross-cultural hostility and subject to dramatic economic change? The following presents a theoretical discussion of the role of "business–society relations" and the importance of social engagement for MNEs, and Japanese corporations in particular, seeking to do business in China.

Given the aim of "constructing a harmonious society" espoused by the Chinese Communist Party, it is increasingly important that corporations be recognized as socially active by the national media. The emergence of the notion of a "harmonious society" in China has further led to greater emphasis on the importance of social engagement, forcing Japanese corporations to live up to various corporate responsibilities imposed by the Chinese government. Such recognition is not only beneficial for localization insofar as it fosters good relations with the local community, but it is also an effective means of attracting the interest of potential investors and expanding the number of corporate stakeholders.

Generally speaking, the research conducted to date has identified two basic theories of "strategic sociality" for the development and cultivation of business–society relations through social engagement initiatives.[16] Given unpredictable markets and the intensified competition arising out of globalization, one school of thought holds that social engagement must be approached purely from the perspective of economic value. Another school of thought, however, believes that social engagement arises out of a profound concern for the underlying social issues and should therefore be approached from the perspective of social value. The following provides an overview of these approaches to strategic sociality.

Yamakura (1993) classifies all business strategies into the following three categories: (1) business structure strategies; (2) international business strategies; and (3) social strategies. According to Yamakura, social strategies are unique in that they are geared towards "achieving a function beyond the domain of corporate productivity" and are therefore not limited to achieving success in the marketplace. Morimoto (1994), in his definition of social strategies as "the basic principle for selecting the methods and resources for fulfilling a corporation's social responsibilities," adopts the hierarchy of social responsibilities developed by Archie B. Carroll (1991). According to Carroll, these responsibilities are comprised of economic, legal, ethical, and philanthropic obligations, with legal responsibilities regarded as an inherent duty and economic responsibilities subsumed under business strategies. Accordingly, it is of primary importance that managers learn to supplement their business tactics with various social strategies.

Yet while these studies stress the importance of social strategies for maintaining corporate legitimacy and garnering support from the community, few if any address the ways in which social strategies are informed by business and economic considerations. Nor do they adequately take into account the complex and sometimes disingenuous relationship between a company's participation in social activities and its pursuit of the bottom line. In his attempt to identify their underlying connection to business strategies, Ansoff (1990) assesses various "social strategies" in terms of their political and profit-earning potential rather than focusing on the social obligations they are meant to fulfill. Matsuno (2006) similarly views social strategies as an effective means of securing a competitive advantage in the marketplace. The notion of social strategies as a core competency that makes economic growth possible is developed further by Burke and Logsdon (1996), who analyze the impact of social strategies on corporate revenue.

The theory of social engagement developed by Martin (2002) is derived from the notion that social strategies are pursued for the sole benefit of the shareholders, though the activities themselves may have nothing to do with the shareholders' self-interest. Within the "virtue matrix" depicting the forces that generate corporate social responsibility, the bottom two quadrants represent the "civil foundation," which consists of norms, customs, and laws that govern corporate practice. Companies engage in practices consistent with the civil foundation either by choice or by necessity, though such engagement represents nothing more than the satisfaction of society's baseline expectations. Martin refers to this behavior as "instrumental" because it explicitly serves the cause of maintaining or enhancing shareholder value.

10.4 Economic Nationalism in China Against Japanese FDI

In several other respects, however, the difficulties facing Japanese corporations are unique among MNEs insofar as they have been confronted with renewed calls to boycott Japanese products in response to various political

Table 10.1. Impact of anti-Japanese demonstrations on Japanese business development

Content	Influence measurement (%) N = 414
Decreased sales due to boycotts of Japanese goods	19.1
Tarnished image of Japanese products	16.4
Worsened relationships with Chinese employees	9.7
Impact on production activities, such as suspension of plant operations	8.5
Difficulty in securing personnel locally	8.0
Canceled or postponed investment projects in China	7.5
Worsened relationships with Chinese customers	6.5
Difficulty in procurement of raw materials and parts	6.3
Decline in exports to China due to reduced rate of factory operations on business partner side	5.8
Downsizing or transfer of present production base in China to a third country	5.6
Other	5.1
Difficulty in collecting bills from customers in China	4.1
Decline in imports from China	2.2

Source: Drafted by author based on the results of "Special survey of Japanese business in China: Impact of the April anti-Japan demonstrations" (June 2005) conducted by JETRO.

disputes. Thus, though there is little evidence that it has had a long-term impact on the general trend of Japan's economic activities, Chinese economic nationalism is viewed by Japanese corporations as a risk of doing business that is likely to continue for some time.

The repercussions of the April 2005 protests, for example, have taken the form of ongoing disputes between labor and management as well as unwillingness on the part of Chinese consumers to purchase Japanese products or invest in Japanese enterprises. According to the results of a June 2005 survey conducted by JETRO (Japan External Trade Organization), anti-Japanese demonstrations have had an appreciably negative effect on Japanese activities in the Chinese market in the form of "decreased sales" (19.1%), "tarnished image of Japanese products" (16.4%), "worsened relationships with Chinese employees" (9.7%), "impact on production activities, such as suspension of plant operations" (8.5%), and "difficulty in securing personnel locally" (8%), among other things (see Table 10.1). During these demonstrations, sales representatives from one of the Japanese manufacturers interviewed for this study conducted field research in response to reports that its products were being withdrawn from stores. They found that competing foreign and domestic enterprises were passing out leaflets "strongly urging storeowners to withdraw Japanese products from their shelves." There was also evidence of discriminatory treatment of Japanese corporations bidding on some of the more high-profile and politically sensitive public works projects.

At the same time, the evidence suggests that Chinese attitudes toward Japan remain somewhat ambivalent. Many of the individuals who participated in the 2005 demonstrations, for example, did so with mixed emotions, while the Chinese media's attempts to highlight government corruption in Japan have gone largely unnoticed among Chinese youth. Although the slogan "do not buy Japanese products," for example, originated from a collective resentment over the continued veneration of Japanese war criminals, there is little evidence that this boycott extended beyond the realm of politics. As reflected in the May 2010 strike by Chinese workers at a Honda transmission factory in southeastern China, the Chinese government has also taken steps to inflame anti-Japanese sentiment in an effort to divert attention away from the domestic origins of its own social unrest. In this respect, the underlying origins of anti-Japanese sentiment in China, as reflected by the political and commercial repercussions of the 2005 protests, go beyond blind economic nationalism or Communist propaganda.

In any case, given such overwhelming evidence of discriminatory treatment, it is essential that Japanese corporations refine their understanding of anti-Japanese hostility in order to improve Sino–Japanese relations and expand market share in China. This would involve working toward rebuilding the trust and confidence of the Chinese populace, including both workers and consumers, and making an effort to conduct business in a manner designed to earn the respect of the local populace. The following section discusses various strategies for achieving such a goal in the context of cultivating "business–society relations."

10.5 Dealing with Economic Nationalism in China

10.5.1 *The Role of Business–Society Relations*

China's evolution from a "planned socialist economy"[17] to a "socialist market economy"[18] and a "harmonious society,"[19] together with the unprecedented rise of Chinese consumerism, have compelled Japanese companies to approach localization in new and creative ways.[20] In the 1990s, when the business model was to import components to be assembled in China and exported to foreign markets, foreign enterprises had little need for direct contact with Chinese society. With the development of China's consumer markets, however, they have now begun to use China as a base for their sales and service departments in addition to manufacturing. In essence, these bases have now become "self-completion companies" equipped to handle production and sales simultaneously. Hence, as China's economy has developed and matured, Japanese companies from the manufacturing industry up have begun to attach greater importance to the Chinese market itself instead of simply using it as a convenient, low-cost production base. This shift from "made in China" to "sold in China," a direct result of China's growing consumer class, has forced Japanese firms to adopt an entirely new approach.

Essentially, effective localization and sustainable development in China are the products of a symbiotic relationship between the business model and local management style of Japanese corporations and the political agenda of the Chinese government. The contributions made by Japanese corporations to Chinese society, as well as their eventual acceptance as good corporate citizens, should enable them to expand market share by gaining the acceptance of Chinese consumers. Accordingly, in order for Japanese corporations to begin to realize their outsized expectations for the Chinese market, they must first learn to prioritize an active participation in grassroots activities outside the scope of their respective businesses.[21] They must realize that economic success in China necessarily depends on addressing economic, environmental, and social issues in a way that benefits local communities and society as a whole in addition to compliance with local laws and regulations.

Given the emergence of economic nationalism discussed above, it is of the utmost importance that Japanese corporations develop the ability to adapt quickly to social and political contingencies while at the same time navigating the changing contours of China's ideological landscape. This necessarily requires that they work toward rebuilding the trust and confidence of the Chinese populace by focusing on social initiatives. Japanese firms doing business in China should also seek to understand and predict changes in China's increasingly strict regulatory framework by attempting to grasp the underlying intentions of the government before pursuing a given strategy.

Thus far, Japanese enterprises have relied on superior product quality and advanced technology to compete in the Chinese marketplace. As the product quality and technical expertise of Chinese companies improve, however, this will no longer constitute a competitive advantage. Moreover, while brand recognition is essential to attract competent personnel and maintain managerial loyalty, recognition and respect for Japanese brands in the Chinese market remains low due to the political tension between the two nations. Japanese brands rarely make it into the top echelon of corporate rankings by the Chinese media, and the social contributions of Japanese companies in China are inadequately publicized. In a market where competition is fierce and technology readily available, brand recognition represents one of the few ways in which corporations can distinguish themselves from their competitors. Insofar as the ability to maintain good relations with local governments and communities also depends on positive brand recognition, effective localization ultimately depends on maintaining a good corporate image.

As a result, Japanese companies with operations in China must not only compete with local businesses and multinational corporations, but also strive to counteract anti-Japanese sentiment by improving their public image. Under the assumption that strong relations between Japan and China are a prerequisite for doing business in China, many Japanese companies have therefore been promoting mutual understanding among their expanding network of stakeholders by seeking to overcome cultural and social differences between the two countries. This is why acceptance as a good corporate citizen, in addition to the adoption of a management style suitable to local conditions, has become increasingly important for Japanese companies to gain the trust of the Chinese populace and to reach out to the Chinese consumer.

For too long, however, Japanese companies have remained stagnant in their economic approach to doing business in China. If anything, the anti-Japanese demonstrations of 2005 made it clear that this traditional approach to localization was ineffective precisely because it did not take into account the role of business–society relations in the Chinese marketplace. Thus, for Japanese companies hoping to succeed in China, the way forward is clear: they must either learn to improve brand recognition by incorporating corporate responsibility initiatives and the notion of "business–society relations" into their localization strategies or continue to lose ground to their Chinese and international counterparts.

10.5.2 *Strategies for Social Engagement*

As discussed above, effective localization in China requires that foreign companies foster better relations with society by focusing on social engagement. Whatever social activities corporations engage in, however, must be conducted strategically to ensure that their underlying conception of social engagement is compatible with that of the host country. There are several concerns that need to be addressed in connection with this issue of cultural compatibility. In the case of Japanese corporations operating in China, distinct strategies must be developed for overcoming the obstacles to business in the Chinese market, keeping up with technological innovations, and navigating local regulations governing commercial transactions.

As a preliminary issue, it is important that corporations be recognized as socially active by the national media. Such recognition is not only beneficial for localization insofar as it fosters good relations with the local community, but it is also an effective means of attracting the interest of potential investors and expanding the number of corporate stakeholders. Second, Japanese corporations must learn to exploit their comparative advantages to navigate China's vast network of management resources, emerging commercial infrastructure, and pro-corporate policies. Such comparative advantages may include anything from superiority in product development and manufacturing methods to innovative marketing techniques and technology. Second, localization demands that Japanese companies go one step further by using these comparative advantages in furtherance of China's own policies and goals, including but not limited to improvements in the domestic economy, the expansion of social welfare, and environmental conservation.

At a time when China's "socialist market economy" is in full swing, there is growing interest, on the part of the government as well as society, in the importance of corporate social responsibility for sustainable development. For Japanese corporations operating in China, brainstorming about what they can do to address the needs and demands of Chinese society, even before such demands materialize, is a prerequisite for expanding market share. As a result, Japanese companies must not only seek to address existing social and environmental problems but also learn to predict the emergence of new issues and structure their localization strategies accordingly. Only when social concerns become the standard for corporate performance can they begin to gain a competitive edge in the Chinese market.

10.5.3 *Case Studies of Social Engagement*

Based on field research conducted between April 2006 and September 2009, the following discussion offers an analysis of the various social activities adopted by two prominent Japanese corporations as part of their localization strategies in China. The purpose of this research was to gain a better understanding of the ways in which Japanese corporations view the inevitable cost of social engagement in connection with its potential benefits for localization.

REDEFINING THE VALUE CHAIN

The localization strategy adopted by NEC (China) is grounded in the belief that corporations can best achieve sustainable development by redefining the value chain through the promotion of environmental awareness.[22] Based on its belief that addressing pollution should be part of its core business, NEC (China)'s environmental strategy is twofold: (1) to reduce the impact of its business operations on the environment; and (2) to provide high-quality products and services that help consumers conserve energy and resources.

In the case of NEC (China), localization begins with so-called "environmental compliance" with China's laws and regulations as well as to the demands of local consumers. Yet mere compliance with environmental requirements is just the beginning, for NEC also makes an effort to design its products so as to comply with proposed regulations that have not yet been passed into law. Since it takes five years for this to occur, NEC is in the practice of designing its products a full five years in advance of China's environmental regulations.

This focus on environmental protection is exemplified by the development of NEC (China)'s line of personal computers. In comparing two models with the same functions and quality, NEC discovered that the energy necessary to run 100 hours for one model was a third of that for the other. It thereby chose to manufacture the first model on the assumption that the Chinese consumer would prefer to save on electricity costs, and that such savings would improve consumer satisfaction and translate into additional sales and revenue—by all accounts a win-win situation. Another example of NEC's innovation is the emergence of QSU ("quick start-up") technology, which it developed in 1999. An ordinary PC requires 30 seconds to warm up, a process that consumes considerable electricity. QSU technology effectively shortened this "warm-up" time to 10 seconds, resulting in a 95% reduction in power consumption, from 130w to 7w.

With the belief that environmental protection should not be limited to the manufacturers themselves, NEC (China) imposes similarly stringent standards on its suppliers. Perhaps even more importantly, the company goes to great lengths to market the energy-saving functions of its products in addition to their effects on the environment. Only when Chinese consumers are aware of these options can their impact on the environment be lessened and the associated savings enjoyed. Hence, the development of "green" technology not only protects the environment (Figure 10.2), but also serves to improve the product's image and to strengthen consumer confidence in the brand—all of which results in enhanced revenue for the corporation.

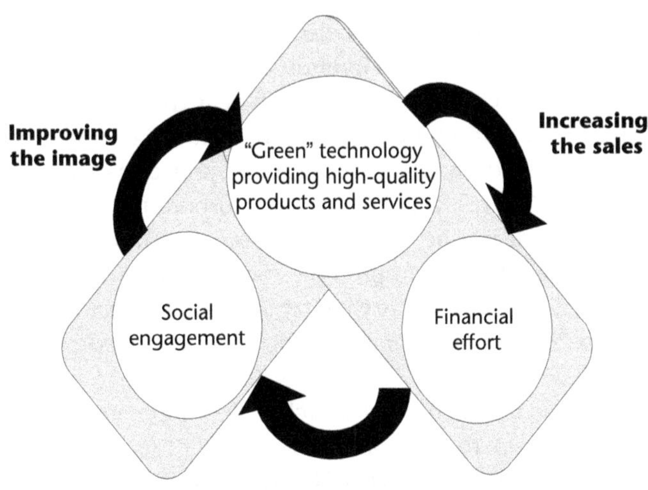

Figure 10.2. NEC (China)'s strategies for social engagement.

GOING TO GREAT LENGTHS

Sony (China) has achieved sustainable development in China by going to great lengths to promote social engagement.[23] In the early stages of China's economic reform, Japanese electronics, which were known for their excellent quality and expensive prices, were hard to come by. Over the years, however, what was once considered prohibitively expensive has now become a ubiquitous component of middle-class Chinese life. Sony remains the leading example of a Japanese electronics corporation that has managed to become nothing less than a way of life for millions of Chinese.

In 2007, with total sales revenue of US$70.92 billion, Sony was listed 69th on Fortune's Global 500. Unlike most other Japanese corporations, overseas sales accounted for half of this revenue, a testament to the company's strong comparative advantage in the overseas market. China is currently Sony's largest independent market after the United States and Japan, no doubt due to its vast population as well as the growing purchasing power of the Chinese consumer class. Eager to take advantage of China's growing market, Sony has invested an enormous amount in its overseas marketing and operations.

In 1991, Sony established offices in both Dalian and Hangzhou, and in 1996 Sony (China) Co., Ltd., was founded. In 2000, in an effort to position China as a base of operations for sales, production, and research development, Sony expanded its business to include such products as digital televisions, portable computers, and semi-conductors. As part of its strategy to redefine the value chain, Sony has also contributed substantial resources to the promotion of environmental protection and energy conservation (Figure 10.3) such that mainland China has rapidly become the epicenter of Sony's global business operations.

Notwithstanding the quality of its electronics, Sony's considerable success in China is partially attributable to its efforts to develop a local business model based on appealing to China's youth, which is at the heart of the country's growing consumerist culture. By targeting the young, Sony's marketing campaign has strengthened its brand recognition and enhanced its corporate image throughout China. Recognizing that corporations that focus exclusively on revenue will not be in a position to gain social recognition, Sony has also gone to great lengths to promote social engagement. In 2006 alone, Sony (China) participated in more than ten large-scale social activities, which ensured its place as one of the most respected Japanese corporations in the country.

In 2001, Sony also founded the Research & Development Center in Shanghai as part of its strategy to secure local management resources while gaining an understanding of the psychology of the Chinese consumer. The purported aim of the Center was to assess the popularity of various technologies in China by hiring local technicians. In essence, however, the Center was established to

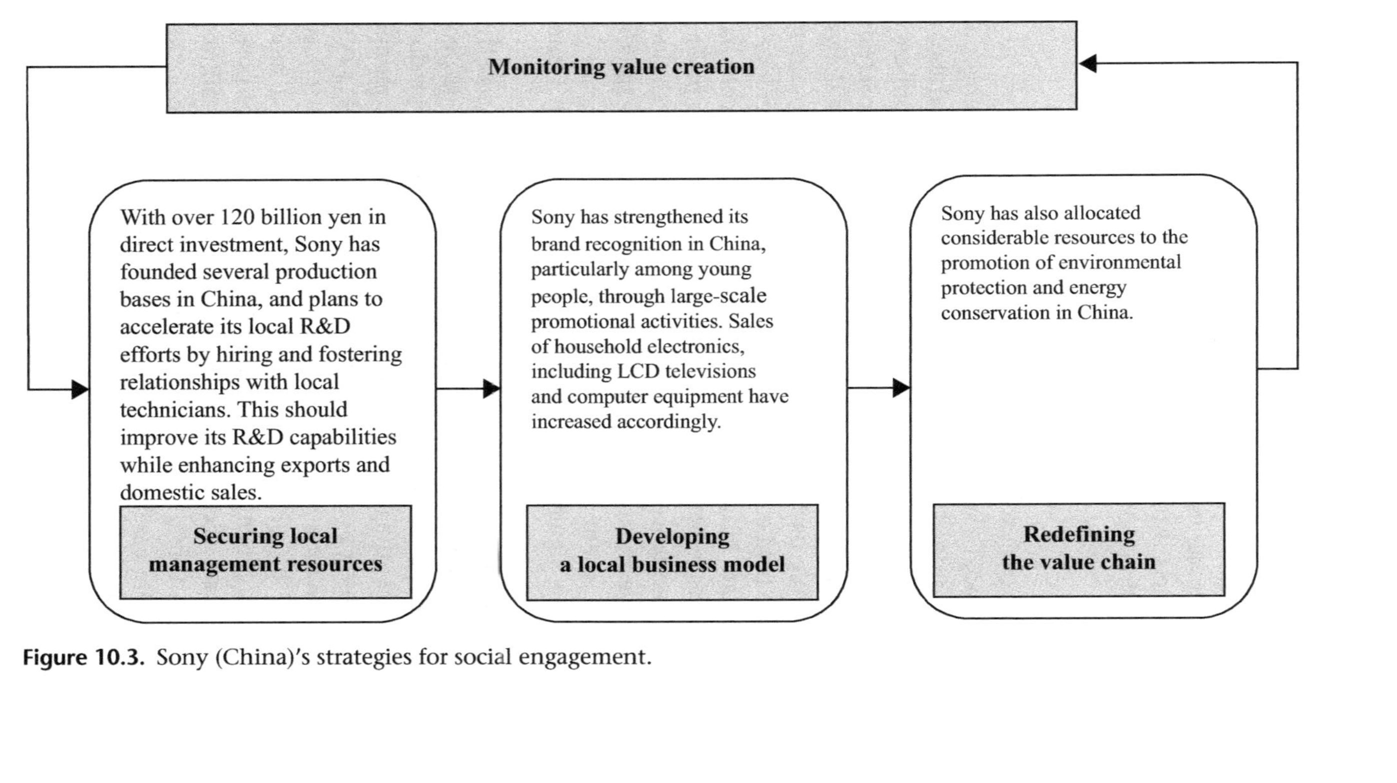

Figure 10.3. Sony (China)'s strategies for social engagement.

answer a fundamental question put forth several years ago by foreign enterprises hoping to enter the Chinese market: how to transform "made in China" to "created in China" (i.e., how to design products suitable for consumption by the Chinese market). With technology one of its strongest advantages in the global marketplace, Japan's development is far ahead of that of China. Sony's China R&D Center was established to bridge this gap by providing a forum for Japanese technicians to communicate with their Chinese counterparts so as to develop technologies designed to meet the unique demands of the Chinese consumer.

REMAINING OBSTACLES TO SOCIAL ENGAGEMENT

Based on the notion of social engagement as a solution to the challenges of localization for Japanese corporations in China, the two cases discussed above strongly support the theory that social activity and economic performance are inextricably linked and that corporations have the capacity to create economic profit by contributing to the collective value of society. As shown in Figure 10.4 below, while participation in social activities was found to increase overheads, it also held enormous potential to facilitate greater localization. Specifically, the data indicate that the decision of Japanese corporations to pursue social engagement within China has measurably improved brand recognition and enhanced profitability by improving shareholder satisfaction, attracting investment, and enhancing productivity. More importantly, however, it has also shown how the efforts of these companies to contribute to society have significantly improved relations between China and Japan.

At the same time, however, it is equally important not to underestimate the importance of China's economic nationalism. The Chinese are a proud people, and China's emergence as an economic superpower is as much a product of their cultural heritage as their political agenda. Proponents of economic nationalism argue that China's economic growth has come at too great a cost to both the general populace and the environment, and that unrestrained growth must be checked by governmental policies geared toward a more sustainable form of development. In the case of Japan, the obstacles posed by this ideological shift are compounded by the history of cross-cultural hostility originating from World War II. Accordingly, Japanese corporations must learn to embrace the emerging emphasis on social responsibility reflected in China's unique brand of economic nationalism by working toward rebuilding the trust and confidence of the Chinese populace. Only by seeking to strengthen mutual understanding between the two cultures can Japanese corporations successfully navigate the risks of doing business in China.

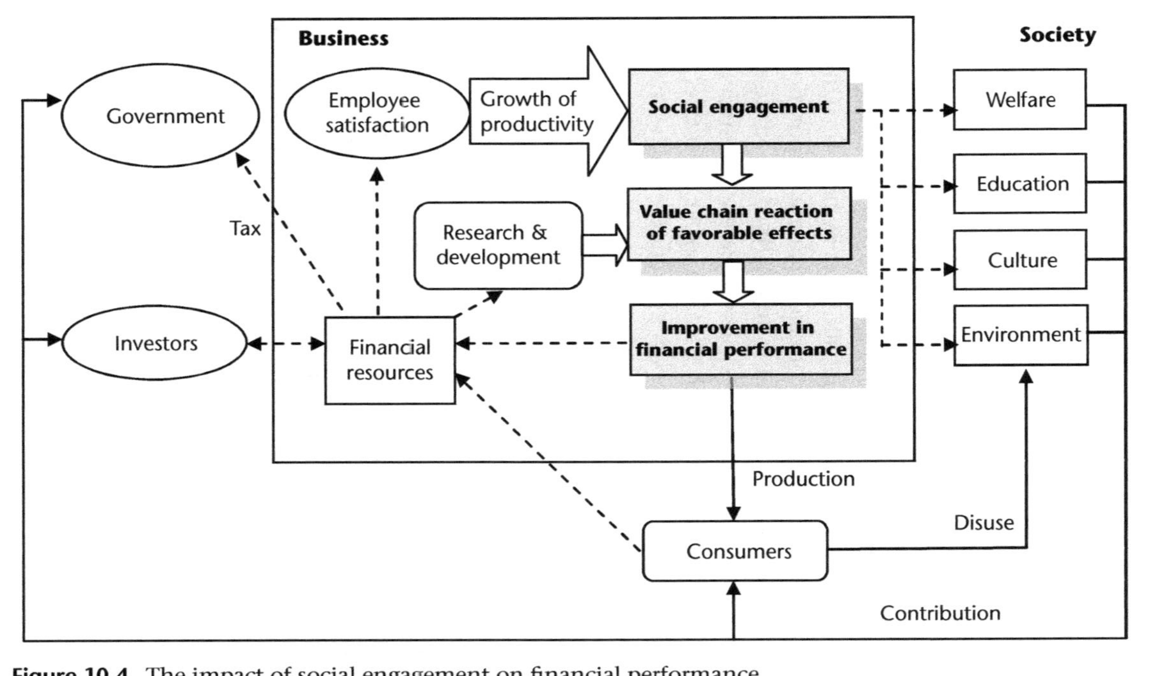

Figure 10.4. The impact of social engagement on financial performance.

Notes: Solid lines represent products and services. Broken lines represent investment.

10.6 Conclusion

As discussed above, society's appraisal of modern corporations is no longer based on economic performance alone, but also on their environmental impact and degree of social engagement. Ideally, these three elements should be of equal importance in formulating strategies for social engagement, yet many Japanese corporations have begun to engage in social activities for the sole purpose of enhancing their reputation in the Chinese market without regard for the underlying causes they purportedly seek to promote. Thus, the ethical incentives for social engagement have not yet been fully incorporated into Japanese corporate culture.

The appraisal of Japanese corporations in China is based on traditional standards of economic achievement as well as instances of social engagement by local stakeholders. The promotion of social activities by both the Chinese government and society at large should encourage Japanese corporations to pay increasing attention to the latter without losing sight of the former. It is hoped that the empirical and anecdotal data collected here will contribute to our understanding of the standards by which Chinese society evaluates Japanese corporations, and demonstrate how a greater awareness of such standards can be used to improve localization performance.

It is well established that social engagement goes a long way to facilitate the localization of Japanese corporations in China. Yet to fully understand the mechanism through which this occurs, it is necessary to analyze corporate responsibility in terms of "social engagement" as well as the "social impact" of such engagement. This chapter deals primarily with the former by discussing corporate activities dedicated to the promotion of various social issues and by gathering empirical and anecdotal evidence to corroborate the effectiveness of such activities. It is also important, however, for corporations to determine the potential impact of these activities in advance, which necessarily involves formulating ways to prevent their potentially harmful effects on society as well as employees of the corporation itself. These are all vital considerations for assessing social engagement and should be the subject of further research.

Notes

1. The Senkaku Islands, also known as the Pinnacle Islands in English and Diaoyu Islands in Chinese, are a group of disputed, uninhabited islands controlled by Japan but claimed by the People's Republic of China. Located roughly northeast of Taiwan, due west of Okinawa, and due north of the end of the Ryukyu Islands in the East China Sea, these islands are regarded by the Japanese government as part of Okinawa Prefecture.

2. Spanning from 1966 until Chairman Mao's death in 1976, the Cultural Revolution was the result of a power struggle within the Chinese Communist Party that manifested itself in wide-scale social, political, and economic violence and chaos, eventually bringing the country to the brink of civil war.
3. The successor to Jiang Zemin as the Paramount Leader of the People's Republic of China, Hu Jintao had been the General Secretary of the Communist Party of China since 2002, President of the People's Republic of China since 2003, and Chairman of the Central Military Commission since 2004. Since assuming power, Hu has reinstated certain controls over the economy and been largely conservative with political reforms. His foreign policy is seen as less conciliatory than that of his predecessor, though China's global influence has increased while he has been in office.
4. Wen Jiabao is the Premier of the State Council of the People's Republic of China and responsible for leading the country's cabinet. He also serves as a member of its Leading Party Members' Group and is the Secretary of the Financial Work Committee of the CPC Central Committee. Since taking office in 2003, Wen ranks third in the hierarchy of the Politburo Standing Committee and has played a key role in the Communist Party's fourth generation of leadership.
5. Relations between the two countries have not improved despite the expansion of the Sino–Japanese labor exchange, which exceeded 5 million in 2007 alone.
6. Following the period of diplomatic rancor that characterized the Junichiro Koizumi administration (2001–6), the bilateral relationship between Japan and China demonstrably improved via breakthrough agreements on territorial disputes, high-level exchanges, and reciprocal port calls by naval vessels.
7. See M. Fackler and I. Johnson, "Arrest in Disputed Seas Riles China and Japan." *The New York Times*, September 19, 2010 ("the episode has fanned growing fears . . . that an increasingly powerful China will become ever more insistent in pressing territorial claims against its neighbors, and in trying to assert military control of ever-wider swaths of the waters around China").
8. Foreign direct investment (FDI) or foreign investment refers to long-term participation by country A in country B. It usually involves participation in management, joint venture, and transfers of technology and expertise. There are two types of FDI: inward foreign direct investment and outward foreign direct investment, resulting in a net FDI inflow (positive or negative) and "stock of foreign direct investment," which is the cumulative number for a given period.
9. The total value of Sino–Japanese trade for fiscal year 2007 was over US$200 billion. See Xinhua, "Sino–Japanese Trade Volume to Top $200b." *China Daily*, October 9, 2006.
10. In April 2004, at least 13 babies in Fuyang and 50 more in the rural areas of Anhui province died of malnourishment from ingesting fake milk powder; 100 to 200 others suffered malnutrition but survived. Local officials in Fuyang arrested 47 people responsible for making and selling the fake formula, and investigators discovered 45 varieties of substandard formula in Fuyang markets. Over 141 factories were responsible for the production of the formula. Chinese officials seized 2,540 bags of fake formula and the State Food and Drug Administration ordered an investigation in May 2004.

11. The use of tainted drugs manufactured by Qiqihar No. 2 Pharmaceutical Company left 11 people dead.
12. The policy of "continuous stable growth" was adopted by the Chinese government in an effort to shift the driving force of economic expansion away from exports and foreign direct investment and towards domestic consumption.
13. Adopted in 1978 by Deng Xiaoping and various pragmatists within the Communist Party, "prioritized economic construction" is a program of economic reform based on the notion of "socialism with Chinese characteristics." The purported goal of this program is to generate sufficient surplus value to finance the modernization of the Chinese economy. Neither the socialist command economy favored by conservatives nor the shift from socialism to communism instigated by the Maoist Great Leap Forward managed to accomplish this. The initial challenge of economic reform was to find a way to motivate workers and farmers to produce a larger surplus and to eliminate imbalances common in command economies. Prioritized economic construction has since managed to bring the poverty rate down from 53% of the population in 1981 to 8% in 2001.
14. The Chinese Communist Party (CCP) is the founding political party of the People's Republic of China and the largest of its kind in the world. While not a governing body recognized by China's constitution, the CCP remains the country's supreme political authority through its control of the state apparatus and the legislative process. Along with the "*xiaokang* society," which aims to create a "basically well-off" middle-class, the construction of the so-called "harmonious society" is the dominant socio-economic vision arising out of Hu Jintao's signature ideology.
15. An important element of China's energy policy is to reduce energy consumption per capita, thereby offsetting the growth in energy supply needed to keep up with population growth. This in turn should reduce energy costs as well as the need for additional power plants, and offer flexibility in choosing preferred methods of energy production.
16. As used in this discussion, the term "social engagement" refers to any corporate activity geared toward cultivating better business–society relations.
17. Referred to as a "command economy," "centrally planned economy," or "command and control economy" in its most extreme form, China's "planned socialist economy" consisted of an economic system managed entirely by the government. In such systems, the state controls all major sectors of the economy and makes all decisions concerning the use of resources and distribution of income. In unplanned or market economies, however, production, distribution, pricing, and investment decisions are made by the private owners of the factors of production based upon their own and their customers' interests. Less extreme forms of planned economies, sometimes referred to as "planned market economies," include those that use indicative planning whereby the state employs subsidies, grants, and taxes to further some overarching macroeconomic plan.
18. The so-called "socialist market economy," also called "socialism with Chinese characteristics," is an economic form practiced in the People's Republic of China.
19. The "harmonious society" refers to the dominant socio-economic vision that is said to be the end result of Hu Jintao's signature ideology based on the pursuit of

"scientific development." Along with the *xiaokang* society, which aims for a "basically well-off" middle-class, the harmonious society was first proposed by the Hu Wen administration during the 2005 National People's Congress and is widely considered to be the ultimate goal of the Chinese Communist agenda. Visible in banners all over China, this ideology reflects the underlying shift in focus from pure economic growth to social balance and harmony.

20. "Localization" can be defined as the process through which foreign-owned corporations effectively utilize local resources so as to enable the management model and style of the host corporation to adapt to the environmental conditions of the local subsidiary.
21. "Grassroots" activities are those driven by the constituents of a community. The term implies that the creation of the movement and the group supporting it are natural and spontaneous, as opposed to having been orchestrated by traditional power structures. Although they are often local, grassroots movements have the potential for widespread impact, such as when the efforts of community volunteers to encourage voter registration affect the outcome of a national election.
22. Additional information concerning NEC (China) is available at http://www.nec.com.cn
23. Additional information concerning Sony (China) is available at http://www.sony.com.cn

References

Ansoff, H.I. (1990). *Implanting Strategic Management.* London: Prentice Hall International Ltd.

Burke, L. and Logsdon, J.M. (1996). "How Corporate Social Responsibility Pays Off." *Long Range Planning,* 29 (4): 495 502.

Carroll, A.B. (1991). "The Pyramid of Corporate Social Responsibility: Toward the Moral Management of Organizational Stakeholders." *Business Horizons,* 34 (4): 39–40.

Hughes, L. and He, Y. (2006). "Hot Economy and Cold Politics? Commerce and Nationalism in Sino-Japanese Relations." 47th Annual Meeting of the International Studies Association, San Diego, Calif., March 22, 2006.

Martin, R.L. (2002). "The Virture Matrix: Calculating the Return on Corporate Responsibility." *Harvard Business Review,* 80: 69–75.

Matsuno, H. (2006). "Kigyo no shakaiteki sekininron." No keisei to tenkai. Kyoto: Minerva Shobo Publishing Company.

Morimoto, M. (1994). *A Study of Corporate Social Responsibility from the Perspective of Management Science.* Tokyo: Hakuto-Shobo Publishing Company.

National Bureau of Statistics of China. (2007). *China Statistical Yearbook.* www.stats.gov.cn [Accessed January 25, 2012].

Xing, Y. (2008). "Japan's Unique Economic Relations with China: Economic Integration under Political Uncertainty." EAI Background Brief No. 410, October 23.

Yamakura, K. (1993). *Interorganizational Relations.* Tokyo: Yuhikaku Publishing.

11

Looking ahead at economic nationalism: concluding remarks

Anthony P. D'Costa

This book began with the proposition that economic nationalism can be practiced under globalization even if states must yield some autonomy over social policy space. We provided several illustrations at both national and sectoral levels as to why and how economic nationalism has been pursued in Asia. However, this kind of nationalism implies that the earlier ideological link between development and social policy is weakened. In other words, under globalization the state is seen as pursuing economic nationalism by concentrating its energies on supporting national capital with the presumption that wider economic benefits will accrue to the society. To capture this shift, the conventional definition of economic nationalism was modified from a focus on protecting domestic capital to alternate forms of mobilizing national resources for economic gain from the world economy (D'Costa 2009). This understanding demands that economic nationalism be seen as a dynamic concept and process, which is historically contingent on new social forces.

It is clear that economic nationalism is alive and well. It is practiced by all of the Asian countries discussed in this volume, some blatantly while others more subtly, with some states pursuing it aggressively and others more defensively. Ongoing state activism is integral to economic nationalism just as it is a product of the balance of class forces and capitalist maturity. When viewed as a dynamic process, economic nationalism is classic protectionism when businesses are young, and it is promotional when national capitalists become capable of competing with other capitalists. In both cases, national economic interests are assumed to be served. However, under the former protectionist approach national economies were less open and thus less subject to the competitive pressures of globalization. Policy intervention could be more effective and better directed in addressing social dimensions of development. Today, under globalization, supporting national business at home and abroad is presumed to create spillover effects such as soft power of the state and economic benefits via tax revenues, dividends, export earnings, and technological learning. States are compelled to forge partnerships with national business to tackle emergent economic challenges and opportunities of globalization in pragmatic ways. States are therefore not static institutions; through their ongoing intervention they learn institutionally to manage their economic affairs under changing contexts of economic globalization.

What is not clear is whether economic nationalism as practiced has served nations well. Going by the East Asian experience, there is ample evidence that economic nationalism, by way of clever and pragmatic state intervention, has indeed paid off (Amsden 1989, 2009). Capitalist development in the region has lifted millions of peasants out of poverty, fostered internationally competitive industries, and made the region one of the world's major economic epicenters. The story is more mixed for South Asia and Latin America. India and Brazil, despite well-intentioned protectionist policies, established an industrial foundation but could not replicate the East Asian economic and industrial dynamism. Today these two countries along with China, all with a history of state activism often bordering on unproductive regulation, are economically dynamic. Intuitively we can infer that past state activism has some bearing on how well states and national businesses respond to globalization. If previous protection of domestic business generated local technological capability and led to high local content, the chances of competing globally when such protection is dismantled are generally favorable. This is evident in several Indian industries such as pharmaceuticals, information technology, and automobiles. By and large, state activism in Asia has contributed to national business capabilities through learning by doing and thus to the general shift in global economic activities. Asia today, boasting three of the world's largest economies, has a combined global share of over 35% of the world's GDP (weighted by purchasing power) (IMF 2006). However, a fundamental question remains: to what extent has economic nationalism distributed the gains from globalization?

It is beyond the scope of this concluding set of remarks to explore the relationship between globalization and equality. Those who have discussed the relationship have not arrived at any definitive answer.[1] However, the issue here is not globalization and equality but rather economic nationalism and equality, mediated by the process of globalization. In other words, if economic nationalism is expected to serve national economic interests, and if citizen well being is a national concern, how well have countries pursuing economic nationalism performed on this front? Put differently, does economic nationalism, justified on grounds of economic growth—often at the behest of national capitalists—meet social objectives such as equality and growth in employment? The "new developmentalism" advanced by Bresser-Pereira (2010) and other heterodox economists incorporates the social dimension of inequality in policy discussions. However, the presumption that states create basic solidarity among classes while pursuing economic nationalism (a form of "new developmentalism") is overstating the neutrality of states and understating how capitalist classes might subvert the state and weaken any serious efforts to redistribute the fruits of capital accumulation. States have class interests and in an era of capitalism the bias is clearly in favor of capital.

The historical record generally shows that where states have intervened with land reforms, public investments in industry, education, technology, health, and infrastructure, along with a conscious policy stance of maintaining income distribution, they have performed relatively well. Even poor economies such as India experienced improvement in an already low Gini coefficient in the pre-reform 1991 period when conventional economic nationalism was strong, compared to the post-reform period when inequality between rural and urban areas widened (Datt 1999: 3517–18). In China the Gini coefficient, despite multiple estimations (Chen et al. 2010), has increased dramatically from about 0.3 in 1981 to 0.45 in 2001 (UNDP China 2008: 22). As argued by Bardhan (2010: 95–103), the source of inequality is generally not globalization but rather lack of investments in infrastructure, restricted access to education, and poor distribution of land. If that is the case, then economic nationalism in high-growth China and India thus far is not serving the citizenry as well as it could since interregional inequality and social polarization are rampant in both. It is therefore doubtful that policies justified on the basis of promoting national interests, such as supporting capital accumulation, will lead to wider social benefits. To make economic nationalism more meaningful, it is therefore incumbent upon states to spread the benefits of growth and development to sectors that tend to get bypassed in the vortex of globalization.

While inequality is generally endogenously generated, globalization cannot be altogether an innocuous process. After all, some of the most egalitarian societies such as Japan and South Korea are experiencing worsening inequality, albeit in small doses. Taking the Japanese case, the reasons are complex and multiple including an ageing population and the inability of young workers to find steady jobs due to the changing structure of the Japanese economy. As the institution of lifetime employment is fading, Japan's labor markets are increasingly veering toward part-time, temporary, not-in-employment-education-training (*NEETO*) types of jobs. For example, already battered by the decade-long recession, part-time employment from 1999 to 2009 further increased for both males and females by 52% (calculated from Ministry of Labour, Health, and Welfare 2010). The share for male workers more than doubled, while the share for females increased by 38%, albeit from a smaller share of male workers to total. These labor market challenges, the stagnant economy, and impending shortages of particular skills due to ongoing demographic and competitive shifts create a case for the need for more immigration, which further raises the ante on economic nationalism in Japan (D'Costa 2008). What kind of economic nationalism the Japanese state might pursue is difficult to say but at the minimum we can expect stemming the economic decline, protecting jobs and wages, and caring for the elderly to top the political agenda. All of these entail additional spending, something that is difficult to increase, in an anti-tax, high public debt environment (see Tanzi 2011: 308). But support for new Japanese industries is only a small piece of the puzzle, while addressing emergent social problems is a larger one.

As we have seen in Chapter 8, Singapore is another case where the pressures of globalization have introduced tensions such as competition for limited real estate between citizens and foreigners. Also, income inequality between unskilled workers and skilled professionals has widened even further. According to the UNDP Human Development Report (2009: 195), Singapore, with high human development indicators (ranked 23rd), suffers from high income inequality (Gini index of 42.5), with the poorest 10% securing just 1.9% of income compared to the richest 10%, who have 32.8%. If Singapore is a successful example of state-managed transformation of an impoverished, resource-poor city-state, globalization today is imposing social costs, whose burden is largely felt by the less skilled and less educated. Hence, governments such as Singapore, when pursuing economic nationalism with a global face, are likely to sacrifice politically less mobilized local communities who might be structural victims of globalization. Alternatively, states in their quest to reap the benefits of globalization, in effect supporting national capitalists in their accumulation process as in India and China, may be structurally incapable of addressing emergent social challenges.[2] The power of capital is strong enough to ensure economic nationalist policies in favor of business, with anticipated trickle-down effects for the wider society. This class bias is a result of capitalist maturity, an outcome for which the state itself was responsible (D'Costa 2005). In the context of hypercompetition in the world economy, the policy space for states to intervene more democratically is substantially reduced since states are now engaged in keeping national economic engines humming in a global context and are not focused on redressing worsening income and other social gaps. Only a political backlash combined with the economic and social limits of inegalitarian development could compel states to reorient policies toward critical social sectors.[3]

Furthermore, systemic capitalist dynamics, unless matched by countervailing policies, are likely to reproduce and exacerbate the concentration of income, rural–urban inequality, regional and capital bias in national output, and uneven industrial and technological development. Thus, in India the rise in the unorganized sector, self-employment, and the secular increase in underemployment (National Commission for Enterprises in the Unorganised Sector 2009: 37; D'Costa 2011: 244), despite rapid economic growth rates and selective internationally competitive industries, is a testament to the challenges of employment creation even in countries that use the state for national economic purposes. The social fallout of contemporary global capitalism is equally stark in China. The much admired, incremental defensive-to-aggressive economic nationalism in China has not served China's rural and urban workers well. Regulated by the *hukou* system, which restricts free movement of rural residents to cities, 100 million or more rural migrants that have fuelled China's unprecedented coastal export sector continue to suffer the indignities of being "illegal" and treated as second-class citizens (Lee and Selden 2007). Additionally, the commodification of production driving down the share of labor to total product value due to low wages and capital-intensive production suggests the social limits of high export-driven economic growth (Chan and Pun 2010; Hung 2012 forthcoming). Such exclusionary developments in the context of massive regional disparity and worsening income distribution suggest that the new kind of economic nationalism as practiced to cope with globalization is inadequate to meet emergent social problems.

Finally, the re-emergence of Asia as an economic center, the coterminous economic erosion and social malaise—if not systematic decline—of the West and Japan, portend a rivalry whose form and effects are difficult to foresee. If Japanese businesses must adhere to China's expectations of corporate social responsibility, if China continues to hold more than a trillion US dollars of US debt, and if the diaspora, especially that of professionals from India and China, continues to expand worldwide, the practice of economic nationalism under these new forms of global enmeshments will not only be difficult but could also detract from the immediate goals of social policy for more inclusive development.[4]

At the same time, intra-Asian interactions and extended regionalism could foster a kind of collaboration not witnessed before, aimed largely to regionally redistribute and stabilize their economies through bilateral and multilateral economic partnerships. The stakes are indeed high with an estimated nearly 800 million poor people (defined as earning under US$1.25 per day) in four of the largest developing Asian countries.[5]

If contemporary economic nationalism is altering the structure of the world economy from its status quo of triad dominance (the USA, Western Europe, and Japan) to unprecedented regional and national rivalries, we can anticipate new forms of capitalist competition between the West and Asia, and for that matter within the more dynamic Asian economies. What might be the effects of the global crisis on the theory and practice of economic nationalism in

Asian countries, especially in terms of domestic social policies, remains an intriguing question. Further research in these areas is likely to generate important global scenarios in which Asia has a vital role and responsibility. It will also enhance our appreciation of the very dynamic phenomenon of economic nationalism in motion and the oft-neglected dimension of recapturing policy space for comprehensive social development in the region.

Notes

1. For a select list of works, see D'Costa (2011: 240).
2. Amsden (2009) may overestimate the economic and social benefits of supporting national private capital if the state does not directly engage in addressing the multiple disequlibria that arise from international integration, be it compressed wages, a mushrooming informal sector, limited formal employment, or spiraling inequality.
3. India's 12th Five-Year Plan (2012–17) reflects this new sentiment, where agriculture, education, health, and social welfare—all neglected sectors under the high growth regimes—are targeted for development (Planning Commission 2011).
4. The pursuit of Mode 4 under the WTO by several developing countries (with India playing a leading role), which would allow the temporary movement of service providers to OECD economies facilitating accumulation, could be a harbinger of renewed economic nationalism bordering on the xenophobic should economic conditions remain dire.
5. The four countries in question are: India with 389 million; Bangladesh 68 million; China 67 million; and Indonesia 43 million (Wan and Sebastian 2011: 10).

References

Amsden, A.H. (1989). *Asia's Next Giant: South Korea and Late Industrialization.* New York: Oxford University Press.

Amsden, A.H. (2009). "Nationality of Firm Ownership in Developing Countries: Who Should 'Crowd Out' Whom in Imperfect Markets?" in M. Cimoli, G. Dosi, and J.E. Stiglitz (eds.), *Industrial Policy and Development: Political Economy of Capabilities Accumulation*, 409–23. Oxford: Oxford University Press.

Bardhan, P. (2010). *Awakening Giants, Feet of Clay: Assessing the Economic Rise of China and India*. Princeton: Princeton University Press.

Bresser-Pereira, L.C. (2010). *Globalization and Competition: Why Some Emergent Countries Succeed while Others Fail*. Cambridge: Cambridge University Press.

Chan, J. and Pun, N. (2010). "Suicide as Protest for the New Generation of Chinese Migrant Workers: Foxconn, Global Capital, and the State." *The Asia-Pacific Journal*, 37 (2): 10.

Chen, J. et al. (2010). "The Trend of the Gini Coefficient of China. Brooks World Poverty Institute." University of Manchester, BWPI Working Paper 109, January.

D'Costa, A.P. (2005). *The Long March to Capitalism: Embourgeoisment, Internationalization, and Industrial Transformation in India*. Basingstoke: Palgrave Macmillan.

D'Costa, A.P. (2008). "The International Mobility of Technical Talent: Trends and Development Implications," in A. Solimano (ed.), *International Mobility of Talent and Development Impact*, 44–83. Oxford: Oxford University Press.

D'Costa, A.P. (2009). "Economic Nationalism in Motion: Steel, Auto, and Software Industries in India." *Review of International Political Economy*, 16 (4): 618–46.

D'Costa, A.P. (2011). "Geography, Uneven Development and Distributive Justice: The Political Economy of IT Growth in India." *Cambridge Journal of Regions, Economy and Society*, 4 (2): 237–51.

Datt, G. (1999). "Has Poverty Declined Since Economic Reforms? Statistical Data Analysis." *Economic and Political Weekly*, 34 (50): 3516–18.

Hung, H. (2012). "China in the Global Crisis: Death Knell of the East Asian Developmental Model?" in A.K. Bagchi and A.P. D'Costa (eds.), *Transformation and Development: The Political Economy of Transition in India and China*. Delhi: Oxford University Press, forthcoming.

IMF (2006). "Asia's Role in the World Economy." *Finance and Development*, 43 (2). http://www.imf.org/external/pubs/ft/fandd/2006/06/picture.htm [Accessed January 25, 2012].

Lee, C.K. and Selden, M. (2007). "China's Durable Inequality: Legacies of Revolution and Pitfalls of Reform." *Japan Focus*. http://www.japanfocus.org/-C_K_-Lee/2329 [Accessed January 25, 2011].

Ministry of Labour, Health and Welfare, Government of Japan. (2010). "Labour Statistics, Part Time Workers Data." http://www.mhlw.go.jp/english/database/db-l/index.html [Accessed January 25, 2011].

National Commission for Enterprises in the Unorganised Sector, Government of India. (2009). *The Challenge of Employment in India: An Informal Economy Perspective*, Volume II, Annexures. New Delhi: National Commission for Enterprises in the Unorganised Sector.

Planning Commission, Government of India. (2011). "Faster, Sustainable and More Inclusive Growth: An Approach to the 12th Five Year Plan." New Delhi: Planning Commission (April; Draft). http://planningcommission.nic.in/plans/planrel/12appdrft/appraoch_12plan.pdf [Accessed January 25, 2011].

Tanzi, V. (2011). *Government versus Markets: The Changing Economic Role of the State*. Cambridge: Cambridge University Press.

UNDP. (2009). *Human Development Report 2009, Overcoming Barriers: Human Mobility and Development*. New York: UNDP.

UNDP China. (2008). *Human Development Report, China 2007/08: Access for All, Basic Public Services for 1.3 Billion People*. Beijing: UNDP China.

Wan, G. and Sebastian, I. (2011). "Poverty in Asia and the Pacific: An Update." Asian Development Bank, ADB Economics Working Paper Series No. 267, August.

Index

Milton Keynes UK
Ingram Content Group UK Ltd.
UKHW020618220923
429161UK00004B/182